SEVENTH EDITION

Reaching Out

Interpersonal Effectiveness and Self-Actualization

David W. Johnson

University of Minnesota

Allyn and Bacon

Boston   London   Toronto   Sydney   Tokyo   Singapore

This book is dedicated to my children, who have significantly contributed to my interpersonal skills and to my self-actualization:

James, David, Jr., Catherine, Margaret, and Jeremiah

Vice President and Editor-in-Chief: Paul A. Smith
Editorial Assistant: Shannon Morrow
Marketing Manager: Brad Parkins
Composition and Prepress Buyer: Linda Cox
Manufacturing Buyer: Megan Cochran
Production Administrator: Deborah Brown
Editorial–Production Service: P. M. Gordon Associates
Text Design and Electronic Composition: Denise Hoffman
Illustrator: Drew Dernavich

Library of Congress Cataloging-in-Publication Data

Johnson, David W., 1940–
    Reaching out : interpersonal effectiveness and self-actualization /
David W. Johnson.—7th ed.
        p.   cm.
    Includes bibliographical references and index.
    ISBN 0–205–30835–X
    1. Interpersonal relations.   2. Interpersonal communication.
3. Interpersonal conflict.   4. Self-actualization (Psychology)
I. Title.
HM1106.J64   1999
302.3'4—dc21   99-37757
                                                                   CIP

Printed in the United States of America
10   9   8   7   6   5   4   04   03   02

Photo Credits
Chapter 1: Mary Ellen Lepionka, p. xii; chapter 2: Robert Harbison, p.38; chapter 3: Mary Ellen Lepionka, p. 92; chapter 4: Robert Harbison, p. 122; chapter 5: Will Hart, p. 166; chapter 6: Robert Harbison, p. 192; chapter 7: Robert Harbison, p. 212; chapter 8: Robert Harbison, p. 248; chapter 9: Robert Harbison, p. 304; chapter 10: Will Faller, p. 346; chapter 11: Mary Ellen Lepionka, p. 382; chapter 12: Robert Harbison, 402.

Contents

Preface   xi

CHAPTER 1

Importance of Interpersonal Skills   1

The Power of Interpersonal Skills   1
The Relationship Imperative   2
Why Improve Your Interpersonal Skills?   5
Your Invitation to Improve Your Interpersonal Skills   6
What's in This Book   7
Interpersonal Interaction and Relationships   9
The Value of Interpersonal Relationships   12
Difficulties in Forming Relationships   19
The Application of Social Science Research to
Interpersonal Skills   23
Learning from Experience   24
Learning Interpersonal Skills   26
Accepting the Invitation   29
■ Comprehension Test A   30
■ Comprehension Test B   31
Summary   36
Answers   37

CHAPTER 2

Self-Disclosure   39

Introduction   39
Being Open with and to Other People   45
Openness with Other Individuals   46
Self-Disclosure and Self-Awareness   51

Self-Awareness Through Feedback from Others   57
Self-Acceptance and Self-Disclosure   62
Self-Disclosure and Self-Presentation   63
■ Comprehension Test A   86
■ Comprehension Test B   87
Self-Diagnosis   88
Summary   89
Answers   91

CHAPTER 3

Developing and Maintaining Trust   93

Introduction   93
Developing and Maintaining Trust   94
Being Trusting and Trustworthy   96
Building Interpersonal Trust   97
Destroying Trust   99
Reestablishing Trust After It Has Been Broken   100
Trusting Appropriately   100
■ Comprehension Test   103
■ Chapter Review   120
Self-Diagnosis   121
Summary   121
Answers   121

CHAPTER 4

Increasing Your Communication Skills   123

Introduction   123
What Is Communication?   124
Effective Communication Versus Misunderstandings   128
■ Comprehension Test A   131
Sending Messages Effectively   132
■ Comprehension Test B   135
■ Comprehension Test C   147
Improving Your Receiving Skills   148

Theory on Listening and Responding   151

■ Comprehension Test D   153

Theory on Selective Perception in Listening
and Responding   155

■ Comprehension Test E   157

■ Comprehension Test F   158

Toward Improved Communication Skills   161

■ Chapter Review   161

Self-Diagnosis   163

Summary   164

Answers   164

CHAPTER 5

Expressing Your Feelings Verbally   167

The Power of Feelings   167

Saying What You Feel   168

What's Going on Inside?   170

■ Comprehension Test A   175

When Feelings Are Not Expressed   176

■ Comprehension Test B   177

Expressing Your Feelings Verbally   178

■ Comprehension Test C   180

Checking Your Perception of Another's Feelings   187

■ Chapter Review   189

Self-Diagnosis   190

Summary   190

Answers   191

CHAPTER 6

Expressing Your Feelings Nonverbally   193

Introduction   193

Nonverbal Communication   194

Importance of Making Your Verbal and Nonverbal
Messages Congruent   205

■ Chapter Review   210

Self-Diagnosis   210

Summary   211

Answers   211

CHAPTER 7

Helpful Listening and Responding   213

Responding to Another Person's Problems   213

Intentions Underlying the Responses   222

■ Comprehension Test A   230

Helping People Solve Their Problems   231

Listening and Responding Alternatives   232

■ Comprehension Test B   234

Phrasing an Accurate Understanding Response   234

■ Chapter Review   245

Self-Diagnosis   246

Summary   246

Answers   247

CHAPTER 8

Resolving Interpersonal Conflicts   249

You Must Negotiate   249

■ Comprehension Test A   260

Conflict Strategies   262

■ Comprehension Test B   267

Negotiating   269

Effective Problem-Solving Negotiating   275

Refusal Skills: This Issue Is Nonnegotiable   297

Negotiation: A Review of the Rules   299

■ Chapter Review   301

Self-Diagnosis   302

Summary   303

Answers   303

CHAPTER 9
Anger, Stress, and Managing Feelings 305

The Nature of Stress 305

Managing Stress Through Social Support Systems 311

The Nature and Value of Anger 312

■ Comprehension Test 315

Rules for Managing Anger Constructively 315

Eliminating Unwanted Feelings from Your Life 329

How to Deal with an Angry Person 339

Anger and Negotiations 342

■ Chapter Review 344

Self-Diagnosis 344

Summary 345

Answers 345

CHAPTER 10
Building Relationships with Diverse Individuals 347

Introduction 347

Step One: Recognize and Value Diversity 349

Step Two: Interact with Diverse Individuals in a Cooperative Context 350

Step Three: Build Pride in Your Historical and Cultural Identity 351

Step Four: Appreciate Others' Historical and Cultural Backgrounds 356

Step Five: Establish a Superordinate Identity 358

Step Six: Reduce Internal Barriers to Constructive Interaction 361

Step Seven: Resolve Conflicts Constructively 370

Step Eight: Internalize Pluralistic Values 371

Other Aspects of Diversity 373

Friendships 377

■ Chapter Review   379

Self-Diagnosis   380

Summary   380

Answers   381

CHAPTER 11
Barriers to Interpersonal Effectiveness   383

Introduction   383

Managing Anxiety and Fear   384

Breathing   389

Progressive Muscle Relaxation   390

Shyness   392

Understanding Your Shyness   393

Building Your Self-Esteem   394

Avoiding Self-Blame   397

Mistakes and Self-Talk   398

■ Chapter Review   400

Self-Diagnosis   400

Summary   401

Answers   401

CHAPTER 12
Epilogue   403

Importance of Interpersonal Skills   403

Interpersonal Effectiveness, Self-Actualization, and Interpersonal Skills   405

Looking Forward   410

Appendix   417

Glossary   421

References   429

Index   431

Exercises

1.1	Your Relationships	4.3	Relationship Statements
1.2	Keeping Friends	4.4	From Their Shoes
1.3	Influential Relationships	4.5	One- and Two-Way Communication
2.1	Friendship Relations	4.6A	Increasing Communication Skills
2.2	Initiating Relationships	4.6B	Increasing Communication Skills
2.3	Name Tagging	4.6C	Increasing Communication Skills
2.4	Sharing Your Past		
2.5	Self-Disclosure and Self-Awareness	4.7	Observing Communication Behavior
2.6	Your Unknown Area		
2.7	Labeling		
2.8	Interviewing	5.1	Describing Your Feelings
2.9	Adjective Checklist	5.2	Ambiguity of Expression of Feelings
2.10	Fantasy Situations	5.3	Is This the Way You Feel?
2.11	Bag Exercise		
2.12	Feedback	6.1	Communication Without Words
2.13	Strength Building		
2.14	Standing Ovation	6.2	Interpreting Others' Nonverbal Cues
2.15	How Self-Accepting Are You?		
2.16	Interpersonal Patterns	6.3	How Do You Express Your Feelings?
2.17	Open and Closed Relationships	6.4	Using Nonverbal Cues to Express Warmth and Coldness
2.18	Who Am I?		
2.19	Self-Description	6.5	Actions Speak Louder Than Words
3.1	How Trusting and Trustworthy Am I?	6.6	Recognizing Cues for Affection or Hostility
3.2	Practicing Trust-Building Skills	6.7	Expressing Your Feelings
3.3	Prisoner's Dilemma Game	6.8	Can You Tell How I Feel?
3.4	Trust-Level Disclosures	6.9	Off Balance
3.5	Nonverbal Trust	6.10	Gaining Acceptance Nonverbally
3.6	Developing Trust		
4.1	Practicing Personal Statements	6.11	Expressing Acceptance Nonverbally
4.2	Describing Others' Behavior		

7.1   Listening and Response Alternatives

7.2   Practicing the Five Responses

7.3   Phrasing an Accurate Understanding Response

7.4   Practicing the Phrasing of an Understanding Response

7.5   Expressing Acceptance Verbally

7.6   Level of Acceptance in Your Group

8.1   My Past Conflict Behavior

8.2   Dividing Our Money

8.3   Nonverbal Conflict

8.4   My Conflict Strategies

8.5   Confronting the Opposition

8.6   Role-Playing the Conflicts

8.7   Which Strategy Would You Use?

8.8   Using the Conflict Strategies

8.9   Disagreeing—The Fallout Shelter

8.10 Which Books Do We Take?

8.11 Feelings in Conflicts

8.12 Differentiating Between Positions and Interests

8.13 Old Lady/Young Girl

8.14 Your Point of View

8.15 Perspective Reversal

8.16 Problem-Solving Negotiations

8.17 Hamlet and His Father's Ghost

8.18 Negotiable Versus Nonnegotiable Issues

8.19 What Are the Rules?

9.1   Can Friends Help You Stay Well?

9.2   Understanding My Anger

9.3   Defusing the Bomb

9.4   Talking to Yourself to Manage Provocations

9.5   Anger Arousers

9.6   Assumptions, Assumptions, What Are My Assumptions?

9.7   Interpretations

9.8   Changing Your Feelings

9.9   How Do I Manage My Feelings?

9.10 Handling Put-Downs

9.11 Protecting Yourself from Put-Downs

10.1 Relating to Diverse Individuals

10.2 My Attitudes Toward Diversity

10.3 Who Am I?

10.4 My Identity

10.5 Aspects of Self

10.6 Cultural, Historical, and Ethnic Heritage Assignment

10.7 Comparing Cultural Identities

10.8 Was de Tocqueville Right or Wrong?

10.9 American Values

10.10 Why Do Stereotypes Endure?

10.11 Stereotyping

10.12 Interacting on the Basis of Stereotypes

11.1 Learning How to Breathe Deeply

11.2 Systematic Muscle Relaxation

11.3 Understanding Your Shyness

11.4 Being Positive About Yourself While Trying Again

12.1 Planning for Improvement

12.2 Your Relationships and Your Skills

12.3 Relationship Survey

12.4 Self-Contract

Preface

Reaching Out provides the theory and experience necessary to develop effective interpersonal skills. It is more than a book that reviews current psychological knowledge on how to build and maintain friendships. It is more than a book of skill-building exercises. The theory and exercises are integrated into an experiential approach to learning about interpersonal skills.

I wish to thank many people for their help in writing this book and in preparing the manuscript. Special thanks are extended to my wife, Linda Mulholland Johnson, who contributed her support to the development and writing of this book. My younger sister, Edythe Holubec, contributed most of the comprehension tests and helped improve many parts of the book. We owe much to the social psychologists who have influenced our theorizing and to the colleagues with whom we have conducted various types of laboratory-training experiences. We have tried to acknowledge sources of the exercises included in this book whenever possible. Some of the exercises presented are so commonly used that the originators are not traceable. If we have inadvertently missed giving recognition to anyone, we apologize.

We wish to thank Drew Dernavich, Nancy Valin Waller, and Thomas Grummett, who drew the cartoon figures appearing in the book.

CHAPTER 1

The Importance of Interpersonal Skills

The Power of Interpersonal Skills

When the English met the French at the battle of Agincourt on Saint Crispin's Day, October 25, 1415, the French outnumbered the English five to one. The French troops were fresh, and the English troops were tired and worn out. The English had little chance of winning. Before the battle King Henry V addressed the English troops. As Shakespeare presented his speech two centuries later, he gave them the option to retreat:

> . . . he which hath no stomach to this fight,
> Let him depart. His passport shall be made,
> And crowns for convoy put into his purse.
> We would not die in that man's company
> That fears his fellowship to die with us.
> This day is called the feast of Crispian.

King Henry inspired his troops with the image of them showing their scars in their old age and telling people about their participation in the battle.

> *And Crispin Crispian shall ne'er go by,*
> *From this day to the ending of the world,*
> *But we in it shall be remembered,—*
> *We few, we happy few, we band of brothers.*
> *For he today that sheds his blood with me*
> *Shall be my brother. Be he ne'er so vile,*
> *This day shall gentle his condition.*
> *And gentlemen in England now abed*
> *Shall think themselves accurst they were not here,*
> *And hold their manhoods cheap whiles any speaks*
> *That fought with us upon Saint Crispin's day.*
>
> —William Shakespeare (*King Henry the Fifth*)

Not only did the English win, but King Henry became the King of France as well as England. King Henry's interpersonal skills (his ability to communicate, disclose his thoughts and feelings, build trust, and inspire commitment) inspired his troops so much that they won the battle. His interpersonal skills changed the course of history.

The Relationship Imperative

> *A friend is one*
> *to whom one may pour*
> *out all the contents*
> *of one's heart,*
> *chaff and grain together*
> *knowing that the*
> *gentlest of hands*
> *will take and sift it,*
> *keep what is worth keeping*
> *and with a breath of kindness*
> *blow the rest away.*
>
> —Arabian Proverb

We are created, not for isolation, but for relationships. At heart, we are not a thousand points of separated light but, rather, part of a larger brightness. *To be alive is to reach out to others.* "People who need people are the luckiest people in the world," a popular song tells us. That includes all of us. Initiating, developing, and maintaining caring and committed relationships is the most important (and often the most underestimated) activity in our lives. From the moment we are born to the moment we die, relationships are the core of our existence. We are conceived within relationships, are born into relationships, and live our lives within relationships. We are dependent on other people for the realization of life itself, for survival during one of the longest developmental periods in the animal kingdom, for food and shelter and aid and comfort throughout our lives, for the love and education necessary for healthy development, for guidance in learning the essential competencies required to survive in our world, and for fun, excitement, comfort, love, and fulfillment. Our relationships with others form the context for all other aspects of our lives.

Whether relationships begin, continue, or end depends largely on our interpersonal skills. The relationships so essential for living productive and happy lives may be lost when the basic interpersonal skills are not learned. To improve the quality and quantity of our relationships, we have to improve our interpersonal skills. The purpose of this book is to provide you with the opportunities to improve your understanding of interpersonal skills and your ability to engage in the skills in ways appropriate to the situation and the other individuals involved.

In this chapter, the specific interpersonal skills needed to build and maintain relationships are introduced (see Figure 1.1). These skills are essential to building and maintaining constructive relationships. While constructive relationships are of great value, there are also numerous difficulties in forming them. Doing so requires mastering a wide variety of interpersonal skills, all of which are discussed in subsequent chapters of this book. The purposes of this chapter, therefore, are for you to

1. Understand the interpersonal skills required to build constructive relationships.
2. Understand the value of constructive relationships.
3. Understand the difficulties in forming constructive relationships.
4. Understand how to master the interpersonal skills.
5. Commit yourself to doing so.

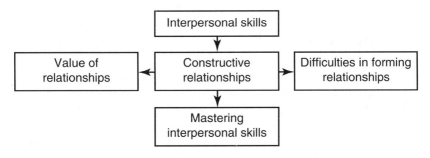

FIGURE 1.1 *Your Interpersonal Skills*

How Skillful Am I? Self-Diagnosis

Each of the following statements describes an action related to interpersonal effectiveness. For each statement mark

5 if you always behave that way
4 if you frequently behave that way
3 if you occasionally behave that way

2 if you seldom behave that way
1 if you never behave that way

When I Am Interacting with Other Individuals,

_____ 1. I disclose information about myself at a level appropriate to the situation and the other individuals present.

_____ 2. I build trust by taking appropriate risks in disclosing information and responding supportively to other individuals' disclosures.

_____ 3. In communicating, I own my ideas, describe (without evaluation) others' actions, and take others' perspectives in phrasing messages.

_____ 4. I describe how I am feeling and ensure that my verbal and nonverbal messages are congruent.

_____ 5. I listen carefully to other individuals' problems and give an appropriate response, depending on the situation and the person.

_____ 6. I face my interpersonal conflicts and define them as problems to be jointly solved. I use the problem-solving negotiation procedure to ensure that the conflicts are resolved constructively.

_____ 7. I recognize and accept my anger and express it appropriately and skillfully.

_____ 8. I manage negative feelings so that they do not interfere with or destroy the quality of my relationships.

_____ 9. I seek out individuals from different backgrounds to enrich my thinking and perspectives.

_____ 10. I face up to my internal barriers to building effective relationships (such as anxiety and shyness) and overcome them.

_____ **Total Score**

Your total score is an indication of your present level of interpersonal skills. As you proceed through this book, these initial impressions may be confirmed, or you may find that there is far more to each skill than you realized at this point. Keep an open mind about the skills and reflect on how you use them throughout each day.

Why Improve Your Interpersonal Skills?

There are many, many reasons why you need to improve your interpersonal skills continuously. Two of the most important are to increase your interpersonal effectiveness and to actualize your potential.

Interpersonal Effectiveness

When you interact with another person, you have no choice but to make some impact, stimulate some ideas, arouse some impressions and observations, or trigger some feelings and reactions. Sometimes you make people react to your behavior much differently than you would like them to. An expression of warmth, for instance, may be seen as your being condescending; an expression of anger may be seen as a joke. Your interpersonal effectiveness depends upon your ability to communicate clearly what you want to communicate, to create the impression you wish, to influence the other person in the way you intend. **Interpersonal effectiveness** is the degree to which the consequences of your behavior match your intentions. You may improve your interpersonal effectiveness by taking action in interacting with another person, assessing the consequences of your behavior and obtaining feedback from others, reflecting and deciding whether those consequences match your intentions, and then engaging in a modified action in the relationship; then repeat the process until your behavior has the consequences you intend it to have.

Self-Actualization

Do your relationships promote the actualization of your potential? Do your relationships result in identifying your talents and abilities and developing them to the fullest extent possible? Your answer is an important indicator reflecting the quality of your relationships. **Self-actualization** is the drive to actualize your potential and take joy and a sense of fulfillment from being all that you can be. You discover what your talents and abilities are in your interpersonal relationships. How other people respond tells you whether you can sing, paint, act, run fast, learn quickly, or understand difficult concepts. Once you begin to actualize your potentialities, you need to be time-competent and autonomous. Being **time-competent** is tying the past and the future to living fully in the present. The self-actualized person appears to be less burdened by guilt, regrets, and resentments from the past than is the non-self-actualized person, and the self-actualized person's aspirations are tied realistically to present goals.

Self-actualization is also dependent on being autonomous. **Autonomous** people have internalized the love, support, and acceptance of

this book has a specific purpose and focuses on specific, essential interpersonal skills. Building and maintaining effective and fulfilling relationships requires that you

1. Disclose yourself to others to let them recognize you as a distinct and unique individual.
2. Build trust between yourself and others.
3. Communicate your ideas and thoughts effectively.
4. Communicate your feelings both verbally and nonverbally.
5. Listen to others' problems constructively and respond in helpful ways.
6. Face conflicts with the other person and resolve them constructively.
7. Manage anger and stress in constructive ways.
8. Value diversity and build relationships with individuals who are different from you.
9. Overcome the internal barriers to relating effectively with others.

Chapter 2, "Self-Disclosure," explains that for a relationship to begin, participants must recognize each other as distinct and unique individuals. All relationships begin with some level of disclosure about who you are and what you hope to accomplish. Your uniqueness and purposes must be clear. You let people know you when you disclose to them how you are reacting to what is currently taking place. Such openness depends on your self-awareness and self-acceptance. If you are unaware of your reactions, you cannot communicate them to another person. If you cannot accept your perceptions and feelings, you will try to hide them. To let them know you, you must first be aware of who you are and accept yourself.

In Chapter 3, "Developing and Maintaining Trust," you learn how to take appropriate risks in letting others know you and respond appropriately when others take such risks with you. The result is a level of trust being built and maintained between the two of you. Once you recognize each other as distinct and unique individuals, the issue of trust becomes central.

Chapter 4, "Increasing Your Communication Skills," explains how you may communicate your ideas, perceptions, conclusions, and theories accurately and unambiguously. Communication skills begin with sending messages that are phrased so that the other person can easily understand them. They also include listening in ways that ensure that you have fully understood the other person. The simultaneous sending and receiving of communications that takes place in interpersonal transactions takes considerable skill. It is through sending and receiving messages that all relationships are initiated, developed, and stabilized.

Chapters 5 and 6 take you through the steps of verbally phrasing your feelings and attitudes, nonverbally indicating how you feel, and ensuring that your verbal and nonverbal messages communicate the same thing. In relationships, it is especially important to communicate warmth and liking. Unless you believe the other person likes you and the other person believes that you like him or her, a relationship will not develop.

Chapter 7, "Helpful Listening and Responding," presents the procedures you use when someone is expressing a problem or concern and wants your help and support. This is an important part of building and maintaining relationships. No matter if the relationship is a business connection or a friendship, at times you will have to listen and respond in helpful, sympathetic, and supportive ways.

Chapter 8 takes you through the steps of defining and resolving interpersonal conflicts in constructive ways. A conflict is a "moment of truth" within a relationship. How you manage conflicts determines whether your relationships are strengthened and maintained, or disintegrate into dislike and divisiveness. Conflicts are inevitable, even among the best of friends, and ensuring that conflicts deepen rather than weaken a relationship involves a vital set of interpersonal skills.

"Anger, Stress, and Managing Feelings," Chapter 9, discusses how you can manage stress and feelings such as anger constructively. Relationships generate stress and are the means by which stress is reduced and managed. Relationships also generate anger and are the means of resolving anger and freeing oneself from negative feelings.

Chapter 10 takes you through the steps of building and maintaining positive relationships with individuals who are from different historical and cultural backgrounds than you. One of the basic laws of nature is that there is strength in diversity. Diversity, furthermore, is increasing in schools, businesses, communities, and societies. How to manage diversity is one of the most complex and important issues in interpersonal relationships.

Chapter 11 focuses on reducing the internal barriers to building and maintaining productive and fulfilling relationships with other people. Those internal barriers include anxiety, shyness, low self-esteem, and fear of failure. There are specific strategies for reducing each of these barriers so that more effective relationships may be developed.

Interpersonal Interaction and Relationships

Your interpersonal skills are your connections to other people. They are the keys to acting appropriately, according to the specific person and situation. There are several ways to describe the interaction among individuals. One way is to focus on the number of people involved. There can

Your Relationships and Your Skills

1. Choose three relationships you are currently involved in. One should be a close, personal friendship, the second should be a good relationship but not a friendship, and the third should be a relationship that is currently not going very well.

2. Consider how each of the skills is being used in each relationship.

3. Formulate at least three goals for using the skills appropriately to improve the quality or effectiveness of each relationship.

---

be dyadic interaction, small-group interaction, large-group interaction, and so forth. A second way is to focus on the formality of the situation. Some situations require a high degree of formality among individuals, and some situations are quite informal. In a formal situation such as a funeral, for example, behavior is governed by rules (be solemn, do not laugh or joke) and rituals (express your condolences) that are almost habit patterns so that upset or nervous people can act appropriately. The interaction in informal situations tends to be less ritualized, rule governed, and habitualized.

A third way to describe the interaction among individuals is to focus on the quality of the relationship (Gergen, 1991). Relationships can be classified on a continuum of personal to impersonal. The difference may be seen on five dimensions (see Table 1.1). The more personal a relationship, the more the relationship is integrated into your identity, the more open you are with the other person, the more distinctive the relationship, the more irreplaceable the relationship, and the more intrinsic the motivation to maintain the relationship. While some relationships are very personal, and others have no personal elements at all, most relationships are not entirely personal or entirely impersonal. Rather, they may be placed on a continuum somewhere between these two positions. There is often some impersonality in a personal relationship and a personal element in even the most impersonal situation. In the former, when you are busy you may keep a conversation with a friend on an impersonal level. In the latter, a bus driver may have a unique sense of humor. A customer's niceness may cheer up your day.

Another way to describe the quality of relationships comes from Martin Buber, one of the most influential theologians of the 20th century. He makes a distinction between relationships based on an "I, it" premise ("I" am a person, and "it" [the other person] is an object to fulfill my needs) and relationships based on an "I, thou" premise ("I" am a person; "thou" [the other person] is a unique individual who changes from moment to moment).

TABLE 1.1   *Personal Versus Impersonal Relationships*

Characteristic	Personal	Impersonal
Integration into identity	The continuation of the relationship impacts your identity, psychological well-being, and emotional happiness.	Whether relationship continues or ends has little impact on your identity, psychological well-being, and feelings.
Openness	Intellectual sharing of ideas and goals, emotional exchange of feelings and reactions, and physical affection such as hugs.	Reveal very little about yourself intellectually and emotionally and keep physical contact minimal.
Distinctive	Interaction based on social rules and roles specific to the relationship (teasing, references to personal life, spontaneous jokes may occur).	Interaction is ritualistic and determined by social rules (use good manners, be honest and fair) and social roles (be polite to elders and persons in authority).
Replaceability	Cannot be replaced. No matter how many relationships in your life, none will be quite like this one.	Easily replaced. Another customer will replace the current one and another bus driver will replace the current one.
Motivation to continue relationship	Intrinsic. The relationship is of value in and of itself.	Extrinsic. The relationship is a means to an end. You relate to an instructor to get a degree and you relate to a customer to make a sale.

Your interpersonal skills are the most important things in your life. Your career success, the quality of your family life, the depth of your friendships, and everything else that is important are directly affected by how able you are to build and maintain appropriate relationships. The value of your relationships is discussed next.

Why Interpersonal Skills Are Important

Rank the following benefits of interpersonal skills from most important to you (1) to least important to you (9).

The Better My Interpersonal Skills,

_____ The more my relationships are humane (they reflect cooperation, compassion, and caring rather than selfishness, indifference, or unkindness).

_____ The better my psychological adjustment and health.

_____ The higher the level of my social, cognitive, and moral development.

_____ The more clearly defined and stronger my personal identity.

_____ The more able I am to actualize my potential.

_____ The better able I am to cope with stress and adversity.

_____ The higher the quality of my life.

_____ The more successful I will be.

_____ The healthier I am physically.

The Value of Interpersonal Relationships

*A real friend is one who walks in
when the rest of the world walks out.*
—Walter Winchell

Interpersonal relationships are not a luxury. They are a necessity. You have to reach out to others. Interpersonal skills are the lifeblood of human relationships. It is through interpersonal skills that you initiate, maintain, and terminate relationships. It is through interpersonal skills that you make your relationships more or less personal and intimate. Through the use of interpersonal skills you increase or decrease the quality of your relationships. It is impossible to discuss relationships without discussing interpersonal skills and vice versa.

The infinite benefits of interpersonal relationships cannot all be listed here. Only a few will be discussed. Relationships are the key to your (a) humanness, (b) psychological health, (c) personal identity, (d) social, cognitive, and moral development, (4) coping with stress and adversity, (5) meaning to and quality of life, (6) self-actualization, (7) educational and career productivity, and (9) physical health (Johnson & Johnson, 1989).

Being Human

How human are you? The answer may reflect the quality of your interpersonal relationships. Your relationships help define your humanity in
two ways. First, it is relationships that have fueled the success of humans
as a species. Humans are a social species whose evolution and success
have been based on cooperation. It is the human ability to join together to
achieve mutual goals that is the primary characteristic that allowed the
species to survive and flourish. Cooperation is to humans what height is
to giraffes and speed is to cheetahs.

Second, the philosophical discussions of what is a "human" has focused on the nature of relationships. Throughout history there have been
numerous attempts to answer the question, "What makes a person human?" The most common answer is that the more your relationships reflect cooperation, responsiveness, consideration, concern, kindness, ten-
derness, caring, love, compassion, and mercy, the more human you are.
To be inhumane is to be unmoved by the suffering of others, to be un-
kind, and to be even cruel and brutal. Humanizing elements cannot be established in a relationship without interpersonal skills. Without the ability to disclose yourself to others, build and maintain trust, communicate
effectively, resolve conflicts constructively, and so forth, you cannot build
and maintain humane and humanizing relationships.

Psychological Health

How healthy are you psychologically? The answer may reflect the quality
of your interpersonal relationships. **Psychological health** is the ability to
build and maintain cooperative, interdependent relationships with other
people. It is your ability to join with other people in achieving mutual
goals that defines how healthy you are. If you are unable to act appropriately, too unskilled to interact with others, or too depressed or anxious
to engage in joint activities, you have psychological problems. Your involvement in caring and supportive relationships builds your psychological health and provides the resources you need to solve problems when
they arise. Positive, supportive relationships are related to psychological
adjustment, lack of neuroticism and psychopathology, lack of psychological distress, self-reliance and autonomy, a coherent and integrated
self-identity, higher self-esteem, increased general happiness, and coping
effectively with stressful situations. Constructive interpersonal relationships, therefore, are both preventive and reparative. You cannot be truly
healthy psychologically without having the interpersonal skills required
to build and maintain positive relationships with other people.

People who, for one reason or another, are unable to establish acceptable relationships tend to develop considerable anxiety, depression, frustration, and alienation. They tend to be afraid and to feel inadequate, helpless, and alone. They often cling to unproductive and unskilled ways of reaching out to others, and they seem unable to change to more successful methods of building and maintaining relationships. Having poor interpersonal skills seems to be a major cause of psychological pathology. Abuse of drugs, criminal acts, and unwanted sexual activity often begin from having poor relationships with authority figures and peers. These problems, furthermore, can result in the loss of long-term goals and opportunities such as attending college, getting a desired job, or even finding the right person to fall in love with. Such psychological problems and antisocial behaviors are avoided when you have high-quality relationships.

Personal Development

Do your relationships promote your social, cognitive, and moral development? The answer is another reflection of the quality of your relationships. Without constructive relationships, infants, children, adolescents, and adults do not grow and develop socially, cognitively, and morally. According to Piaget and Kohlberg, as a person cooperates on the environment with other people, he or she moves from preoperational to concrete operational to formal operational reasoning. As a person's cognitive reasoning advances, so does his or her moral reasoning. The higher forms of moral reasoning are based on formal reasoning.

According to Vygotsky, (a) all reality is socially constructed within relationships, and (b) healthy social and cognitive development depend on engaging in cooperative efforts with individuals who are somewhat more socially and cognitively advanced than you are. Without interpersonal interaction, a clear view of reality cannot be developed. As you strive to make sense of the world and determine what is real and what is illusory, you depend on other people to validate your perceptions and impressions. While you can touch a leaf or smell a flower, you cannot tell what is fair or unfair, good or bad, or beautiful or ugly without checking your perceptions and opinions with the perceptions and opinions of others. In order to make sense of the world, you need to share your perceptions and reactions with other people and find out whether or not other people perceive and react similarly. Healthy social and cognitive development is based on these shared perceptions of reality.

Finally, it is from your family, peers, friends, colleagues, and teachers that you learn new skills and competencies and acquire knowledge, frames of reference, attitudes, and values. As you grow and develop, there are an ever-expanding number of people with whom you must build and maintain relationships. Your interpersonal skills must become more and more refined and sophisticated as you interact with older persons and a broader range of individuals.

Personal Identity

Do your relationships clarify and enrich your self-definition of who you are as a person? The answer to this question reflects the quality of your relationships. It is through your relationships that you build a positive and coherent personal identity. Your **identity** defines who you are as a person. You create your identity through three processes. First, you (a) note how the people you are interacting with are responding to you and seek feedback as to how they perceive you and (b) view yourself as others view you. From the reflections of others, you develop a clear and accurate picture of yourself. When others view you as a worthwhile, valuable person, you tend to view yourself similarly. Second, you incorporate into yourself characteristics that you admire in other people. If one of your heroes is hardworking, you try to be hardworking. Third, in your relationships with other people you adopt social roles such as "student" or "engineer" that become part of your self-definition. It is within your relationships that you discover who you are as a person. The more other people confirm you, indicate that you are normal, healthy, and worthwhile, the stronger your identity tends to be.

Constructively Coping with Stress

Do your relationships provide the resources that help you manage stress and deal with adversity in constructive ways? The answer reflects the quality of your relationships. It is during major life transitions that stress tends to be highest and social support may be most needed. When one moves from school to a job, when one loses or changes jobs, when one gets married, when one gets divorced, when one's spouse or parents die, or when one moves from one part of the country to another, stress is high and social support is an important resource for coping. Positive and supportive relationships provide the caring, information, resources, and feedback you need to cope with stress. They decrease the number and severity of stressful events in your life. They reduce your anxiety and help you appraise the nature of the stress and your ability to deal with it constructively. Discussions with supportive peers help you perceive the meaning of the stressful event, regain mastery over your life, and enhance your self-esteem. Such discussions have helped such diverse populations as runaways, addicted individuals, unmarried mothers, cancer patients, first-time parents, the bereaved, rape victims, stepparents, parents of acting-out teenagers, teenage children of acting-out parents, and all sorts of other individuals experiencing adversity, challenges, and stress.

Productivity and Success

> *A friend is a present you give yourself.*
> —Robert Louis Stevenson

Do your relationships provide the resources and assistance you need to be productive? The answer reflects the quality of your relationships. One of the most well established principles of the social sciences is that people working together to achieve mutual goals are far more productive than are the same number of people all working in isolation (Johnson & Johnson, 1989). Almost without exception, any meaningful job requires the efforts of more than one individual. Curing cancer, building a sky-scraper, bringing a product to market, funding a new company, all require the efforts of many different people working together. Even in school, more complex and interesting assignments are better done by students working together than working alone.

In most situations, therefore, when you are asked to complete a meaningful task, you also will be asked to work jointly with others in doing so. Most people realize that technical competencies are needed to be successful. Many people may be less aware that *interpersonal skills are just as important to employability, productivity, and career success.* A national survey found that employers value five types of skills: verbal communication skills, responsibility, interpersonal skills, initiative, and decision-making skills. In 1982 the Center for Public Resources published a nationwide survey of businesses, labor unions, and educational institutions that found that 90 percent of the people fired from their jobs were fired for poor job attitudes, poor interpersonal relationships, inappropriate behavior, and inappropriate dress. Being fired for lack of basic and technical skills was infrequent.

The heart of most jobs, especially higher paying, more interesting jobs, is leading others, getting others to cooperate, coping with complex power and influence issues, and helping solve people's problems in working with each other. To do so you need the interpersonal skills to motivate others to achieve goals, negotiate and mediate, get decisions implemented, exercise authority, and develop credibility.

Quality of Life

> *From the standpoint of everyday life . . . there is one thing you do know; that man is here for the sake of other men—above all, for those upon whose smile and well-being your own happiness depends, and also for the countless*

unknown souls with whose fate you are connected by a bond of sympathy.
Many times a day I realize how much my own outer and inner life is built
upon the labors of my fellow men, both living and dead, and how earnestly I
must exert myself in order to give in return as much as I have received.
   —Albert Einstein

Do your relationships provide meaning and happiness to your life? The answer obviously reflects the quality of your relationships. The quality of your life is indicated by the answers to two questions: "What makes my life meaningful?" and "What makes my life happy?" Life is a search for daily meaning as well as for daily bread. And the primary determinant of meaning is other people. When a national sample of people was asked, "What is it that makes your life meaningful?" almost all respondents said, "Friends, parents, siblings, spouses, lovers, children, and feeling loved and wanted by others." When the same sample was asked, "What makes your life happy?", the most common answer was "Intimate relationships." In a number of national surveys most people considered it very important to have "a happy marriage, a good family, and good friends." Less importance was given to work, housing, beliefs, and financial security. There is no simple recipe for producing happiness, but all of the research indicates that for almost everyone a necessary ingredient is some kind of satisfying, close, personal, intimate relationship.

Physical Health

You must love another or die.
   —W. H. Auden

Do your relationships provide the support, trust, and openness that promote your physical health? Your answer reflects the quality of your relationships. Loneliness kills. Relationships create and extend life. Positive, supportive relationships have been found to be related to living longer lives, recovering from illness and injury faster and more completely, and experiencing less severe illnesses. People who are connected with others live longer than isolated people do in every age and ethnic/racial group and across all diseases. The mortality rate of divorced white American men under 65 (as opposed to their married counterparts) is double for strokes and lung cancer, 10 times as high for tuberculosis, 7 times as high for cirrhosis of the liver, and double for stomach cancer. Premature death from heart disease is significantly more frequent among the "lonely"—the divorced, widowed, and single, both old and young. People who lacked social and community ties were found to be twice as likely to die from any cause during a 9-year period as were people who had such relationships.

Individuals involved in relationships with others recover from illness faster and experience less severe illnesses than do individuals who are isolated and without friends. A higher percentage of married people, for example, survive cancer at nearly every age. Divorced people, as opposed to the widowed or the never married, faced the greatest risks of all. Divorced adults are at severely greater risk for mental and physical illness, automobile accidents, alcoholism, and suicide.

Friendships

Ingredients of Friendship

A *Psychology Today* survey of friendship revealed how important the following qualities are in a friend. The percentages represent the number of people who said that particular quality was "important" or "very important."

Keeps confidences	89%	Similar education	17%
Loyalty	88%	About my age	10%
Warmth, affection	82%	Physical attractiveness	9%
Supportiveness	76%	Job accomplishments	8%
Frankness	75%	Similar income	4%
Sense of humor	74%	Similar occupation	3%

What Friends Do Together

According to *Psychology Today,* here is what friends did together within the past month.

Female	Male	Activity
90%	78%	Had an intimate talk.
84%	80%	Had a friend ask you to do something for him or her.
84%	77%	Gone to dinner in a restaurant.
80%	75%	Asked your friend to do something for you.
75%	70%	Had a meal at home or at your friend's home.
67%	64%	Gone to a movie, play, or concert.
62%	64%	Gone drinking together.
62%	49%	Gone shopping.
45%	55%	Participated in sports.
41%	53%	Watched a sporting event.

Interpersonal skills help. Recent studies in Europe have found that heart-disease-prone individuals are characterized by anger, hostility, and aggression while cancer-prone individuals are characterized by (a) the inability to express emotions such as anger, fear, and anxiety, (b) the inability to cope with stress, and (c) a tendency to develop feelings of hopelessness, helplessness, and finally depression. The key change for cancer-prone individuals is to stop being overly passive and to take more initiative in their relationships. The key change for heart-disease-prone individuals is to abandon their tendencies toward hostility and aggression and become more constructive in the way they deal with conflict. The interpersonal skills required by both changes can be taught.

Difficulties in Forming Relationships

A friend is one before whom I may think aloud.
—Ralph Waldo Emerson

It is not always easy to initiate, develop, and maintain positive relationships. It takes work and considerable skill. Major difficulties include (a) the complex and constantly changing nature of relationships, (b) the slowness with which positive feelings and impressions are built, and (c) the fragility of relationships. These three factors and many more point to the difficulty in developing friendships.

Interacting with others is a dynamic process. You and the other person change, your behavior is inconsistent, and the situations you find yourself in change. The interaction is constantly shifting and changing as you and the other person respond and react to each other. Sometimes communication will be clear. Other times you may misunderstand each other. Sometimes you will have common goals and needs; other times your goals and needs will conflict. Everything you do will affect the relationship to some degree. Everything the other person does will affect your perceptions and feelings about the other person and the relationship. Managing the dynamics of relationships is often difficult.

Difficulties I Have in Forming Relationships

1. _____

2. _____

3. _____

4. _____

Potential for Loneliness Quotient

Read the statements in each *row* of the following table. Place an *x* in front of the statement that best describes you. You cannot choose both. Then total each column. The more *x*'s you have in Column B, the greater your potential for loneliness.

Column A	Column B
_____ I have lived in the same location most of my life.	_____ I frequently move to different locations.
_____ I spend lots of time in doing things with friends and conversing face-to-face.	_____ I spend lots of time watching TV, listening to music, using the computer, or reading.
_____ I have intimate conversations with friends and neighbors and we know each other's lives well.	_____ I have superficial contacts and conversations with most people.
_____ I reflect on my relationships and plan how I can act differently to improve them.	_____ I am like I am. Nothing can be done about it.
_____ I consciously work to improve my interpersonal skills.	_____ I rarely think of how my interpersonal skills can be improved.
_____ **Total**	_____ **Total**

Many of the difficulties in initiating, building, and maintaining relationships revolve around the *crude law of relationships:* Positive perceptions of and feelings toward another person are hard to acquire but easy to lose; negative perceptions of and feelings toward another person are easy to acquire and hard to lose. It takes many positive interactions to build a strong relationship with another person. Positive relationships usually build slowly. One negative experience can end a relationship. Relationships can end very quickly. A perception of another person as "kind," for example, may develop as you see the person act in sympathetic and generous ways toward others. But one instance of deliberate cruelty changes your perception of the person dramatically. The same result can happen in the reverse order. The sight of a person kicking a dog on a single occasion creates a memorable impression of meanness, and repeated evidence of kindness would not wipe out the impression that the person can be cruel.

Despite the difficulties in building relationships, loneliness can push most people into the effort to do so. The experience of feeling lonely is a central fact of human existence. Everyone feels lonely sometime. It is one of the most common human experiences. Loneliness is not the same as physical isolation. You can feel lonely in a crowd and happy in complete solitude. Instead, *loneliness* is a state of dejection or grief caused by feeling alone. It can result from **social isolation** (not having friends who share your interests and concerns and provide a sense of community) or **emotional isolation** (not having deep personal relationships that provide a sense of attachment). Most people feel painfully lonely at times. Whether or not they stay so depends largely on their interpersonal skills.

Loneliness has been aggravated by a number of contemporary developments. One is a *nomadic lifestyle* (as opposed to living in the same community for several generations). The average American moves 14 times in a lifetime. About 40 million Americans change their home addresses at least once every year. The extended family (in which children, parents, and grandparents lived in the same household, or at least within short walking distance of one another) has almost disappeared in modern America. The people you know and love today may be hundreds of miles away tomorrow. Several times during your life you may be faced with beginning anew with people you do not know. Very few adults today retain friendships formed during their childhood. The dramatic change in mobility has had a profound effect on friendship patterns, on the family, and on the whole fabric of human interaction.

Second, relationships are limited in terms of the *energy individuals are willing and able to commit* and the context within which the relationship occurs. Historically, before computers, television, stereos, and movies, the primary source of entertainment was other people. Leisure time was spent with friends, neighbors, and colleagues. Economic conditions forced people into community support systems. Today, many people are economically independent, have self-entertainment devices (such as computers and televisions), and are overcommitted and busy without a great deal of flexible time to spend with friends. Relationships at work and school may be quite positive without extending into leisure activities. The limited nature of relationships contributes to feelings of social and emotional isolation. Many people feel isolated from others and believe that even their friends do not know them well and do not care for them intensely.

Third, in addition to increased mobility and isolation, the *impersonality of life* has radically changed friendship patterns. Historically, people lived in close-knit communities where everyone knew each other and provided support and help in troubled times. Their lives were intertwined, and everyone knew each other well. Today, people live lives independent of those living around them and often do not know the names of those who live next door. Someone in the neighborhood could lose money in a bad investment or have a death of a relative and no one would know or provide help and support. In addition, many people know little about the personal lives of business associates or the checkout clerk at the supermarket.

Fourth, lonely people may *misattribute the causes of difficulties in forming and maintaining constructive relationships.* When deciding what is causing their loneliness, they decide it is something (a) stable and unchanging rather than unstable and open to change and (b) internal rather than external such as other people and the situation. They blame aspects of themselves—their shyness, personality, fear of rejection, or lack of social skills—for their social and emotional isolation and believe they cannot change these characteristics (see Figure 1.2). By believing that the cause of their loneliness is inside them and cannot be changed, they perpetuate their loneliness and do not take action to end it.

Finally, lonely people may *lack interpersonal skills* in their interactions with others and are less socially responsive. Their lack of skills causes them to be socially cautious and avoid situations in which they could be rejected. Connecting with others is hard work. Friendships are like money—easier made than kept. It takes interpersonal skills to build and maintain a positive relationship. Despite their value, most people take interpersonal skills for granted. Mastering the skills required to build and maintain positive relationships is not automatic or easy. It takes training and it takes practice. You must reach out with sensitivity and grace.

Locus of Causality

		Internal	External
Stability	Stable	I'm lonely because I have all these faults and problems. I'll never be worth getting to know. Some people have what it takes to make friends, and some people don't. I don't.	Other people are cold and impersonal. None of them are interested in the same things I am. They already have their friends, and they do not want any more. I better leave.
	Unstable	I'm lonely now, but I won't be for long. I'll improve my social interaction skills. I'll meet new people. I'll participate in new activities.	The first year in college is always the worst. There are lots of nice people here. I'm sure they will seek me out soon. I could be discovered any day! Things will get better.

FIGURE 1.2 *Causal Attributions for Loneliness.* How people explain the causes of their loneliness may influence how long they stay lonely. An internal, stable attribution is associated with prolonged loneliness.

Loneliness

Roots of Loneliness	Historical Situation
Individual nomadic lifestyle	Living in the same community for generation after generation
Impersonality of lifestyle	Knowing neighbors well, neighborhood support systems
Lack of time and energy in relationships	Long periods of time spent together
Interpersonal incompetence	Interpersonal competence
Believe causes are unchangeable aspects of themselves and others	Believe causes are changeable aspects of themselves and others

Overcoming the nomadic lifestyle, impersonality of life, limited nature of relationships, faulty attribution of causes of problems, and lack of interpersonal skills in order to build and maintain caring and committed friendships is not easy. There is nothing easy about building and maintaining constructive relationships. Relationships are not always positive. There are many examples of human indifference to others' suffering and problems, prejudice toward others, and even abuse, exploitation, and violence. You have to work constantly on the interpersonal skills required to relate effectively to others and build and maintain constructive relationships.

Before the specific interpersonal skills are discussed, there is a need to understand the importance of applying social science knowledge to interpersonal skills, for individuals to be cooriented about how interpersonal skills are expressed in relationships, as well as to understand the procedure for learning from experience and the steps in learning interpersonal skills.

The Application of Social Science Research to Interpersonal Skills

We have at our disposal a vast amount of social science research on interpersonal interaction. The basic skills that determine a person's interpersonal effectiveness have been identified from the results of the social-psychological research on interpersonal relationships, the author's research, and the research on effective therapeutic relationships. In addition, much of the material in this book has been used in a variety of training programs aimed at increasing interpersonal skills. The evaluation of these programs indicates that the material in this book is effective in increasing the interpersonal skills of readers. This book translates the theory and research into a form useful to individuals who wish to increase their interpersonal skills, filling the gap between the research on interpersonal interaction and the development of interpersonal skills. To make this book as readable as possible, however, a minimum of footnotes and references to research and theory are included. Any person concerned with increasing his or her interpersonal skills and any practitioners who work with people will be able to understand and use the material in this book and find this book helpful.

Learning from Experience

Knowing is not enough; we must apply. Willing is not enough; we must do.
—Johann Wolfgang von Goethe

Aesop tells the story of the lion, the bear, and the fox. The bear was about to seize a stray goat when the lion leaped from another direction on the same prey. The bear and the lion then fought furiously for the goat until they had received so many wounds that both sank down unable to continue the battle. Just then the fox dashed up, seized the goat, and made off with it as fast as he could go, while the lion and the bear looked on in helpless rage. "How much better it would have been," they said, "to have shared in a friendly spirit." The bear and the lion had learned from their direct experience an important lesson in the advantages of cooperation over competition.

We all learn from our experiences. From touching a hot stove we learn to avoid heated objects. From dating we learn about male-female relationships. Every day we have experiences we learn from. Learning by experience is a process of making generalizations and conclusions about your own direct experiences. It emphasizes experiencing directly what you are studying, building a personal commitment to learn, and being responsible for organizing the conclusions you draw from your experiences.

Everyone needs to become competent in taking action and simultaneously reflecting on the action in order to learn from it. Integrating thought with action requires that you plan an action, engage in it, and then reflect on how effective it was. Patterns of behavior that are effective tend to be repeated over and over until they function automatically. Such

My Action Theories

Think of ways you behave in certain situations. If you were caught stealing a cookie, for example, what would you do? How would that create the result you want? List five situations you have recently found yourself in. Describe what you did and what you expected to result as a consequence of your actions. You have just identified one of your action theories.

Situation	If I Do . . .	Then the Result Will Be . . .
1. _____	_____	_____
2. _____	_____	_____
3. _____	_____	_____
4. _____	_____	_____
5. _____	_____	_____

habitual behavioral patterns are based on theories of action. An **action theory** is a theory as to what actions are needed to achieve a desired consequence in a given situation. All theories have an "if . . . then . . ." form. An action theory states that in a given situation if we do *x,* then *y* will result. Examples of action theories can be found in almost everything you do. If you smile and say hello, then others will return the smile and greeting. If you apologize, then the other person will excuse you. All your behavior is based on theories that connect your actions with certain consequences.

Action theories are the heart of experiential learning. Experiential learning can be conceived of in a simplified way as a four-stage cycle: (1) take action on the basis of one's current action theory, (2) assess consequences and obtain feedback, (3) reflect on how effective actions were and reformulate/refine the action theory, and (4) implement the revised action theory by taking modified action (see Figure 1.3). As learners engage in these four steps, they must perceive themselves as being capable of implementing the procedures and strategies contained in the theory, perceive these procedures and strategies as being appropriate to their social world, and develop positive attitudes toward the theory and its implementation. This process of continuous improvement is repeated over and over again until expertise in the use of group skills is developed.

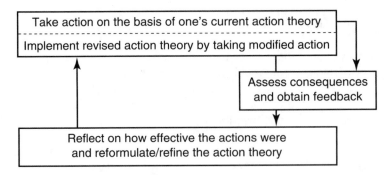

FIGURE 1.3   *Experiential Learning Cycle*

Learning Interpersonal Skills

For things we have to learn before we can do them, we learn by doing them.
—Aristotle

Learning from your experiences is especially useful when you want to learn skills. Socially skilled individuals are not born; they are made. No one wants to ride in an airplane with a pilot who has read a book on how to fly but has never actually flown a plane. Seeing a movie about love is not the same as experiencing love. Reading a book on physical conditioning exercises will not make you fit. Studying books on golf, swimming, or horseback riding will not make you an expert golfer, swimmer, or horseback rider. Learning interpersonal skills is no different. Hearing a lecture on friendship is not the same as having a friend. Reading about how to communicate is not enough to make you skillful in communicating with others; you need practice and experience in good communication skills.

You are not born with interpersonal skills, nor do they magically appear when you need them. You have to learn them. Interpersonal skills are learned just as any other skill is learned. Learning how to resolve a conflict is no different from learning how to play the piano or throw a football. All skills are learned the same way, according to the following steps:

1. **Understand why the skill is important and how it will be of value to you.** To want to learn a skill, you must see a need for it. You need to know that you will be better off with the skill than without the skill.

2. Understand what the skill is, what are the component behaviors you have to engage in to perform the skill, and when it should be used. To learn a skill, you must have a clear idea of what the skill is, and you must know how to perform it. Often it is helpful to observe someone who has already mastered the skill perform it several times while describing it step by step. Apprentices, for example, watch masters of their craft perform the skill over and over again.

3. Find situations in which you can practice the skill over and over and over again while a "coach" watches and tells you how well you are performing the skill. There are four levels of guided practice. The first level of guided practice consists of practicing successive approximations of the interpersonal skill while others provide scaffolding on how to do so. *Scaffolding* is support, in the form of reminders, prompts, and help, that you require to approximate the expert use of the interpersonal skills. As you practice the skills again and again, the scaffolding is gradually faded until you use the skill by yourself; doing it on your own is called soloing. The second level of guided practice consists of using the interpersonal skills while articulating and explaining out loud how to do so to your "coach." This ensures that the scaffolding is internalized and that self-monitoring and self-correcting on how to engage in the skill take place. The third level is independent practice. You engage in the skill while self-monitoring and self-correcting your efforts. In effect, you give yourself feedback. This solidifies your sense of self-efficacy and commitment to use the skills. Finally, you decontextualize your use of the skills by using them in a variety of groups and in a variety of different situations. Try practicing the skill for a short time each day for several days until you are sure you have mastered it completely.

4. Assess how well the interpersonal skills are being implemented. The key to assessing how well you engage in the skill is to realize that your behavior approximates what you ideally wish and that, through practice and the process of experiential learning (i.e., progressive refinement), the approximations get successively closer and closer to the ideal. Remember, you have to sweat in practice before you can perform in concert! Short-term failure is part of the process of gaining expertise, and long-term success is inevitable when short-term failure is followed by persistent practice, obtaining feedback, and reflecting on how to implement the *interpersonal* skills more competently. Receiving feedback, furthermore, is necessary for correcting mistakes in learning a skill and for identifying problems you are having in mastering the skill. Through feedback you find out how much progress you are making in mastering the skill. Feedback lets you compare how well you are doing with how well you want to do.

5. Keep practicing until the skill feels real and it becomes an automatic habit pattern! Most skill development goes through the following steps:

  a. Self-conscious, awkward engagement in the skill. Practicing any new skill feels awkward, and *interpersonal* skills are no exception. The first few times someone throws a football, plays a violin, or paraphrases, it feels strange.

  b. Feelings of phoniness while engaging in the new skill. After a while the awkwardness passes, and enacting the skill becomes more smooth. Many individuals, however, feel that the skill is unauthentic or phony. Encouragement is needed to move through this stage.

  c. Skilled but mechanical use of the skill.

  d. Automatic, routine use where the skill is fully integrated into your behavioral repertoire and seems like a natural action to engage in.

You have to practice the skills long enough to go through the stages of skill development. The more you use a skill, the more natural it feels. It is then, when you apply the skills to real situations, that the skills will gain the fire and life that may sometimes be lacking when you practice.

6. Load your practice toward success. Set up practice units that you can easily master. It always helps to feel like a success as you practice a skill.

7. Get friends to encourage you to use the skill. Your friends can help you learn by giving you encouragement to do so. The more encouragement you receive, the easier it will be for you to practice the skill.

8. Help others learn interpersonal skills. Harvey S. Firestone said, "It is only when we develop others that we permanently succeed." Nothing is completely learned until it is taught to someone else. By helping others learn *interpersonal* skills, you will enhance your own expertise.

With most skills there is a period of slow learning, then a period of rapid improvement, then a period where performance remains the same, and then another period of rapid improvement, and then another plateau, and so forth. You have to practice the interpersonal skills long enough to make it through the first few plateaus and integrate the skills into your behavioral repertoire. To become skillful in interacting with others, you must practice, practice, practice. Once learned, a social skill is automatic, and you will not need to rethink consciously how to do it when interacting with another person.

The best way to learn about the skills and to master them is through structured exercises. As you read this book you will be asked to partici-

Steps in Learning Interpersonal Skills

Choose an interpersonal skill to learn. Check off each step as you achieve each step of the process for learning a skill.

_____ 1. I understand the need for the skill.

_____ 2. I understand the verbal and nonverbal actions needed to engage in the skill. I watch others engage in the skill.

_____ 3. I engage in the skill under the direction of someone who has already mastered the skill.

_____ 4. I listen carefully to and reflect on the feedback on how well I am engaging in the skill.

_____ 5. I engage in the skill again in a modified, improved way.

_____ 6. I repeat steps 3, 4, and 5 over and over again.

_____ 7. I independently use the skill until it becomes an automatic habit pattern.

_____ 8. I teach the skill to someone else.

pate in skill-building exercises and practice activities. You will be asked to support and encourage the efforts of other readers to do likewise. Each chapter has a series of exercises that provide opportunities to experience, practice, and master the interpersonal skills as well as to read about them. Improving your interpersonal competence is an exciting and exhilarating experience, but in doing so it is often helpful to remember the stages of skill learning involved. Do not worry about feeling awkward the first time you implement a skill. Persevere and practice and soon the awkwardness will pass. In learning any skill it is helpful to remember the following advice. "You have to sweat on the practice field before you perform on the playing field!" "You got to study the lessons before you get the grades!" "You got to make the call before you get the sale!"

Accepting the Invitation

At this point you should understand that (a) interpersonal skills are required to build constructive relationships, (b) constructive relationships are of great value, (c) there are difficulties in forming constructive relationships, and (d) there are specific procedures to master interpersonal skills. At the beginning of this chapter, you were invited to increase your interpersonal skills. It is now time to decide whether you wish to accept the invitation or not. You accept simply by going on to the next chapter. You are then committed to increasing your interpersonal competence.

■ COMPREHENSION TEST A

Demonstrate your understanding of the following concepts by matching the definitions with the appropriate concept. Find a partner. Compare answers.

Concept	Definition
_____ 1. Interpersonal skills	a. Positive perceptions of and feelings toward another person are hard to acquire but easy to lose; negative perceptions of and feelings toward another person are easy to acquire and hard to lose.
_____ 2. Interpersonal effectiveness	
_____ 3. Self-actualization	
_____ 4. Time competence	b. Sum total of your ability to interact effectively with other people.
_____ 5. Autonomy	
_____ 6. Psychological health	c. Internalize the love, support, and acceptance of others so that they can apply values and principles flexibly in order to act in ways that are appropriate to the current situation.
_____ 7. Loneliness	
_____ 8. Crude law of relationships	
_____ 9. Action theory	d. Ability to build and maintain cooperative, interdependent relationships with other people.
	e. Tying the past and future to living fully in the present.
	f. Degree to which the consequences of your behavior match your intentions.
	g. A theory as to what actions are needed to achieve a desired consequence in a given situation.
	h. State of dejection or grief caused by feeling alone.
	i. Drive to actualize your potential and take joy and a sense of fulfillment from being all that you can be.

■ COMPREHENSION TEST B

Demonstrate your understanding of the following concepts by matching the definitions with the appropriate concept. Find a partner. Compare answers.

Concept

_____ 1. Self-disclosure

_____ 2. Trust

_____ 3. Communication

_____ 4. Feelings

_____ 5. Nonverbal messages

_____ 6. Conflict of interests

_____ 7. Anger

_____ 8. Diversity

_____ 9. Barriers

Definition

a. Perception that a choice can lead to gains or losses, that whether you gain or lose depends on the other person's behavior, that the loss will be greater than the gain, and that the person will likely behave so that you will gain rather than lose.

b. Facial expressions, tone of voice, gestures, and posture.

c. Individuals from different historical, cultural, ethnic, and economic backgrounds.

d. Sending a message with the conscious intent of affecting the receiver's behavior.

e. Obstacles or obstructions that prevent a person from engaging in effective behavior.

f. A defensive emotional reaction that occurs when we are frustrated, thwarted, or attacked.

g. When the actions of one person attempting to reach his or her goals prevent, block, or interfere with the actions of another person attempting to reach his or her goals.

h. Revealing how you are reacting to the present situation.

i. Internal physiological reactions to your experiences.

Keeping an Interpersonal Skills Journal

As you go through this book you may wish to keep a journal in which you record what you are learning about interpersonal skills and your own interpersonal competence. A *journal* is a personal collection of writing and thoughts that have value for the writer. It has to be kept up on a regular basis. The entries should be important to you in your effort to make this book useful. You may be surprised how writing sharpens and organizes your thoughts. The journal will be of great interest to you after you finish this book.

Each day you should make an entry about interpersonal skills in your journal. These entries should help you

1. Collect thoughts related to interpersonal skills (the best thinking often occurs when you are driving to or from school, about to go to sleep at night, and so forth).

2. Collect newspaper and magazine articles and references that are relevant to interpersonal skills.

3. Keep summaries of conversations and anecdotal material that are unique or interesting or that illustrate things related to interpersonal skills.

 **EXERCISE 1.1**

Your Relationships

Make new friends And keep the old. One is silver, The other gold.
  —Children's song

The purpose of this exercise is to reflect on your current relationships. The procedure is as follows:

1. On a piece of paper draw a circle in the center about the size of a 50-cent piece. Write your name inside this circle.

2. Draw a number of smaller circles (25-, 5-, 10-cent sizes) around the big circle. These circles represent your relationships.

3. Think about the persons with whom you have the strongest and closest bonds. Fill in the various circles with their names. List the people you care for, have warm feelings for, and are comfortable with. List the people you would like to talk with if you were having a hard time. Think of who you

would like to share a meal with or receive a letter from. The more personal the relationship, the larger the circle the name should appear in.

   a. Draw the circles and jot down names quickly, just as they come to mind.

   b. Include the people who have been supportive of and personally close to you all through your life as well as those who are supportive of and personally close to you now.

   c. Do not worry about being "fair" or reasonable or logical. This exercise is for you alone.

4. You may wish to jog your memory by referring to your address book. Think of places you have lived and the friends you had there. Think of friends from work, old school buddies, and neighborhood friends. Think of the social, religious, and political groups you belong to and the people you have grown close to in those associations.

5. As you list friends' names, you may find yourself wishing to be in closer touch with some of them. There may be others that you find yourself wanting to call or write to or even buy a small present for. There may be people you feel deeply for but have not been able to express your feelings to. There may be people with whom you would like to initiate deeper and more meaningful relationships. If so, list those names on a second sheet of paper.

6. When you have finished, review each name and remember the experiences you have had with that person. A sample of a completed diagram is in Figure 1.4.

Relationships Assessment 1

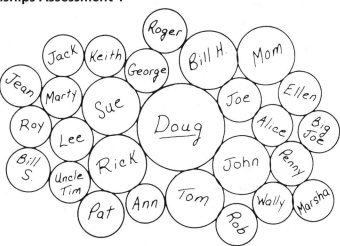

FIGURE 1.4 *Sample Relationships Diagram*

Relationships Assessment 2

People I Would See, Call, or Write	*People I Would Like to Deepen a Relationship With*	*People I Would Like to Begin a Relationship With*
1. _____	_____	_____
2. _____	_____	_____
3. _____	_____	_____
4. _____	_____	_____
5. _____	_____	_____
6. _____	_____	_____

 EXERCISE 1.2

Keeping Friends

Friendship is like money—easier made than kept. You may meet many people in your lifetime and make many acquaintances. But true friends are rare. Friends are earned, and once found, they must be treasured. Doing so requires as much care as tending a garden. The following questions may help you consider whether you are increasing or decreasing the quality of your friendships.

1. Do you enjoy doing favors for people you care about?
2. Do you publicly find fault with other people?
3. Can you keep a secret?
4. When a friend receives public recognition for his or her efforts, do you secretly wish it was you being recognized?
5. Are you generally cheerful and happy?
6. Do you see friends only if they will do things you like to do?
7. Do you feel free to share your reactions and feelings with your friends?
8. When a friend hurts your feelings, do you decide the person is not really your friend and avoid him or her?
9. Do you promise to do things and then forget about them?
10. Do you sometimes tell others things a friend told to you in confidence?
11. Is it easy to see good qualities in others?

12. Do you seek out activities and projects that you and your friends can do together?

13. Are you often depressed and negative?

14. Do you feel genuinely happy when a friend succeeds?

15. Do you hide your "true self" from your friends?

16. When you are angry with a friend, do you sit down with him or her and try to solve the problem?

Answers

1. Yes	5. Yes	9. No	13. No
2. No	6. No	10. No	14. Yes
3. Yes	7. Yes	11. Yes	15. No
4. No	8. No	12. Yes	16. Yes

Analysis

14–16 correct answers: You have friends because you are a friend to others. You are open, trustworthy, reliable, supportive, cooperative, committed, and caring, each a true art.

10–13 correct answers: You have friends, but some of them stick with you despite your faults.

5–9 correct answers: You find yourself looking for friends, but unable to find them. Look at yourself carefully and plan some changes.

 EXERCISE 1.3
Influential Relationships

1. In the first column, write the names of ten people who have influenced your life in positive ways. They may be relatives, friends, teachers, or perhaps someone you have never met. Complete this step before moving on to the rest of the exercise.

2. In the second column, write what that influence has been.

3. In the third column, rate your gratitude for this person's influence from 1 (little gratitude) to 5 (extreme gratitude).

4. In the fourth column, write what you would like to communicate to this person if you were to express your gratitude.

Names	Influence	Gratitude	Communication
_____	_____	_____	_____
_____	_____	_____	_____
_____	_____	_____	_____
_____	_____	_____	_____
_____	_____	_____	_____
_____	_____	_____	_____
_____	_____	_____	_____
_____	_____	_____	_____
_____	_____	_____	_____
_____	_____	_____	_____

5. You also influence other people. Make a list of people whose lives you have influenced. Consider sharing with those people why you enjoy being part of their lives.

Summary

This book is a guidebook for improving your interpersonal skills. The book has two purposes: increasing your understanding of the interpersonal skills required to build and maintain effective interpersonal relationships and increasing your ability to perform the skills. **Interpersonal skills** are the sum total of your ability to interact effectively with other people. Whenever you interact with other people, whether they are friends, family members, acquaintances, business associates, or store clerks, interpersonal skills are a necessity. You disclose yourself to others to let them recognize you as a distinct and unique individual, build trust between yourself and others, communicate your ideas and thoughts effectively, listen to others' problems constructively and respond in helpful ways, face conflicts and resolve them constructively, manage anger and stress in constructive ways, build relationships with individuals who are different from you, and overcome the internal barriers to relating effectively with others.

Your relationships have great value. They become integrated into your identity, are places where you can share your ideas and emotions, become irreplaceable, and become important aspects of your life. Your interpersonal skills are the lifeblood of your relationships and the connections between you and other people. They pervade every aspect of your life, defining your humanness, determining your psychological health, defining your identity, ensuring your health development, allowing you to cope with stress and adversity, providing meaning to your life, promoting the actualization of your potentialities, increasing your productivity, and even increasing your physical health.

Developing good relationships is not always easy. There are difficulties. The nature of your relationships is constantly changing, trust and caring are slow to build, and relationships are fragile—one wrong action can destroy years of friendship. The more you move locations, isolate yourself in front of a TV or computer, keep conversations superficial, believe you cannot change yourself, and ignore the need to improve your interpersonal skills, the less likely you are to be involved in the relationships you need.

These barriers can be overcome when you make a conscious decision to learn from your experiences and follow the process for learning interpersonal skills. By following the experiential learning cycle and the steps in learning interpersonal skills, you can master the interpersonal skills. These procedures are inherent in this book.

Answers

Comprehension Test A: 1. b; 2. f; 3. i; 4. e; 5. c; 6. d; 7. h; 8. a; 9. g.

Comprehension Test B: 1. h; 2. a; 3. d; 4. i; 5. b; 6. g; 7. f; 8. c; 9. e.

CHAPTER 2

Self-Disclosure

Introduction

By letting you know me, I allow you to like me. By disclosing myself to you, I create the potential for trust, caring, commitment, growth, self-understanding, and friendship. How can you care for me if you do not know me? How can you trust me if I do not demonstrate my trust in you by disclosing myself to you? How can you be committed to me if you know little or nothing about me? How can I know and understand myself if I do not disclose myself to friends? To like me, to trust me, to be committed to our relationship, to facilitate my personal growth and self-understanding, and to be my friend, you must know me.

I let you know me when I disclose to you how I am reacting to what is currently taking place. Such openness depends on my self-awareness and self-acceptance. In order for me to feel free to disclose myself to you, I must accept and appreciate myself (see Figure 2.1). If I am unaware of my reactions, I cannot communicate them to you. If I cannot accept my perceptions and feelings, I will try to hide them. When I let you know me, trust is built if you react positively, and trust is destroyed if you react negatively. This chapter will focus on self-awareness and the disclosure of oneself to other people. A later chapter will focus on self-acceptance.

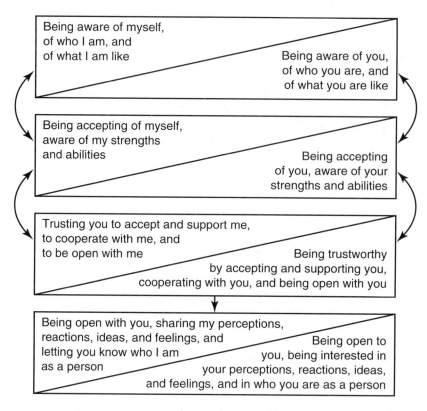

Being aware of myself, of who I am, and of what I am like

Being aware of you, of who you are, and of what you are like

Being accepting of myself, aware of my strengths and abilities

Being accepting of you, aware of your strengths and abilities

Trusting you to accept and support me, to cooperate with me, and to be open with me

Being trustworthy by accepting and supporting you, cooperating with you, and being open with you

Being open with you, sharing my perceptions, reactions, ideas, and feelings, and letting you know who I am as a person

Being open to you, being interested in your perceptions, reactions, ideas, and feelings, and in who you are as a person

FIGURE 2.1 *An Open Relationship = Self-Awareness, Self-Acceptance, Trust*

 EXERCISE 2.1
Friendship Relations

The following exercise is based on the Johari Window. The objectives of the exercise are to examine your and the group's receptivity to feedback, willingness to self-disclosure, and willingness to take risks in relations with friends. The procedure for the exercise is as follows:

1. Working by yourself, complete the Friendship Relations Survey.

2. Score the results, according to the instructions given.

3. Follow the directions on the Friendship Relations Survey Summary Sheet that follows to get the final results of the survey for yourself and your group.

4. Form into groups of six. Complete a new Friendship Relations Survey Summary Sheet for the group as a whole, using the average of the members' scores. The group average is found by adding the scores of every member and dividing by the number of persons in the group.

5. Discuss the results in the group, using the following questions:
   a. What are your thoughts and feelings about when it is appropriate to receive feedback from your friends and to self-disclose to them?
   b. What are your thoughts and feelings about when you want other members of the group to give feedback to you and when you want to self-disclose to them?
   c. Do you have a conservative or a risky group?
   d. How does trust affect your receptivity to feedback and willingness to give feedback?
   e. Would you like to change the way you are now behaving?
   f. What changes in your behavior would be productive and useful in developing better relationships with your friends?

Friendship Relations Survey

This questionnaire was written to help you assess your understanding of your behavior in interpersonal relationships. There are no right or wrong answers. The best answer is the one that comes closest to representing your quest for good interpersonal relationships. In each statement, the first sentence gives a situation, and the second sentence gives a reaction. For each statement, indicate the number that is closest to the way you would handle the situation.

5 You always would act this way.   **2** You seldom would act this way.
4 You frequently would act this way. **1** You never would act this way.
3 You sometimes would act this way.

   Try to relate each question to your own personal experience. Take as much time as you need to give a true and accurate answer for yourself. Remember, there is no right or wrong answer. Trying to give the "correct" answer will make your answer meaningless to you. Be honest with yourself.

1. You work with a friend, but some of her mannerisms and habits are getting on your nerves and irritating you. More and more you avoid interacting with or even seeing your friend.

Never   1—2—3—4—5   Always

2. In a moment of weakness, you give away a friend's secret. Your friend finds out and calls you to ask about it. You admit to it and talk with your friend about how to handle secrets better in the future.

Never   1—2—3—4—5   Always

3. You have a friend who never seems to have time for you. You ask him about it, telling him how you feel.

Never   1—2—3—4—5   Always

4. Your friend is upset with you because you have inconvenienced him. He tells you how he feels. You tell him he is too sensitive and is over-reacting.

Never   1—2—3—4—5   Always

5. You had a disagreement with a friend, and now she ignores you when-ever she's around you. You decide to ignore her back.

Never   1—2—3—4—5   Always

6. A friend has pointed out that you never seem to have time for him. You explain why you have been busy and try for a mutual understanding.

Never   1—2—3—4—5   Always

7. At great inconvenience, you arrange to take your friend to the doctor's office. When you arrive to pick her up, you find she has decided not to go. You explain to her how you feel and try to reach an understanding about future favors.

Never   1—2—3—4—5   Always

8. You have argued with a friend and are angry with her, ignoring her when you meet. She tells you how she feels and asks about restoring the friend-ship. You ignore her and walk away.

Never   1—2—3—4—5   Always

9. You have a secret that you have told only to your best friend. The next day, an acquaintance asks you about the secret. You deny the secret and decide to break off the relationship with your best friend.

Never   1—2—3—4—5   Always

10. A friend who works with you tells you about some of your mannerisms and habits that get on his nerves. You discuss these with your friend and look for some possible ways of dealing with the problem.

Never   1—2—3—4—5   Always

11. Your best friend gets involved in something illegal that you believe will lead to serious trouble. You decide to tell your friend how you disapprove of his involvement in the situation.

Never   1—2—3—4—5   Always

12. In a moment of weakness, you give away a friend's secret. Your friend finds out and calls you to ask about it. You deny it firmly.

Never   1—2—3—4—5   Always

13. You have a friend who never seems to have time for you. You decide to forget her and to start looking for new friends.

    Never   1—2—3—4—5   Always

14. You are involved in something illegal, and your friend tells you of her disapproval and fear that you will get in serious trouble. You discuss it with your friend.

    Never   1—2—3—4—5   Always

15. You work with a friend, but some of her mannerisms and habits are getting on your nerves and irritating you. You explain your feelings to your friend, looking for a mutual solution to the problem.

    Never   1—2—3—4—5   Always

16. A friend has pointed out that you never seem to have time for him. You walk away.

    Never   1—2—3—4—5   Always

17. Your best friend gets involved in something illegal that you believe will lead to serious trouble. You decide to mind your own business.

    Never   1—2—3—4—5   Always

18. Your friend is upset because you have inconvenienced him. He tells you how he feels. You try to understand and agree on a way to keep it from happening again.

    Never   1—2—3—4—5   Always

19. You had a disagreement with a friend, and now she ignores you whenever she's around you. You tell her how her actions make you feel and ask about restoring your friendship.

    Never   1—2—3—4—5   Always

20. A friend who works with you tells you about some of your mannerisms and habits that get on his nerves. You listen and walk away.

    Never   1—2—3—4—5   Always

21. At great inconvenience, you arrange to take your friend to the doctor's office. When you arrive to pick her up, you find she had decided not to go. You say nothing but resolve never to do any favors for that person again.

    Never   1—2—3—4—5   Always

22. You have argued with a friend and are angry with her, ignoring her when you meet. She tells you how she feels and asks about restoring the friendship. You discuss ways of maintaining your friendship, even when you disagree.

    Never   1—2—3—4—5   Always

23. You have a secret that you have told only to your best friend. The next day, an acquaintance asks you about the secret. You call your friend and ask her about it, trying to come to an understanding of how to handle secrets better in the future.

Never   1—2—3—4—5   Always

24. You are involved in something illegal, and your friend tells you of her disapproval and fear that you will get in serious trouble. You tell your friend to mind her own business.

Never   1—2—3—4—5   Always

Friendship Relations Survey Answer Key

In the Friendship Relations Survey there are 12 questions that deal with your willingness to self-disclose and 12 questions that are concerned with your receptivity to feedback. Transfer your scores to this answer key. Reverse the scoring for all questions that are starred; that is, if you answered 5, record the score of 1; if you answered 4, record the score of 2; if you answered 3, record the score of 3; if you answered 2, record the score of 4; and if you answered 1, record the score of 5. Then add the scores in each column.

Willingness to Self-Disclose	Receptivity to Feedback
*1. _____	2. _____
3. _____	*4. _____
*5. _____	6. _____
7. _____	*8. _____
*9. _____	10. _____
11. _____	*12. _____
*13. _____	14. _____
15. _____	*16. _____
*17. _____	18. _____
19. _____	*20. _____
*21. _____	22. _____
23. _____	*24. _____
Total _____	Total _____

On the Friendship Relations Survey Summary sheet, add the totals for receptivity to feedback and willingness to self-disclose to arrive at an index of interpersonal risk taking, which you will use in Chapter 3.

Friendship Relations Survey Summary Sheet

Draw horizontal and vertical lines through your scores and the group's scores on receptivity to feedback and willingness to self-disclose. The results should look like the Johari Window.

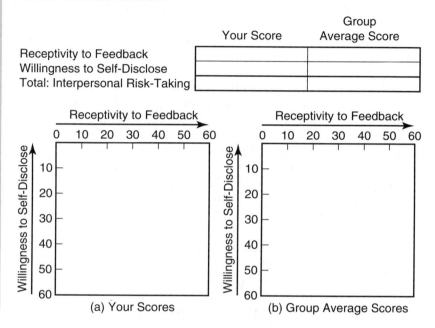

	Your Score	Group Average Score
Receptivity to Feedback		
Willingness to Self-Disclose		
Total: Interpersonal Risk-Taking		

(a) Your Scores   (b) Group Average Scores

Being Open with and to Other People

Relationships may be classified on a continuum from open to closed. **Openness** in a relationship refers to participants' willingness to share their ideas, feelings, and reactions to the current situation. On a professional basis, relationships among collaborators who are working to achieve mutual goals tend to be quite open, while relationships among competitors who are seeking advantages over each other tend to be quite closed. On a personal level, some relationships (such as friendships) are very open, while other relationships (such as casual acquaintances) are relatively closed. The more open participants in a relationship are with each other, the more positive, constructive, and effective the relationship tends to be.

Openness has two sides. To build good relationships you must be both open *with* other people (disclosing yourself to them) and open *to* others (listening to their disclosures in an accepting way). Usually, the more that people know about you, the more likely they are to like you. Yet self-disclosure does carry a degree of risk. For just as knowing you better is likely to result in a closer relationship, sometimes it could result in people liking you less. "Familiarity breeds contempt" means that some people may learn something about you that detracts from the relationship. Because disclosing is risky, some people prefer to hide themselves from others in the belief that no reaction is better than a possible negative reaction. "Nothing ventured, nothing gained," however, means that some risk is vital to achieving any worthwhile goal. To build a meaningful relationship you have to disclose yourself to the other person and take the risk that the other person may reject rather than like you.

The other side of the coin is responding to the other person's self-disclosures. Being open to another person means showing that you are interested in how he or she feels and thinks. This does not mean prying into the intimate areas of his or her life. It means being willing to listen in an accepting way to his or her reactions to the present situation and to what you are doing and saying. Even when a person's behavior offends you, you may wish to express acceptance of the person and disagreement with the way he or she behaves.

In order for the relationship to build and develop, both individuals have to disclose and be open to other people's disclosures. Openness depends on three factors: self-awareness, self-acceptance, and trust. Openness, self-awareness, and self-acceptance are discussed in this chapter. Trust is discussed in the next chapter.

Openness with Other Individuals

You are *open with* other persons when you disclose yourself to them, sharing your ideas, feelings, and reactions to the present situation, and letting other people know who you are as a person. To be open with another person you must (a) be aware of who you are, (b) accept yourself, and (c) take the risk of trusting the other person to be accepting of you. Openness thus can be described as being dependent on self-awareness (S), self-acceptance (A), and trust (T) (O = S A T). Commonly, openness is known as self-disclosure.

What Is Self-Disclosure?

Self-disclosure is revealing to another person how you perceive and are reacting to the present situation and giving any information about yourself and your past that is relevant to an understanding of your perceptions and reactions to the present. Effective self-disclosure has a number of characteristics:

1. **Self-disclosure focuses on the present, not the past.** Self-disclosure does not mean revealing intimate details of your past life.

Making highly personal confessions about your past may lead to a temporary feeling of intimacy, but a relationship is built by disclosing your reactions to events you both are experiencing or to what the other person says or does. A person comes to know and understand you not through knowing your past history but through knowing how you react. Past history is helpful only if it clarifies why you are reacting in a certain way.

2. **Reactions to people and events include feelings as well as facts.** To be self-disclosing often means to share with another person how you feel about events that are occurring.

3. **Self-disclosures have two dimensions—breadth and depth.** As you get to know someone better and better, you cover more topics in your explanations (breadth) and make your explanations more personally revealing (depth).

4. **In the early stages of a relationship, self-disclosure needs to be reciprocal.** The amount of self-disclosure you engage in will influence the amount of self-disclosure the other person engages in and vice versa. The polite thing to do is to match the level of self-disclosure offered by new acquaintances, disclosing more if they do so and drawing back if their self-disclosure declines. Once a relationship is well established, strict reciprocity occurs much less frequently.

Impact of Self-Disclosure on Relationships

Healthy relationships are built on self-disclosure. A relationship grows and develops as two people become more open about themselves to each other. *If you cannot reveal yourself, you cannot become close to others, and you cannot be valued by others for who you are.* Two people who let each other know how they are reacting to situations and to each other are pulled together; two people who stay silent about their reactions and feelings stay strangers.

There are many ways in which self-disclosure initiates, builds, and maintains relationships. *First, self-disclosure enables you and other people to get to know each other.* Most relationships proceed from superficial exchanges to more intimate ones. At first, individuals disclose relatively little to another person and receive relatively little in return. When initial interactions are enjoyable or interesting, exchanges become (a) broader, involving more areas of your life and (b) deeper, involving more important and sensitive areas. In terms of breadth, from discussing the weather and sports, as the relationship develops you may discuss a wider range of topics (such as your family, your hopes and dreams, issues at work, and so forth) and share more diverse activities (such as going to movies or plays together, going bike riding or playing tennis together, and so forth).

In terms of depth, you might willingly talk with a casual acquaintance about your preferences in food and music but reserve for close friends discussions of your anxieties and personal ambitions. The longer people interact, the more topics they tend to be willing to discuss and the more personally revealing they tend to become. This does not mean that getting to know another person is a simple process of being more and more open. You do not simply disclose more and more each day. Rather, there are cycles of seeking intimacy and avoiding it. Sometimes you are candid and confiding with a friend, and other times you are restrained and distant. The development of caring and commitment in a relationship, however, results from the cumulative history of self-disclosure in the relationship.

Second, self-disclosure allows you and other individuals to identify common goals and overlapping needs, interests, activities, and values. In order to know whether a relationship with another person is desirable, you have to know what the other person wants from the relationship, what the other person is interested in, what joint activities might be available, and what the other person values. Relationships are built on common goals, interests, activities, and values. If such information is not disclosed, the relationship may end before it has a chance to begin.

Third, once common goals have been identified, self-disclosure is necessary to work together to accomplish them. Working together requires constant self-disclosure to ensure effective communication, decision making, leadership, and resolution of conflict. Joint action to achieve mutual goals cannot be effective unless collaborators are quite open in their interactions with each other.

Just as relationships are built through self-disclosure, *relationships can deteriorate for lack of self-disclosure.* Sometimes people hide their reactions from others through fear of rejection, fear of a potential or ongoing conflict, or feelings of shame and guilt. Whatever the reason, if you hide how you are reacting to the other person, your concealment can hurt the relationship, and the energy you pour into hiding is an additional stress on the relationship. Hiding your perceptions and feelings dulls your awareness of your own inner experience and decreases your ability to disclose your reactions even when it is perfectly safe and appropriate to do so. The result can be the end of the relationship. Being silent is not being strong—strength is the willingness to take a risk by disclosing yourself with the intention of building a better relationship.

Benefits of Self-Disclosure

We disclose information to another person for many reasons. *First, you begin and deepen a relationship by sharing reactions, feelings, personal information, and confidences.* This topic has already been discussed.

Second, self-disclosure improves the quality of relationships. We disclose to those we like. We like those who disclose to us. We like those to whom we have disclosed. Overall, it is through self-disclosure that caring is developed among individuals and commitment to each other is built.

Third, self-disclosure allows you to validate your perception of reality. Listeners provide useful information about social reality. The events taking place around us and the meaning of other people's behavior are often ambiguous, open to many different interpretations. By seeing how a listener reacts to your self-disclosures, you get information about the correctness and appropriateness of your views. Other people may reassure you that your reactions are "perfectly normal" or suggest that you are "blowing things out of proportion." If others have similar interpretations, we consider our perceptions to be valid. Comparing your perceptions and reactions with the reactions and perceptions of others is called **consensual validation.** Without self-disclosure, consensual validation could not take place.

Fourth, self-disclosure increases your self-awareness and clarifies your understanding of yourself. In explaining your feelings in watching a sunset or why you like a certain book, you clarify aspects of yourself to yourself. In sharing your feelings and experiences with others, you may gain greater self-understanding and self-awareness. Talking to a friend about a problem, for example, can help you clarify your thoughts about a situation. Sharing your reactions with others results in feedback from others, which contributes to a more objective perspective on your experiences.

Fifth, the expression of feelings and reactions is a freeing experience. Sometimes it helps to get emotions and reactions "off your chest." After a difficult day at work, it may release pent up feelings by telling a friend how angry you are at your boss or how unappreciated you feel. Even sharing long-term feelings of insecurity with a trusted friend may free you from such feelings. Simply being able to express your emotions is a reason for self-disclosure.

Sixth, you may disclose information about yourself or not as a means of social control. You may deliberately refrain from talking about yourself to end an interaction as quickly as possible or you may emphasize topics, beliefs, or ideas that you think will make a favorable impression on the other person.

Seventh, self-disclosing is an important part of managing stress and adversity. Communicating intimately with another person, especially in times of stress, seems to be a basic human need. By discussing your fear, you free yourself from it. By sharing your anxiety, you gain insight into ways to reduce it. By describing a problem, you see ways to solve it. The more you seek out a friend in times of adversity and discuss the situation openly, the more you will be able to deal with the stress and solve your problem.

Benefits of Self-Disclosure

Form a pair. Rank order the following benefits of self-disclosure from most important (1) to least important (8).

_____ To begin and deepen a relationship.

_____ To improve the quality of and caring within a relationship.

_____ To determine whether your reactions and perceptions are accurate.

_____ To clarify and increase your self-understanding and self-awareness.

_____ To free yourself from feelings by getting them "off your chest."

_____ To control your current interactions.

_____ To help you manage stress and adversity.

_____ To be known intimately and accepted for who you are.

Finally, self-disclosure fulfills a human need to be known intimately and accepted. Most people want someone to know them well and accept, appreciate, respect, and like them.

Keeping Your Self-Disclosures Appropriate

You only self-disclose when it is appropriate to do so. Just as you can disclose too little, you can also be too self-disclosing. Refusing to let anyone know anything about you keeps others away. Revealing too many of your reactions too fast may scare others away. Typically, a relationship is built gradually and develops in stages. Although you should sometimes take risks in sharing your reactions with others, you should ensure that the frequency and depth of your reactions are appropriate to the situation. When you are unsure about the appropriateness of your self-disclosures, you may wish to follow these guidelines:

1. I make sure my disclosures are not a random or isolated act but rather part of an ongoing relationship.

2. I focus my disclosures on what is going on within and between persons in the present.

3. I am sensitive to the effect a disclosure will have on the other person. Some disclosures may upset or cause considerable distress. What you want to say may seem inappropriate to the other per-

son. Most people become uncomfortable when the level of self-disclosure exceeds their expectations.

4. I only disclose when it has a reasonable chance of improving the relationship.

5. I continue only if my disclosures are reciprocated. When you share your reactions, you should expect disclosure in return. When it is apparent that self-disclosures will not be reciprocated, you should limit the disclosures you make.

6. I increase my disclosures when a crisis develops in the relationship.

7. I gradually move my disclosures to a deeper level. Self-disclosures may begin with the information acquaintances commonly disclose (such as talking about hobbies, sports, school, and current events) and gradually move to more personal information. As a friendship develops, the depth of disclosure increases as well. Disclosures about deep feelings and concerns are most appropriate in close, well-established relationships.

8. I keep my reactions and feelings to myself when the other person is competitive or untrustworthy. While relationships are built through self-disclosure, there are times when you will want to hide your reactions. If a person has been untrustworthy and if you know from past experience that the other person will misinterpret or overreact to your self-disclosure, you may wish to keep silent.

Self-Disclosure and Self-Awareness

Chilon, a Spartan philosopher, after visiting the Oracle of Delphi in 556 B.C., wished to leave some of his wisdom as an offering to Apollo in appreciation for the Oracle's services. On a column in the antechamber he carved, "Know thyself." Later, Shakespeare told us, "To thine own self be true." Western civilization has taken this advice to heart. Hundreds of books have been written dealing with how to get to know yourself, and the *Oxford English Dictionary* lists more than 100 words that focus on the self, from *self-abasement* to *self-wisdom*. A great deal of effort is expended to increase self-awareness. When your attention is focused on yourself, you are **self-aware.** Self-awareness is the key to self-knowledge, self-understanding, and self-disclosure.

Being open with another person begins with being aware of who you are and what you are like. To disclose your feelings and reactions, you must be aware of them.

How Self-Aware Am I?

How self-aware are you? The following questions may help you decide (adapted from Fenigstein, Scheier, & Buss, 1975). Rate yourself on a scale from 1 (disagree) to 5 (agree). The higher your score, the more self-aware you tend to be.

_____   1. I am constantly trying to figure myself out.

_____   2. I am concerned about what other people think of me.

_____   3. I am always examining my motives.

_____   4. I often worry about making a good impression.

_____   5. I am sensitive to changes in my mood.

_____   6. Whenever I get the chance, I look in a mirror.

_____   7. I often fantasize about myself.

_____   8. I am self-conscious about the way I look.

_____   **Overall Total**

_____   **Total, Questions 1, 3, 5, 7: Private Self-Awareness**

_____   **Total, Questions 2, 4, 6, 8: Public Self-Awareness**

Benefits of Self-Awareness

Try this experiment. Set your watch to beep every hour. When it beeps write down what you are doing and what you are thinking. Do this for one week. Then count the number of times you were thinking about yourself. Two researchers who conducted such a study found that less than 8 percent of all recorded thoughts were about the self. For the most part, attention was focused on work and other activities. When participants were thinking about themselves, they reported feeling relatively unhappy and wished they were doing something else. The truth is, however, that there are so many benefits of self-awareness that it would take a whole book just to discuss them. Some of the major benefits are described in the following paragraphs.

Self-awareness helps you identify the actions that you need to take to behave competently in different situations. The more self-aware you are, the more able you are to control your behavior and the greater is your ability to adapt your behavior to changing circumstances. The more aware you are of your need to be independent, the less likely you are to accept money from your parents. If you see yourself as overweight, you may be less likely to eat candy and dessert. The more aware you are of your love for your mother, the more likely you are to send her flowers on Mother's Day. Overall, the more aware you are of yourself, the more able you are to regulate your actions and behave appropriately in different situations.

Self-awareness helps you present yourself appropriately and create the impression you want. Self-monitoring theory focuses on your ability to interact effectively with different people in different situations. **Self-monitoring** is the tendency to regulate your behavior to meet the demands of social situations. Individuals who are high on self-monitoring seem to have a repertoire of selves from which to draw. They are sensitive to self-presentation concerns, poised, ready, and able to modify their behavior as they move from one situation to another. They often act like very different people in different situations and with different individuals. Low self-monitors are less concerned about the social propriety of their behavior and express themselves in a consistent manner from one situation to the next, exhibiting what they regard as their true and honest self.

Self-awareness increases your social sensitivity. The more self-aware you are, the more effort you may make to learn about other people and to evaluate social situations. You may pay attention to information about people you are going to meet and interact with and tailor your behavior to fit the demands of the interaction.

Self-awareness increases your ability to communicate effectively. To be an effective communicator, you must formulate and coordinate both verbal and nonverbal messages. Your self-awareness may be the basis for your skills in using your face and voice to communicate particular emotions.

Self-awareness leads to self-understanding that enables you to solve personal problems. Psychotherapy, for example, is sought to increase self-awareness, to increase self-understanding, to increase your ability to solve personal problems, and to deal with adverse situations. The better you understand yourself, the more able you are to face difficult situations and successfully cope with stress.

Self-awareness helps you be the person you want to be. Self-awareness enables you to evaluate your actions against a standard and to adjust what you are doing so you will meet the standard. Self-awareness thus helps you behave in ways that are consistent with your personal values and socially accepted ideals. When you see a person in distress, for example, you are more likely to provide help when you are aware of your personal values.

Self-awareness is so central to your life that it affects almost everything you do. Yet despite its necessity and centrality, there are some dangers of being self-aware.

The Dangers of Self-Awareness

I refuse to be intimidated by reality anymore. . . . Reality is the leading cause of stress amongst those in touch with it. . . . Now, since I put reality on a back burner, my days are jam-packed and fun-filled.
—Trudy the Bag Lady in *Search for Intelligent Life in the Universe*

The first danger is that awareness may lead to depression over not living up to your own standards. The more self-aware you are, the more aware you may be of the discrepancy between your actions and your internal standards. This comparison can result in a temporary loss of self-esteem. When placed in front of a mirror, for example, many people tend to be uncomfortable. *Self-awareness theory* proposes that the discrepancy between actual and ideal selves can motivate either a change in behavior or an escape from self-awareness (see Figure 2.2). The danger is that awareness of the discrepancy will result in depression, withdrawal from self-awareness through denial or mood altering drugs such as alcohol, and continued dysfunctional and incompetent behavior.

The second danger is that unproductive self-awareness can result in being self-absorbed. There is a difference between being self-aware and self-absorbed. While self-awareness helps you behave more appropriately and competently, self-absorbed people are more likely to suffer from alcoholism, depression, anxiety, and other clinical disorders. In response to failure, a depressed person will focus his or her attention inwardly (without finding behaviors that can reduce the discrepancy) longer than will a nondepressed person. A negative self-image results. Alcohol is sometimes used to reduce self-awareness, so that the discrepancy between what you want to be and what you are is not so clear. Individuals who have failed on a task, for example, tend to drink more wine than those who have succeeded. Many people expect alcohol to grant mental relief from their problems.

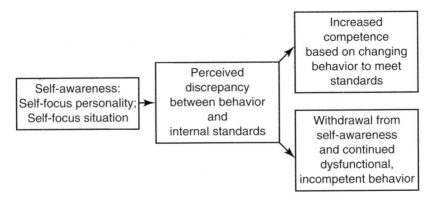

FIGURE 2.2   *Self-Discrepancy Resulting from Self-Awareness*

The Dangers of Lack of Self-Awareness

There are also dangers to lack of self-awareness. As self-awareness declines, a change in consciousness can take place in which the individual attends less to internal standards of conduct, reacts more to the immediate situation, and is less sensitive to long-term consequences of behavior. Behavior can slip out from the bonds of cognitive control, and individuals act on impulse. Mob violence is often caused by such *deindividuation.*

Ways of Becoming More Self-Aware

Given the multitude of benefits of self-awareness and its role in self-disclosure, you need to take Chilon's advice to heart and work to know yourself. There are a number of ways of becoming more self-aware. *The first way is introspection.* You can look inward and examine the "inside information" that you, and you alone, have about your thoughts, feelings, and motives. Introspection does help you become more aware of who you are and how you are feeling and reacting. Unfortunately, self-scrutiny is not always present, possible, or accurate. Most people spend very little time thinking about themselves. The reasons they feel or behave the way they do can be hidden from conscious awareness. In trying to understand their behavior, people sometimes make up reasons for their actions that come to mind easily and seem plausible but are probably incorrect. Introspection is almost always a good idea, but it has its limits.

The second way to increase your self-awareness is to observe yourself. **Self-perception theory** focuses on this procedure. It states that you understand your attitudes and emotions partly by inferring them from observations of your behavior or the circumstances in which your behavior occurs. By "watching" what you do, you become aware of what you are like as a person, much as outside observers form judgments of you on the basis of what they see. Often your behavior is a reliable guide to your inner feelings. When you become more self-aware, you usually focus on one facet of yourself. Asking you to look in a mirror physically focuses you on your appearance, while playing a tape recording of you speaking focuses you on your voice. When you become aware of some aspect of yourself, you typically evaluate it, considering how this aspect of you measures up to some internal rule or standard. Sometimes you make mistakes about the reasons for your behavior, leading to mistaken conclusions about yourself. You tend to do so when

1. External influences on your behavior are subtle and you mistakenly think your behavior reflects your personality. Going to a party with an outgoing, extroverted person can cause you to be more outgoing, and you may ascribe this result to your own personality.

2. External influences on your behavior are so conspicuous that you underestimate how much they are influencing your behavior. When a group of friends are all encouraging you to ask someone for a date, you may do so believing that you have decided to do so on your own.

3. The causes of your emotional arousal are unclear, so you form mistaken conclusions about what you are feeling. According to the **two-factor theory of emotion,** you first experience physiological arousal and then seek an appropriate label for the feeling. You may not always be right. Some people have misinterpreted being scared as affection for the person they are with (which is why you take your dates on scary rides at the amusement parks).

Your own behavior, however, is usually a useful guide to your thoughts and feelings.

Third, your self-awareness is increased when you explain your feelings, perceptions, reactions, and experiences to another person. When you put your feelings and reactions in words, they become clearer, better organized, and take on new meanings. Explaining your reactions and feelings to other people can also lead to new insights into yourself and your experiences. Most types of psychotherapy and many classroom learning procedures are based on the premise that oral explanation results in higher-level reasoning and deeper-level understanding.

A fourth way of becoming more self-aware is to compare yourself to others. **Social comparison** is gauging your own attitudes, emotions, attributes, and abilities by comparing them to those of other people. Some comparisons are easy to make. There is little room for error in deciding whether your hair is blond or brunette or how old or tall you are. There are no objective standards, however, for determining how kind, considerate, insightful, intelligent, extroverted, or socially astute a person you are. To make such judgments, you must compare yourself to other people. In the absence of objective measures of evaluation, comparing yourself to others provides a subjective measuring tool. You discover your similarities and uniqueness and form an impression of what you are like. From knowing others you know yourself.

A fifth way of becoming more self-aware is to interact with a wide variety of diverse people. Much of your self-awareness arises from your experiences and interactions with other people. As you get to know others, you get to know yourself. You learn very little about yourself while hiding in a closet and avoiding others. The wider the variety of your experiences with many different people, the better you get to know yourself. By having friends from different cultures and backgrounds, you become more sophisticated about their cultures, and at the same time you become more aware of your own culture and of who you are as a person.

Ways of Increasing Self-Awareness

Form a pair. Rank order the following ways of increasing self-awareness from most important (1) to least important (6).

_____ Engaging in introspection.

_____ Observing yourself.

_____ Explaining yourself to others.

_____ Comparing yourself to others.

_____ Interacting with diverse individuals.

_____ Seeking feedback from others

Sixth, you can increase your self-awareness by requesting feedback from other people as to how they see you and how they are reacting to your behavior. This is such an important aspect of becoming more self-aware that it is discussed in detail in the next section.

Self-Awareness Through Feedback from Others

The Relationship Between Self-Disclosure and Feedback

Feedback from other people can (a) confirm your view of yourself or (b) reveal to you aspects of yourself and consequences of your behavior you did not know. From the feedback you receive from others you increase your self-awareness and construct a **looking-glass self** (i.e., adopt, over time, other people's views of you). Your self-awareness is especially increased when you receive feedback from others who have different perspectives and see you differently than you see yourself.

The relationship between disclosure, feedback, and self-awareness is represented in the Johari Window (see Figures 2.3, 2.4, and 2.5), named after its two originators, Joe Luft and Harry Ingham (Luft, 1969). They believed that (a) there are certain things you know about yourself and certain things you do not know about yourself and (b) there are certain things other people know about you and certain things they do not know. As a relationship grows and develops, (a) you disclose more and more, enlarging your free area and reducing your hidden area, and (b) you receive more and more feedback, reducing your blind area and enlarging your free area. Through reducing your hidden area you give other people information to react to, thus enabling them to give more informed and precise feedback, which in turn reduces your blind area. Through reducing your blind area, you increase your self-awareness; this development helps you to be even more self-disclosing with others.

	Known to Self	Unknown to Self
Known to Others	Free to self and others	Blind to self, free to others
Unknown to Others	Free to self, hidden to others	Unknown to self and others

FIGURE 2.3 *Johari Window*

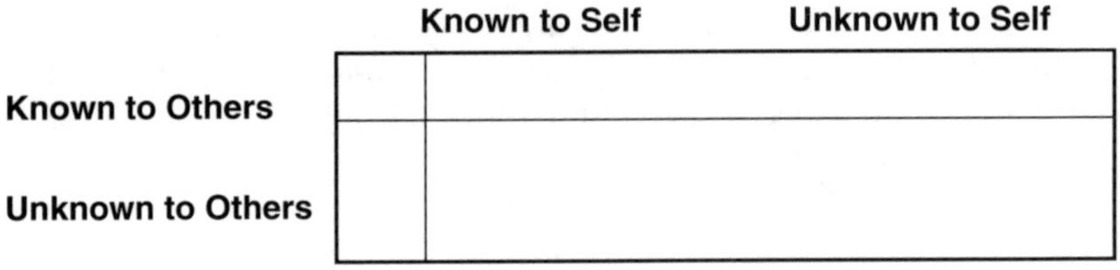

	Known to Self	Unknown to Self
Known to Others		
Unknown to Others		

FIGURE 2.4 *At the Beginning of a Relationship*

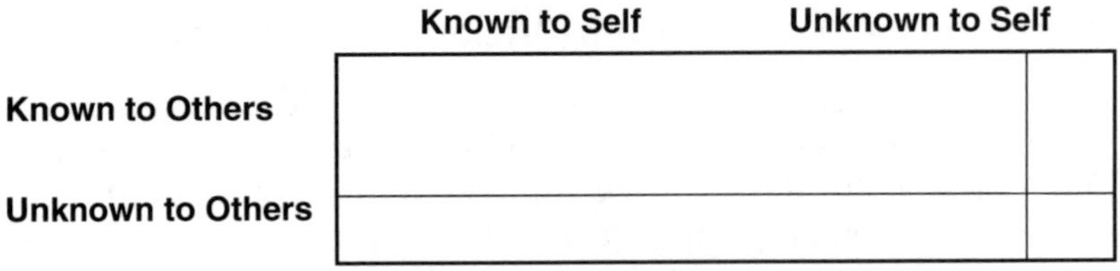

	Known to Self	Unknown to Self
Known to Others		
Unknown to Others		

FIGURE 2.5 *At the End of a Relationship*

Principles

1. Self-disclosure reduces the hidden area.
2. Feedback reduces the blind area.
3. Together they reduce the unknown area.

How to Give Constructive Feedback

When other people disclose how they are reacting to your behavior, they are giving you feedback. **Feedback** is information that allows you to compare your actual performance with standards of performance. In interpersonal relationships it is other people disclosing how they are perceiving and reacting to your behavior. You use feedback to determine the effectiveness of what you are doing. Receiving feedback from other people to increase our self-awareness begins in infancy, when parents tell us what a good person we are, how math is our best subject, how talented we are at playing the piano, and how we should be less shy and more outgoing. Later in childhood, feedback from peers becomes important. Are we picked early or late for athletic teams, do many or few people want to be our friend, and do we get invited to birthday parties? In school we get direct feedback on our academic performance. The *purpose* of all of this feedback is to provide constructive information to help us become aware of how others perceive our behavior and are affected by it.

You both give and receive feedback. Feedback given to another person should be nonthreatening and nondemanding. If you make the other person defensive, the feedback will be unhelpful because the person will tend not to hear and understand it correctly. You also let the person receiving the feedback decide whether or not his or her behavior is to be continued or changed. By increasing other people's self-awareness through feedback, you provide them with a more informed choice for future behavior. Some characteristics of helpful feedback are the following:

1. **Focus your feedback on the person's behavior, not on the person's personality.** Refer to what the person does, not to what you imagine his or her traits to be. Thus, you might say that the person "talked frequently in the meeting" rather than saying the person "is domineering." The former is an observation of what you see and hear and the latter is an inference about the person's character.

2. **Be descriptive, not judgmental.** Refer to what occurred, not to your judgments of right or wrong, good or bad, or nice or naughty. You might say, "You do not pronounce words clearly, and you speak too softly to be heard," rather than, "You are a terrible public speaker." Judgments arise out of a value system. Descriptions represent neutral reporting.

3. **Focus your feedback on a specific situation rather than on abstract behavior.** What a person does is always related to a specific time and place. Feedback that ties behavior to a specific situation increases self-awareness. Instead of saying, "You do not listen to other people," say, "When you and John were talking just now you looked out the window and seemed to be thinking of something else."

4. Focus your feedback on the "here and now" not on the "there and then." The more immediate the feedback, the more helpful it is. Instead of saying, "Last year you didn't speak to me in the hallway," say, "Hey, I just said hello and you didn't reply. Is something wrong?"

5. Share your perceptions and feelings, not advice. By sharing perceptions and feelings you leave other people free to decide for themselves how to use the feedback in the light of their own goals in a particular situation at a particular time. When you give advice, you tell other people what to do with the information and thereby take away their freedom to determine for themselves what is for them the most appropriate course of action. You can give feedback such as, "You look away and blush whenever Jose says hello to you," without giving advice such as, "You are too shy. Go ask Jose for a date."

6. Do not force feedback on other people. Feedback is given to help people become more self-aware and to improve their effectiveness in relating to other people. It is not given to make you feel better. Feedback should serve the needs of the receiver, not the needs of the giver. Giving feedback does release tension and increase the giver's energy, but feedback should not be forced on the receiver. Even if you are upset and want more than anything else in the world (at that moment) to give a friend some feedback, do not give it if your friend is too upset, defensive, or uninterested to understand it.

7. Do not give people more feedback than they can understand at the time. If you overload other people with feedback, it reduces the chances that they will use it. When you give people more feedback than they can understand, you are satisfying some need for yourself rather than helping the people become more self-aware.

8. Focus your feedback on actions that the person can change. It does no good to tell people that they have a lopsided head, that you don't like the color of their eyes, or that they are missing an ear. These are things the other person cannot change. It is helpful to give your perceptions of the effectiveness of a person's actions.

The giving and receiving of feedback require courage, skill, understanding, and respect for yourself and others. Feedback is a sign of involvement in and commitment to the relationship. Do not give it lightly. Make sure you are willing to be responsible for what you say and to clarify as much as the receiver wants. Be sure the timing of your feedback is appropriate. Excellent feedback presented at an inappropriate time may do more harm than good. Finally, remember that the purpose of feedback is to increase other people's self-awareness and feelings that "I am liked, I am respected, I am appreciated, I am capable, I am valued." To invest in a relationship by providing accurate and realistic feedback is a sign of caring and commitment.

Seeking Constructive Feedback

The above guidelines provide a framework for receiving feedback. When you want feedback, you ask for feedback on your behavior, not your personality. You ask the person to be descriptive, not judgmental. You focus the feedback on a specific situation, not on abstract, broad impressions. You focus the feedback on the immediate, not past situations. Make it clear that you want the other person's perceptions and feelings, not advice. Only listen to feedback when you want it, not when the other person wants to give it. When you have received as much feedback as you can comprehend and process, ask for the feedback to stop. Finally, only reflect on feedback that relates to aspects of yourself you have control over and can change.

Giving and Receiving Feedback

Giving Constructive Feedback	Receiving Feedback Constructively
Give feedback on others' behavior, not personality.	Ask for feedback on your behavior, not personality.
Give descriptive, not judgmental feedback.	Ask for descriptive, not judgmental feedback.
Give feedback on others' actions in a specific situation, not in the abstract.	Ask for feedback about your actions in a specific situation, not in abstract.
Give feedback on immediate behavior, not on the past.	Ask for feedback in the immediate situation, not in past situations.
Share your perceptions and feelings, not advice.	Ask for perceptions and feelings, not advice.
Give feedback only when other people ask you to.	Do not let people force feedback on you.
Do not give people more feedback than they can understand at the time.	Only receive as much feedback as you can comprehend and process.
Focus your feedback on actions that the person can change.	Only reflect on feedback on aspects of yourself you can change.

Self-Acceptance and Self-Disclosure

Show me the sensible person who likes himself or herself? I know myself too well to like what I see. I know but too well that I'm not what I'd like to be.
—Golda Meir

Even if you are aware of many different aspects of yourself, you may not disclose what you know if you do not find it acceptable. To be self-disclosing, it helps to be self-accepting. **Self-acceptance** is viewing yourself and your actions with approval or satisfaction, or having a high regard for yourself or, conversely, a lack of cynicism about yourself.

There is a common saying: "I can't be right for someone else if I'm not right for me!" There are at least five ways you can increase your self-acceptance. First, you can make conclusions about yourself on the basis of how you think other people see you. If other people like you, you tend to like yourself. This is called **reflected self-acceptance.** Second, you can believe that you are intrinsically and unconditionally acceptable. This is

 How I Reason About Myself

Working individually, rank the ways of deriving conclusions about your self-worth from 1 (most likely what I would do) to 5 (least likely what I would do). Write out the reasons for the order of your ranking.

Find a partner. Share your ranking and reasons. Listen carefully to his or her ranking and reasons. Make any modifications to your ranking you want to. Then find a new partner and repeat the process.

_____	Reflected self-acceptance	You make conclusions about yourself on the basis of how you think other people see you. If other people like you, you tend to like yourself.
_____	Basic self-acceptance	You believe you are intrinsically and unconditionally acceptable.
_____	Conditional self-acceptance	You base your conclusions about your self-worth on how well you meet external standards and expectations.
_____	Self-evaluation	You estimate how positively your attributes compare with those of your peers.
_____	Real–ideal comparison	You judge how your real self compares with your ideal self, that is, the correspondence between what you think you are and what you think you should be.

called **basic self-acceptance.** Third, you can base your conclusions about your self-worth on how well you meet external standards and expectations. This is known as **conditional self-acceptance.** It is characterized by "if-then" logic. "If I meet the external standards and expectations placed on me by other people, then I am of value. If I do not, then I am worthless." Fourth, you can estimate how positively your attributes compare with those of your peers. This is called **self-evaluation.** Fifth, you can judge how your real self compares with your ideal self, that is, the correspondence between what you think you are and what you think you should be. This is known as **real–ideal comparison.** Most people use one or more of these procedures for making judgments about their self-worth. It is important that you learn not only to accept yourself but also learn a constructive method of judging your self-worth from the information that is available to you. Usually, an unconditional, basic self-acceptance is viewed as the most constructive way to determine your self-acceptance.

Being self-accepting is important for many reasons. First, the more self-accepting you are, the greater your self-disclosure tends to be. The greater your self-disclosure, the more others accept you. And the more others accept you, the more you accept yourself. Second, considerable evidence abounds that self-acceptance and acceptance of others are related. If you think well of yourself, you tend to think well of others. Third, the more self-accepting you are, the more you tend to assume that others will like you, an expectation that often becomes a self-fulfilling prophecy. Finally, a high level of self-acceptance is reflected in psychological health.

Self-Disclosure and Self-Presentation

The image of myself which I try to create in my own mind that I may love myself is very different from the image which I try to create in the minds of others in order that they may love me.
—W. H. Auden

Self-disclosure is based on self-awareness, self-acceptance, and taking the risk of revealing yourself to others. Self-disclosure takes place in an ongoing social interaction in which you choose how you wish to present yourself to others. Most people are concerned about the images they present to others. The fashion industry, the cosmetic companies, diet centers, and the search for new drugs that grow hair, remove hair, whiten teeth, freshen breath, and smooth out wrinkles, all exploit our preoccupation with physical appearance. Manners, courtesy, and etiquette are all responses to concern about the impressions our behavior makes.

In *As You Like It*, William Shakespeare wrote, "All the world's a stage, and all the men and women merely players." Erving Goffman (1959) put

Shakespeare's thought into social science by arguing that life can be viewed as a play in which each of us acts out certain scripted lines. Our scripts are a reflection of the social face or social identity that we want to present to others. **Self-presentation** is the process by which we try to shape what others think of us and what we think of ourselves. It is part of **impression management**—the general process by which you behave in particular ways to create a desired social image.

In presenting yourself to others, you have to recognize that there are many complex aspects of yourself. It is as if you have a number of selves that are tied to certain situations and certain groups of people with whom you interact. The self you present to your parents is usually different from the self you present to your peers. You present yourself differently to your boss, subordinates, colleagues, customers, neighbors, same-sex friends, opposite-sex friends, and strangers. When you are playing tennis, the aspect of yourself that loves physical exercise and competition may be most evident. When you attend a concert, the aspect of yourself that responds with deep emotion to classical music may be most evident. In church, your religious side may be most evident. In a singles bar, your interest in other people may be most evident. In different situations and with different people, different aspects of yourself will be relevant.

In presenting yourself to others, you have to vary your presentation to the audience. Societal norms virtually require that you present yourself in different ways to different audiences. You are expected to address someone considerably older than you differently from the way you address your peers. You are expected to address the president of the United States differently from how you address your next-door neighbor. In formal situations you are expected to act in ways different from how you would act in informal situations. Depending on the setting, the role relationship, and your previous experience with the person, you are expected to monitor your behavior and present yourself accordingly.

In presenting yourself to others, you basically have two motives: strategic self-presentation and self-verification. **Strategic self-presentation** consists of efforts to shape others' impressions in specific ways in order to gain influence, power, sympathy, or approval. Job interviews, personal ads, political campaign promises, and a defendant's appeal to a jury are examples. Your goal may be to be perceived as likable, competent, moral, dangerous, or even helpless, depending on the situation and the relationship. You communicate who you are and what you are like through your clothes, appearance, posture, eye contact, tone of voice, manners, and gestures. There are many people who believe that you will be perceived in quite different ways depending on your style of dress, manner, and cleanliness. Clothing, they believe, transmits messages about the wearer's personality, attitudes, social status, behavior, and group allegiances. People who wear clothes associated with high status tend to have more influence than those wearing low-status clothes. Somber hues (grays, dark blues, or browns) of clothing seem to communicate ambition, a taste for moderate risks and long-range planning, and a preference for tasks that have clear criteria for success and failure. Attention to clothes, posture, eye contact, tone of voice, manners, and gestures may be especially important for first impressions.

Related to strategic self-presentation are ingratiation and self-promotion. **Ingratiation** describes acts that are motivated by the desire to get along and be liked. When people want to be liked, they put their best foot forward, smile a lot, make eye contact, nod their heads, express agreement with what is said, and give compliments and favors. **Self-promotion** describes acts that are motivated by a desire to "get ahead" and be respected for one's competence. When people want to be respected for their competence, they try to impress others by talking about themselves and immodestly showing off their knowledge, status, and exploits.

The second self-presentation motive is **self-verification**—the desire to have others perceive us as we genuinely perceive ourselves. This is sometimes known as **open self-presentation,** which consists of efforts to let others see you as you believe yourself to be. People generally are quite motivated to verify their existing self-view in the eyes of others. People, for example, often selectively elicit, recall, and accept feedback that confirms their self-conceptions. This statement does not mean that they wish to fool others about who they are. People often work hard to correct others whose impressions of them are mistaken. They may want to make a good impression, but they also want others (especially their friends) to have an accurate impression, one that is consistent with their own self-concept.

Self-presentation and impression management are part of everyone's life. Some people do these things more consciously and successfully than others. People differ in their ability to present themselves appropriately and create the impression they want. The more self-monitoring you are, the more sensitive you tend to be to strategic self-presentation concerns, poised, ready, and able to modify your behavior as you move from one situation to another.

The self is an enduring aspect of human personality, an invisible "inner core" that is stable over time and slow to change. The struggle to "find yourself" or "be true to yourself" is based on this view. Yet at least part of the self is malleable, molded by life experiences and different from one situation to the next. In this sense, the self is multifaceted and has many different faces. Each of us has a private self consisting of our innermost thoughts and feelings, memories, and self-views. We also have an outer self, portrayed by the roles we play and the way we present ourselves in public. In fulfilling our social obligations and presenting ourselves to others, we base our presentations on the complexity of our personalities, the social norms specifying appropriate behavior, and the motives of revealing who we really are, verifying our views of ourselves, and creating strategic impressions.

EXERCISE 2.2
Initiating Relationships

The following is a simple exercise in initiating relationships. The objectives of this exercise are

1. To initiate relationships with other individuals whom you do not know.

2. To share initial feelings and thoughts with other individuals.

3. To take risks in revealing yourself to other individuals.

4. To experience a variety of ways to disclose yourself to others.

5. To encourage openness, trust, risk taking, and feedback with other individuals.

The Activities

1. Everyone stand up and mill around the room, making sure that you pass by everyone present. Greet each person nonverbally. This greeting may be a handshake, a smile, a wink, a sock on the arm, or any other nonverbal way you may think of to say hello. After five minutes of milling, find a person you do not know. If you know everyone present, find the person you know least well.

2. Sit down with the person; each of you then take 2½ minutes to introduce yourself to the other. Do this by discussing the question of who you are as a person.

3. Turn around and find someone else near you whom you do not know or know least well of the other people present. Sit down with your new partner; each of you then take 2½ minutes to discuss the most significant experience you have had recently.

4. Find someone else you do not know. Sit down with your new partner and take five minutes (2½ minutes each) to exchange views on what you hope to accomplish by participating in this program.

5. Find another person whom you do not know. Sit down with your new partner and take five minutes (2½ minutes each) to share a fantasy or daydream that you often have. It may be connected with success, such as becoming president of the United States, or it may be connected with love, such as meeting a terrific person who immediately falls in love with you, or it may be about what you would like to do with your next vacation.

6. Now form a group no larger than 10 or 12 people. Try to be in a group with as many of the individuals as you have talked with in the previous activities. In the group discuss
    a. How you feel about the different members on the basis of the previous activities, first impression, or past experience if you knew them previously.
    b. Which activity you felt was most helpful in getting to know the person you were interacting with.
    c. What you have learned from this exercise.
    d. What individuals in the group need to share if you are to get to know them during this session.
    e. Anything else that seems relevant to initiating relationships. This discussion may continue for as long as you like.

7. Alternative topics for discussion in pairs are
    a. What animal I would like to be and why.
    b. What song means the most to me and why.
    c. What it is that I like most about myself.
    d. How I would change myself if I had complete power to do so.
    e. What my most significant childhood experience was.
    f. What my immediate impressions of you are.
    g. The ways in which we are similar or different.

 EXERCISE 2.3

Name Tagging

The other members of your group or class are your major resources for learning. Look around the room and see who is here to facilitate your learning. The purpose of this exercise is to get to know the other participants while at the same time letting them know more about you.

1. Working alone, write your first name in the center of a three-by-five-inch index card. Write it large enough so other people can read it at some distance. Then,
    a. In the *upper left-hand corner* write the names of two places: where you were born and your favorite place.
    b. In the *upper right-hand corner* write two of your favorite activities. These may be sports, hobbies, pastimes, jobs, or other ways you spend your time.
    c. In the *lower right-hand corner* write two things: Something pleasant you have experienced in the past few months and something pleasant you are looking forward to in the next few months.
    d. In the *lower left-hand corner* write three adjectives or adverbs that describe you.

2. Pin the card on the front of your shirt or blouse.

3. Mill around and meet as many other participants as possible in the time allowed (about 15 minutes). Discuss each other's cards.

4. Keep your name tag and wear it at subsequent course sessions until you know everyone present and they know you.

Muncie, Indiana	Mountain Climbing
Lake Berg, British Columbia	Running Marathons

DAVID

Intense	Vacation in Mexico
Fun-Loving	Backpacking in Yellowstone
Hard-Working	National Park

EXERCISE 2.4
Sharing Your Past

The purpose of this exercise is to let other people get to know you by sharing your family history with them and to get to know them by learning more about their past. The procedure is as follows:

1. Fill in the following chart with the names (first and last) of your grandparents and parents. If you are not sure of all the names, ask your parents what they are. If you did not grow up with your parents, use whatever parent figures you have.

Maternal grandfather	Maternal grandmother	Paternal grandfather	Paternal grandmother
Mother		Father	
You			

2. In small groups (from two to seven members), give your answers to the following questions and listen carefully to the answers of the other group members.

  a. Maternal grandfather:
    (1) Where was he born and raised?
    (2) What was his early life like?
    (3) What are (were) his outstanding characteristics?
    (4) What is (was) his career?
    (5) Can you trace any of your characteristics or attitudes to him?
    (6) Do any family traditions (activities, foods, etc.) come from him?

  b. Maternal grandmother:
    (1) Where was she born and raised?
    (2) What was her early life like?
    (3) What are (were) her outstanding characteristics?
    (4) What is (was) her career?
    (5) Can you trace any of your characteristics or attitudes to her?
    (6) Do any family traditions (activities, foods, etc.) come from her?

  c. Paternal grandfather:
    (1) Where was he born and raised?
    (2) What was his early life like?
    (3) What are (were) his outstanding characteristics?
    (4) What is (was) his career?
    (5) Can you trace any of your characteristics or attitudes to him?
    (6) Do any family traditions (activities, foods, etc.) come from him?

  d. Paternal grandmother:
    (1) Where was she born and raised?
    (2) What was her early life like?
    (3) What are (were) her outstanding characteristics?
    (4) What is (was) her career?
    (5) Can you trace any of your characteristics or attitudes to her?
    (6) Do any family traditions (activities, foods, etc.) come from her?

  e. Father:
    (1) Where was he born and raised?
    (2) What was his early life like?
    (3) What are (were) his outstanding characteristics?
    (4) What is (was) his career?
    (5) Can you trace any of your characteristics or attitudes to him?
    (6) Do any family traditions (activities, foods, etc.) come from him?

  f. Mother:
    (1) Where was she born and raised?
    (2) What was her early life like?
    (3) What are (were) her outstanding characteristics?
    (4) What is (was) her career?
    (5) Can you trace any of your characteristics or attitudes to her?
    (6) Do any family traditions (activities, foods, etc.) come from her?

3. In the same small groups, discuss the following questions:
   a. How did you feel about doing this exercise?
   b. Did you learn anything new about yourself?
   c. Is it important for you to know about your family?
   d. How do you think an adopted person deals with this issue? (If you are adopted, how do you deal with it?)
   e. How did you react to what other members of your group said about their family roots?

 ### EXERCISE 2.5
Self-Disclosure and Self-Awareness

The purpose of this exercise is to allow participants to focus on three of the areas described in the Johari Window: the free area, the blind area, and the hidden area. It is to be used with people who know each other, at least a little. Each participant needs a number of three-by-five-inch index cards. The procedure is as follows:

1. Working by yourself, review the material on the Johari Window. Then on a sheet of paper, write down several of your characteristics that you think other people in the room know (free area) and several of your characteristics that you think no one in the room knows (hidden area). Leave room on your paper to add characteristics in your blind area.

2. Form into groups of five. Each member takes five three-by-five-inch index cards. Working by yourself, write a different group member's name on the front of each card (make one for yourself also). Turn the cards over and write two positive characteristics of the person whose name appears on the front. On your own card write two positive characteristics you think the other group members do not know about you (from your hidden area) that you are willing to have them know.

3. Collect all the cards, shuffle them, and place them face down in a pile in the center of the group. Then, one by one, take each card, read the description aloud, and decide by group consensus to whom the card belongs (do not look at the name on the card). Place the card, with the name still facing down, in front of the person the group decides it belongs to. Repeat this procedure until all the cards have been distributed.

4. One by one, members of the group turn the cards they have been given face up. Each member gives his or her reactions to the cards received. If someone receives a card that does not belong to him, the card is given to the person it really belongs to. The group then discusses
   a. Why the cards were given to the right or wrong person.
   b. Whether the descriptions on the cards are accurate for the people for whom they are intended.
   c. What has been learned from the exercise.

5. Working by yourself, take the cards you received and classify them into the free, hidden, and blind areas of the Johari Window. If your cards mention any characteristics you did not write down at the beginning of the exercise, add them to your sheet. Pay special attention to characteristics that are in your blind area.

Self-Awareness Sheet

Name: _____   Date: _____

Free Area

1. _____   6. _____
2. _____   7. _____
3. _____   8. _____
4. _____   9. _____
5. _____   10. _____

Hidden Area

1. _____   6. _____
2. _____   7. _____
3. _____   8. _____
4. _____   9. _____
5. _____   10. _____

Blind Area

1. _____   6. _____
2. _____   7. _____
3. _____   8. _____
4. _____   9. _____
5. _____   10. _____

 EXERCISE 2.6
Your Unknown Area

The purpose of this exercise is to increase your awareness of aspects of yourself that may be in your unknown area. The procedure is as follows:

1. As the instructor reads a list of topics, write down in a "free association" way the first responses that come into your mind.

2. Study your written responses. What conclusions about yourself as a person can you make from your responses? What characteristics, needs, goals, fears, or worries do your responses reflect?

3. Form into groups of five members. If you feel comfortable doing so, share your responses with the group and ask for their help in describing what you have learned about yourself. If a member of your group does not wish to report her responses, protect her right to remain silent. Be supportive of those group members who do reveal their responses to the group.

4. Working by yourself, summarize on a sheet of paper what you have learned about yourself from the exercise.

Topics

Tools	Musical instrument	Fruit
Geographic location	Vacation	Article of clothing
Color	Human	God or goddess
Hero or heroine	Legendary figure	Piece of furniture
Season of the year	Food	Retreat
Weapon	Animal	Protect

 **EXERCISE 2.7**

Labeling

The purpose of this exercise is to provide feedback concerning first impressions. Each participant needs ten blank name tags or labels. The procedure is as follows:

1. The instructor gives each participant ten blank name tags or labels and a copy of the Category List.

2. Participants copy each category on a separate blank name tag or label.

3. Participants then mill around the room and choose a person who best fits each category. Then they attach a category label on the clothing of the person and engage in a one-minute conversation with the person.

4. Participants form groups of five and discuss reactions to being labeled (or not labeled) by people's first impressions. Did you learn anything about yourself?

Category List

Happy	Warm	Fun
Smart	Friendly	Spontaneous
Sincere	Aloof	Aggressive
Mysterious		

EXERCISE 2.8

Interviewing

The purpose of this exercise is to get acquainted with other members of a group. Each participant needs a copy of the Interview Sheet. The procedure is as follows:

1. Choose a partner. Make sure it is a person you would like to know better. Choose five questions from the Interview Sheet and interview your partner. He or she will then interview you by asking you five of the questions. Each of you will later introduce the other to a group, so you may want to take notes.

2. Form groups of six. Each person introduces his or her partner to the group.

3. Pick a new partner and repeat the interview and introduction procedure. The whole process may be repeated as often as there is time for.

4. Discuss in your group
   a. How it feels to be interviewed and introduced.
   b. Whether you learned anything about yourself from the experience.

Interview Sheet

What is difficult for you to do?

What is a favorite joke of yours?

How do you define friendship?

What value is most important to you?

When do you feel most comfortable?

If you weren't what you are, what would you be?

How do you deal with your own anger?

Where do you go to be alone?

What is your favorite object?

What do you most often dream about?

Whom do you trust the most?

When do you feel most uncomfortable?

Where would you most like to live?

What is easy for you to do?

Under what circumstances would you tell a lie?

What is your major life goal?

What is one thing your worst enemy would say about you?

What is one thing your best friend would say about you?

EXERCISE 2.9
Adjective Checklist

This exercise is aimed at providing an opportunity for participants to disclose their view of themselves to the other members of their group and to receive feedback on how the other group members perceive them.

1. Members should each go through the list of adjectives and circle the six adjectives they think are most descriptive of themselves.

2. Each member of the group then tells the group which adjectives he circled. Members of the group then tell the person what adjectives they would have checked if they were to describe him. Do not spend more than 5 to 10 minutes on each person in the group.

able	dependent	helpful
accepting	derogatory	helpless
adaptable	determined	honorable
aggressive	dignified	hostile
ambitious	disciplined	idealistic
annoying	docile	imaginative
anxious	dogged	immature
authoritative	domineering	impressionable
belligerent	dreamy	inconsiderate
bitter	dutiful	independent
bold	effervescent	ingenious
brave	efficient	innovative
calm	elusive	insensitive
carefree	energetic	insincere
careless	extroverted	intelligent
caring	fair	introverted
certain	fearful	intuitive
cheerful	foolish	irresponsible
clever	frank	irritable
cold	free	jealous
complex	friendly	jovial
confident	genial	juvenile
conforming	gentle	kind
controlled	giving	knowledgeable
courageous	greedy	lazy
cranky	gruff	learned
critical	guilty	lewd
cynical	gullible	liberal
demanding	happy	lively
dependable	hard	logical

loving	proud	silly
malicious	quarrelsome	simple
manipulative	questioning	sinful
materialistic	quiet	skillful
maternal	radical	sly
mature	rational	sociable
merry	rationalizing	spontaneous
modest	reactionary	stable
mystical	realistic	strained
naïve	reasonable	strong
narcissistic	reassuring	stubborn
negative	rebellious	sympathetic
nervous	reflective	taciturn
neurotic	regretful	tactful
noisy	rejecting	temperamental
normal	relaxed	tenacious
objective	reliable	tender
oblivious	religious	tense
observant	remote	thoughtful
obsessive	resentful	tough
organized	reserved	trusting
original	resolute	trustworthy
overburdened	respectful	unassuming
overconfident	responsible	unaware
overconforming	responsive	uncertain
overemotional	retentive	unconcerned
overprotecting	rigid	uncontrolled
passive	sarcastic	understanding
paternal	satisfied	unpredictable
patient	scientific	unreasonable
perceptive	searching	unstructured
perfectionist	self-accepting	useful
persuasive	self-actualizing	vain
petty	self-assertive	vapid
playful	self-aware	visionary
pleasant	self-conscious	vulnerable
pompous	self-effacing	warm
powerful	self-indulgent	willful
pragmatic	self-righteous	wise
precise	selfish	wishful
pretending	sensible	withdrawn
pretentious	sensitive	witty
principled	sentimental	worried
progressive	serious	youthful
protective	shy	zestful

EXERCISE 2.10
Fantasy Situations

Self-disclosure is most clearly accomplished when you tell others directly how you are reacting to the present situation. Yet many times we reveal ourselves in indirect ways, for example, by the jokes we tell, the things we find funny, the books we are interested in, or the movies we see. All these actions and attitudes tell other people something about ourselves. Often we may learn something about ourselves we were not fully aware of by analyzing our dreams, our daydreams, our interests, our values, or our humor. The following exercise lets you use your imagination in ways that may lead to a greater awareness of yourself and also may help you get to know others in a different and interesting way.

The following are a series of fantasy situations. They deal with initiating relationships with lonely people or giving help to individuals who seem to need it. The procedure for the exercise is as follows:

1. Divide into groups of three.

2. The leader presents an unfinished fantasy situation.

3. Each member of the triad thinks about his or her ending to the fantasy situation.

4. In the triad each person tells her ending to the fantasy situation.

5. Each person tells the other members of the triad what she has learned from the endings given to the fantasy situation about herself and about the other two members.

6. Switch partners and repeat steps 2, 3, 4, and 5. Do this for a series of situations, switching partners after each situation.

7. In the group as a whole, discuss what you have learned about yourself and the other members.

The Fantasy Situations

1. You are walking down a dark street. Up ahead you see a streetlight. You walk nearer and nearer to the streetlight. Underneath the streetlight is a girl crying. What do you do? What happens?

2. You are eating lunch in a school cafeteria. You get your lunch and walk into the lunchroom. The lunchroom is crowded and noisy with lots of people laughing and shouting and having a good time. Off in a corner is a boy sitting all alone at a table. What do you do? What happens?

3. You are going to a party. You enter the party, take off your coat, find something to drink, and talk to a couple of friends. Standing all by himself in the middle of the room is a person you don't know. After 10 minutes, the person is still standing by himself. What do you do? What happens?

4. You are at a basketball game. It is halftime. You are talking with several of your friends. A person whom you casually met the week before is nearby. He is making obnoxious and embarrassing remarks to the people he is with. They all leave. You walk over to him, and he insults you. What do you do? What happens?

5. You are sitting in class. Several persons in the class are making belittling comments about another student. The student is obviously having his feelings hurt. He catches your eye and looks at you. What do you do? What happens?

6. You are watching a group of friends in front of a restaurant. A person whom they consider odd and strange walks up to them and tries to join in the conversation. They ignore her. Finally one of your friends says, "Why don't you get lost?" The person turns away. What do you do? What happens?

7. You are sitting in a classroom. A student you don't know has constantly bugged the teacher and caused trouble ever since the class began several months ago. Although he is often funny, everyone is fed up with his behavior. He comes into the room and takes a seat next to you. What do you do? What happens?

8. There is a new student in the school. You have often heard her say that your school is not nearly as good as the school she previously attended and that the students at your school are "really just unreal" and "really think they're cool" while she praises the students at her previous school. You meet her walking out of the school door. What do you do? What happens?

EXERCISE 2.11
Bag Exercise

This exercise is to be used in connection with the presentation of the Johari Window. The exercise focuses on the thinking through of the things about yourself that you commonly share with other individuals (your free areas) and the things that you do not commonly share with other individuals (your hidden areas). In addition, it opens up the opportunity for each group member to receive feedback on how the others see him or her. The materials needed for the exercise are

1. A ten-pound paper bag for each person.
2. One or two popular magazines, such as *People,* for each person.
3. Construction paper of several different colors.
4. Yarn, string, and some small toys or any other objects that will help in constructing the bags.
5. Crayons, paints, or pencils for drawing.
6. Tape, paste, or glue.

The procedure for the exercise is as follows:

1. Each person in the group gets a paper bag. Various materials described in the preceding list are scattered around the room.
2. Each person spends half an hour building his or her bag. On the outside of the bag you should attach things that represent aspects of yourself that you commonly share with other people. On the inside of the bag you should place things that represent aspects of yourself that you do not commonly share with others. You may cut pictures, words, phrases, or slogans out of the magazines, draw designs or pictures, make objects out of the construction paper, or use anything else that seems relevant in portraying the free and hidden aspects of yourself.
3. After everyone has finished, a group meeting is begun in which anyone may volunteer to talk about his bag. You may want to talk just about the outside of the bag, or you may feel like talking about part or all of what you have inside your bag. Everyone should feel free to share as much or as little as they would like to. You may want to keep working on your bag for a few days, adding things to the outside and inside, and then share it with the group at a later date.
4. After a person has shared part or all of his bag, the other members of the group may wish to comment on how their perceptions of the person match what they have heard. You may feel that the person left out qualities that you appreciate in him or perceive him as having. You may be surprised by finding that something the person felt was in his free area you have never seen in his behavior. Whatever your impressions of the person and your reactions to his bag, you should feel free to share them with him, using the characteristics of good feedback.
5. So that everyone who wants to may share her bag, you may want to put a time limit on how long the group may focus upon one person. Try to ensure that everyone who wants to share part or all of her bag has the opportunity to do so within the time limit set for the session.

EXERCISE 2.12
Feedback

Many of the exercises described in this chapter involve giving and receiving feedback. Feedback from others is the primary means by which you can increase your self-awareness. Since your ability to self-disclose depends upon your awareness of what you are like, it is important for you to receive as much feedback as possible from others on their impressions of you and how they are reacting to your behavior in the group. If not much feedback has been given and received during the other exercises, the group may wish to spend some time sharing their impressions of, and reactions to, each other. This can be done simply by stating, "My impression of you is . . . ," or "My reactions to your behavior are . . . ," or "The way I feel about you is . . ." Be sure to observe the rules for constructive feedback.

Sometimes you may be unsure of what your impressions are of another person or of how you are reacting to his or her behavior. One way to clarify your impressions of, and reactions to, a person is to associate some animal, bird, song, color, weather, movie, book, food, or fantasy with the person. You may want to ask yourself, "What animal do I associate with this person: a puppy, a fox, a rabbit?" Or you may wish to ask yourself, "What books do I associate with this person; what songs do I associate with this person?" Finally, you may wish to ask yourself, "What fantasies do I associate with this person? Is he a knight in shining armor, an innkeeper in medieval England, a French chef, a conforming business executive, a professional singer?" Through telling that person what animal, song, color, weather, movie, food, book, or fantasy you associate with him or her you may clarify your impressions and reactions and provide the other person with some interesting, entertaining, and helpful feedback.

EXERCISE 2.13
Strength Building

Accepting and appreciating yourself is related to being aware of your strengths and assets. We all have many strengths. We all have strengths we are not using fully. We all can develop new strengths. A *strength* is any skill, ability, talent, or personal quality that helps you to be effective and productive. You increase your self-acceptance as you become more aware of your strengths and develop new ones. The more you see yourself as having real skills, abilities, talents, and other personal strengths, the more you will value and accept yourself.

In this exercise you will concentrate on identifying your strengths and determining how they can be used most productively to build personal relationships. The objectives of this exercise are to increase your self-acceptance

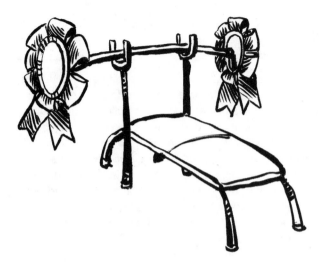

through the increased awareness of your strengths and to increase your awareness of how your strengths can be used to develop fulfilling relationships with other individuals. In this exercise you will be asked to discuss your strengths openly with the other group members. This is no place for modesty; an inferiority complex or unwillingness to be open about your positive attributes is not a strength. You are not being asked to brag, only to be realistic and open about the strengths that you possess. The procedure for the exercise is

1. Think of all the things that you do well, all the things which you are proud of having done, all the things for which you feel a sense of accomplishment. List all your positive accomplishments, your successes, of the past. Be specific.

2. Divide into pairs and share your past accomplishments with each other. Then, with the help of your partner, examine your past successes to identify the strengths you utilized to achieve them.

3. In the group as a whole, each person should share the full list of his strengths. Then ask the group, "What additional strengths do you see in my life?" The group then adds to your list other qualities, skills, and characteristics that you have overlooked or undervalued. The feedback should be specific; that is, if one member tells another he has a strength, he must back his feedback up with some evidence of behavior that demonstrates the strength.

4. After every group member has shared her strengths and received feedback on further strengths that others see in her life, each member should then ask the group, "What might be keeping me from utilizing all my strengths?" The group then explores the ways you can free yourself from factors that limit utilizing your strengths.

5. Think about your past successes and your strengths. Think about how your strengths may be utilized to improve the number or quality of your close relationships. Then set a goal for the next week concerning how you may improve either the number or the quality of your close relationships. Plan how utilizing your strengths will help you accomplish this goal.

 EXERCISE 2.14
Standing Ovation

The purpose of this exercise is to provide you with the opportunity to receive considerable recognition and acceptance by your peers. The procedure is as follows:

1. Stand in a circle of at least six people. The larger the group, the better.
2. One at a time, each member goes to the center of the group and states his or her name, and then the group cheers and claps for that person. Make each member feel special, valued, and recognized.

 EXERCISE 2.15
How Self-Accepting Are You?

How do you tell if you are self-accepting? One way is to list all the assets you have. If you can list 200 to 300 assets, then you are very self-accepting. Another way is to see if you can plan how to use your assets when you get into a stressful or problem situation. Finally, you can measure yourself against the following checklist, which summarizes much of the research conducted on self-accepting people (Hamachek, 1971). Write *yes* if the item fits you, write *no* if it does not.

_____ I strongly believe in certain values and principles. I am willing to defend them, even in the face of strong group opposition. I feel personally secure enough to change them if new experiences and new evidence suggest I am in error.

_____ I am capable of acting on my own best judgment. I do so without feeling overly guilty or regretting my actions, even if other people disapprove of what I have done.

_____ I do not spend a lot of time worrying about what is coming tomorrow, what has happened to me in the past, or what is taking place in the present.

_____ I am confident in my ability to deal with problems, even in the face of failure and setbacks.

_____ I feel equal to other people as a person. I do not feel superior or inferior. I feel equal even when there are differences in specific abilities, family backgrounds, job prestige, or amount of money earned.

_____ I take for granted that I am a person of interest and value to others, at least to the people I associate with.

_____ I can accept praise without the pretense of false modesty; I can accept compliments without feeling guilty.

_____ I am inclined to resist the efforts of others to dominate me.

_____ I am able to accept the idea and admit to others that I am capable of feeling a wide range of impulses and desires. These range from being angry to being loving, from being sad to being happy, from feeling deep resentment to feeling deep acceptance.

_____ I am able to genuinely enjoy myself in a wide variety of activities. These include work, play, loafing, companionship, and creative self-expression.

_____ I am sensitive to the needs of others, to accepted social customs, and particularly to the idea that I cannot enjoy myself at the expense of others.

 **E X E R C I S E 2 . 16**
Interpersonal Patterns

This exercise focuses upon your interaction with other individuals. It may help you think about how you behave when you initiate a relationship with another person or how you act in a group. The procedure for the exercise is as follows:

1. Divide into groups of three. Each person fills out the adjective checklist.

2. Analyze the meaning of the adjectives you checked by following the instructions that follow the checklist.

3. Share with the other two members of your triad the results of the exercise and ask for their comments on whether they perceive you in the same way as or differently than the results of this exercise indicate.

The 20 verbs in the following list describe some of the ways people feel and act from time to time. Think of your behavior in feelings and actions while interacting with other people. Check the five verbs that best describe your behavior in interaction with others.

_____ acquiesces	_____ coordinates	_____ leads
_____ advises	_____ criticizes	_____ obliges
_____ agrees	_____ directs	_____ relinquishes
_____ analyzes	_____ disapproves	_____ resists
_____ assists	_____ evades	_____ retreats
_____ concedes	_____ initiates	_____ withdraws
_____ compiles	_____ judges	

There are two underlying factors involved in the list of adjectives: dominance (authority or control) and sociability (intimacy or friendliness). Most people tend to like to control things (high dominance) or to let others control things (low dominance). Similarly most people tend to be very warm and personal (high sociability) or to be somewhat cold and impersonal (low sociability). In the following boxes circle the five adjectives you used to describe yourself. The set in which three or more adjectives are circled out of the five represents your interpersonal pattern.

	High Dominance	Low Dominance
High Sociability	Advises Coordinates Directs Initiates Leads	Acquiesces Agrees Assists Complies Obliges
Low Sociability	Analyzes Criticizes Disapproves Judges Resists	Concedes Evades Relinquishes Retreats Withdraws

EXERCISES 2.17
Open and Closed Relationships

Are most of your relationships open or closed? Read through Table 2.1 carefully and classify yourself on each dimension. Do you have relationships you wish to make more open? Do you have relationships you wish to make more closed? What actions are needed to make a relationship more open? What acts are needed to make a relationship more closed? Discuss your conclusions with another member of your group.

Each of the aspects of open and closed relationships summarized in Table 2.1 will be discussed in this book.

TABLE 2.1 *Open and Closed Relationships*

	Closed ◄――――――――――――――――――――――► Open			
Content being discussed	Of concern to no one (weather talk).	Technical topics and issues.	Perceptions, reactions, ideas, and feelings.	Relationship between the two persons.
Time reference	No time reference (jokes and abstractions)	Distant past or future being discussed.	Recent past or future being discussed.	The imme-diate "here and now" discussed.
Awareness of your reactions and feelings	You never focus your attention on yourself and try to ignore, repress, and deny perceptions, feelings and reactions.		You are constantly aware of your perceptions, reactions, and feelings.	
Openness with own ideas, feelings, intentions	Your statements are generalizations, abstract ideas, intellectualizations; feelings are excluded as irrelevant, inappropriate, and nonexistent.		You state your personal reactions (attitudes, values, preferences, feelings, experiences, and observations of the present); feelings are included as helpful information about the present.	
Feedback from other people	Feedback from others is avoided, ignored, not listened to, and perceived as being hostile attacks on your personality.		Feedback from others is asked for, sought out, listened to, and used to increase your self-awareness; it is perceived as helpful to your growth and effectiveness.	
Acceptance of yourself	You believe that once you are known you will be disliked and rejected and, therefore, you hide your "real" self and try to make the impression you think will be most appreciated by other people.		You express confidence in your abilities and skills; you can discuss your positive qualities without bragging and false modesty; you used your abilities in the past to achieve your goals and are confident you will do so again.	

TABLE 2.1 *Continued*

	Closed ◄——————————————————► Open	
Openness to others' ideas, feelings, reactions	You avoid and disregard others' reactions, ideas, and perceptions; you are embarrassed and repelled by others' feelings; you reject other people and try to better them; you refuse to listen to their reactions to your behavior.	You listen to and solicit others' reactions, ideas, and feelings; you cooperate fully with them; you see their value and strengths even when you disagree with them; you ask others for feedback on your behavior.
Acceptance of other people	You evaluate the other person's actions, communicate that the other is unacceptable, show disregard for other as a person.	You react without evaluation to the other's actions, communicate that the other is acceptable, value the other as a person.

E X E R C I S E   2 . 1 8

Who Am I?

	Personal Characteristics	Demographic Characteristics	Abilities, Competencies
1.	_____	_____	_____
2.	_____	_____	_____
3.	_____	_____	_____
4.	_____	_____	_____
5.	_____	_____	_____
6.	_____	_____	_____
7.	_____	_____	_____
8.	_____	_____	_____
9.	_____	_____	_____
10.	_____	_____	_____

EXERCISE 2.19

Self-Description

Who am I? What am I like? How do others perceive me? What are my strengths as a person? In what areas do I want to develop greater skills? At this point you have participated in a series of exercises aimed at increasing your self-awareness, self-acceptance, and skills in self-disclosing. You should now sit down and try to summarize what you have learned about yourself. Take a sheet of paper and write a description of what you are like. Use the five questions posed at the beginning of this paragraph as a guide.

■ COMPREHENSION TEST A

Demonstrate your understanding of self-disclosure by matching the definitions with the appropriate characteristic. Check your answers with a partner, and explain the reasoning for your answers. The answers are at the end of the chapter.

Concept	Definition
_____ 1. Self-disclosure	a. General process by which you behave in particular ways to create a desired social image.
_____ 2. Consensual validation	
_____ 3. Self-awareness	b. Process by which we try to shape what others think of us.
_____ 4. Social comparison	
_____ 5. Self-monitoring	c. Regulating your behavior to meet the demands of social situations.
_____ 6. Self-awareness theory	
_____ 7. Objective self-awareness	d. Becoming aware of some aspect of yourself and evaluating it by considering how it measures up to some internal rule or standard.
_____ 8. Deindividuation	
_____ 9. Looking-glass self	e. Comparing your perceptions and reactions with the reactions and perceptions of others.
_____ 10. Feedback	
_____ 11. Self-acceptance	
_____ 12. Self-presentation	f. Revealing to another person how you are reacting to the present situation.
_____ 13. Impression management	
_____ 14. Ingratiation	g. Self-presentation acts motivated by the desire to get along and be liked.
_____ 15. Self-promotion	
_____ 16. Self-verification	h. Desire to have others perceive us as we genuinely perceive ourselves.

i. Information that allows you to compare your actual performance with standards of performance. In interpersonal relationships it is other people disclosing how they are perceiving and reacting to your behavior.

j. Theory that self-focused attention leads people to notice self-discrepancies, thereby motivating either a change in behavior or an escape from self-awareness.

k. The loss of a person's sense of individuality and the reduction of normal constraints against deviant behavior.

l. Gauging your attitudes, emotions, attributes, and abilities by comparing them to those of other people.

m. Seeing yourself as other people see you.

n. Viewing yourself and your actions with approval or satisfaction, or having a positive regard for yourself.

o. Focusing your attention on yourself.

p. Self-presentation acts motivated by a desire to get ahead and be respected for one's competence.

■ COMPREHENSION TEST B

Test your understanding of this chapter by answering true or false to the following statements. Answers are at the end of the chapter.

True   False   1. Self-disclosure should be aimed at making the other person improve his or her behavior.

True   False   2. Self-disclosure should be a two-way street, a shared understanding of how each person is reacting to the present situation.

True   False   3. Self-disclosure involves risk taking.

True   False   4. Statements are more helpful if they are tentative, specific, and informing.

True   False   5. Wait to discuss disturbing situations until after your feelings have built up for a while.

True   False   6. It is often helpful to describe your reactions to the other person's behavior.

True   False   7. It is often helpful to disclose full details of your past life.

True   False   8. An example of constructive self-disclosure is when Edythe says to David, "Stop bothering me!"

True   False   9. An example of constructive self-disclosure is when David says to Edythe, "You look angry. Are you?"

True   False   10. An example of constructive self-disclosure is when Edythe says to David, "I feel hurt and rejected by your failure to answer my questions."

True   False   11. Self-acceptance means that you regard yourself highly and are aware of your strengths.

True   False   12. Because self-acceptance gives you the confidence to be self-disclosing, it leads to your being accepted by others, which further increases your self-acceptance.

True   False   13. It is not necessary, psychologically, to be self-accepting.

True   False   14. The more self-accepting you are, the less you will be accepting of others.

True   False   15. The best feeling about your self-worth is an unconditional basic self-acceptance.

Self-Diagnosis

This chapter has focused on being self-disclosing, self-aware, and self-accepting. Giving and receiving feedback was also covered. On a scale from 1 (poorly mastered) to 5 (highly mastered) rate the degree to which you have mastered each skill. Then choose two skills to improve on in the next week.

Rating   Skill

_____   Disclosing my perceptions and reactions appropriately.

_____   Using my experiences, self-disclosures, and feedback to increase my self-awareness.

_____   Giving feedback constructively.

_____   Receiving feedback constructively.

_____   Increasing my self-acceptance.

_____   Appropriately presenting myself to others.

Skills I Will Improve in the Next Week

1. _____

2. _____

Summary

In every relationship you need to decide how well you wish the other person to know you and build an appropriate level of openness. To be open with another person you must (a) be aware of who you are, (b) accept yourself, and (c) take the risk of trusting the other person to be accepting of you (O = S A T). There are two sides of openness: How open you are with other persons (disclosing yourself to them) and how open you are to others (listening to their disclosures in an accepting way). Self-disclosure is revealing to another person how you perceive and are reacting to the present situation and giving any information about yourself and your past that is relevant to an understanding of your perceptions and reactions to the present. Self-disclosure focuses on the present, includes feelings as well as facts, has both breadth and depth, and should be reciprocal in the early stages of a relationship.

Healthy relationships are built on self-disclosure. If you cannot be open with other people, you cannot become close to others, and you cannot be valued by others for who you are. Self-disclosure enables you and other people to get to know each other, identify common goals, and work together to achieve those goals. Self-disclosure not only begins and improves the quality of relationship, but it also validates your perception of reality, increases your understanding of yourself, frees you from negative emotions, controls your interaction with others, helps you manage stress and adversity, and fulfills your needs to be known intimately and accepted. In keeping your disclosures appropriate, there are a set of guidelines to follow.

You cannot disclose unless you are self-aware. Self-awareness comes from focusing your attention on yourself. It leads to self-knowledge and self-understanding. Self-awareness is the basis for self-disclosure. It helps you identify the actions that you need to take, present yourself appropri-

ately, increase your social sensitivity, increase your ability to communicate effectively, and solve personal problems, and it helps you be the person you want to be. There are dangers to self-awareness. It may lead to
depression over not living up to your standards and self-absorption. There
are also dangers to lack of self-awareness, such as becoming deindividual-
ized so that you behave on impulse rather than according to your internal
standards of conduct. You can increase your self-awareness through introspection, self-observation, explaining yourself to others, comparing
yourself to others, interacting with diverse individuals, and seeking feedback. There is a reciprocal relationship among self-disclosure, self-awareness, and feedback. The more self-aware and self-accepting you are, the
more you can let others know about you, the better the feedback you can
receive, which increases your self-awareness.

Feedback from others is an important way to increase your self-
awareness. Feedback is information that allows you to compare your actual performance with standards of performance. In interpersonal relationships it is other people disclosing how they are perceiving and
reacting to your behavior that you use to determine the effectiveness of
what you are doing. There are rules for both giving and receiving feedback, such as focusing it on behavior, not on personality, and being descriptive, not judgmental.

Self-awareness is not enough to ensure accurate self-disclosure. Actions and thoughts that you are ashamed of or that other people would
find objectionable you hide and keep to yourself. You only disclose what
you accept. Self-acceptance is viewing yourself and your actions with approval or satisfaction, or having a high regard for yourself. You increase
your self-acceptance through receiving feedback and viewing yourself as
others view you, believing you are intrinsically acceptable, meeting standards, comparing yourself with others, and deciding you are reaching
your ideal. Self-acceptance allows you to disclose yourself to others.

Finally, self-disclosure can be selective so that you present a certain
impression to other people. Self-presentation is the process by which you
try to shape what others think of you and what you think of yourself.
Self-presentation is more difficult than it sounds because there are many
complex aspects of yourself, because your presentation has to be varied to
match the audience and situation, and because it is motivated by wanting
to create a positive impression and by experiencing self-verification.

Self-disclosure is a risk. Others may reject you once they get to know
you. You may drive people away when you want to draw them closer.
Taking the risks involved in disclosing yourself requires trust. The next
chapter will build on the skills of self-disclosure, self-awareness, and self-
acceptance by showing you how to build and maintain trust in a relationship.

Answers

Comprehension Test A: 1. f; 2. e; 3. o; 4. l; 5. c; 6. j; 7. d; 8. k; 9. m; 10. i; 11. n; 12. b; 13. a; 14. g; 15. p; 16. h.

Comprehension Test B: 1. false; 2. true; 3. true; 4. true; 5. false; 6. false; 7. false; 8. false; 9. true; 10. true; 11. true; 12. true; 13. false; 14. false; 15. true.

CHAPTER 3

Developing and Maintaining Trust

Introduction

I am afraid to tell you who I am, because, if I tell you who I am, you may not like who I am, and it's all that I have.
—John Powell

Good relationships bring us joy and affirmation. To develop a good relationship, trust must be established. You achieve this purpose by letting other people know you, though doing so can be risky. Others may hurt or reject you. In order to build trust appropriately, you must know and accept yourself. You need to have the skills to deal with rejection. And, you must know how to build trust in relationships.

In studying this chapter you should seek to (1) understand what trust is and what it is not, (2) understand how trust is developed and maintained in a relationship, (3) know the difference between appropriate and inappropriate trust, (4) experience a situation in which trust is either developed or destroyed, and (5) diagnose your skill level in building and maintaining trust in a relationship. Achieving these goals will not be easy, as trust is one of the hardest social skills to understand and implement.

Developing and Maintaining Trust

Aristotle once said, "A true friend is one soul in two bodies." In order for two people to get to know each other that well, they must trust each other. Trust is essential for relationships to grow and develop. The first crisis most relationships face involves the ability of two individuals to trust each other. In order to build a relationship, you must learn to create a climate of trust that reduces your own and the other person's fears of betrayal and rejection and promotes the hope of acceptance, support, and confirmation. Trust is not a stable and unchanging personality trait. Trust is an aspect of relationships that constantly changes and varies. Everything individuals do increases or decreases the trust level in their relationship. The actions of both people are important in establishing and maintaining trust.

What is trust and how do you create it? Trust is a word everyone uses, yet it is a complex concept and difficult to define. Perhaps the best definition is by Deutsch (1962), who proposed that trust includes the following elements:

1. You are in a situation where a choice to trust another person can lead to either beneficial or harmful consequences for your needs and goals. Thus, you realize there is a risk involved in trusting.

2. You realize that whether beneficial consequences or harmful consequences result depends on the actions of another person.

3. You expect to suffer more if the harmful consequences result than you will gain if the beneficial consequences result.

4. You feel relatively confident that the other person will behave in such a way that the beneficial consequences will result.

When you choose to trust another person involves the perception that the choice can lead to gains or losses, that whether you will gain or lose depends upon the behavior of the other person, that the loss will be greater than the gain, and that the other person will probably behave in such a way that you will gain rather than lose. Sounds complicated, doesn't it? In fact, there is nothing simple about trust. An example may help. Imagine you are participating in a class discussion. You begin to contribute to the discussion, knowing you will gain if you contribute good ideas that other members accept but lose if your ideas are laughed at and belittled. Whether you gain or lose depends on the behavior of other group members. You will feel more hurt if you are laughed at than you will feel satisfaction if your ideas are appreciated. Yet you expect the other group members to consider your ideas and accept them. The issue of trust is captured in the question every group member asks: "If I express myself openly, will what I say be used against me?"

Another example may help. Trust is when you lend your older brother your bicycle. You can gain his appreciation or lose your bike; which one happens depends on him. You will suffer more if your bike is wrecked than you will gain by his appreciation, yet you really expect him to take care of your bike. (Sad experience has led an unnamed person to recommend that you never lend your bike to your older brother!)

Helpful Hints About Trust

1. **Trust is a very complex concept to understand.** It may take a while before you fully understand it.

2. **Trust exists in relationships, not in someone's personality.** While some people are more naturally trusting than others, and it is easier for some people to be trustworthy than others, trust is something that occurs between people, not within people.

3. **Trust is constantly changing as two people interact.** Everything you do affects the trust level between you and the other person to some extent.

4. **Trust is hard to build and easy to destroy.** It may take years to build up a high level of trust in a relationship, then one destructive act can ruin it all.

5. **The key to building and maintaining trust is being trustworthy.** The more accepting and supportive you are of others, the more likely they will disclose their thoughts, ideas, theories, conclusions, feelings, and reactions to you. The more trustworthy you are in response to such disclosures, the deeper and more personal the thoughts a person will share with you. When you want to increase trust, increase your trustworthiness.

6. **Trust needs to be appropriate.** *Never* trusting and *always* trusting are inappropriate.

7. **Cooperation increases trust, competition decreases trust.** Trust generally is higher among collaborators than among competitors.

8. **Initial trusting and trustworthy actions within a relationship can create a self-fulfilling prophecy.** The expectations you project about trust often influence the actions of other people toward you.

Being Trusting and Trustworthy

You can bring your credibility down in a second. It takes a million acts to build it up, but one act can bring it down. . . . People are suspicious because for several thousand years that suspicion was warranted . . . we try very hard not to do things that will create distrust.
—Howard K. Sperlich

The level of trust within a relationship is constantly changing according to individuals' ability and willingness to be trusting and trustworthy. You **trust** when you are willing to risk beneficial or harmful consequences by making yourself vulnerable to other people. More specifically, you are trusting when you are **self-disclosing** and willing to be openly accepting and supportive of others. **Openness** is the sharing of information, ideas, thoughts, feelings, and reactions to the issue being discussed. **Sharing** is the offering of your resources to other people in order to help them achieve their goals.

> **TOSS**
> **T**rusting is
> **O**penly
> **S**elf-Disclosing and
> **S**haring

You are **trustworthy** when you are willing to respond to another person's risk taking in a way that ensures that the other person will experience beneficial consequences. More specifically, you are trustworthy when you express acceptance of, support for, and cooperativeness toward the other person, as when you reciprocate his or her disclosures. **Acceptance** is the communication of high regard for another person and his or her statements. **Support** is the communication to another person that you recognize he or she has the strengths and capabilities needed to manage productively the situation he or she is in. **Cooperative intention** is the expression that you want to work together to achieve a mutual goal. There is considerable evidence that the expression of warmth, accurate understanding, and cooperative intentions increases trust in a relationship, even when there are unresolved conflicts between the individuals involved (Johnson, 1971; Johnson & Matross, 1977; Johnson & Noonan,

1972). *Reciprocating the other person's self-disclosures occurs when you share something about yourself in response to the other person's disclosures to you.* Appropriate reciprocation increases trust and influences the other person to be even more self-disclosing (Johnson & Noonan, 1972).

Acceptance is probably the first and deepest concern to arise in a relationship. *Acceptance is the key to reducing anxiety and fears about being vulnerable.* Defensive feelings of fear and distrust are common blocks to the functioning of a person and to the development of constructive relationships. Certainly, if a person does not feel accepted, the frequency and depth of disclosures to another person will decrease. Accepting another person's disclosures and supporting his or her willingness to trust you does not mean that you agree with everything he or she says. You can express acceptance and support and at the same time express different ideas and opposing points of view. *The key to building and maintaining trust is being trustworthy.* The more accepting and supportive you are of others, the more likely they will disclose their thoughts, ideas, theories, conclusions, feelings, and reactions to you. The more trustworthy you are in response to such disclosures, the deeper and more personal the thoughts a person will share with you. When you want to increase trust, increase your trustworthiness.

TURN

Trustworthiness is

Unwavering acceptance and support

Reciprocating the other

Nourishing the relationship by signalling cooperative intentions

Building Interpersonal Trust

Ralph Waldo Emerson once said, "The only way to have a friend is to be one." He was calling attention to the fact that how you behave in a relationship affects how the other person acts toward you. Trust has two sides. Trust is established through a sequence of trusting and trustworthy actions (see Figure 3.1). If Person A takes the risk of being open and sharing, he may be either confirmed or disconfirmed, depending on whether Person B responds with acceptance or rejection. If Person B takes the risk

Person B

	High Acceptance, Support, and Cooperativeness	Low Acceptance, Support, and Cooperativeness
High Openness and Sharing	Person A { Trusting / Confirmed } Person B { Trustworthy / Confirmed }	Person A { Trusting / Disconfirmed } Person B { Untrustworthy / No risk }
Low Openness and Sharing	Person A { Distrusting / No risk } Person B { Trustworthy / Disconfirmed }	Person A { Distrusting / No risk } Person B { Untrustworthy / No risk }

Person A (vertical label at left)

FIGURE 3.1   *The Dynamics of Interpersonal Trust*

of being accepting, supportive, and cooperative, she may be confirmed or disconfirmed, depending on whether Person A is disclosing or nondisclosing. Interpersonal trust is *built* through risk and confirmation and is *destroyed* through risk and disconfirmation. Without risk there is no trust, and the relationship cannot move forward. The steps in building trust are these:

1. Person A takes a risk by sharing his thoughts, information, conclusions, feelings, and reactions to the immediate situation and to Person B.

2. Person B responds with acceptance, support, and cooperativeness, and reciprocates Person A's openness by sharing her own thoughts, information, conclusions, feelings, and reactions to the immediate situation and to Person A.

An alternative way in which trust is built is as follows:

1. Person B communicates acceptance, support, and cooperativeness toward Person A.

2. Person A responds by sharing his thoughts, information, conclusions, feelings, and reactions to the immediate situation and to Person B.

Destroying Trust

Friendships require high trust. For trust to develop, one person has to let down his or her guard and become vulnerable to see whether the other person abuses that vulnerability. Many such tests are necessary before the trust level between two people becomes very high. *Just one betrayal, however, may create distrust and, once established, distrust is extremely resistive to change.* Distrust is difficult to change because it leads to the perception that despite the other person's attempts to make up, betrayal will recur in the future.

> **Behaviors That Decrease Trust (LOSER)**
> **L**aughing at the other person
> **O**penly moralizing about another's behavior
> **S**ilent, poker-face, or rejecting actions
> **E**valuating the other in your response
> **R**efusing to reciprocate in openness and sharing

There are three types of behavior that will decrease trust in a relationship. The first is the use of rejection, ridicule, or disrespect as a response to the other's openness. Making a joke at the expense of the other person, laughing at his disclosures, moralizing about her behavior, being evaluative in your response, or being silent and poker-faced, all communicate rejection and will effectively silence the other person and destroy some of the trust in the relationship. The second is the nonreciprocation of openness. To the extent that you are closed and the other person is open, he will not trust you and will feel overexposed and vulnerable. The third type of behavior that will decrease trust in a relationship is the refusal to disclose your thoughts, information, conclusions, feelings, and reactions after the other person has indicated considerable acceptance, support, and cooperativeness. If a person indicates acceptance and you are closed and guarded in response, she will feel discounted and rejected.

Reestablishing Trust After It Has Been Broken

How can trust, once lost, be regained? The following guidelines may help. To reestablish trust, you should

1. Establish cooperative goals that neither person can achieve alone but are so compelling that each person will join in to achieve them. Such goals are often referred to as **superordinate goals.**

2. Increase dependence on each other's resources (resource interdependence) so that no one person has a chance of succeeding on his or her own.

3. Openly and consistently express cooperative intentions.

4. Reestablish credibility by making certain that your actions match your announced intentions. You must always keep your word.

5. Be absolutely and consistently trustworthy in your dealing with others. Acceptance and support of others is critical.

6. Periodically test the waters by engaging in trusting actions and making yourself vulnerable to the other persons.

7. Apologize sincerely and immediately when you inadvertently engage in untrustworthy actions.

8. Strive to build a tough but fair reputation by
   a. Initially and periodically responding cooperatively to others who act competitively (even when you know in advance that the others plan to compete).
   b. Using a tit-for-tat strategy that matches the other person's behavior if the other continues to compete. When the competitors realize that their competitiveness is self-defeating and that the best they can hope for is mutual failure, they may start cooperating.

Trusting Appropriately

Should you always trust others? Of course not. Some people behave in very untrustworthy ways and you should not make yourself vulnerable to them. You need to be able to tell when it is appropriate to be trusting and when it is not. You must develop the capacity to size up situations and make an enlightened decision about when, whom, and how much to trust others. Remember not to reveal yourself so fast to another person that he

or she is overpowered and bewildered. And remember that there are situations in which trust is inappropriate and destructive to your interests.

Never trusting and *always* trusting are inappropriate. Trust is appropriate only when you are relatively confident that the other person will behave in such a way that you will benefit rather than be harmed by your risk, or when you are relatively sure the other person will not exploit your vulnerability. In some situations, such as competitive ones, trust is not appropriate. When you have a mean, vicious, hostile boss who has taken advantage of your openness in the past, it is inappropriate to engage in trusting behavior in the present.

Trusting as a Self-Fulfilling Prophecy

Tom joins a new group expecting the members to dislike and reject him. He behaves, therefore, in a very guarded and suspicious way toward the other group members. His actions cause them to withdraw and look elsewhere for a friendly companion. "See," he then says, "I was right. I knew they would reject me." Sue, who joins the same group at the same time Tom does, expects the members to be congenial, friendly, and trustworthy. She initiates warmth and friendliness, openly discloses her thoughts and feelings, and generally is accepting and supportive of the other members. Consequently, she finds her fellow members to be all that she expected. Both Tom and Sue have made a self-fulfilling prophecy.

A **self-fulfilling prophecy** is, in the beginning, a false definition of a situation that evokes a new behavior, one that makes it possible for the originally false impression to come true. The assumptions you make about other people and the way in which you then behave often influence how other people respond to you, thus creating self-fulfilling prophecies in your relationships. People usually conform to the expectations others have of them. If other people feel that you do not trust them and expect them to violate your trust, they will often do so. If they believe that you trust them and expect them to be trustworthy, they will often behave that way. The perception of others as untrustworthy is probably a major source of tension leading to conflict. The history of labor/management strife, interracial violence, war, and revolution demonstrates the power of distrust. The lack of trust helps create conflict, and conflict leads to increased distrust. There is often a vicious circle of distrust, causing conflict, which increases distrust, which increases conflict.

In building trust in a relationship, your expectations about the other person may influence how you act toward that person, thus setting up the possibility of a self-fulfilling prophecy. There is a lot to be said for assuming that other people are trustworthy.

Personal Proclivity to Trust

While trust exists in relationships, not in people, there has been some attempt to measure individual differences in willingness to trust others. Rotter (1971) developed the **Interpersonal Trust Scale** to distinguish between people who have a tendency to trust others and those who tend to distrust. A high truster tends to say, "I will trust a person until I have clear evidence that he or she cannot be trusted." A low truster tends to say, "I will not trust a person until there is clear evidence that he or she can be trusted." High trusters tend to be more trustworthy than low trusters. High trusters, compared with low trusters, are (a) more likely to give others a second chance, respect the rights of others, and be liked and sought out as friends (by both low- and high-trust people), and (b) less likely to lie and be unhappy, conflicted, or maladjusted.

Trust in Friendships

There are two kinds of interpersonal trust that occur in friendships: reliability and emotional trust. We trust in other people's reliability when we believe they will do what they have promised to do. We trust others emotionally when we believe that they are concerned about how we feel and will act to protect our welfare. Friends who are more comfortable relying on each other are more satisfied with the relationship and are able to work together more cooperatively on solving problems. Trust may be the crucial factor in creating a stable and long-lasting friendship.

Trust in Groups

An essential aspect of group effectiveness is developing and maintaining a high level of trust among group members. The more members trust each other, the more effectively they will work together (Deutsch, 1962, 1973; Johnson, 1974). To complete tasks and achieve goals, group members are required to disclose more and more of their ideas, thoughts, conclusions, feelings, and reactions to the immediate situations and to each other. Once they do, other group members are required to respond, hopefully with acceptance, support, and cooperativeness. If group members express an opinion and do not get the acceptance they need, they may withdraw from the group. If they are accepted, they will continue to risk disclosing their thoughts and observations and continue to develop their relationships with other members. Group members will more openly express their thoughts, feelings, reactions, opinions, information, and ideas when the trust level is high. When the trust level is low, group members will be evasive, dishonest, and inconsiderate in their communications.

Creating distrust within a group is a bad idea for several reasons. First, when group members distrust other members to do their share of the work, for example, they will loaf themselves rather than risk looking like a "sucker" who did the bulk of the work (Baron, Kerr, & Miller, 1992). Second, when group members cannot trust each other, they often compete simply to defend their own best interests. Such competition is self-defeating in the long run, for it initiates a negative cycle. Distrust creates competition, which creates greater distrust, which creates greater competition. Third, distrust creates destructive conflict among group members.

■ COMPREHENSION TEST

Test your understanding of building trust by answering true or false to the following statements. Answers are at the end of the chapter.

True   False   1. Trust involves a risk that can lead to either harmful or beneficial consequences.

True   False   2. Your own behavior determines whether there are beneficial or harmful consequences from your trusting actions.

True   False   3. When you trust another person, you will gain more from the beneficial consequences than you will suffer from the harmful ones.

True   False   4. When you engage in trusting behavior, you are relatively confident that the other person will be accepting.

True   False   5. In responding to another person's self-disclosures, you should be noncommittal and nonjudgmental.

True   False   6. It does not matter if the other person reciprocates your self-disclosures or not.

True   False   7. When someone self-discloses, he or she will feel disconfirmed if the other person is not accepting.

True   False   8. When people communicate acceptance, then you can risk trusting them.

True   False   9. An example of trusting behavior would be Jane telling Frank about a personal problem.

True   False   10. An example of trustworthy behavior would be Frank listening noncommittally to Jane.

True   False   11. Trust is necessary for stable cooperation.

True   False   12. An ingredient of trust is the awareness that you are taking a chance of gaining or losing by it.

Match the following elements of trust with their definitions:

a. Openness
b. Sharing
c. Acceptance
d. Support
e. Cooperative intentions
f. Trust
g. Trustworthiness

_____ 13. The communication of high regard for another person and his contributions to the joint effort.

_____ 14. Offering your materials and resources to others to help obtain the goal.

_____ 15. The expectation that you and the other person will help each other.

_____ 16. Sharing information, ideas, thoughts, feelings, and reactions to the issue.

_____ 17. Openness and sharing with others.

_____ 18. Expressing acceptance, support, and cooperative intentions.

_____ 19. Communicating that you recognize another person's strengths and believe she is capable.

EXERCISE 3.1

How Trusting and Trustworthy Am I?

There is always a risk that someone will be rejecting and competitive when you attempt to build a relationship. In order for two people to trust each other, each has to expect the other to be trustworthy, and each has to engage in trusting behavior. This exercise allows you to compare the way you see your trust-building behavior in the group with the way other people see your trust-building behavior. The procedure for this exercise is as follows:

1. Complete the questionnaire "Understanding Your Trust Actions." Score your responses.

2. Take out a slip of paper for each member of your group. Write the name of one of the members on each slip of paper. Write (1) openness and sharing, and (2) acceptance, support, and cooperativeness on each slip of paper. Then rate the members of your group from 1 to 7 (Low 1—2—3—4—5—6—7 High) on how open and accepting you perceive each to be. Here is an example of a completed slip:

Member receiving feedback	Edythe
1. Openness and sharing	3
2. Acceptance, support, and cooperativeness	6

Rate group members individually on the basis of how you think they have behaved during the entire time your group has met together.

3. Hand each member his or her slip. If there are six members in your group, you should have five ratings of yourself, and each of the other members should end up with five slips. Compute an average of how the other members see your behavior by adding all your ratings for openness and dividing by the number of slips and adding all your ratings for acceptance and dividing by the number of slips.

4. Record in the Johnson Trust Diagram your average openness and acceptance by (1) drawing a dotted line for the results of the feedback slips you received and (2) drawing a solid line for the results of your questionnaire. Both the questionnaire and the feedback results should be recorded in the Johnson Trust Diagram.

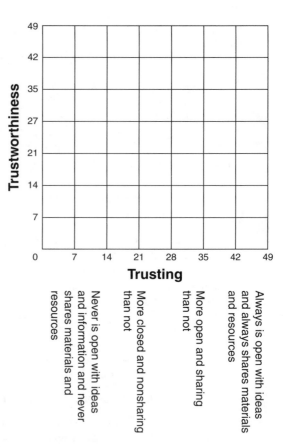

Always expresses acceptance, support, and cooperative intentions to other members

Expresses acceptance, support, and cooperative intentions more often than not

Expresses rejection, nonsupport, and competitive intentions more often than not

Always expresses rejection, nonsupport, and competitive intentions to other members

Trustworthiness

Trusting

Never is open with ideas and information and never shares materials and resources

More closed and nonsharing than not

More open and sharing than not

Always is open with ideas and always shares materials and resources

Johnson Trust Diagram

5. Discuss in the group how similar your self-perception and the perceptions of other group members are of your openness and acceptance. If there is a difference between the two, ask the group to give more specific feedback about your behavior and how it relates to trust in the group. Then discuss how to build trust with people in situations outside of the group.

Understanding Your Trust Actions

The following is a series of questions about your behavior in your group. Answer each question as honestly as you can. There are no right or wrong answers. It is important for you to describe your behavior as accurately as possible. Answers should range between 1 (not true of me) and 7 (very true of me).

1. I offer facts, give my opinions and ideas, and provide suggestions and relevant information to help the group discussion.

   Never   1—2—3—4—5—6—7   Always

2. I express my willingness to cooperate with other group members and my expectations that they will also be cooperative.

   Never   1—2—3—4—5—6—7   Always

3. I am open and candid with my dealings with the entire group.

   Never   1—2—3—4—5—6—7   Always

4. I give support to group members who are on the spot and struggling to express themselves intellectually or emotionally.

   Never   1—2—3—4—5—6—7   Always

5. I keep my thoughts, ideas, feelings, and reactions to myself during group discussions.

   Never   1—2—3—4—5—6—7   Always

6. I evaluate the contributions of other group members in terms of whether their contributions are useful to me and whether they are right or wrong.

   Never   1—2—3—4—5—6—7   Always

7. I take risks in expressing new ideas and current feelings during a group discussion.

   Never   1—2—3—4—5—6—7   Always

8. I communicate to other group members that I am aware of, and appreciate, their abilities, talents, capabilities, skills, and resources.

   Never   1—2—3—4—5—6—7   Always

9. I offer help and assistance to anyone in the group in order to bring up the performance of everyone.

   Never   1—2—3—4—5—6—7   Always

10. I accept and support the openness of other group members, supporting them for taking risks and encouraging individuality in group members.

    Never   1—2—3—4—5—6—7   Always

11. I share any materials, books, sources of information, or other resources I have with the other group members in order to promote the success of individual members and the group as a whole.

    Never   1—2—3—4—5—6—7   Always

12. I often paraphrase or summarize what other members have said before I respond or comment.

    Never   1—2—3—4—5—6—7   Always

13. I level with other group members.

        Never   1—2—3—4—5—6—7   Always

14. I warmly encourage all members to participate, giving them recognition for their contributions, demonstrating acceptance and openness to their ideas, and generally being friendly and responsive to them.

        Never   1—2—3—4—5—6—7   Always

Your Trust Behavior

In order to get a total score, write the number you circled for each question in the following tables. Reverse the scoring for the starred questions. (If you circled 2, write 6; if you circled 1, write 7; 4 remains the same.)

Trusting *Openness and* *Sharing*	**Trustworthy** *Acceptance and* *Support*
1. _____	2. _____
3. _____	4. _____
*5. _____	*6. _____
7. _____	8. _____
9. _____	10. _____
11. _____	12. _____
13. _____	14. _____
Total _____	Total _____

If a person has a score of 35 or over, classify him/her as being trusting or trustworthy, whichever better applies. If someone has a score of under 35, classify him/her as being distrustful or untrustworthy, whichever better applies.

EXERCISE 3.2
Practicing Trust-Building Skills

This exercise provides you with an opportunity to practice the trust-building skills needed for relationships to grow and develop. The procedure for the exercise is as follows:

1. Form groups of six members and choose one member to observe, using the observation sheet that follows.

2. Complete the Genetic Traits Task.

3. Discuss the following questions in your group:
   a. Who engaged in what types of trust-building behaviors?
   b. What feelings do members of the group have about their participation in the group?
   c. Was trust increased or decreased by participating in this exercise?

Observation Sheet

1. Contributes ideas				
2. Describes feelings				
3. Paraphrases				
4. Expresses acceptance and support				
5. Expresses warmth and liking				

Trusting behaviors = 1 and 2
Trustworthy behaviors = 3, 4, and 5

Genetic Traits Task

Working as a group, estimate the number of people in your city (or school) who possess each of the following genetic traits. Establish the frequency of occurrence of each genetic trait, first in your group, then in the entire room. On the percentage of occurrence in your group and the room, estimate the number of people in your city (or school) who possess each trait.

1. Dimples in the cheeks versus no dimples.
2. Brown (or hazel) eyes versus blue, gray, or green eyes.
3. Attached versus free earlobes (an earlobe is free if it dips below the point where it is attached).
4. Little-finger bend versus no bend (place your little fingers together with your palms toward you—if your little fingers bend away from each other at the tips, you have the famous "little finger bend").
5. Tongue roll versus no tongue roll (if you can curl up both sides of your tongue to make a trough, you have it, and it's not contagious).
6. Hairy versus nonhairy middle fingers (examine the backs of the middle two fingers on your hands and look for hair between the first and second knuckle).

7. Widow's peak versus straight or curved hairline (examine the hairline across your forehead and look for a definite dip or point of hair extending down toward your nose).

 EXERCISE 3.3
Prisoner's Dilemma Game

The game you are about to play is called the Prisoner's Dilemma game. It is a game in which a player has to choose between increasing his own immediate gain or increasing the total gain of both players. It derives its name from the following situation:

> Two suspects are taken into custody and separated. The District Attorney is certain that they are guilty of a specific crime, but he does not have adequate evidence to convict them at a trial. He points out each prisoner's alternatives to him: to confess to the crime that the police are sure they have committed, or not to confess. If they both do not confess, then the District Attorney states he will book them on some very minor but trumped-up charge such as petty larceny and illegal possession of a weapon for which they would both receive minor punishments; if they both confess they will be prosecuted, but he will recommend less than the most severe sentence; but if one confesses and the other does not, then the confessor will receive lenient treatment for turning state's evidence, whereas the latter will get "the book" slapped at him. (Luce and Raiffa 1957, p. 95)

Neither prisoner is aware of the other prisoner's decision. The decision of each will be very much affected by his prediction of what the other prisoner will do. Both decisions will be very much affected by the extent to which each trusts the other not to confess. The important properties of this dilemma appear in the Prisoner's Dilemma Matrix.

Prisoner's Dilemma Matrix

In the matrix it is clear that the number of points a person receives from a choice depends not only upon his own choice, but upon what the choice of the other person is. If Person I chooses *A*, how many points he receives depends upon whether Person II chooses *C* or *D*. If Person I chooses *A*, and Person II chooses *C*, each will receive 10 points. If Person I chooses *A*, and Person II chooses *D*, Person I will lose 25 points and Person II will gain 25 points. If Person I chooses *B*, and Person II chooses *C*, Person I will gain 25 points and Person II will lose 25 points. And if Person I chooses *B* and Person II chooses *D*,

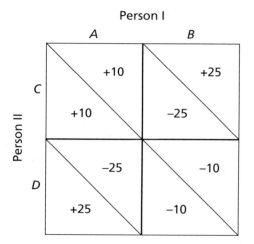

both will lose 10 points. Study this matrix until you are sure you understand it. Then answer the following questions. Answers are at the end of the chapter.

1. If Person II chooses C and Person I chooses A, Person I receives _____ points and Person II receives _____ points.

2. If Person II chooses C and Person I chooses B, Person I receives _____ points and Person II receives _____ points.

3. If Person II chooses D and Person I chooses A, Person I receives _____ points and Person II receives _____ points.

4. If Person II chooses D and Person I chooses B, Person I receives _____ points and Person II receives _____ points.

When you understand the matrix, you are ready to play the Prisoner's Dilemma game. The objective of the game is to provide an experience in which trust is either built and maintained or violated and diminished. To play the game each person needs a small pad of paper and a pencil. The procedure for the game is as follows:

1. Pair up with another person in the group. Sit back-to-back so that you cannot see the other player. Each person should have a pencil and a small pad of paper. One person is designated as Person I and the other as Person II.

2. When the leader gives the signal, each person should make his or her choice (Person I chooses between A and B, Person II chooses between C and D). Next, when the leader gives the signal, each person passes a slip of paper with the choice written on it over his or her shoulder to the other player. You may not speak; no communication to the other player other than the choice you make is allowed.

3. This step is repeated ten times. Each player should keep track of the number of points he or she has on the record sheet.

4. At the end of the tenth choice, the two players can discuss anything they want to with each other for 10 minutes.

5. Ten more choices are made, following the procedure outlined in step 2.

6. At the end of the 20th choice, total your gains and losses. Then fill out the questionnaire "Impressions of Other's Behavior."

7. In the group as a whole, discuss the following questions:
   a. What were your feelings and reactions about yourself and the other player during the game?
   b. How many points did you make during the game? How many did the other player make?
   c. How did you describe the other player's behavior during the game? How did he or she describe your behavior during the game?
   d. Did the two of you trust each other? Were the two of you trustworthy?
   e. How did it feel to have your trust violated (if that happened to you)? How did it feel to violate the other player's trust?
   f. How was trust built during the game (if it was)?
   g. What effect did the period of communication have upon the way you played the game? Did it affect the way you felt about the other player's behavior?

The essential psychological feature of the Prisoner's Dilemma game is that there is no possibility for rational individual behavior in it unless the conditions for mutual trust exist. If each player chooses B and D to obtain either maximum gain or minimum loss for himself, each will lose. But it makes no sense to choose the other alternative, A and C, which could result in maximum loss, unless you can trust the other player. If you have to play the game, you either develop mutual trust or resign yourself to a loss by choosing competitively (that is, choosing B and D) in order to minimize your loss.

There has been a great deal of research on trust using the Prisoner's Dilemma game. Some of the conclusions from that research are these:

1. Trust is often difficult to build but very easy to destroy. It may take two players a long time to arrive at a point where both consistently choose A and C, and any deviation to B and D may destroy all possibility of a cooperative solution to the dilemma.

2. Inappropriate trust may be just as dysfunctional as no trust at all; when a person consistently makes a trusting choice (A or C) and the other player consistently chooses B or D, the player exploiting the first person's trust will often feel little or no guilt, rationalizing that anyone who keeps making himself or herself vulnerable deserves to be taken advantage of.

3. How the situation is defined will affect how easily trust may be built. If the game is defined as a problem-solving situation that the two individuals must solve, trust is relatively easy to build. If the game is defined as a competitive situation in which you must win more points than the other player, trust is very difficult to build.

Record Sheet: Prisoner's Dilemma Game

	Your choice	Other's choice	Your gain or loss	Your total	Other's gain or loss	Other's total
1.						
2.						
3.						
4.						
5.						
6.						
7.						
8.						
9.						
10.						
11.						
12.						
13.						
14.						
15.						
16.						
17.						
18.						
19.						
20.						

Thus in a situation in which you are attempting to increase trust, you may want to avoid violating the other person's trust, avoid trusting the other person if he or she consistently behaves in untrustworthy ways, and ensure that the situation is defined as a problem-solving situation, not a competitive one.

Impressions of Other's Behavior

Indicate your impression of the other player's behavior during the game by checking the appropriate adjectives in the following list. You may know the other player; if so, ignore everything you have felt about the person in the past and rate *only* your impressions of his or her behavior during the game.

_____ warm	_____ cold
_____ trustworthy	_____ untrustworthy
_____ fair	_____ unfair
_____ generous	_____ selfish
_____ congenial	_____ uncongenial
_____ cooperative	_____ competitive
_____ kind	_____ unkind
_____ trustful	_____ untrustful

 EXERCISE 3.4
Trust-Level Disclosures

The purpose of this exercise is for members of the group to disclose to one another their perceptions of the depth of the trust level in their relationship. Once this information is out in the open, the members of the group can discuss how trust could be increased in their relationship. Openly discussing issues concerning one's relationships is perhaps the most effective way to increase the closeness of the relationship. The procedure for the exercise is as follows:

1. Pick the individual whom you trust least in the group and pair off with him.

2. For 15 minutes, share your perceptions of why the trust level is low in your relationship. Try to avoid being defensive or hostile. Try to understand as fully as possible why the other person feels the way he does.

3. For the next 10 minutes, share your impressions of how the trust level in the relationship can be increased. This step may involve stating how you are going to behave differently or how you would like the other to behave differently. Be as specific as possible.

4. Answer the following questions with your partner:
   a. To what extent is the lack of self-disclosure by one or both persons contributing to the relatively low level of trust in the relationship?
   b. To what extent is the lack of communicated support and acceptance by one or both persons contributing to the relatively low level of trust in the relationship?

5. Now find the person in the group whom you trust the most. Pair up with her.

6. For 15 minutes, share your understanding of why the trust level is high in your relationship. Try to understand as fully as possible why each of you feels the way you do.

7. For 10 minutes, share your impressions of how the trust level in the relationship can be increased even more. This step may involve stating how you are going to behave differently or how you would like the other to behave differently. Be as specific as possible.

8. Answer the following questions with your partner:
   a. To what extent is the level of self-disclosure by one or both persons contributing to the relatively high level of trust in the relationship?
   b. To what extent is the communication of acceptance and support by one or both persons contributing to the relatively high level of trust in the relationship?

In this exercise it is possible to focus on two important aspects of building and maintaining trust in a relationship. The first is the risk you and your partners took in self-disclosure. The second is the response you and your partners made to the other person's risk taking. Both the risks and the responses are crucial elements in building trust in a relationship.

How do you self-disclose your perceptions of, and your feelings about, your relationship with another person in ways that will result in a closer relationship? This question will be answered in depth in the next chapter, which focuses on communication. But if your self-disclosures include the following four elements, you have a good chance of successfully moving the relationship closer.

1. *Statement of your intentions:* For example, "I'm worried about our relationship. I want to do something that will help us become better friends."

2. *Statement of your expectations about how the other person may respond:* For example, "I think you may be uncomfortable about my bringing this up but I hope that you will listen and try to understand what I am saying."

3. *Statement of what you will do if the other person violates your expectations:* For example "If you shut me off, I will be hurt and will become defensive."

4. *Statement of how trust will be reestablished if he violates your expectations and you make your response:* For example, "if you cut me off and I become defensive, then we'll have to spend an evening talking about old times to get ourselves back together again."

To the extent that these four points become clear in the conversation in which you take a risk, you may feel more confident that the relationship will not be damaged even if the risk turns out badly.

The response you make to another person's risk taking is crucial for building trust in the relationship. The other person will feel it is safe to take risks in self-disclosure to the extent that she feels she will receive support when necessary and acceptance rather than rejection. To ensure that the relationship grows you should do the following:

1. Make sure the other person feels supported for taking the risk.

2. If you disagree with what he or she is saying, make sure that it is clear that it is his or her ideas you are rejecting, not him or her as a person.

3. Make sure you disclose your perceptions and feelings about the relationship. Always reward openness with openness when you are dealing with friends or individuals with whom you wish to develop a closer relationship.

 EXERCISE 3.5
Nonverbal Trust

Taking a risk that makes you vulnerable to another person and receiving support can take place in a variety of nonverbal as well as verbal ways. One of the interesting aspects of the development of trust in a relationship is that sometimes the sense of physical support can be as powerful a developer of trust as can a sense of emotional support. Your group may like to try some of the following nonverbal exercises. Each of them is related to the development of trust. Before you attempt the exercises, however, you should carefully consider the following points:

1. No one with a bad back or another physical condition that might be adversely affected should participate in an exercise in which participants might be handled roughly.

2. Although these nonverbal exercises can be used as a form of play, they should be used only for educational purposes. That is, they should be done for a specific learning purpose, such as learning more about the development of trust, and they should be discussed thoroughly after they have been done.

3. Do not enter into an exercise unless you plan to behave in a trustworthy manner. If you cannot be trusted to support another person, do not enter into an exercise in which you are responsible for physically supporting someone. No one should be allowed to fall or to suffer any injury.

4. No group pressure should be exerted upon individuals to participate. Participation should be strictly voluntary. If you do not feel like volunteering, however, you may find it interesting to analyze why. You may learn something about yourself and your relationships with the other members of the group from such an analysis. A lack of trust in the group or in other individuals might lead you to refuse to participate; on the other hand, a sense of adventure and fun might lead you to volunteer even though you do not trust the group or other individuals.

Trust Circle

The group stands facing into a closed circle. A volunteer, perhaps a person who wishes to develop more trust in the group, is handed around the inside of the circle by the shoulders and upper torso. He should stand with his feet in the center of the circle, close his eyes, and let the group pass him around or across their circle. His feet should not move from the center of the circle. After as many people who want to try it have been passed around the circle, discuss the following questions:

1. How did it feel to be on the inside of the circle? What were you thinking about; what was the experience like?

2. How did it feel to be a part of the circle, passing others around? What were you thinking about; what were you experiencing? Did you feel differently with different people in the center? Did the group behave differently when different people were in the center?

3. Some of the groups take a great deal of care in passing a person around and are very gentle; other groups engage in aggressive play and toss the person from side to side. What did your group do? What does it signify about the group and members?

Trust Walk

Each member of the group pairs up with another person. One person is designated as the guide, the other as a blind person. The blind person should close her eyes and the guide will lead her around the room. The guide should grasp the wrists of the blind person and, either from the side or from behind, guide the blind person around the room, planning as "rich" an experience as possible for the blind person using all the senses other than sight. Various touching experiences such as feeling the wall, the covering of a chair, the hair or face of another person are all interesting. If you can go outdoors, standing in the sun or the wind is enjoyable. In a large room, trust in the guide can be tested by running across the room, the blind person keeping her eyes shut. After 15 minutes, reverse roles and repeat. After everyone has been both a guide and a blind person, discuss the following questions in the group as a whole:

1. How did it feel to be the blind person?
2. What were some of the best experiences your guide gave you?
3. What did you learn about the guide?
4. What did you learn about the blind person?
5. How did it feel to be the guide?
6. At this point, how do the two of you feel about each other?

Trust Cradle

The group forms two lines by the side of a volunteer. The volunteer leans back, and the group picks him up, someone supporting his head. The volunteer should close his eyes and relax as much as possible. The group rocks him forward and backward. Slowly the group raises the person up, rocking him all the time, until he is as high as they can lift him. The group then slowly lowers the person to the floor, rocking him back and forth all the time. This can be repeated with several or all of the members of the group, depending upon the amount of time available. Afterward, the group as a whole should discuss the following questions:

1. How did it feel to be cradled? What were you thinking of while the group was cradling you? What were you experiencing?
2. How did it feel to cradle the different members of the group? Did you have different feelings with different people?
3. How has trust in the group been affected by the experience?

Trust Fall

Partners stand, one with her back turned to the other's front. With her arms extended sideways, she falls backward and is caught by her partner. Reverse roles and repeat. You may like to try the exercise with several different group partners. Then discuss in the group as a whole the following questions:

1. How did it feel to fall? Did you doubt that the other would really catch you?

2. How did it feel to catch your partner? Did you doubt that you would be able to catch him?

3. How has trust in the individuals who caught you been affected?

Elevated Trust Passing

The group lines up in a straight line, each person facing the back of the person in front of him. The person at the beginning of the line is lifted high and is passed over the top of the others to the end of the line, where he is slowly brought down. The person now at the head of the line is lifted high and is passed over the top of the others to the end of the line. If a group member does not wish to be passed, he moves to the end of the line when he finds himself at the head of the line. The exercise continues until all members who want to have been lifted and passed.

1. How did it feel to be passed?

2. What were you thinking; what were you experiencing?

3. How did it feel to pass the other members of the group?

4. How has trust in the group been affected by the exercise?

 EXERCISE 3.6
Developing Trust

The objectives for this exercise are for the members of the group to arrive at a summary statement concerning the ways in which trust can be built in a relationship. The procedure for the exercise is the following:

1. Divide into groups of four.

2. Arrive at the ten most important things a person can do to develop trust in a relationship. Take 20 minutes for this.

3. Share the results across the group.

4. As a whole, rank the ten most important aspects of developing trust from the most important to the least important.

Did your list include any of the following: progressively disclosing oneself to the other person; making sure your behavior regarding the other person is consistent; following through on your commitments to the other person; expressing warmth and acceptance to the other person; avoiding being judgmental of the other person; being trustworthy; being honest?

■ CHAPTER REVIEW

Test your understanding of this chapter by taking the following quiz. Answers are at the end of the chapter.

True   False   1. In a trust situation, you can be either accepted or rejected.

True   False   2. In a trust situation, you should prepare for rejection in order to keep from getting hurt.

True   False   3. Once you develop trust in a situation, you will not have to work on the relationship anymore.

True   False   4. What you expect from a situation can determine what you will get.

True   False   5. Risk trusting in every situation.

True   False   6. Your response to another person's self-disclosure determines your trustworthiness.

True   False   7. An example of good risk taking is when Helen tells Roger how she expects him to respond to her self-disclosure.

True   False   8. A good response to risk taking is when Roger interrupts Helen to make his own self-disclosures.

9. What four elements should you have in a conversation when you are taking a risk in self-disclosure in a relationship?
   a. An initial statement of neutral interest
   b. A statement of your intentions
   c. A statement of your expectations and how the other person may respond
   d. A comment about how good the other person looks
   e. A statement of what you will do if the other person violates your expectation
   f. A statement of how the other person bothers you
   g. A statement of how trust will be reestablished

10. When the other person takes a risk in self-disclosure, what three things should you work into the conversation?
    a. Support of the other person for taking the risk
    b. Complete acceptance of the other person's ideas
    c. Your nervousness in self-disclosing
    d. If you disagree, your rejection of the person's ideas but not of the person
    e. Your own openness in response to the other person's openness
    f. How much you've learned from reading this book

Self-Diagnosis

This chapter has focused on the skills involved in engaging in trusting and trust-worthy behavior. On a scale from 1 (poorly mastered) to 5 (highly mastered) rate the degree to which you have mastered each skill. Then choose two skills to improve on in the next week.

Rating	Skill
_____	Expression of warmth and cooperative intentions
_____	Taking appropriate risks with self-disclosure
_____	Responding to another person's self-disclosures with acceptance and support
_____	Reciprocating another person's self-disclosures

Skills I Will Improve in the Next Week

1. _____

2. _____

Summary

At this point, you should understand what trust is and when it is appropriate to engage in trusting and trustworthy actions. You should also have an understanding of how to develop and maintain trust in a relationship. However, in order for you to self-disclose appropriately and effectively, you need to communicate effectively. The next chapter deals with increasing your communication skills.

Answers

Comprehension Test: 1. true; 2. false; 3. true; 4. true; 5. false; 6. false; 7. true; 8. true; 9. true; 10. false; 11. true; 12. true; 13. c; 14. b; 15. e; 16. a; 17. f; 18. g; 19. d.

Prisoner's Dilemma: 1. +10, +10; 2. +25, −25; 3. −25, +25; 4. −10, −10.

Chapter Review: 1. true; 2. false; 3. false; 4. true; 5. false; 6. true; 7. true; 8. false; 9. b, c, e, g; 10. a, d, e.

CHAPTER 4

Increasing Your Communication Skills

Introduction

"What creature walks on four legs in the morning, on two at noon, and upon three in the evening?" If you were walking on the high mountain road leading to the Greek city of Thebes, you might be asked this riddle by the legendary Sphinx. Failure to answer correctly would result in your death. The Sphinx had the body of a lion, the wings of an eagle, and the torso and head of a woman. The riddle of the Sphinx was the last remnant of the lore of Egypt's Great Sphinx, who had the form of a human-headed lion and was built to guard the Pharaoh's tombs. As an enigmatic and all-knowing creature of mystery, the Sphinx symbolizes the lack of clarity in communication both in expression and words.

To live is to communicate! All life communicates in some way. Animals and insects communicate by means of chemicals, movements, and sounds. Humans use all of these to communicate, but they add words: a unique system based on symbols that stand for the objects and ideas to which humans refer. The importance of communication cannot be overemphasized. Communication is the foundation for all interpersonal relationships, and our daily lives are filled with one communication experience after another. Through communication we reach some understanding of each other, learn to like, influence, and trust each other, begin and end relationships, and learn more about ourselves and how others perceive us. Through communication we learn to understand others as individuals and we help others to understand us. Any discussion of interpersonal skills must emphasize the skills of communicating effectively.

What Is Communication?

Our basic social nature demands that we seek out communication with other people. All of us have personal needs that can be satisfied only by relating to others. Interpersonal communication reflects our mutual need to establish contact and join our efforts to achieve mutual goals. The very process of communication—exchanging messages to achieve understanding of each other's perceptions, ideas, and experiences—makes people interdependent. It takes two to communicate, and through the act of communicating with another person we begin or maintain a relationship. What prompts communication is our desire for someone else to know what we know, to value what we value, to feel what we feel, and to decide what we decide.

Communication has been described in many different ways. One view of communication differentiates between quantitative and qualitative communication. The quantitative view differentiates among communication between two people, communication among members of a small group, communication to large audiences, and communication to mass audiences. The qualitative view differentiates between personal and impersonal communication. Another view of communication describes communication as being focused on content or on the relationship. Finally, communication as been viewed as (a) a linear process in which a sender creates a message and sends it through a channel to a receiver, who interprets the message and replies, and (b) a transactional process in which individuals create, send, receive, and interpret messages simultaneously. It is this latter description that is emphasized in this chapter.

Two people sensing each other through sight, sound, touch, or smell will have a continuous effect on each other's perceptions and expectations of what the other is going to do. Communication is much more than the exchange of words; all behavior conveys some message and is, therefore, a form of communication. **Interpersonal communication** can be broadly defined as any verbal or nonverbal behavior that is perceived by another person, but is more commonly defined as a message sent by a person to a receiver (or receivers) with a conscious intent of affecting the receiver's behavior. Communication is initiated in order to change the other person in some way. A person sends the message "How are you?" to evoke the response "Fine." A teacher shakes his head to get two students to stop throwing erasers at him. Under this more limited definition, any signal aimed at influencing the receiver's behavior in any way is a communication.

This definition of communication does not mean that an orderly sequence of events in time always exists in which a person thinks up a message and sends it, and someone else receives it. Communication among people is a process in which everyone receives, sends, interprets, and infers all at the same time, and there is no beginning and no end. All communication involves people sending one another symbols to which certain meanings are attached. These symbols can be either verbal (all words are symbols) or nonverbal (all expressions and gestures are symbols). The exchange of ideas and experiences between two people is possible only when both have adopted the same ways of relating a particular non-

Ways of Defining Communication

View	Definition
Quantitative	Differentiates among dyadic communication, communication in small groups, communication to large audiences, and mass communication.
Qualitative	Difference between personal and impersonal communication.
Content	Statements about the subject being discussed.
Relational	Statements about how the parties feel toward each other and their relationship.
Linear	A sender encodes ideas and feelings into a message and sends it through a channel to a receiver, who decodes the message and gives the sender feedback by his or her reaction.
Transactional	We encode, send, receive, and decode messages simultaneously, not in a back-and-forth manner. A transactional view of communication recognizes that it is difficult to isolate a single discrete "act" of communication from the events that precede and follow it.

verbal, spoken, written, or pictorial symbol to a particular experience. And all communication affects the relationship between two people, one way or the other.

Figure 4.1 represents a model of the process of communication between two individuals. In this model the communicator is referred to as the sender and the person at whom the message is aimed is the receiver. The message is any verbal or nonverbal symbol that one person transmits to another. The channel is the means of conveying the message to the receiver; the sound waves of the voice or the light waves involved in seeing words on a printed page are examples of channels. Because communication is a process, sending and receiving messages often takes place simultaneously; a person can be speaking and at the same time paying close attention to the receiver's nonverbal responses.

Communication between two people may be viewed as consisting of seven basic elements:

1. The intentions, ideas, and feelings of the sender and the way she decides to behave, all of which lead to her sending a message that carries some content.

2. The encoding of the message by the sender—she translates her ideas, feelings, and intentions into a message appropriate for sending.

3. Sending the message to the receiver.

4. The channel through which the message is translated.

5. The decoding of the message by the receiver—he interprets its meaning. The receiver's interpretation depends on how well the receiver understands the content of the message and the intentions of the sender.

6. An internal response by the receiver to this interpretation of the message.

7. The amount of noise in the preceding steps. Noise is any element that interferes with the communication process. In the sender, noise refers to such things as the attitudes, prejudices, and frame of reference of the sender and the appropriateness of her language or other expression of the message. In the receiver, noise refers to such things as his attitudes, background, and experiences that affect the decoding process. In the channel, noise refers to (a) environmental sounds, such as static or traffic, (b) speech problems, such as stammering, and (c) annoying or distracting mannerisms, such as a tendency to mumble. To a large extent, the success of communication is determined by the degree to which noise is overcome or controlled.

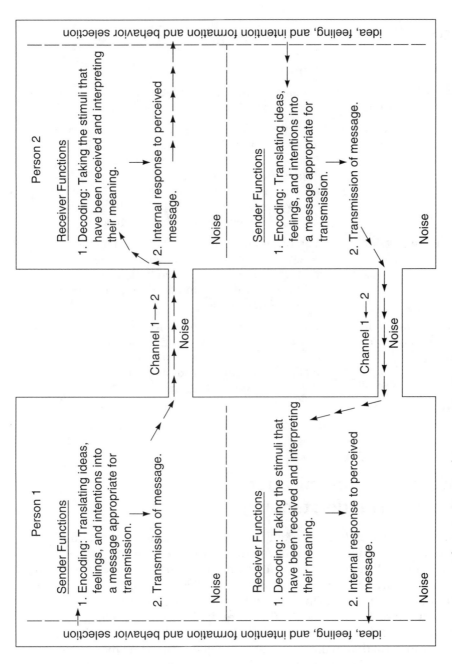

FIGURE 4.1 *The Interpersonal Communication Process*

Principles of Communication

Principle	Explanation
We communicate with (not to) others.	Communication is not something we do *to* others, it is an activity we do *with* them.
Communication can be intentional or unintentional.	Sometimes you may carefully plan and practice an apology to a friend. Other times people overhear private conversations, see an expression that was meant to be hidden, or observe what a person does when he or she believes no one is watching. In such cases, messages are not encoded in a planned way.
Communication is irreversible.	You cannot un-ring a bell. You cannot un-receive a message. Once a message is transmitted, it can never be taken back, erased, or changed. Words said and deeds done cannot be retrieved or undone.
Communication is unrepeatable.	Communication is a continuous, ongoing process, and therefore it cannot be repeated exactly the same way or with exactly the same meaning. The same words and actions are different each time they are spoken or performed.

Effective Communication Versus Misunderstandings

Communication is like ballroom dancing. You cannot waltz alone. You must have a partner whose movements coordinate with and complement your actions. When you move forward, your partner moves backward. When you turn to your right, your partner glides to the left. No two partners are quite the same. One partner may be more graceful or more skilled than another. How you waltz, therefore, varies from one partner to another. A great dancer considers and adapts to the skill level of his or her partner in ways that make them both look good. The same may be said for communication. Like dancing, communication requires at least one partner. The actions of both must be coordinated in ways that complement each other. Communication becomes a unique creation that arises out of the way in which the partners interact. Since each person is unique, the way in which communication transpires is unique to that relationship.

How do you tell whether communication is effective? **Effective communication** when the receiver interprets the sender's message the way the sender intended it. If John tries to communicate to Jane that it is a wonderful day and he is feeling great by saying "Hi" with a warm smile, and if Jane interprets John's "Hi" as meaning John thinks it is a beautiful day and is feeling well, then effective communication has taken place. If Jane interprets John's "Hi" as meaning he wants to stop and talk with her, then ineffective communication has taken place.

Why is it so common for two individuals not to understand each other? One source of communication failures arises from the sender's inaccurate expression of the message or lack of verbal ability. The sender can use the wrong words or make critical grammatical errors. Perhaps the most common source of misunderstanding results from the receiver's interpreting the meaning of a message differently from what the sender intended. Since intentions are private, a sender's intentions must be inferred by the receiver. I know my intentions, but I must make inferences about yours. You know your intentions, but you must infer mine. Difficulties in communication often result from the failure of the receiver to understand correctly the intentions of the sender.

Emotional and social sources of noise, however, are much more troublesome. People are often so angry, upset, or preoccupied that they just do not listen to what others are saying. Or they can be so interested in what they have to say that they listen to others only to find an opening to get the floor. Sometimes individuals are so sure that they know what the other person is going to say that they distort the message to match their expectations. A man who has a very low opinion of himself, for example, may ask a woman for a date and take her statement "Let me think for a minute" as a refusal.

Sometimes individuals listen in order to evaluate and make judgments about the speaker and the message, an approach that in turn makes the speaker guarded and defensive in what he or she is trying to say. An example occurs when a person is presenting an argument and the receiver is constantly saying, "That's stupid; that's wrong." The speaker then becomes very careful about what he is saying.

At times individuals understand the words a communicator is using without understanding the real underlying meaning of what he or she is trying to say. For example, a person may say, "It is a nice day," in an attempt to change the subject, and the receiver may think the speaker is really interested in the weather. All of these problems in communication will be discussed more fully later in the chapter.

Finally, a lack of trust can (a) reduce the amount of information the sender shares and (b) increase the receiver's suspiciousness of what little information is communicated. Increasing communication between two individuals results in greater accuracy of understanding only when trust is high.

Thus misunderstanding may arise from the sender's lack of verbal ability, the receiver interpreting the meaning of a message differently from what the sender intended, the receiver's emotional noise, the receiver being highly evaluative of the sender and the message, the receiver missing the point, and lack of trust by either the sender or the receiver or both. These are only a few of the sources of misunderstandings. When you stop to think of how many ways individuals can misunderstand each other, it seems at times a wonder that any effective communication can take place at all. What can be concluded is that effective communication takes considerable skill, both in sending and receiving messages.

False Principles	Misconceptions
If you say it, the other person will understand.	Words are not meaning. Saying it does not mean it will be understood.
The more communication, the better.	At times, talking too much is a mistake. Excessive communication can aggravate or even create a problem.
Any problem can be solved if people communicate with each other.	At times, the more clearly you communicate, the greater the problems become and the more hurt and angry people become.
Some people are born communicators; some are not.	Communication is not a natural ability. There is no aptitude for communicating skillfully. It takes training and practice.

◼ COMPREHENSION TEST A

Test your understanding of what communication is by taking the following quiz. Answers are at the end of the chapter.

True   False   1. If you are alive, you have to communicate something.

True   False   2. It takes two to communicate.

True   False   3. In interpersonal communication, the sender wants to affect the receiver's behavior in some way.

True   False   4. Communication is an orderly sequence of events in which a person thinks up a message and sends it, and the message is received.

True   False   5. A person's attitude can be noise that interferes with communication.

True   False   6. Effective communication exists when the receiver gets the message that was sent.

True   False   7. Effective communication is a little old lady hitting a burglar over the head with her umbrella.

True   False   8. Effective communication is your reading this book and trying to answer this question.

9. What are the seven basic elements of communication?
   a. The subject of the conversation, around which all communication occurs
   b. The intentions of the communicator
   c. The receiver's reactions to the sender
   d. Encoding
   e. Transmission of the message
   f. The receiver's understanding of the content of the message and the sender's intention
   g. The preferred style of thinking of the sender
   h. The channel through which the message is sent
   i. The internal response of the receiver
   j. Noise
   k. The categories of response the receiver has in mind
   l. Expressing acceptance and support

10. What are three common communication faults of the receiver?
   a. Not giving the sender undivided attention
   b. Turning off the sender's hearing aid
   c. Relating the conversation to something the speaker does not know about
   d. Thinking about her replies instead of paying attention to the sender
   e. Listening for details rather than the essential message
   f. Listening to the essential but missing details

Communication Skills

Sending Skills

1. Speak for yourself by using personal pronouns when expressing thoughts, ideas, reactions, and feelings.

2. Describe other people's actions without making value judgments.

3. Use relationship statements when they are appropriate.

4. Take the receiver's perspective into account when sending your messages.

5. Ask for feedback about the receiver's understanding of your message.

6. Describe your feelings.

7. Make your nonverbal messages communicate clearly what you are feeling.

8. Make your nonverbal messages congruent with your words.

Receiving Skills

1. Paraphrase accurately without making value judgments about the sender's thoughts, reactions, perceptions, needs, and feelings.

2. Negotiate the meaning of the sender's messages.

3. Describe what you think the other person is feeling and then ask if you are correct.

4. Understand what the message means from the sender's perspective.

Sending Messages Effectively

How can you send messages effectively? What can you do to ensure effective communication of your ideas and feelings? In this and the following three chapters we discuss the answers to these questions. There are several ways senders of a message can increase the likelihood that they will be understood. The three basic requirements are understandable messages, credibility of the sender, and optimal feedback on how the message is affecting the receiver.

The skills of sending messages effectively include the following:

1. Clearly "own" your message by (a) using personal pronouns such as *I, me,* and *my* and (b) letting others know what your thoughts and feelings are. You "disown" your messages when you use expressions such as "most people," "some people,"and "our group," making it difficult to tell whether you really think and feel what you are saying or are simply repeating the thoughts and feelings of others. This skill is covered in this chapter.

2. Describe the other person's behavior without including any judgment, evaluation, or inferences about the person's motives, personality, or attitudes. When reacting to the behavior of other people, be sure to describe their behavior ("You keep interrupting me") rather than evaluating it ("You're a rotten, self-centered egotist who won't listen to anyone else's ideas"). This skill is covered in this chapter.

3. Describe the ways the relationship can be changed to improve the quality and quantity of interaction among the individuals involved. In order to maintain and improve a relationship, the quality of the relationship needs to be discussed and reflected on periodically.

4. Make the message appropriate to the receiver's frame of reference. The same information will be explained differently to an expert in the field than to a novice, to a child than to an adult, or to your boss than to a co-worker. Perspective taking is covered in this chapter.

5. Ask for feedback concerning the way your messages are being received. In order to communicate effectively you must be aware of how the receiver is interpreting and processing your messages. The only way to be sure is to continually seek feedback as to what meanings the receiver is attaching to your messages. This is known as two-way communication and is covered in this chapter.

6. Describe your feelings by name, action, or figure of speech. When communicating your feelings, it is especially important to be descriptive. You may describe your feelings by name ("I feel sad"), by actions ("I feel like crying"), or by figures of speech ("I feel down in the dumps"). The description will help communicate your feelings clearly and unambiguously. This skill is covered in Chapter 5.

7. Use nonverbal messages to communicate your feelings. Nonverbal messages are very powerful but inherently ambiguous. When people cry, for example, it may be because they are sad, happy, angry, or even afraid. When utilized with verbal messages, however, nonverbal messages clarify, strengthen, enrich, emphasize, and frame the message.

8. Make your verbal and nonverbal messages congruent with each other. Every face-to-face communication involves both verbal and nonverbal messages. Usually these messages are congruent, so by smiling and expressing warmth nonverbally, a person can be saying that she has appreciated your help. Communication problems arise when a person's verbal and nonverbal messages are contradictory; if a person says, "Here is some information that may be of help to you," with a sneer and in a mocking tone of voice, the meaning you receive is confused by the two different messages being sent simultaneously. This topic is covered in Chapter 6.

9. Be redundant. Repeating your messages more than once and using more than one channel of communication (such as pictures and written messages as well as verbal and nonverbal cues) will help the receiver understand your messages.

One of the most important elements in interpersonal communication is the credibility of the sender. **Sender credibility** refers to the receiver's belief in the trustworthiness of the sender's statements. Several dimensions affect the credibility of the sender:

1. The reliability of the sender as an information source—the sender's dependability, predictability, and consistency.
2. The intentions of the sender or the sender's motives. The sender should be open as to the effect he or she wants the message to have upon the receiver.
3. The expression of warmth and friendliness.
4. The majority opinion of other people concerning the trustworthiness of the sender. If all your friends tell you the sender is trustworthy, you will tend to believe it.
5. The sender's relevant expertise on the topic under discussion.
6. The dynamism of the sender. A dynamic sender is seen as aggressive, emphatic, and forceful and tends to be viewed as more credible than a more passive sender.

A highly credible sender is one who is perceived in a favorable light on all of these dimensions. A source low in credibility, in contrast, is one who is perceived in a negative light on any one of the dimensions. Unless you appear credible to the receiver, he or she will discount your message and you will not be able to communicate effectively with him or her. Sender credibility is often discussed as the perceived trustworthiness of the sender, and therefore credibility relates to the discussion of trust in Chapter 3.

Each individual in a relationship is constantly commenting on his definition of the relationship implicitly or explicitly. Every message exchange (including silence) defines the relationship implicitly since it expresses the idea "this is the sort of relationship where this sort of message may be given."
—Donald Jackson (1959)

■ COMPREHENSION TEST B

Test your understanding of sending understandable messages and having good credibility by marking the following questions true or false. The answers are given at the end of the chapter.

True   False   1. It is important to express what you think, not what other people think.

True   False   2. It is important that your verbal and nonverbal messages go together.

True   False   3. If you express yourself clearly, you will not need to repeat your message.

True   False   4. Evaluating and interpreting other people's behavior is a necessary part of effective communication.

True   False   5. As long as you express yourself clearly, you need not check on how your message is being received.

True   False   6. You must be seen as high on all the credibility dimensions in order to have high credibility.

True   False   7. The opinions of other people can influence how trustworthy the receiver sees the sender.

True   False   8. A passive sender is more credible than an aggressive one.

True   False   9. An example of good communication is Frank calling Edye a pig after she eats all the Christmas cookies.

True   False   10. An example of good credibility is a happily married psychiatrist giving his sister careful, loving advice on how to improve her marriage.

Sending Skill 1: Taking Ownership

One of the most basic sending skills is speaking for oneself. When you speak for yourself, you take responsibility for and acknowledge ownership of your thoughts, opinions, observations, and feelings. You speak for yourself when you use the personal pronoun *I, me, my, mine*. **Personal statements** are messages referring to yourself—about what you are feeling, what you are doing, what you are thinking, how you see yourself and your behavior, and so on (e.g., "I think . . . ," "I feel . . . ," and "I want . . ."). The more you speak for yourself, the clearer your messages will be. The less you speak for yourself, the more confused your messages will be. Whenever you refer to yourself, the discussion target is personal. Personal statements reveal who you are to the receiver and increase the personal quality of the relationship. They also communicate personal involvement and trust in the relationship. Not owning your messages is a symbol of mistrust and decreases the possibilities of a closer relationship developing between you and the person with whom you are talking.

There are two ways you can confuse the ownership of your messages. The first is to speak for no one. To speak for no one you can substitute words like "it," "some people," "everyone," or "one" for a personal pronoun. Or you can use no pronoun at all. As a result, it is not clear who is the owner of the ideas or feelings. Examples are "Most people believe that students from Southeast Central are chickens!" or "It is commonly believed that students from Southeast Central have a big yellow streak down their backs!"

The second way to confuse ownership of a message is to speak for others. When you speak for others you substitute pronouns such as *you* or *we* (or the person's name) for a first-person-singular pronoun. Examples are "Bill doesn't like you—he thinks you are a lousy boss" and "We are bored, bored, bored!" Speaking for other people may make them angry or, at the very least, boxed in by your statements. Other people will be confused as to what your thoughts, feelings, and needs are.

EXERCISE 4.1
Practicing Personal Statements

Find a partner and decide which of the following are personal statements (P), which speak for no one (N), and which speak for someone else (O). Answers are at the end of the chapter.

_____   1. Everyone here hates Bill.

_____   2. I love you.

_____   3. I hate you.

_____   4. Rumor has it that you are a beautiful person.

_____   5. We think flying is for the birds.

_____   6. Anyone can tell from looking at your face that you feel terrible.

_____   7. I want to find a better job.

Then discuss with your partner the following questions.

1. In making statements about your strengths, to what extent were the statements clearly personal ones?

2. What is your reaction to making personal statements and to receiving personal statements?

3. How do you think personal statements help develop a relationship and improve communication between the sender and the receiver?

Sending Skill 2: Be Descriptive, Not Evaluative

Describing the other's behavior promotes effective communication by providing information without creating defensiveness or closed-mindedness. A **behavioral description** is a message that includes the specific behaviors you have observed and does not include any judgment or evaluation or any inferences about the person's motives, personality, or attitudes. You may practice this skill in Exercise 4.2.

EXERCISE 4.2
Describing Others' Behavior

To communicate effectively and clearly, you need to describe other people's behavior without passing judgment. Working with a partner, put a

> *D* for each statement that *describes* a person's behavior.
> *J* for each statement that *judges* a person's behavior.

Agree on each answer. Then combine with another pair and compare answers. Discuss each statement until everyone agrees.

Statements

_____ 1. Sam interrupted Sally.

_____ 2. Mark is very sincere.

_____ 3. I do not like Sally.

_____ 4. Mark is very shy.

_____ 5. Today on the way to school, I saw three butterflies..

_____ 6. Jane is trying to make me mad.

_____ 7. Sam changed the subject.

_____ 8. Sam contributed six ideas to our discussion.

Sending Skill 3: Relationship Statements

Happiness is having good relationships. With some people, you will automatically become friends or enemies. But most relationships do not just happen. They have to be built and maintained. At times your relationships will be smooth and enjoyable. At other times, conflicts and problems will arise and will have to be solved. At such times, you will have to sit down with the other person and discuss the current problems in the relationship and negotiate a solution. During such a conversation, you will need to make relationship statements.

A **relationship statement** is a message describing how you view the relationship or some aspect of the way the two of you are interacting with each other. A good relationship statement indicates clear ownership (refers to *I, me, my,* or *mine*) and describes how you see the relationship. "I think we need to talk about our disagreement yesterday" is a good relationship statement. A poor relationship statement speaks for the other person and makes judgments about the relationship. Relationship statements change the relationship; they consider clearly where the relationship is and what needs to happen in order for it to develop. Making relationship statements clarifies where two individuals stand and facilitates the expression of feelings and perceptions that can lead to a deeper, more satisfying relationship. Relationship statements also decrease the possibility of faulty communication.

 E X E R C I S E 4 . 3
Relationship Statements

Find a partner. Decide which of the following are good relationship statements (*R*) and which are poor ones (*No*). Then review your answers for all poor relationship statements. Decide which ones are about a person and not a relationship (*P*), which ones make a judgment about the relationship (*J*) rather than describing how you perceive the relationship, and which ones speak for the other person (*O*) rather than for the speaker. Agree on the answer for each question and then check your answer and read the explanation in the answer section following the questions.

_____ 1. We really enjoyed ourselves last night.

_____ 2. Our relationship is really lousy!

_____ 3. For the past two days you have not spoken to me once. Is something wrong with our relationship?

_____ 4. You look sick today.

_____ 5. You really make me feel appreciated and liked.

_____ 6. You are angry again. You are always getting angry.

_____ 7. My older brother is going to beat you up if you don't stop doing that.

_____ 8. This job stinks.

_____ 9. I'm concerned that when we go to lunch together we are often late for work in the afternoon.

Answers

1. "We really enjoyed ourselves last night." This is a poor relationship statement because it speaks for the other person as well as for oneself. It should be marked *O*.

2. "Our relationship is really lousy!" This is a poor relationship statement because it judges the quality of the relationship rather than describing some aspect of the relationship. It should be marked *J*.

3. "For the past two days you have not spoken to me once. Is something wrong with our relationship?" This is a good relationship statement because it describes how the speaker sees one aspect of the relationship. It describes the speaker's perceptions of how the two people are relating to one another. Label it *R*.

4. "You look sick today." This is a poor relationship statement because it focuses on a person, not on a relationship. It should be marked *P*. The person may look sick, but such a statement does not describe how the two people are relating to each other. It could be reworded as a good relationship statement as follows: "For the past 15 minutes you have been holding your head in your hands. Are you not feeling well, or is what I'm saying giving you a headache?"

5. "You really make me feel appreciated and liked." This is a good relationship statement because the speaker is describing one aspect of how the speaker and the other person relate to each other. Label it *R*.

6. "You are angry again. You are always getting angry." This is a poor relationship statement because it speaks for the other person. It should be marked *O*. A good relationship statement would be "You look angry. You have frequently looked angry to me during the past two days. Is there a problem about our relationship that we need to discuss?"

7. "My older brother is going to beat you up if you don't stop doing that." This statement focuses on two other people (the older brother and the receiver). It should be marked *P*.

8. "This job stinks!" Definitely a judgment (*J*). To be a good relationship statement, it would have to be something like the following: "I get so angry and upset at the way you treat me that I dislike working here."

9. "I am concerned that when we go to lunch together we are often late for work in the afternoon." This is a relationship statement and should be marked *R*. It describes an aspect of the relationship in that the two people manage their lunches together in such a way that they end up being late for work in the afternoon.

Sending Skill 4: Understanding the Other's Perspective

Meg and Marge attend the same college. Meg is very wealthy, having inherited a great deal of money from her grandparents. Marge, whose parents are very poor, earns barely enough money to pay her tuition, buy books, and live inexpensively. They both buy tickets for the state lottery in which they could win up to $5,000. Two months later, they both receive letters. Meg reads her letter and says, "Hey, I won $5,000 in that lottery. Imagine that." Marge reads her letter, starts jumping up and down and screams, "I won! I won! I won $5,000!!! I won $5,000! I won! I won!" She throws her arms around her friend, both crying and laughing at the same time. She is too excited to eat or sleep.

Why did Meg and Marge react so differently to the news that they had each won $5,000 in the state lottery?

Different people have different perspectives. You see things from your shoes, I see things from my shoes, and our perspectives will never be quite the same. Misunderstandings often occur because we assume that everyone sees things from the same perspective as we do. If we like Italian food, we assume that all our friends like Italian food. If we are interested in sports, we assume that everyone is interested in sports. If we get angry when someone laughs at our behavior, we assume that being laughed at angers everyone. If we think the boss is stupid, we are sur-

prised when a co-worker thinks the boss is brilliant. As children, we can see things only from our perspective. As we become adults, we learn that different people have different perspectives, and we learn how to understand other people's perspectives.

You can have two different perspectives at two different times. When you are a tired clerk who wants to go home early to get ready for an important date, a customer's behavior may seem unreasonable. When you are a manager who is trying to increase sales, the same customer behavior may seem very understandable. On Monday, if a clerk overcharges you, you may laugh it off. But on Tuesday, when you have been overcharged at the last three stores you have visited, a careless clerk may make you angry. If you have been lifting 100-pound bags of cement and someone tosses you a 40-pound bag, it will seem very light, but if you have been lifting 20-pound bags, the 40-pound bag will seem very heavy. As your experiences, assumptions, career, and values change, your perspective will change.

The same message can mean two entirely different things to two different people. If you tease a classmate, he may laugh. But if you tease a prominent professor, she may get angry and throw you out of class. Different perspectives result in the message being given different meanings. From one perspective, a message may be interpreted as a joke. From another perspective, the same message may be interpreted as hostile insubordination.

Perspective taking is a vital skill for communicating effectively. To phrase your messages effectively, you need to take into account the perspective of the receiver. When deciding how to phrase a message, you need to consider

1. The receiver's perspective.
2. What the receiver already knows about the issue.
3. What further information the receiver needs and wants about the issue.

By taking these factors into account, you can phrase the message so the receiver can easily understand it.

To be skilled in receiving messages accurately, you need to understand the sender's perspective. When deciding what a message means, you need to take into account

1. The sender's perspective.
2. The meaning of the message from the sender's perspective.

By taking these factors into account, you can decide accurately what the sender wanted to communicate with the message.

There is no skill more important for effective communication than taking into consideration the other person's perspective. Try standing in someone else's shoes; it will considerably improve your communication with that person.

EXERCISE 4.4
From Their Shoes

The purpose of this exercise is to provide some practice in phrasing messages so they are appropriate to the receiver's perspective. The procedure is as follows:

1. Form into groups of four and read the story entitled "The Typists," which follows. As a group, write out what Jim might say to Sally, John Adams, and Dr. Elizabeth Smith. Then read the story entitled "The Laboratory Technicians." Write out what Edythe might say to Buddy, Helen, Dr. Smith, and Mrs. Jonathan.

2. In your group, discuss the following questions:
   a. How do your group's answers compare with the answers of the other groups?
   b. What did you learn about making messages appropriate to the perspective of the receiver?
   c. How do you find out what another person's perspective is?

The Typists

Sally and Jim are typists for a small publishing firm. Sally and Jim often tease each other about who is the faster typist. Their boss, John Adams, asks Jim to type a manuscript for one of their authors, whose name is Dr. Elizabeth Smith. Dr. Smith is a well-known authority in mathematical psychology. The manuscript is very complicated. It contains a great many mathematical equations that are hard to type. It contains a lot of psychological jargon that Jim does not understand. It has handwritten notes all over it that are impossible for him to read. Dr. Smith, for example, has written sentences filled with psychological jargon, in small and sloppy handwriting and in ink that is smeared all over the page. It takes Jim hours trying to figure out what the handwritten notes say. Since he does not know what half the words mean, he cannot be sure whether he has typed the notes correctly or not. The math included in the manuscript, furthermore, is very complicated. It all has to be double-checked to make sure it is correctly typed. This process has taken hours and hours of proofreading and correcting mistakes. All in all, Jim hates the manuscript. But he is working hard to finish it correctly. To top it all off, Jim is using an old typewriter that is difficult to type on. He asked his boss, John, for a word processor several weeks ago, but so far John has not tried to get him one.

One morning Sally looks over at Jim, smiles, and says, "That manuscript is really taking you a long time to type. How come?" Then John walks in and asks, "Jim, I have other typing for you to do, and you're still working on Dr. Smith's manuscript. Why is it taking you so long?" Then Dr. Smith phones Jim and says, "Look! I have to revise the manuscript before next month! I need a clean, typed copy immediately. Why haven't you finished it?"

If you were Jim, would you say the same thing to Sally, John, and Dr. Smith? If you phrased your answers differently, what would you take into account about the persons? In phrasing his messages to each person, Jim might take the following into account:

1. Who the person is.

2. What his or her position in the company is.

3. How much the person knows about the condition and content of the manuscript.

4. What the nature of the relationship between Jim and the person is.

5. How appropriate it is to be fully honest about
   a. Jim's feelings about the manuscript.
   b. The facts about why it is so hard to type.

The Laboratory Technicians

Buddy and Edythe are laboratory technicians in a large hospital. They have worked with each other for just a few days and do not know each other very well. One morning their supervisor, Helen, asks them to do a rush job on a blood sample. Helen is Edythe's older sister. Helen states that Dr. Smith is very worried about the patient. The tests, therefore, have to be done perfectly. The patient's name is Mrs. Jonathan. Edythe has never met either Dr. Smith or Mrs. Jonathan.

Edythe quickly conducts a series of blood tests. The results indicate that Mrs. Jonathan has blood cancer. As she finishes writing the results of the tests, Buddy comes over and asks, "What'd you find?" Then Helen rushes in and asks, "What were the results of the blood tests for Dr. Smith?" Dr. Smith then calls on the phone for a quick report from Edythe. Finally, later in the day, Mrs. Jonathan calls up Edythe and says, "Look! I'm the person paying the bills! I want to know the results of my blood tests! And don't tell me to ask Dr. Smith! I already did and he won't tell me!"

If you were Edythe, would you say the same thing to Buddy, Helen, Dr. Smith, and Mrs. Jonathan? If the answer is no, what would you take into account in replying to each person? You might want to take the following factors into consideration:

1. Who the person is.
2. What his or her position in the hospital is.
3. How much the person knows about blood tests and blood cancer.
4. What the nature of the relationship between Edythe and the person is.
5. How appropriate it is to be fully honest about the results of the blood tests.

 EXERCISE 4.5
One- and Two-Way Communication

The objective of this exercise[1] is to demonstrate the differences between a situation in which two-way communication exists and one in which communication goes only one way. For this exercise each participant needs two pieces of paper and a pencil. The leader needs copies of Square Arrangement I and Square Arrangement II, which are given in the Appendix. The leader should copy Tables A–C onto a blackboard or a large sheet of paper.

Table A   Medians for Trials I and II

Medians	I	II
Time elapsed		
Guess accuracy		
Actual accuracy		

Table B   First Trial

Number Correct	Guess	Actual
5		
4		
3		
2		
1		
0		

1. Adapted from an exercise in H. Leavitt, *Managerial Psychology* (University of Chicago Press, 1958), pp. 118–28.

Table C   Second Trial

Number Correct	Guess	Actual
5		
4		
3		
2		
1		
0		

Procedure

1. The leader selects a sender and two observers. (If the group has fewer then seven members, select only one observer.) The sender should be a person who communicates well and who speaks clearly and loudly enough to be heard.

2. The sender is seated either with her back to the group or behind a screen. She is given Square Arrangement I. The leader should be careful that the group members do not see the diagram of squares that the sender will describe. The sender is told to study the first arrangement carefully for 2 minutes in order to be prepared to instruct the group members on how to draw a similar set of squares on their paper.

3. The first observer is asked to note the behavior and reactions of the sender during the exercise and to make notes for later comment. The second observer is asked to make notes on the behavior and reactions of the group members. Facial reactions, gestures, posture, and other nonverbal behaviors may be observed.

4. The group is given these instructions: The sender is going to describe a drawing to you. You are to listen carefully to her instructions and draw what she describes as accurately as you can. You will be timed, but there is no time limit. You may ask no questions of the sender and give no audible response. You are asked to work independently.

5. Tables A–C are shown in the front of the room. The sender is then told to proceed to give the instructions for drawing the first figure of squares as quickly and accurately as she can. The leader should ensure that there are no questions or audible reactions from the group members.

6. When the sender has completed giving the instructions for Square Arrangement I, the leader records the time it took to do so in the proper space in the first table. Each member of the group is asked to write down on his paper the number of squares he thinks he has drawn correctly in relation to the preceding one.

7. The leader instructs the sender to face the group members. She gives the sender Square Arrangement II and tells her to study the relationship of the squares in this new diagram for 2 minutes in preparation for instructing the group members on how to draw it.

8. The group is then given these instructions: "The sender is going to describe another drawing to you. This time she will be in full view of you, and you may ask as many questions as you wish. She is free to reply to your questions or amplify her statements as she sees fit. She is not, however, allowed to make any hand signals while describing the drawing. You will be timed, but there is no time limit. Work as accurately and rapidly as you can."

9. The sender is told to proceed.

10. When the sender has completed giving instructions for the second figure, the time is again recorded in the appropriate space of Table A. The group members are asked to guess the number of squares they have drawn correctly and to record the number on their papers.

11. A median for guessed accuracy on the first drawing is obtained by recording the number of group members who guessed zero, the number who guessed one, and so on in Table B. The median guessed number is found by counting from zero the number of group members guessing each number until you reach half the members of the group. The median is then recorded in Table A.

12. The method is repeated to get the median of accurate guesses for the second drawing.

13. Members are shown the master drawing for the first set of squares, and the relationship of each square to the preceding one is pointed out. Each square must be in the exact relationship to the preceding one as it appears on the master drawing to be counted as correct. When this step has been completed, the members are asked to count and record the actual number right. A similar count is taken for the second chart.

14. The median for accuracy for the first and second drawings is obtained and placed in Table A.

15. The following questions are discussed:
    a. What may be concluded from the results in terms of time, accuracy, and level of confidence?
    b. What did the observers record during the exercise? How did the behavior of the sender and the group members vary from one situation to the other? The group members and the sender should comment on what they were feeling during the two situations.
    c. How does this exercise compare with situations you find yourself in at work, school, or home? How might you change your behavior in relating to your friends and acquaintances as a result of what you have experienced during this exercise?

Sending Skills 5: Ensuring Two-Way Communication

One of the best ways a sender can make sure messages are received correctly is to obtain feedback on the effects the message is having on the receiver. **Feedback** in communication occurs when the sender receives information from the receiver on how the message is being decoded and received. *One-way communication* occurs when the sender is not able to determine how the receiver is decoding the sender's message. In such cases, inaccuracies in communication may occur, continue, and never be uncovered. *Two-way communication* occurs when the sender is able to obtain feedback concerning how the receiver is decoding the sender's message. The response the receiver makes to the message can subsequently cause the sender to modify messages to communicate more accurately with the receiver. Two-way communication facilitates understanding in communication, which in turn helps such things as developing a fulfilling relationship and being able to work together effectively.

The typical result of Exercise 4.5 is that one-way communication is quicker and less accurate, and the level of confidence of the receiver is lower. Two-way communication takes more time, but it is also likely to be more accurate, and the level of confidence of the receiver is higher. Two-way communication promotes more accurate understanding between the sender and the receiver and builds a more cooperative relationship between the two. The sender, however, usually is more disturbed and frustrated during the two-way communication process.

Just as the sender can increase the accuracy of communication by transmitting his message through a variety of channels, it is also an aid to accuracy if feedback is available in a variety of channels. Feedback does not have to be only verbal. Nonverbal cues such as facial expression, posture, gestures, sighs, and tone of voice when asking questions are often indications of how your message is being interpreted by the receiver.

■ COMPREHENSION TEST C

Test your understanding of one- and two-way communication by answering true or false to the following statements. Answers are at the end of the chapter.

True   False   1. Feedback is the process by which the receiver tells the sender how the message is being received.

True   False   2. Feedback is the primary process for clearing up misunderstandings in communication.

True   False   3. Feedback is not given in one-way communication.

True   False   4. One-way communication is quicker than two-way communication.

True   False   5. One-way communication is more frustrating to the sender than two-way communication.

True   False   6. Two-way communication is usually more accurate than one-way communication.

True   False   7. The confidence level of the receiver is higher in two-way communication.

True   False   8. Helen is getting feedback when Edye tells her how delicious her Christmas cookies are.

True   False   9. Edye is getting feedback when Buddy makes a face after taking a bite of her cookies.

True   False   10. David is getting feedback when no one buys his cookies.

Improving Your Receiving Skills

All communication affects the relationship between the sender and the receiver. It moves the relationship forward or backward, or keeps it the same. Communication can deepen a relationship, or it can make the relationship more distant and impersonal. Many problems found in relationships stem from failures to communicate effectively. In addition to sending skills, effective communication depends on receiving skills. Four key receiving skills are paraphrasing, negotiating for meaning, perception checking, and taking the sender's perspective in interpreting the message.

Exercise 4.6 A–C will illustrate the skills involved in deepening relationships through communication. The activities are designed to lead you from engaging in an irrelevant, somewhat destructive conversation to using the tools of communicating effectively. The exercise

1. Allows you to experience both effective and ineffective communication procedures.
2. Provides skill practice in how to listen effectively and how to respond constructively to messages sent by another person.
3. Provides skill practice in how to send effective messages that facilitate the development of personal relationships.
4. Introduces several key concepts on communication, such as listening with understanding, selective perception, personal statements, and relationship statements.

The session consists of three steps. The first two steps contrast effective and ineffective ways of listening and responding. The third step provides practice in applying the sending and receiving skills emphasized in the first two steps. In each step a combination of experience, theory, and discussion will be used.

Step	Constructive Action	Destructive Action
1	Paraphrasing	Irrelevant response
2	Negotiating for meaning	Asyndetic response
3	Practice	

The suggested procedures may at first seem deceptively simple. Once you attempt them, however, you may find them more difficult than you expected. You will also find that they are very powerful when skillfully used. Your communication skills will especially improve if you become involved in the exercises and consciously attempt both to learn as much as possible and enjoy yourself. If you try the activities willingly and with enthusiasm, you can have a lot of fun while learning.

EXERCISE 4.6A
Increasing Communication Skills

Step 1: Not Listening Versus Listening Closely; Irrelevant Response Versus Relevant Response

Part 1: Discussion on Listening

Find a partner and answer the following questions. What types of problems make it difficult for two persons to understand each other? What failures in sending, listening, and responding cause communication gaps? List at least four reasons why two persons may fail to communicate effectively with each other.

1. _____

2. _____

3. _____

4. _____

Do your suggestions include the following?

1. Inaccurate expression of one's thoughts

2. Failing to listen to all that is being said

3. Trying to say too much in one statement

4. Two individuals not talking about the same thing while they are in a conversation with each other

Part 2: Not Listening and Irrelevant Response

Combine with another pair to form a group of four.

1. Conduct a discussion on establishing friendships. Allow 5 minutes of discussion. During the discussion, you must talk about the assigned topic, but what you say must be unrelated to what others in the group say. It is as though you did not hear them.

2. After the discussion, jot down answers to the following questions to use later.
    a. How did it feel to make a statement and have no one respond to it?

    _____

    _____

    b. How did it feel to ignore a statement made by others in the group?

    _____

    _____

Part 3: Close Listening and Relevant Response

Within the group of four divide into pairs. Designate one member of each pair A, the other B.

1. A makes a statement to B either about himself, about B, or about the relationship between them. Try not to make bland statements, but say something that you have some feelings about and that can have real meaning for both of you.

2. B paraphrases A's statement, restating A's remark in his or her own words. There is no discussion of the statements. A simply makes the statement; B paraphrases it back. Some *general rules for paraphrasing* responses are these:
    a. Restate the other person's expressed feelings and ideas in your own words; don't mimic or parrot the exact words of the other person.
    b. Preface reflected remarks with "You feel . . . ," "You think . . . ," "It seems to you that . . . ," "It sometimes appears to you that . . . ," and so on.
    c. Avoid any indication of approval or disapproval. Refrain from blaming, interpreting, giving advice, or persuading.

3. A makes a second statement to B; B paraphrases it.

4. A makes a third statement to B; B paraphrases it.

5. Reverse the process. B makes three statements to A; after each one A paraphrases it back.

6. Jot down answers to the following questions to use later:
   a. How did it feel to make a statement and have your partner paraphrase it?

   _____

   _____

   b. How did it feel to paraphrase a statement made by your partner?

   _____

   _____

7. Discuss your experiences in the group of four. Some questions you may use in the discussion are as follows:
   a. Did you find that you had difficulty in listening to others during the exercise? Why?
   b. Did you find that you were not getting across what you wanted to say?
   c. What was your reaction to the paraphrasing of your partner? Was your partner receiving what you intended to send?
   d. Was your partner's manner of presentation affecting your listening ability? In what way?
   e. What were the differences in your feelings during the two types of experiences?

Theory on Listening and Responding

Give every man thine ear, but few thy voice.
   —William Shakespeare (Polonius in *Hamlet*)

To speak precisely and to listen carefully present a challenge. You have just been through an exercise in which you both sent and received messages. There are several common faults that people often make when they communicate. Were you guilty of any of these mistakes in communicating?

_____ Not organizing your thoughts before speaking

_____ Including too many (and sometimes unrelated) ideas in your messages

_____ Making short statements that did not include enough information and repetition to be understood

_____ Ignoring the amount of information the receiver already had about the subject

_____ Not making your message appropriate to the receiver's point of view

_____ Not giving your undivided attention to the sender

_____ Thinking about your reply before listening to everything the sender had to say

_____ Listening for details rather than for the entire message

_____ Evaluating whether the sender was right or wrong before you fully understood the message

These are not the only mistakes you can make in communicating, but they all need to be avoided if you are to be effective in communicating with other people.

The way you listen and respond to another person is crucial for building a fulfilling relationship. You can either listen and respond in ways that make the relationship more distant and impersonal, or you can listen and respond in ways that bring you and the sender into a closer, more personal relationship. It is crucial in a close relationship for you to communicate that you have clearly heard and understood the sender. It is characteristic of impersonal relationships for the receiver to communicate that he has not heard and has not understood the sender. When you listen accurately and respond relevantly, you communicate to the sender, "I care about what you are saying, and I want to understand it." When you fail to listen and respond irrelevantly, you communicate to the sender, "I don't care about what you are saying, and I don't want to understand it." The previous exercises have highlighted these two different ways of listening and responding.

The keystone to good listening is paraphrasing. **Paraphrasing** is restating, in your own words, what the person says, feels, and means. Although paraphrasing sounds simple, it can be difficult to do. Yet it has powerful effects on both the sender and the receiver. Listening intently to what a person says and demonstrating your understanding of how it seems to him or her tends to increase trust, reduces the sender's fears about revealing him- or herself to you, decreases the sender's defensiveness about what he or she is communicating, increases the sender's insight into and understanding of what he or she is saying, and increases the sender's self-acceptance. It also facilitates the sender's psychological health and growth.

Paraphrasing also has powerful effects on the person doing it. First, it helps you avoid judging and evaluating. When you are restating, you are not passing judgment. Second, it increases your understanding of the sender's messages. Your restating gives the sender direct feedback as to how well you understand the messages. If you do not fully understand, the sender can add messages until you do. If you are interpreting the message differently from the way he intended it, the sender can clarify. Being able to clarify and elaborate are important for making sure effective communication is taking place. Third, it communicates your cooperative intent. Paraphrasing communicates to the sender that you want to understand what he is saying. It shows that you care about him or her enough to listen carefully, that you are interested, that you take what he or she is saying seriously, and that you want to understand. Finally, paraphrasing helps you get into the sender's shoes. It helps you see the message from the sender's perspective. By restating the message as accurately and fairly as possible, you begin to see things from the sender's frame of reference.

How do you improve your skills in listening empathetically to others? One way is simply to follow this rule the next time you get deeply involved in a conversation: *Each person can speak up for himself only after he has first restated the ideas and feelings of the previous sender accurately and to the sender's satisfaction.* This means that before presenting your own message and point of view, it is necessary for you to take the other's frame of reference and understand his or her thoughts and feelings so well that you could accurately paraphrase them. Sound simple? Try it. You may find it difficult. This rule is especially useful in arguments and conflicts. You will find that your conflicts will become much more constructive and productive if you are able to follow the paraphrasing rule successfully.

■ COMPREHENSION TEST D

You may wish to assess your comprehension of the preceding material on listening and responding by answering the following questions. Answers are at the end of the chapter.

1. What is the effect of judgmental or evaluative responses on communication?
   a. They increase the accuracy of communication.
   b. They encourage the sender to elaborate on her statements.
   c. They increase the sender's fears about disclosing his ideas and feelings to the receiver.
   d. They spice up the conversation.
   e. They increase the sender's defensiveness about what she is saying.
   f. They alienate the sender.

2. What are three rules for effective paraphrasing?
   a. Repeat the sender's words exactly and with the same inflections.
   b. Restate the sender's message in your own words.
   c. Preface your paraphrasing with such remarks as "You feel . . . ."
   d. Indicate whether you approve or disapprove of his message.
   e. Do not indicate any approval or disapproval of the sender's statements.

3. How does giving an understanding response—paraphrasing—facilitate communication?
   a. It helps the receiver to see the expressed ideas and feelings from the sender's frame of reference.
   b. It communicates to the sender that the receiver cares about the message and wants to understand it.
   c. It increases the amount of time two individuals talk with each other.

 EXERCISE 4.6B
Increasing Communication Skills

Step 2: Partial Listening Versus Listening for Meaning: Asyndetic Response Versus Attending and Negotiation for Meaning Response

Part 1: Partial Listening and Asyndetic Responding

Divide into groups of four.

1. Conduct a discussion about establishing a friendship, resolving a conflict with a friend, or some other related topic. Discuss the topic for 5 minutes.

2. During the discussion you listen to what the others say but only for the purpose of using some small part of their statements to change the discussion to something more interesting to you. In other words, you acknowledge their statement but use it only as a polite way of introducing your own ideas into the conversation. This is called an **asyndetic response.**

3. Jot down answers to the following questions for use in a later discussion:
   a. How did it feel having others change the subject right after your statement?

   _____

   _____

   b. How did it feel changing the subject right after others had made a statement?

   _____

   _____

Part 2: Listening for Meaning, and Attending and Negotiating for Meaning Response

Divide into pairs. Designate one person A, and the other B.

1. A makes a statement about herself, about B, or about their relationship.

2. B responds by saying, "What I think you mean is . . . ." (He then says what he thinks A meant.) He does not try to speculate about why he thinks that

or about why A might be saying that. He simply tells A exactly what he thinks A meant by the statement, A and B then negotiate until they are in complete agreement about what A really meant, and A is able to respond to B with, "Yes, that is exactly what I meant." Do not add to or go beyond the original meaning, and do not try to analyze each other. Simply attempt to get at the exact meaning of what was said.

3. A makes a second statement. B responds with, "What I think you mean is . . . ." The two then negotiate the exact meaning of the statement.

4. A makes a third statement. B responds as before.

5. Reverse the process. B makes three statements, and A responds.

6. Answer these questions:
   a. How did it feel to make a statement and have my partner reply with what he thought it meant, then for us to negotiate the exact meaning of the statement?

   _____

   _____

   b. How did it feel to listen to my partner's statement and respond with what I thought it meant, then for us to negotiate the exact meaning of the statement?

   _____

   _____

7. Discuss the experiences in your group of four. Here are some questions you may use in the discussion:
   a. Did you always communicate what you wanted to communicate?
   b. Did you find the listener responding to only part of what you said?
   c. Was it ever unclear what the speaker had in mind? What made it unclear?

Theory on Selective Perception in Listening and Responding

Did you notice that in responding to your partner's statement you sometimes selected part of the message to respond to and did not respond to other parts? This kind of thing is common in communication. Most communication is so complex that we have to be selective about what we perceive and what we respond to. A message has too many aspects, both verbal and nonverbal, for a receiver to respond to all of them. Even when a person says, "How are you?" a receiver may ignore the tone of voice, facial expression, gestures, and the appropriateness of the message to the situation and respond only to the usual meaning of the words. Or the receiver may decide that the tone of voice, facial expression, and situation are such that the real message is sarcasm, then ignore the usual meaning of the words and respond with an insult. You are always selecting part of what is being communicated and deciding what is the most appropriate response. This selective perception is one of the sources of noise in the communication process. To reduce its potentially disruptive effects you must understand (a) the factors involved in selective perception and (b) how to negotiate the meaning of the sender's messages.

Some of the factors that influence what you respond to in a message are your (a) expectations, (b) wants and needs, and (c) beliefs and atti-tudes. If you expect a person to act unfriendly, you will be sensitive to anything that can be perceived as unfriendliness. If your past experiences have led you to expect certain people to be hostile, you will be sensitive to any expression that can be seen as hostile. Such sensitization may make you blind to friendly expressions.

If you need and want someone to give you support, however, you may be highly sensitive to any expressions that can be perceived as sup-portive. If you are hungry you may be sensitive to any messages about food. If you want to go home after a long evening you may be sensitive to how tired others are. Your wants and your needs constantly affect what you perceive in interpersonal communication situations.

Finally, you tend to be more sensitive to perceiving messages that are consistent with your beliefs and attitudes. You will tend to misperceive or fail to perceive messages that are opposite to your opinions, beliefs, and attitudes. You even learn and remember material that is consistent with your beliefs and attitudes much better than material inconsistent with your beliefs and attitudes.

In listening and responding appropriately to others, it is important to be aware of your expectations, wants and needs, and beliefs and attitudes and the likelihood of selectivity in what you perceive. You should be ready to change your interpretation of the sender's messages when it be-comes evident that you may have misperceived. Your interpretations of what messages mean will always be tentative until confirmed by the sender; that is one reason it is so important to negotiate the meaning of a message before you respond to it. Negotiating for meaning occurs when the receiver states what he or she perceives the meaning of the sender's message to be and asks for the sender to agree or clarify. The general rules for the negotiating for meaning response are these:

1. Describe in your own words the perceived meaning of the sender's message.
2. Preface your description with "What I think you mean is . . . ," "Is this what you mean?" and so on.
3. Avoid any indication of approval or disapproval.

■ COMPREHENSION TEST E

You may wish to answer the following questions to see how well you have understood the material on selective perception. Answers are at the end of the chapter.

1. What is selective perception?
   a. Responding to all the aspects, both verbal and nonverbal, of a message
   b. Responding only to a few of the verbal and nonverbal aspects of a message
   c. The name of a famous racehorse

2. Which of the following are factors that influence selective perception?
   a. Self-disclosure
   b. Expectations
   c. The weather
   d. Needs, wants, desires
   e. Opinions, attitudes, beliefs
   f. Trust

3. How can you avoid misunderstandings that result from selective perception?
   a. Do not try to communicate.
   b. Keep all interpretations of messages tentative until confirmed by the sender.
   c. Do not have expectations, needs, or opinions.

 EXERCISE 4.6C

Increasing Communication Skills

Step 3: The Use of Effective Communication Skills— Clarifying Personal Strengths and Clarifying Relationships

Clarifying Strengths

Divide into pairs.

1. A takes 3 minutes to share with B what A considers to be his or her personal strengths, talents, and abilities (things A does well, likes about him- or herself, and thinks others like about him or her).

2. B bombards A with observations about A's strengths and personal assets. In each case, when A receives an item of feedback he or she responds by (a) paraphrasing the feedback and (b) negotiating its meaning. Do not take more than 5 minutes to do this.

3. Reverse roles and repeat the same process.

▪ COMPREHENSION TEST F

Test your understanding of the previous communication skills by answering true or false to the following statements. Answers are at the end of the chapter.

True   False   1. Evaluative responses encourage the sender to elaborate on her statements.

True   False   2. Paraphrasing is restating the ideas and feelings of the sender before responding.

True   False   3. Paraphrasing shows that you care about what the other person is saying.

True   False   4. Paraphrasing helps the receiver understand the sender's message.

True   False   5. In selective perception, you respond to only part of the communication.

True   False   6. Our own needs, attitudes, and expectations can bring about selective perception.

True   False   7. The way to avoid misunderstandings due to selective perception is to avoid having any expectations, needs, or opinions.

True   False   8. The more you speak for yourself, the more confused your message will be.

True   False   9. When you make good personal statements, you talk about the other person's personal life.

True   False   10. Relationship statements focus mainly on the other individual in the relationship.

EXERCISE 4.7
Observing Communication Behavior

You have just been through a series of short experiences on effective and ineffective communication behavior. You may wish to sharpen your skills in recognizing such behavior. The procedure for this exercise is as follows:

1. Pick a group to observe, or sit down in a crowded area in which a number of conversations are going on.

2. Using the observation sheets that follow, count the number of times each type of effective or ineffective communication behavior takes place.

3. Within a week's time, discuss in the group the results of your observations. What general conclusions can you draw from what the members of your group observed?

Observation Sheet for Ineffective Communication

1. The receiver fails to listen to the message.

   _____

   _____

2. The receiver listens only to part of the message in order to say what he wants to say rather than responding fully to the message.

   _____

   _____

3. The receiver distorts the message to conform with his expectations of what he thought the sender was going to say.

   _____

   _____

4. The receiver is listening in order to make judgments and evaluations of the sender, thus making the sender defensive and guarded in formulating the message.

   _____

   _____

5. The receiver understood the words of the message but not the underlying meaning.

   _____

   _____

6. The sender uses general pronouns and nouns to refer to her own feelings and ideas.

   _____

   _____

7. Other ineffective communication behaviors.

   _____

   _____

Observation Sheet for Effective Communication

1. The receiver paraphrases the sender's remarks.

   _____

   _____

2. The receiver checks out the meaning of the sender's remarks.

   _____

   _____

3. The receiver does not give evaluations or judgments about the sender's remarks.

   _____

   _____

4. The receiver keeps his interpretation of the sender's remarks tentative until he checks it out with the sender.

   _____

   _____

5. The receiver focuses upon the meaning of the message, not the specific words.

   _____

   _____

6. The sender uses personal statements.

   _____

   _____

7. The sender uses relationship statements.

   _____

   _____

8. Other effective communication behaviors.

   _____

   _____

Toward Improved Communication Skills

The difficulties in establishing effective communication between individuals are very real. What, then, can be done to improve understanding? One thing is the development of an atmosphere of mutual confidence and trust through the use of personal and relationship statements. Second, the use of communication skills such as paraphrasing, negotiating meaning, and making your responses relevant to the sender's message improves understanding. You may also facilitate the development of close, personal relationships by making your messages reflect personal and relationship statements and by making your responses reflect a recognition of the other person's strengths and capabilities. Through the use of such skills, you can consciously make the most of your chances to develop close, fulfilling relationships with other people.

■ CHAPTER REVIEW

Demonstrate your understanding of communication by matching the definitions with the appropriate characteristic. Check your answers with a partner and explain the reasoning for your answers.

Concept	Definition
_____ 1. Interpersonal communication	a. Receiver interprets the sender's message the way the sender intended.
_____ 2. Effective communication	b. Receiver's belief in the trustworthiness of the sender's statements.
_____ 3. Ownership of message	c. The sender receiving information from the receiver on how the message is being decoded and received.
_____ 4. Sender credibility	
_____ 5. Communication feedback	
_____ 6. One-way communication	d. A message sent by a person to a receiver (or receivers) with a conscious intent of affecting the receiver's behavior.
_____ 7. Two-way communication	e. Using personal pronouns such as *I*, *me*, and *my*.
_____ 8. Paraphrasing	

Concept	**Definition**
_____ 9. Asyndetic response	f. Receiver states what he or she perceives the meaning of the sender's message to be and asks for the sender to agree or clarify.
_____ 10. Negotiating for meaning	
_____ 11. Relationship statement	g. A message describing how you view the relationship or how you view some aspect of the relationship.
_____ 12. Behavioral description	h. Sender is not able to determine how the receiver is decoding the sender's message.

f. Receiver states what he or she perceives the meaning of the sender's message to be and asks for the sender to agree or clarify.

g. A message describing how you view the relationship or how you view some aspect of the relationship.

h. Sender is not able to determine how the receiver is decoding the sender's message.

i. Restating the other person's message and expressed feelings in your own words.

j. Sender receives feedback concerning how the receiver is decoding the sender's message.

k. A message that includes the specific behaviors you have observed and does not include any judgment or evaluation or any inferences about the person's motives, personality, or attitudes.

l. Acknowledging another's statement but using some small part of it in order to introduce your own ideas into the conversation.

Test your understanding of how to increase your communication skills by answering true or false to the following statements. Answers are at the end of the chapter.

True   False   13. Interpersonal communication is a message sent with a conscious attempt to affect the receiver's behavior.

True   False   14. The factors that most interfere with communication are external, not internal.

True   False   15. In effective communication, the receiver must interpret the message the way the sender intended.

True   False   16. Sending messages effectively involves owning your messages.

True   False   17. If a sender is lacking in credibility, she will have trouble communicating.

True   False   18. Getting feedback from the receiver helps eliminate misunderstandings.

True   False   19. Paraphrasing involves giving your opinion of the sender's message.

True   False   20. Relationship statements describe how one person feels about how both people are relating.

True   False   21. Most people have the same perspective.

True   False   22. Different perspectives result in the same message having different meanings.

Self-Diagnosis

In this chapter a series of communication skills have been discussed. On a scale from 1 (poorly mastered) to 5 (highly mastered) rate the degree to which you have mastered each skill. Then choose two skills to improve on during the next week.

Rating	Skill
_____	Speak for yourself by using personal pronouns when expressing thoughts, ideas, reactions, and feelings.
_____	Describe other people's actions without making value judgments.
_____	Use relationship statements when they are appropriate.
_____	Take the receiver's perspective into account when sending your messages.
_____	Ask for feedback about the receiver's understanding of your message.
_____	Paraphrase accurately without making value judgments about the sender's thoughts, reactions, perceptions, needs, and feelings.
_____	Negotiate the meaning of the sender's messages.
_____	Understand what the message means from the sender's perspective.
_____	Recognizing when effective or ineffective communication is taking place.

Skills I Will Improve in the Next Week

1. _____

2. _____

Summary

Interpersonal communication is the sending of a message to a receiver with the conscious intent of affecting the receiver's behavior. Communication contains seven basic elements: sender's intentions, sender's encoding of message, sending the message, channel through which message is sent, the receiver's decoding of the message, the receiver's internal response, and the amount of noise in the process. Communication is not a step-by-step linear process, however. Everything takes place simultaneously. Communication is effective when the receiver interprets the sender's message the way the sender intended it. There are, however, many ways in which misunderstandings occur. Effective communication, therefore, takes both sending and receiving skills. Sending messages effectively requires taking clear ownership of your message and describing (not judging) the other person's behavior. Statements about the relationship are important for improving the quality of interaction. Two-way communication tends to take more time but is far more effective than one-way communication. Communication is enhanced when you make the message appropriate to the receiver's frame of reference. Other sending skills include describing your feelings and making your verbal and nonverbal messages congruent with each other. The more credible you are, the more effective your communication tends to be. Receiving messages effectively requires paraphrasing and negotiating for meaning. These skills take continual practice to perfect. The next chapter will discuss how to become more aware of your feelings and more skillful in communicating them effectively.

Answers

Comprehension Test A: 1. true; 2. true; 3. true; 4. false; 5. true; 6. true; 7. true; 8. true; 9. b, d, e, f, h, i, j; 10. a, d, e.

Comprehension Test B: 1. true; 2. true; 3. false; 4. false; 5. false; 6. true; 7. true; 8. false; 9. false; 10. true.

Practicing Personal Statements (Exercise 4.1): 1. O; 2. P; 3. P; 4. N; 5. O; 6. N; 7. P.

Comprehension Test C: 1. true; 2. true; 3. true; 4. true; 5. false; 6. true; 7. true; 8. true; 9. true; 10. true.

Comprehension Test D: 1. c, e, f; 2. b, c, e; 3. a, b.

Comprehension Test E: 1. b; 2. b, d, e; 3. b.

Comprehension Test F: 1. false; 2. true; 3. true; 4. true;
5. true; 6. true; 7. false; 8. false; 9. false; 10. false.

Chapter Review: 1. d; 2. a; 3. e; 4. b; 5. c; 6. h; 7. j; 8. i;
9. l; 10. f; 11. g; 12. k; 13. true; 14. false; 15. true; 16. true;
17. true; 18. true; 19. false; 20. true; 21. false; 22. true.

CHAPTER 5

Expressing Your Feelings Verbally

The Power of Feelings

Coach Joe Newton is one of the nation's winningest high school cross-country coaches, one of only two high school coaches ever named to a U.S. Olympic track team staff, a coach who has developed more than 150 all-state track and field athletes and won the state championship meet 17 times, and a demanding second father to several hundred runners at York Community High School in Illinois (reported in *Sports Illustrated*, October 4, 1993). Newton's success comes from a combination of building intense team cooperation and forming a personal relationship with each runner. Newton creates team cooperation by having his team run together as a pack. In a race, team members bunch together toward the front of the field rather than running individually. He plays down individual stars in favor of team cooperation. Each year the hundred or so members of his cross-country team run together six days a week, preparing for a championship meet that only seven of them can enter. When those seven face off against the other teams, all of Newton's athletes know they have helped forge a team that will perform up to its potential, win or lose. As part of the emphasis on team cooperation, Newton makes daily contact with all his runners. He gives everybody a nickname. Newton checks each runner in at the beginning of each practice, taking care to make eye contact and welcome the student to the practice. He checks each runner out at the end of each practice, shaking each runner's hand. During each practice, Newton makes a point of calling out each runner's name at least once. All the runners receive direct daily feedback from Newton on how they are doing. Each runner knows that Newton is paying attention to what the runner is doing and appreciates the runner's hard work. This combination of team cooperation and personal encouragement from the coach inspires ordinary runners to work hard for four years and become extraordinary as a team.

The expression of positive feelings and the feelings generated by being part of a team are powerful motivators. Expressing exactly what you are feeling, however, is not always easy.

Saying What You Feel

Feeling the warmth, support, acceptance, and caring of close friendships is one of the most exciting aspects of being alive. And feelings are especially wonderful when they are shared with other people. One of the most rewarding aspects of relationships is sharing personal feelings. The more you share your feelings with other people, the happier and more meaningful your life will be. Yet one of the characteristics of our society is that we are not given much training in how to express feelings in such a way that there will be little chance of misunderstanding. Years and years of our education focus on communicating ideas clearly and unambiguously, yet relatively little education is given in communicating feelings clearly and unambiguously. And although the words that describe aspects of friendships, such as *like, love, dislike,* and *hate,* are among the most frequently used in the English language, our language has relatively few words that label feeling states. Sanskrit, for example, is reputed to have more than nine hundred words describing various feeling states, but English has fewer than fifty, if one excludes slang and figures of speech.

To experience emotions and express them to another person is not only a major source of joy, but also necessary for your psychological well-being. It is natural to have feelings. The capacity to feel is as much a part of being a person as is the capacity to think and reason. A person without feelings is not a person at all; he or she is a machine. The quest of individuals who really enjoy life is to feel a greater range of emotions and to build relationships in which emotions are aroused and allowed positive expression. Feeling and expressing caring for another person, feeling and expressing love for another person, even feeling and expressing anger toward another person are all potentially highly rewarding and beautiful experiences. And it is through experiencing and sharing feelings that close friendships are built and maintained.

There is a wide variety of feelings you may have while relating to other people. Here is a partial list of the feelings you may experience:

happy	confused	cautious	proud
pleased	surprised	confident	anxious
daring	silly	glad	grieving
bored	lonely	excited	confused
satisfied	elated	delighted	overjoyed
uncomfortable	apathetic	fearful	frightened
ecstatic	hopeful	embarrassed	humiliated
angry	weary	supported	accepted
shy	scared	discontented	
loved	appreciated	sad	

Feelings are internal physiological reactions to your experiences. You may begin to tremble, sweat, or have a surge of energy. Your heart may beat faster. Tears may come. Although feelings are internal reactions, they do have outward signs. Sadness is inside you, but you cry or frown on the outside. Anger is inside you. But you may stare and shout at the person you are angry with. Feelings are always internal states, but you use overt behaviors to communicate your feelings to other people.

It is often difficult to express feelings. Whenever there is a risk of being rejected or laughed at, expressing feelings becomes very difficult. The more personal the feelings, the greater the risk you may feel. It is also sometimes difficult to control your expression of your feelings. You may cry when you don't want to, get angry when it is best not to, or even laugh at a time it disturbs others. Expressing feelings appropriately often means thinking before you communicate them.

Having feelings is a natural and joyful part of being alive and being human. Feelings provide the cement holding relations together as well as the means for deepening relationships and making them more personal. The accurate and constructive expression of feelings, furthermore, is one of the most difficult aspects of building and managing your relations with other people. The purpose of this chapter is to provide the material and experiences necessary for becoming more skillful in appropriately saying how you feel.

What's Going on Inside?

You can't enjoy your feelings if you aren't aware of them. You can't express feelings you refuse to acknowledge. You can't communicate feelings you refuse to accept as yours. To accept your feelings you have to be aware of them and accept them as yours. You have to own them. And you have to communicate effectively. That is what this chapter is about.

Feelings are internal reactions to your experiences. To be aware of your feelings you have to be aware of how you are reacting to what is currently taking place around you. There are five aspects of such internal reactions (Miller, Nunnally, & Wachman, 1975):

1. You gather information about what is going on through your five senses (seeing, hearing, touching, tasting, smelling).
2. You decide what the information means by interpreting the meaning of the information you sense.
3. You have a feeling based on your interpretation.

4. You decide how you intend to express your feeling.

5. You express your feeling.

Here is an example. I see you sitting in the library, a book open in front of you, but you are looking around the room (sensing). I think you must be looking for an excuse to stop studying so that you can go to lunch (interpreting). I feel sorry that you can't take a break from studying (feeling). I want to give you a chance to enjoy yourself for a few minutes (intending). So I ask you if you'd like to eat lunch with me (expressing).

When we are relating to other people, we sense, interpret, feel, intend, and express all at the same time. It all happens faster than you can read a word. *Everything happens so fast that it seems as though it is only one step instead of five!* To become aware of the five steps you have to slow down the process. Being aware of, and understanding, the five aspects of experiencing and expressing a feeling give you the basis for skillfully and appropriately communicating your feelings and for changing negative feelings (such as anger, depression, guilt, hopelessness, frustration, and fear) to positive ones. Each of the five steps, therefore, will be discussed in more detail in the following subsections.

Sensing

The only way you can gather information is through your five senses: seeing, hearing, touching, tasting, and smelling. All information about the world and what is taking place in your life comes to you through one of the five senses. You look, listen, touch, taste, and smell to be aware of your immediate experiences. These senses give you *descriptive* information only. You hear a person's voice get louder. You see a person frown. You feel his fist hit your nose. You smell and taste the blood dripping from your nose. *Such sensory information only describes what is taking place. It does not place any meaning on what is happening.*

Interpreting: Deciding What It Means

After your senses make you aware of what is going on, you have to decide what the information means. *The information is neutral: You decide what it means.* Interpretations are yours; they take place inside you. They are not in another person's behavior or in the events that take place in your life. Different people interpret the same sensory information quite differently. For example, one friend may interpret the fact that your voice is loud to mean that you are angry. Another friend may decide that your loud voice means you are nervous. The sensory information (your voice is loud) they have is the same, but they interpret it in two different ways.

When you are interacting with your friends and acquaintances, or even with strangers, your interpretations of what the information gathered by your senses means depends on at least three things:

1. The information you receive through your senses.
2. What you think is causing the other person's actions.
3. The assumptions you make about what is good or bad, what you do or do not need, and what causes what in the world. (Your assumptions are an important part of your perspective, which was discussed in the previous chapter.)

The information you receive through your senses has already been discussed, so we will now look at deciding what is causing another person's actions. When someone's voice gets louder, you look around to see what's causing it. If you see a huge dog with its teeth embedded in the person's leg, you decide that pain and fear are causing her voice to get louder. If you see someone else tickling her, you interpret the loud voice as indicating happiness. If you notice that the person has just paid $1,000 for a new stereo, and it fell apart when she picked it up to take it home, you decide her loud voice means she is angry.

What you decide is causing the person's actions will influence your interpretation of the meaning of the information you sense. Let's take another example. You feel pain on your nose. You see that a fist of another person has just landed on your nose. You then decide whether the person intended to hit you, or whether it was an accident. If it was an accident, you will be less angry than if you decide the person did it on purpose. If you decide the person intended to hit you, you decide whether he had just cause (you were kicking him at the time) or whether he did not have just cause (he is a mean, nasty person). All of this happens so fast that for the most part you are not aware that it is going on. Your interpretations follow your gathering of information much faster than a speeding bullet!

Finally, your perspective influences your interpretations. Your assumptions especially influence what you decide the sensory information means. If you *assume* that people are as mean and nasty as goblins, your interpretation of someone's fist landing on your nose may be biased. You may immediately jump to the conclusion that this is another example of how mean and nasty people are. Or, if you *assume* that people are basically gentle and harmless creatures, you may jump to the conclusion that the person hit you accidentally. Your assumptions and your overall perspective have a powerful effect on your interpretations.

First you sense, then you interpret, and finally you feel. Your interpretations determine your feelings. Every feeling you have is based on an interpretation about the meaning of the information you sense. You can, therefore, control what you feel. By changing your interpretations, you can change your feelings. This does not mean that changing your feelings is easy. Most people make interpretations so automatically that it seems difficult to change them. But it can be done if they want to work at it. Chapter 9 explains how feelings such as anger, depression, resentment, fear, frustration, and guilt can be changed and controlled.

Feeling

You sense, you interpret, then you feel. Your feelings are a spontaneous reaction to your interpretations. You may hear and see an acquaintance say, "Hope you're feeling well this morning!" How you feel in response to the statement is based on what you decide it means. If you think the acquaintance is being sarcastic, you may feel angry. If you think the acquaintance is expressing liking and concern for you, you will feel warmth and appreciation. All this happens immediately and automatically. The important thing to remember is that the acquaintance's actions did not cause your feeling; your feeling was caused by your interpretation of the meaning of the person's statement.

Feelings promote an urge to take action. They prepare your body for action. If you feel angry, for example, your muscles tense, adrenaline is pumped into your bloodstream, your heart begins to beat faster, all of which prepares you for either running away or physically fighting. Feelings activate the physiological systems within your body so that they are ready for action. Because of the action-urge aspect of feelings, it takes energy to hide your feelings from yourself and others. That means the more you are aware of your feelings, accept them as yours, and express them to others, the more energy you will have for enjoying yourself and your friendships. In addition, you will be able to communicate more easily and effectively.

It is unhealthy, both physically and psychologically, to avoid expressing your feelings. Yet many people do try to avoid or ignore their feelings. Some people believe that what they are not aware of does not exist and can't hurt them. Yet the repression and denial of feelings such as anger can lead to physiological damage caused by the failure to take action and reestablish a homeostatic state within one's body. Ulcers and headaches are commonly thought to result from chronically repressed anger. And the repression of feelings can lead to a self-alienation that leaves a person confused as to what motivates and causes his or her behavior.

Feelings will keep trying to be expressed until you do so in a way that ends them. Sadness, for example, can be expressed by crying and talking to an understanding friend. Walking around with a smile on your face will not end the sadness inside of you. When you refuse to express your feelings, they start to control you. If you are holding sadness inside, for example, you will begin to avoid anything that makes you sad. When your friends become sad you will get angry at them. Pretty soon your whole life is organized around avoiding sadness because you are afraid that otherwise your own sadness will come out.

You *do not* control feelings by holding them inside. You *do not* control feelings by pretending they really don't exist. You *do* control feelings by accepting them as being yours and expressing them. You let them happen. Don't fight them or hold them back. Be aware of them. Take responsibility for them. They are yours. Usually things will be all right if you let your feelings take their natural course. It is even helpful to try to feel them more. If you are happy, feel happier. If you are sad, feel sadder. The important thing is to allow them to exist and to be appropriately expressed. Feelings don't have to be justified, explained, or apologized for. As you become more and more aware of your feelings, you will recognize what they are telling you about yourself and the situation you are in. *You control feelings by being aware of them, accepting them, giving them direction, and expressing them appropriately.* And if you are constantly depressed, anxious, or unhappy, you can change your feelings by changing the interpretations you are making.

Feelings activate your body physically so it is ready for action. Feelings urge you to take action to express them. What is lacking is a sense of direction. Do you run? Do you fight? Do you hug? Do you move toward another person? Do you move away? Feelings get the body ready for action. But they do not give you a sense of direction. It is your intentions that give you a sense of direction.

Intending

Your senses provide you with information about what is taking place within your environment. Your interpretations give the information meaning. Your feelings are your reactions to your interpretations. Your **intentions** are your guides to action, pointing out how the feelings can be expressed. They are your immediate goals as to what you want to have happen as a result of your feeling the way you do.

Intentions give your feelings direction. A few examples of intentions are as follows:

to reject	to love	to play	to be caring
to cooperate	to clarify	to help	to share
to avoid	to hurt	to demand	to understand
to praise	to persuade	to accept	to defend yourself
to protest	to support	to resign	to try harder

Intentions are important because they have such power over your actions. They organize your actions in expressing your feelings. They identify what you want to do to express your feelings. They guide your actions so that your feelings are terminated through expression.

Once you decide how to express your feelings, the next step is taking action and actually expressing them.

Expressing

You say it. You act it out. You smile. You frown. You laugh. You cry. You jump up and down. You run screaming out of the building. You burn this book. Your words and nonverbal actions express your sensations, interpretations, feelings, and intentions. This chapter focuses on expressing your feelings verbally in a way that is easily understood. The next chapter deals with the nonverbal expression of feelings. Chapter 9 discusses how you can control your feelings by modifying your interpretations.

■ COMPREHENSION TEST A

Test your understanding of the preceding material by answering true or false to the following statements. Answers are at the end of the chapter.

True   False   1. Feelings are external events that force a reaction from you.

True   False   2. Feelings are internal reactions to your experiences.

True   False   3. Expressing feelings is a sign of weakness.

True   False   4. Expressing feelings is a psychological necessity and a source of joy.

True   False   5. Your senses gather information about what is happening and give meaning to it.

True   False   6. You interpret the information that your senses gathered and decide what it means and whether it's good or bad.

True   False   7. Your previous assumptions will influence your interpretations of an event.

True   False   8. Your feelings are caused by the event you are responding to.

True   False   9. Controlling feelings means that you hold them inside.

True   False   10. Your intentions are your guides on how to express your feelings.

When Feelings Are Not Expressed

One of the most frequent sources of difficulty in building and maintaining good relationships is communicating feelings. We all have feelings about the people we interact with and the experiences we share, but many times we do not communicate these feelings effectively. Problems arise in relationships not because we have feelings but because we are not effective in communicating our feelings in ways that strengthen our relationships. When we repress, deny, distort, or disguise our feelings, or when we communicate them in an ineffective way, we are asking for trouble in our relationships.

There are several difficulties that arise when feelings are not recognized, accepted, and expressed constructively.

1. Suppressing and denying your feelings can create relationship problems. If you suppress your feelings, it can result in increased conflicts and barriers that cause deterioration in the relationship. A friend's actions may be irritating, and as the irritation is suppressed, anger and withdrawal from the relationship may result.

2. Suppressing and denying your feelings can interfere with the constructive diagnosis and resolution of relationship problems. Maintaining a relationship requires an open expression of feelings so that difficulties or conflicts can be dealt with constructively. There is a common but mistaken belief that being rational, logical, and objective requires you to suppress and ignore your feelings. Nothing is further from the truth! If you want to be effective in solving interpersonal problems, you need all the relevant information (including feelings) you can get. This means that your feelings need to be conscious, discussable, and controllable.

3. Denying your feelings can result in selective perception. When feelings are unresolved, your perceptions of events and information may be affected. If you are denying your anger, you may perceive all hostile actions but be completely blind to friendly overtures. Threatening and unpleasant facts are often distorted or not perceived. Unresolved feelings tend to increase blind spots and selective perception.

4. Suppressing your feelings can bias your judgments. It is common for people to refuse to accept a good idea because someone they dislike suggested it, or to accept a poor idea because someone they like is for it. If you are aware of your feelings and manage them constructively, you will be far more unbiased and objective in your judgments.

5. Implying a demand while expressing your feelings can create a power struggle. Many times feelings are expressed in ways that demand changes in the receiver's behavior. If someone says to you, "You make me angry when you do that," she is indirectly saying, "Stop doing it." Or if a friend says, "I like you, you are a good friend," he may be indirectly demanding that you like him. When feelings imply demands, a power struggle may result over whether or not the demands are going to be met.

6. Other people often ask you to suppress or deny your feelings. A person may say, "Don't feel that way" whenever you express a feeling. If you say, "I feel depressed," he will say, "Cheer up!" If you say, "I'm angry," she will say, "Simmer down." If you say, "I feel great," she will say, "The roof will cave in any moment now." All these replies communicate: "Don't feel that way. Quick, change your feeling!"

■ COMPREHENSION TEST B

Test your understanding of expressing your feelings constructively by answering true or false to the following statements. Answers are at the end of the chapter.

True	False	1.	Problems arise in relationships because we have feelings.
True	False	2.	Feelings should be ignored when making rational decisions.
True	False	3.	If feelings are communicated effectively, the relationship will be strengthened.
True	False	4.	If feelings are ignored, an idea may be disliked because the person suggesting it is disliked.
True	False	5.	Blind spots happen when facts are ignored or distorted on account of unresolved, unpleasant feelings about them.
True	False	6.	Unresolved feelings will tend to increase blind spots.
True	False	7.	Expressing feelings may imply a demand for the other person to do something.
True	False	8.	People often respond to expressions of feelings by telling others to deny them.
True	False	9.	If someone tells you that he is sad, you should say something to make him happy.
True	False	10.	If someone tells you that your actions make her unhappy, she may be asking you to change.

Expressing Your Feelings Verbally

There are two ways of communicating feelings: verbally and nonverbally. If you want to communicate clearly, your verbal and your nonverbal expression of feelings must agree or be congruent. Many of the communication difficulties experienced in relationships spring from giving contradictory messages to others by indicating one kind of feeling with words, another with actions, and still another with nonverbal expressions. This chapter focuses on the verbal expression of feelings. The next chapter focuses on the nonverbal expression of feelings. The congruence between the verbal and nonverbal expression of feelings is emphasized in both chapters.

Communicating your feelings depends on your being aware of your feelings, accepting them, and being skillful in expressing them constructively. When you are unaware or unaccepting of your feelings, or when you lack skills in expressing them, your feelings may be communicated indirectly through

1. **Labels:** "You are rude, hostile, and self-centered" versus "When you interrupt me I get angry."

2. **Commands:** "Shut up!" versus "I'm annoyed at what you just said."

3. **Questions:** "Are you always this crazy?" versus "You are acting strangely, and I feel worried."

4. **Accusations:** "You do not care about me!" versus "When you do not pay attention to me I feel left out."

5. **Sarcasm:** "I'm glad you are early!" versus "You are late; it has delayed our work, and that irritates me."

6. **Approval:** "You are wonderful!" versus "I like you."

7. **Disapproval:** "You are terrible!" versus "I do not like you."

8. **Name Calling:** "You are a creep!" versus "You are embarrassing me."

Such indirect ways of expressing feelings are common. But they are ineffective because they do not give a clear message to the receiver. And the receiver often will feel rejected and put down by the remarks. We are taught how to describe our *ideas* clearly and correctly. But we are rarely taught how to describe our *feelings* clearly and correctly. We express our feelings, but we do not usually name and describe them. Here are four ways you can describe a feeling.

1. Identify or name it: "I feel angry." "I feel embarrassed." "I like you."

2. Use sensory descriptions that capture how you feel: "I feel stepped on." "I feel as if I'm on cloud nine." "I feel as if I've just been run over by a truck." Because we do not have enough names or labels to describe all our feelings, we make up ways to describe them.

3. Report what kind of action the feeling urges you to do: "I want to hug you." "I want to slap your face." "I want to walk on your face."

4. Use figures of speech as descriptions of feelings: "I feel like a stepped-on toad." "I feel like a pebble on the beach."

You describe your feelings by identifying them. A description of a feeling must include

1. A personal statement—refer to *I, me, my,* or *mine.*

2. A feeling name, simile, action urge, or figure of speech.

Anything you say can convey feelings. Even the comment, "It's a warm day," can be said so that it expresses resentment or irritation. To build and maintain a friendship or any relationship, you must be concerned with communicating your feelings clearly and accurately, especially the feelings of warmth, affection, and caring. If you convey your feelings by commands, questions, accusations, or judgments, you will tend to confuse the person with whom you are interacting. When you want to express your feelings, your ability to describe them is essential for effective communication.

When you describe your feelings, expect at least two results. First, describing your feelings to another person often helps you to become more aware of what it is you actually do feel. Many times we have feelings that seem ambiguous or unclear to us. Explaining them to another person often clarifies our feelings to ourselves as well as to the other person. Second, describing your feelings often begins a dialogue that will improve your relationship. If other people are to respond appropriately to your feelings, they must know what the feelings are. Even if the feelings are negative, it is often worthwhile to express them. Negative feelings are signals that something may be going wrong in the relationship, and you and the other person need to examine what is going on in the relationship and figure out how it may be improved. By reporting your feelings, you provide information that is necessary if you and the other person are to understand and improve your relationship. When discussing your relationship with another person, describing your feelings conveys maximum information about what you feel in a more constructive way than giving commands, asking questions, making accusations, or offering judgments.

■ COMPREHENSION TEST C

Test your understanding of expressing feelings by answering true or false to the following statements. Answers are at the end of the chapter.

True   False   1. Indirect methods of communicating feelings are often quite effective.

True   False   2. Indirect methods of communicating feelings do not give a clear message to the receiver.

True   False   3. Eight indirect ways to communicate feelings are labels, commands, questions, accusations, sarcasm, approval, disapproval, and name calling.

True   False   4. Describing your feelings can help you become aware of your feelings.

True   False   5. Describing your feelings can begin a dialogue that will improve your relationship.

True   False   6. You should describe only positive feelings if you want to maintain relationships.

True	False	7. A feeling description must include a personal statement and the name of a feeling.
True	False	8. "I think you stink!" is a good feeling description.
True	False	9. Feeling descriptions can be figures of speech or sensory descriptions.
True	False	10. "I feel like a low-down toad" is a good feeling description.

 EXERCISE 5.1

Describing Your Feelings

The objectives of this exercise are to help you recognize when you are displaying feelings without describing them, to explain how you may express your feelings verbally in a way that communicates them effectively, and to give you a chance to practice the latter. In the following list, each of the ten items consists of two or three statements. One statement is a description of a feeling; the others are expressions that do not describe the feeling involved. The procedure for the exercise is as follows:

1. Divide into groups of three.

2. Work individually. In item 1 put a *D* before the sentence that describes the sender's feelings. Put a *No* before the sentence that conveys feeling but does not describe what it is. Mark the answers for item 1 only; do not go on to item 2 yet.

3. Compare your answers to item 1 with those of the other two members of your triad. Discuss the reasons for any differences.

4. Turn to the answers that follow the list and read the answer for item 1. Discuss the answer in your triad until you all understand the point.

5. Repeat steps 2, 3, and 4 for item 2. Then continue the same procedure for each item until you have completed all ten.

1. _____ a. Stop driving this fast! Slow down right now!

   _____ b. Your driving this fast frightens me.

2. _____ a. Do you have to stand on my foot?

   _____ b. You are so mean and vicious. You don't care if you cripple me for life!

   _____ c. I am annoyed at you for resting your 240-pound body on my foot.

3. _____ a. I feel ecstatic about winning the *Reader's Digest* Sweepstakes!

   _____ b. This is a wonderful day!

4. _____ a. You're such a helpful person.

   _____ b. I really respect your ideas; you're so well informed.

5. _____ a. Everyone here likes to dance with you.

   _____ b. When I dance with you I feel graceful and relaxed.

   _____ c. We all feel you're a great dancer.

6. _____ a. If you don't start cleaning up after yourself, I'm moving out!

   _____ b. Did you ever see such a messy kitchen in your life?

   _____ c. I am afraid you will never do your share of the housework.

7. _____ a. This is a very interesting book.

   _____ b. I feel this is not a very helpful book.

   _____ c. I get very excited when I read this book.

8. _____ a. I don't feel competent enough to contribute anything of worth to this group.

   _____ b. I'm not competent enough to contribute anything worthwhile to this group.

9. _____ a. I'm a born loser; no one will ever like me!

   _____ b. Sue is a rotten creep! She laughed when I told her my score on the test!

   _____ c. I'm depressed because I flunked that test.

10. _____ a. I feel warm and comfortable in my group.

    _____ b. Someone in my group always seems to be near when I need company.

    _____ c. I feel everyone cares that I'm part of this group.

Answers

1. a. No   Commands like these communicate strong feelings, but they do not name the feeling that underlies the commands.

   b. D   This statement both expresses and names a feeling. The person communicates the feeling by describing himself as frightened.

2. a. No   A feeling is implied through a question, but the specific feeling underlying the question is not described.

    b. No   This statement communicates considerable feeling through an accusation, but it is not clear whether the accusation is based on anger, hurt, fear, or some other feeling.

    c. D   The person describes the feeling as annoyance. Note that the speaker also "owns" the feeling by using the personal pronoun "I."

3. a. D   The speaker describes herself as feeling ecstatic.

    b. No   This statement communicates positive feelings without describing what they are. The speaker appears to be commenting on the weather when in fact the statement is an expression of how the speaker feels. We cannot tell whether the speaker is feeling proud, happy, caring, accepted, supported, or relieved.

4. a. No   The speaker makes a value judgment communicating positive feelings about the other person, but the speaker does not describe the feelings. Does the speaker admire the other person or like the other person, or is the speaker only grateful?

    b. D   The speaker describes the positive feelings as respect.

5. a. No   This statement does name a feeling (likes) but the speaker is talking for everyone and does not make clear that the feeling is personal. A description of a feeling must contain *I, me, my,* or *mine* to make clear that the feelings are within the speaker. Does it seem more friendly for a person to say, "I like you," or "Everybody likes you"?

    b. D   The speaker communicates clearly and specifically the feeling the speaker has when dancing with the other person.

    c. No   First, the speaker does not speak for himself, but rather hides behind the phrase "we feel." Second, "You're a great dancer" is a value judgment and does not name a feeling. Note that merely placing the word *feel* in front of a statement does not make the statement a description of feeling. People often say *feel* when they mean *think* or *believe.*

6. a. No   This statement communicates general and ambiguous negative feelings about the person's behavior. It refers to the condition of the apartment or house and the speaker's future behavior, but not the speaker's inner feelings.

    b. No   The speaker is trying to communicate a negative feeling through a rhetorical question and a value judgment. Although it is clear the feeling is negative, the specific feeling is not described.

c. D   The speaker describes fear as the negative feeling connected
           with the other person's housework.

Note: Notice that in 6a and 6b the feelings could easily have been in-
           terpreted as anger. Many times the expression of anger results
           from an underlying fear. Yet when the receiver tries to re-
           spond, she may understand that the other person is angry
           without comprehending that the basic feeling to be re-
           sponded to is a feeling of fear.

7. a. No   The speaker communicates a positive value judgment that
            conveys feelings, but the specific feelings are not described.

   b. No   The speaker uses the words "I feel" but does not then describe
            or name a feeling. Instead, the speaker gives a negative value
            judgment. What the speaker actually meant was "I believe" or
            "I think" the book is not very good. People commonly use the
            word *feel* when they mean *think* or *believe.* Consider the dif-
            ference between, "I feel you don't like me" and "I believe
            (think) you don't like me."

   c. D   The speaker describes a feeling of excitement while reading
            this book.

   Note: Many times people who say they are unaware of what they
            feel—or who say they don't have any feelings about some-
            thing—state value judgments about recognizing that this is
            the way their positive or negative feelings get expressed. Many
            times useless arguments can be avoided if we are careful to
            describe our feelings instead of expressing them through value
            judgments. For example, if Joe says the book is interesting and
            Fred says it is boring, they may argue about which it really is. If
            Joe, however, says he was excited by the book and Fred says
            he was frustrated by it, no argument should follow. Each per-
            son's feelings are what they are. Of course, discussing what it
            means for Joe and Fred to feel as they do may provide helpful
            information about each person and about the book.

8. a. D   Speaker communicates a feeling of incompetence.

   b. No   Warning! This statement is potentially hazardous to your
            health! Although it sounds much the same as the previous
            statement, it states that the speaker actually is incompetent—
            not that the speaker currently feels incompetent. The speaker
            has passed a negative value judgment on himself and labeled
            himself as incompetent.

   Note: Many people confuse *feeling* with *being.* A person may feel in-
            competent yet behave very competently or a person may feel
            competent and perform very incompetently. A person may

feel hopeless about a situation that turns out not to be hopeless once his behavior is given an appropriate focus. *A sign of emotional maturity is that a person does not confuse feelings with the reality of the situation.* An emotionally mature person knows she can perform competently, even though she feels incompetent. She does not let her feelings keep her from doing her best because she knows the difference between feelings and performance and knows that the two do not always match.

9. a. No The speaker has evaluated himself—passed a negative value judgment on himself by labeling himself a born loser.

   b. No This statement also communicates a negative value judgment, but against another person rather than of oneself. Although the statement contains strong feelings, the feelings are not specifically named or described.

   c. D The speaker states he feels depressed, Statements 9a and 9c highlight the important difference between passing judgment on yourself and describing your feelings.

   Note: Feelings are constantly changing and are by no means written in concrete once they occur. To say that you are now depressed does not imply that you will or must always feel the same. If you label yourself as a born loser, however, you imply a permanence to a feeling of depression by defining it as a trait rather than as a temporary affective response. You can *feel* anger without being an *angry person.* You can *feel* shy without being a *shy person.* Many people try to avoid new situations and activities by labeling themselves. "I'm not artistic," "I'm not a good public speaker," and "I can't participate in groups" are examples. If we could recognize what our feelings are beneath such statements, maybe we would be more willing to risk doing things we are somewhat fearful of.

10. a. D The speaker communicates a feeling by describing it and taking ownership of it.

    b. No The speaker communicates a positive feeling but does not take direct ownership of it and does not say whether the feeling is happiness, gratitude, supportiveness, or what.

    c. No Instead of "I feel" the speaker should have said "I believe." The last part of the statement really tells what the speaker believes the others feel about her. It does not tell what the speaker feels. Expressions 10a and 10c relate to each other as follows: "Because I believe that everyone cares whether I am part of this group, I feel warm and comfortable."

EXERCISE 5.2
Ambiguity of Expression of Feelings

The objective of this exercise is to increase your awareness of the ambiguity or unclearness in expressing feelings in ways that are not descriptive. Each of the following statements presents an interpersonal situation. The procedure for the exercise is as follows:

1. Divide into groups of three.

2. For each situation in the list that follows these instructions, write descriptions of *two different* feelings that might have given rise to the expression of feelings in the statement.

3. Compare your answers with the answers of the other members of your trio. Discuss them until you understand each other's answers.

4. In the group as a whole, discuss the results of ambiguity in expressing feelings in interpersonal relationships.
   a. What happens when persons make ambiguous statements of feeling? How do other persons respond? How do they feel?
   b. Why would you state feelings ambiguously? In what circumstances would you be ambiguous rather than descriptive? What would be the probable consequence?

Situations

1. A woman asks her boyfriend, "Why can't you ever be any place on time?" What might the woman have said that would have described her feelings openly?

2. You notice that a person in the group who was talking a lot has suddenly become silent. What might the person have said that would have described his feelings openly?

3. During a group meeting, you hear John tell Bill, "Bill, you're talking too much." What might John have said that would have described his feelings openly?

4. Sally abruptly changed the subject after Ann made a comment. What might Sally have said that would have described her feelings openly?

5. A man told his girlfriend, "You shouldn't have bought me such an expensive gift." What might the man have said that would have described his feelings openly?

6. You hear a passenger say to a taxi driver, "Do we have to drive this fast?" What might the passenger have said that would have described his feelings openly?

7. Sam says to Jane, "You're really wonderful." What might Sam have said that would have described his feelings openly?

Checking Your Perception of Another's Feelings

Feelings are internal reactions, and we can tell what people are feeling only from what they tell us and from their overt actions. Overt actions include such things as smiles, frowns, shouts, whispers, tears, and laughter. When other people describe their feelings to us, we can usually accept their feelings to be what they say they are. But if other people express their feelings indirectly (such as through sarcasm) or nonverbally (such as through a frown), we often need to clarify how they actually feel. A basic rule in interpersonal communication is that before you respond to a person's feelings, you need to check to make sure you really know what the other person actually feels.

The best way to check out whether or not you accurately understand how a person is feeling is through a perception check. A **perception check** has three parts:

1. You describe what you think the other person's feelings are.

2. You ask whether or not your perception is accurate.

3. You refrain from expressing approval or disapproval of the feelings.

"You look sad. Are you?" is an example of a perception check. It describes how you think the person is feeling, then it asks the person to agree with or correct your perception, and it does both without making a value judgment about the feeling. A perception check communicates the message, "I want to understand your feeling; is this the way you feel?" It is an invitation for other people to describe their feelings more directly. And it shows you care enough about the person to want to understand how the person feels. Perception checking will help you avoid actions you later regret because they are based on false assumptions about what the other person is feeling.

Checking out our impressions of how others are feeling is an important communication skill. Our impressions are often biased by our own fears, expectations, and present feelings. If we are afraid of anger and expect other people to be angry, then we may think they are angry when in fact they are not. If we feel guilty, we may think other people are about to reject us. We frequently misperceive how other people are feeling, and it is therefore essential that we check out our perceptions before taking action.

 EXERCISE 5.3
Is This the Way You Feel?

The purpose of this exercise is to provide an opportunity to increase your understanding of perception checking by indicating which of the listed statements are perception checks and which are other types of statements. The procedure is as follows:

1. Working by yourself, read each of the statements. On a separate sheet of paper write your answers.

   Put a *PC* for each perception check.

   Put a *J* for each statement that makes a judgment about the other person.

   Put an *O* for each statement that speaks for the other person rather than for yourself.

   Put a *Q* for each question that does not include a description of your perceptions of the other person's feelings.

2. Form groups of four. Review the answers of each member for each statement. Discuss any disagreements until all members agree on the answer. Answers are at the end of the chapter.

3. Go around the group and have members check out their perceptions of how other members are feeling.

Statements

1. _____ Are you angry with me?
2. _____ You look as if you are upset about what Sally said. Are you?
3. _____ Why are you mad at me?
4. _____ You look as if you feel put down by my statement. That's stupid!
5. _____ What is it about your boss that makes you resent her so much?
6. _____ Are your feelings hurt again?
7. _____ You look unhappy. Are you?
8. _____ Am I right that you feel disappointed that nobody commented on your suggestion?

9. _____ Why on earth would you get upset about that? That's pretty crazy!

10. _____ I get the impression you are pretty happy with my work. Are you?

11. _____ Are you feeling rejected?

12. _____ If you are dumb enough to get angry about that, the hell with you!

13. _____ You're always happy!

14. _____ I'm not sure whether your expression means that I'm confusing you or hurting your feelings. Which one is it?

15. _____ Half the time you're laughing. The other half of the time you're staring off into space. What's going on?

■ CHAPTER REVIEW

Test your understanding of how to express your feelings verbally by answering true or false to the following statements. Answers are at the end of the chapter.

True   False   1. You become aware of your feelings by being aware of how you are reacting to what is happening around you.

True   False   2. You express your feelings after you have gone through the process of sending, interpreting, feeling, and intending.

True   False   3. The best way to express your feelings is to describe how the other person feels.

True   False   4. How you feel about a situation reflects how the situation really is.

True   False   5. "Everyone likes you!" is an example of a good feeling description.

True   False   6. A perception check is done to make sure a person really understands how you feel.

True   False   7. In a perception check, you describe what you think the other person's feelings are and ask whether you are right, without showing approval or disapproval.

True   False   8. A perception check will help you understand the other person's message.

True   False   9. We often receive an inaccurate impression of someone else's feelings because of our fears and anger.

True   False   10. "You look happy! Is that the way you feel?" is an example of a good perception check.

Self-Diagnosis

This chapter has focused on expressing feelings verbally. On a scale from 1 (poorly mastered) to 5 (highly mastered) rate the degree to which you have mastered each skill. Then choose two skills to improve in the next week.

Rating	Skill
_____	Understanding the process of having and expressing feelings (sensing, interpreting, feeling, intending, expressing)
_____	Making a personal statement
_____	Describing a feeling by name, simile, action urge, figure of speech
_____	Using perception checks (describing your perception of other's feelings, asking whether the perception is correct, without indicating approval or disapproval)
_____	Avoiding the indirect expression of feelings through commands, questions, accusations, and so on

Skills I Will Improve in the Next Week

1. _____

2. _____

Summary

In every relationship you decide which feelings you wish to communicate verbally to the other person and which you wish to keep private. **Feelings** are internal physiological reactions to your experiences. Having feelings is a natural and joyful part of being alive. You cannot enjoy or consciously communicate your feelings, however, if you are not aware of them. There are five aspects to being aware of your feelings: gathering information through your senses, deciding what the information means, experiencing the appropriate feeling, deciding how to express your feeling, and expressing it. Feelings may be expressed verbally and nonverbally. Expressing feelings verbally must include (a) a personal statement and (b) a description of the feeling. Four ways to describe a feeling include identifying or naming it, using sensory descriptions ("I feel I have just been hit by a pile driver!"), describing an action urge ("I want to leap and shout"), or using a figure of speech ("I feel like a drop of water in the ocean"). Indirect expression of feelings creates ambiguity and misunderstandings. When clarifying other people's feelings, you may use a **perception check,** which has three parts (describing your perception of the other's feelings, asking whether your perception is correct, and refraining from expressing approval or disapproval). The next chapter will help you learn the skills of constructively expressing your feelings nonverbally.

Answers

Comprehension Test A: 1. false; 2. true; 3. false; 4. true; 5. false; 6. true; 7. true; 8. false; 9. false; 10. true.

Comprehension Test B: 1. false; 2. false; 3. true; 4. true; 5. true; 6. true; 7. true; 8. true; 9. true; 10. true.

Comprehension Test C: 1. false; 2. true; 3. true; 4. true; 5. true; 6. false; 7. true; 8. false; 9. true; 10. true.

Is This the Way You Feel? (Exercise 5.3):   1. Q; 2. PC; 3. O; 4. J; 5. O; 6. Q; 7. PC; 8. PC; 9. J; 10. PC; 11. Q; 12. J; 13. O; 14. PC; 15. PC.

Chapter Review: 1. true; 2. true; 3. false; 4. false; 5. false; 6. false; 7. true; 8. true; 9. true; 10. true.

CHAPTER 6

Expressing Your Feelings Nonverbally

Introduction

When we speak we rarely trust words alone to convey our messages. We shift our weight, stand close to the other person or far away, wave our arms, smile or frown, speak loudly or softly, touch or don't touch, or use other nonverbal behaviors to emphasize or clarify what our words mean. We communicate by the way we sit or stand, straighten our clothing, place our hands, manipulate a glass, and so forth. Consciously and unconsciously we use nonverbal behaviors to communicate our feelings, liking, and preferences as well as to reinforce the meaning of our words.

Many people have great difficulties in communicating clearly and accurately to other individuals how they feel, despite the fact that awareness, acceptance, and expression of feelings are crucial for psychological health and for building and maintaining fulfilling relationships. Expressing warmth and liking is especially important for establishing and keeping friendships. The previous chapter focused on constructive ways of

The Power of Friendship

William Manchester wrote of an insight he had on revisiting Sugar Loaf Hill in Okinawa, where 34 years before he had fought as a Marine. He stated that he understood, at last, why he secretly left a military hospital and, in violation of orders, returned to the front and almost certain death. "It was an act of love. Those men on the line were my family, my home. They were closer to me than I can say, closer than any friends had been or ever would be. They were comrades; three of them had saved my life. They had never let me down, and I couldn't do it to them. I had to be with them, rather than let them die and me live with the knowledge that I might have saved them." He concluded that men do not fight for flag or country, for the Marine Corps or glory or any other abstraction. "They fight for their friends."

expressing feelings verbally. This chapter focuses on the skills necessary for effective nonverbal expression of feelings. The objectives of this chapter are to

1. Remind you of the importance of the congruence between your verbal and nonverbal messages in communicating your feelings to another person clearly and accurately.

2. Increase your awareness of how you communicate feelings to others.

3. Provide skill practice in expressing feelings nonverbally.

Nonverbal Communication

Actions speak louder than words. Because nonverbal messages tend to be less conscious we tend to believe them even more than the words people say. In communicating effectively with other individuals it may be more important to have a mastery of nonverbal communication than fluency with words. In a normal two-person conversation, the verbal components carry less than 35 percent of the social meaning of the situation, while more than 65 percent is carried by nonverbal messages (Ambady & Rosenthal, 1992; Knapp & Vangelisti, 1995). That statement may seem surprising to you, but we communicate by our manner of dress, physique, posture, body tension, facial expression, degree of eye contact, hand and body movements, tone of voice, continuities in speech (such as rate, duration, nonfluencies, and pauses), spatial distance, and touch, as well as by words. In order to communicate effectively with other people, therefore, you must be as concerned with the nonverbal messages you are sending as with the verbal ones, if not more so. It is the nonverbal messages that most clearly and powerfully communicate liking and disliking, acceptance and rejection, and interest and boredom.

Eye contact is one nonverbal way to provide information (such as liking, attentiveness, competence, and credibility), regulate interaction (eye contact has an important role in initiating communication and in maintaining a conversation once it has begun), express intimacy (people look more at others whom they like than at those they dislike), exercise social control (eye contact increases when we attempt to be persuasive), and facilitate the accomplishment of tasks (eye contact helps to closely coordinate behavior). Facial expressions convey a variety of emotions, and these basic emotional expressions can be identified by people of very different cultures. Cultures may differ, however, in the *display rules* that govern the circumstances in which an emotion will be expressed. Interpersonal distance is a more abstract form of communication, but it, too, is an important means of conveying information. Four major zones (intimate, personal, social, and public) define the distances between people that accompany different types of interchange.

In comparison with verbal language, nonverbal behavior is very limited. Usually nonverbal messages are used to communicate feelings, likings, and preferences, and they customarily either reinforce or contradict messages that are communicated verbally. Feelings, in particular, are communicated more by nonverbal messages than by the words a person uses. Facial expressions and tone of voice are especially important in communicating feelings. Smiles, for example, communicate friendliness, cooperativeness, and acceptance of other individuals. There appears to be more eye contact between people who like each other than between people who do not like each other. Emotional meanings are communicated quite accurately through voice tone and inflection.

The problem is that it is often difficult to know for sure what another person really feels. People often say one thing but then do another. Someone can seem to like you but never say so. A person can say he or she likes you, but somehow you do not feel the statement is sincere. Feelings are often misunderstood and misinterpreted for two major reasons: (1) the ambiguity of nonverbal messages and (2) the frequent contradictions between verbal and nonverbal messages.

Since nonverbal messages are inevitably ambiguous, the receiver cannot be sure about what the sender is feeling. For one thing, the same feeling can be expressed nonverbally in several different ways. Anger, for example, can be expressed by jumping up and down or by a frozen stillness. Happiness can be expressed through laughter or tears. Any single nonverbal message, furthermore, can arise from a variety of feelings. A blush may show embarrassment, pleasure, nervousness, or even anger. Crying can be caused by sadness, happiness, excitement, grief, pain, or confusion. Also there are wide differences among social groups as to the meaning of many nonverbal messages. Standing close to the receiver may be a sign of warmth to a person from one cultural background and a sign of aggressiveness and hostility to a person from another cultural background. In understanding nonverbal messages, the receiver must interpret the sender's actions. As these actions increase in ambiguity, the chance for misinterpretation increases.

It is often difficult to make accurate judgments about the feelings of other people because of the different degrees of feelings or contradictory kinds of feelings being expressed simultaneously through verbal and nonverbal messages. We have all been in situations in which we have received or sent conflicting messages on verbal and nonverbal channels. The parent who screams, "I WANT IT QUIET AROUND THIS HOUSE!" or the teacher who says, "I've always got plenty of time to talk to a student," are examples. Sometimes a person may say, "I like you," but communicate nonverbally, "Don't come close to me," by using a cold tone of voice, looking worried, and backing away. When receiving such conflicting messages through two different channels, we tend to believe the messages that we perceive to be harder to fake. These are often the nonverbal ones. You are, therefore, more apt to believe the nonverbal communication than the verbal one. Such contradictory communications are known as double binds and can make the receiver anxious and suspicious.

When communicating your feelings, it pays to take special care that your verbal and nonverbal messages are congruent. It is when your verbal and nonverbal messages are redundant and reinforce and complement each other that you will be most successful in effectively communicating what you feel. Especially when communicating liking and acceptance, avoid stooped shoulders and downcast eyes (signs of depression and disappointment), and keep your posture erect with your head held high (signs of self-acceptance and well-being). Keep good eye contact because it communicates that you are open to communication, involvement, and feedback. People tend to avoid eye contact when they want to hide their feelings, when they are tense, when they are interacting with someone they dislike, or when they are attempting to cut off social contact.

Nonverbal messages, then, are more powerful in communicating feelings than are verbal messages, but are also more ambiguous and difficult to interpret accurately. To communicate your feelings clearly and accurately to another person, you need to be skillful in both the verbal and nonverbal ways of expressing feelings. Above all, you need to make your verbal and nonverbal messages congruent with each other. The following exercises will help you become more aware of the ambiguity of nonverbal messages and of how you presently communicate feelings nonverbally, and they will help you become more skillful in the use of nonverbal cues to communicate feelings.

Nonverbal Behavior

Characteristics

All nonverbal behavior communicates. If it is observed, it communicates.

Nonverbal communication is culturally bound. The same gesture will have different meanings in different cultures.

Nonverbal communication is primarily about the relationship (affinity, control, respect).

Nonverbal communication supports, enhances, or contradicts verbal statements in many different ways.

Nonverbal communication is inherently ambiguous (crying can mean several different things).

Types

Body orientation: degree to which you face toward or away from someone with your body, feet, head.

Posture: body position as you sit, stand, walk.

Gestures: movement of hands, arms, and head.

Facial expressions and eye movements reflect surprise, fear, anger, disgust, happiness, sadness.

Voice: tone, speed, pitch, volume, number and length of pauses, and inflections make up a paralanguage.

Touch: functional (haircut), social (handshake), friendship (clap on back), aggression (shoves), sexual arousal (kisses).

Clothing indicates economic level, education level, social position, trustworthiness, sophistication, level of success, moral character.

Use of space and distance: how close or far away you stand, the boundaries you set around yourself.

EXERCISE 6.1
Communication Without Words

The objective of this exercise is to increase your awareness of the ambiguity of expressing feelings in nonverbal or in behavioral ways. A series of situations are presented. Each involves the expression of feelings through certain nonverbal behaviors. The procedure for the exercise is as follows:

1. Divide into groups of three.

2. For each situation describe *two different* feelings (within the person named) that might have given rise to such a nonverbal expression of feelings.

3. Compare your answers with the answers of the other members of your trio. Discuss until you understand each other's answers.

4. In the group as a whole, share your feelings and reactions to the exercise. What did you learn? How would you react if someone in the group behaved similarly to the people in the situations described? Are there any times when the nonverbal expression of feelings is more effective than the verbal description of feelings?

The Situations

1. Helen, who had been talking a lot in the group, suddenly became silent. Describe two feelings that might have caused Helen to do so.

2. Without expression, Dale suddenly changed the subject of the group's discussion. What are two different feelings that might have been responsible for Dale's changing the subject?

3. Whenever Keith made a comment in the group, he watched the leader's face. What are two different feelings that might have led Keith to watch the leader so intently?

4. While the group discussion was going on, Betty became more and more tense and restless. Finally, she got up abruptly and left the room without saying a word. Describe two different feelings that might have caused Betty to leave.

5. Roger was describing in a serious manner a fight he and a friend had had earlier. In the middle of his discussion, Dale began to laugh. Describe two different feelings that might have caused Dale to laugh.

E X E R C I S E   6 . 2

Interpreting Others' Nonverbal Cues

The objectives of this exercise are (1) to demonstrate the ambiguity of nonverbal cues in communicating feelings and (2) to illustrate how many different feeling reactions the same nonverbal cues can give. For this exercise you need from five to ten pictures cut out of magazines. Each picture should have at least one person in it who is expressing a feeling. The procedure for this exercise is as follows:

1. Number the pictures. Pass each picture around the group.

2. Each person answers the following questions about each picture:
   a. How do the individuals in the picture feel?
   b. How does this picture make you feel?

3. The group then shares their answers for each picture.
   a. How similar were your interpretations of what the individuals in the pictures felt?
   b. How similar were the feelings you had in response to the pictures?
   c. If you have dissimilar answers, what makes the pictures so ambiguous?
   d. Could different people interpret your own nonverbal cues in as many different ways as the group interpreted the nonverbal cues of the individuals in the pictures?

 E X E R C I S E   6 . 3

How Do You Express Your Feelings?

The objective of this exercise is to increase your self-awareness of the ways in which you express your feelings. Several descriptions of feelings you may have experienced are presented. For each of these you are to report two different ways that you express such feelings. The first answer should be something you would say that would express your feelings. The second answer should report how you might express such feelings by actions and without using words. The procedure for this exercise is as follows:

1. Divide into groups of three.

2. Write out your answers to the various situations.

3. Compare your answers with the answers of the other members of your trio. Discuss until you understand each other's answers. Then discuss these questions:
   a. What did I learn about the way I usually express my feelings?
   b. In what ways would it be helpful for me to change the ways I usually express my feelings?
   c. In what ways would it be helpful for each of us to change the ways we usually express feelings?

4. In the group as a whole, share your feelings and reactions to the exercise. Then list as many principles for constructively expressing feelings as you can think of.

The Descriptions

1. When you feel bored with what is going on in a discussion, how do you usually express your feelings?

   Using words: _____

   Without using words: _____

2. When you feel very annoyed with another person with whom you want to build a better relationship, how do you usually express your feelings?

   Using words: _____

   Without using words: _____

3. When another person says or does something to you that hurts your feelings deeply, how do you usually express your feelings?

   Using words: _____

   Without using words: _____

4. An acquaintance asks you to do something that you are afraid you cannot do well. You also want to hide the fact that you feel inadequate. How do you express your feelings?

   Using words: _____

   Without using words: _____

5. You feel affection and fondness for someone else but at the same time can't be sure the other person feels the same way about you. How do you usually express your feelings?

   Using words: _____

   Without using words: _____

6. Your close friend is leaving town for a long time, and you feel alone and lonely. How would you usually express your feelings?

Using words: _____

Without using words: _____

 EXERCISE 6.4

Using Nonverbal Cues to Express Warmth and Coldness

The objective of this exercise is to increase your skills in the use of nonverbal cues to express warmth. In order to increase your awareness of the nonverbal cues that express warmth, you will be asked to role-play the expression of coldness as well as the expression of warmth. Some of the nonverbal cues that can indicate either warmth or coldness are shown in the following list.

Nonverbal cue	*Warmth*	*Coldness*
Tone of voice	Soft	Hard
Facial expression	Smiling, interested	Poker-faced, frowning, uninterested
Posture	Lean toward other; relaxed	Lean away from other; tense
Eye contact	Look into other's eyes	Avoid looking into other's eyes
Touching	Touch other softly	Avoid touching other
Gestures	Open, welcoming	Closed, guarding oneself, and keeping other away
Spatial distance	Close	Distant

The Procedure

1. Divide into pairs. Designate one person A and the other B.

2. Person A makes three statements about his childhood in a warm way. Then person A makes three statements about his childhood in a cold way.

3. Person B gives person A feedback of how successfully he role-played the nonverbal expression of warmth and coldness.

4. Reverse roles and repeat steps 2 and 3.

5. Find a new partner. Repeat steps 2 and 3 with your new partner. This time discuss the characteristics of a person you want as a friend.

6. Find a new partner. Repeat steps 2 and 3 with your new partner. This time discuss what you could do to improve your relationship with your partner.

7. Discuss the exercise in the group as a whole.
   a. Did you find it easy to role-play warmth and coldness? Why or why not?
   b. How well did each of you master the skills of expressing warmth and coldness nonverbally?
   c. Are there other ways to express warmth nonverbally?
   d. What were your reactions and feelings to the exercise?

8. Go around the group and give each other feedback concerning the typical nonverbal messages you send in the group. How would you describe each other's nonverbal behavior? What is most distinctive about each other's nonverbal behavior? If you were to suggest one way for each person to change his nonverbal behavior, what would it be?

Expressing warmth is a vital skill for building and maintaining fulfilling relationships. More than any other behavior, warmth communicates liking, concern, and acceptance of another person. You should practice the nonverbal expression of warmth until you are sure that you can communicate it effectively when you want to.

 EXERCISE 6.5
Actions Speak Louder Than Words

The following exercise will give you a chance to practice nonverbal communication of feelings. You may not use words and sounds during this exercise, but must communicate only by nonverbal means, such as facial expressions, eye contact, gestures, posture, and touch. The procedure for the exercise is as follows:

1. Form groups of six. Sit on the floor in a circle. Do not use a table. Deal out a deck of ordinary playing cards until everyone has the same number of cards and there are at least three cards left in the draw-deck. The draw-deck is placed face down in the center of the circle.

2. The winner of the game is the person who gets rid of all her cards first. You get rid of your cards by correctly identifying the feelings expressed by other group members and by accurately communicating feelings to the other group members.

3. Group members take turns expressing one feeling. To begin, the person on the dealer's left selects a card from her own hand and lays it face down in front of her. She is now the expresser. The remaining group members are to identify the feeling she expresses. Then she expresses nonverbally the feeling on the card. The feeling each card represents is listed in item 9. The other people check their hands to see if they have a card that matches the feeling that was expressed. If so, they place the card(s) face down in front of them. If not, they pass.

4. When all the cards are down for the first round, they are all turned face up at the same time. If one or more of the receivers have matched the expresser's card, the expresser puts her card and all the matching cards face down on the bottom of the draw-deck.

5. Any group member who put down a wrong card must return it to his hand and draw an additional penalty card from the top of the draw-deck. You draw the same number of penalty cards from the draw-deck as the number of cards you put down in front of you.

6. If no other group member matched the expresser's card, then the expresser failed to communicate and she returns her card to her hand and draws a penalty card from the draw-deck. In this case the other people return their cards to their hands but *do not* draw penalty cards.

7. When you have two or three cards representing the same feeling, you must play all the cards if you play one of them. If you have several queens, for example, you must play all of them, if you play queens at all. So, as expresser or receiver, you may get rid of two or three cards. Or you may have to draw two or three penalty cards.

8. The expresser may use any nonverbal or unspoken behavior she wishes in order to communicate accurately the feeling she is portraying. No words may be spoken or sounds made. You may wish to use your hands, your head, and your whole body, and you may involve other group members by touching them or engaging them in a nonverbal interchange.

9. Each card represents a different feeling.

2 = contentment	9 = anger
3 = shyness	10 = hope
4 = indifference	Jack = happiness
5 = fear	Queen = joy
6 = frustration	King = warmth
7 = loneliness	Ace = love
8 = sorrow	Joker = admiration

10. Discuss the following questions:
    a. Was it difficult or easy to express feelings nonverbally? Why or why not?
    b. Was it difficult or easy to interpret the nonverbal expressions? Why or why not?
    c. What nonverbal messages were most and least understandable?
    d. What did I learn about myself from this exercise?

 EXERCISE 6.6
Recognizing Cues for Affection or Hostility

This exercise is aimed at providing you with an opportunity to see if you can tell the difference between messages indicating affection and messages indicating hostility. Twenty messages are listed. In the spaces provided, write an *A* if you think the message indicates affection and an *H* if you think the message indicates hostility. Then check your answers with the answers at the end of the chapter. Discuss with your group members any that you missed until you are sure you understand them.

_____ 1. Looks directly at the other person and gives undivided attention.

_____ 2. Greets the person in a cold, formal manner.

_____ 3. Engages in friendly humor.

_____ 4. Yawns or shows other signs of boredom.

_____ 5. Has a relaxed posture and does not appear tense or nervous.

_____ 6. Sits close to the other person.

_____ 7. Interrupts repeatedly.

_____ 8. Leans toward the other person as an expression of interest.

_____ 9. Sits relatively far away.

_____ 10. Responds directly and openly to the other person's request to know one's opinions, values, attitudes, and feelings.

_____ 11. Exhibits a cold, nonreceptive facial expression.

_____ 12. Uses the other person's vocabulary in explaining things.

_____ 13. Makes encouraging, reassuring remarks to the other person.

_____ 14. Lays traps for the other person (e.g., "A minute ago you said . . . and now you are contradicting yourself!").

_____ 15. Makes casual physical contact with the other person as an expression of liking (e.g., pat on the back, touch on the arm).

_____ 16. Says, "That stupid remark is about what I would expect from someone like you."

_____ 17. Shows consideration for the physical comfort of the other person by taking the person's coat, offering a more comfortable chair, adjusting the window, and so forth.

_____ 18. Sneers and appears amused when the other person is sharing personal feelings.

_____ 19. Hedges or rebuffs the other person when asked a personal question.

_____ 20. During the conversation looks repeatedly at the clock, out the window, away from the other person, or at papers on the desk.

Importance of Making Your Verbal and Nonverbal Messages Congruent

There is no way to overemphasize the importance of making congruent your verbal and nonverbal messages for communicating feelings. If you wish to express warmth, your words, facial expression, tone of voice, posture, and so on must all communicate warmth. Contradictory messages will only indicate to the other person that you are untrustworthy and will create anxiety about the relationship. Some psychologists have stated that receiving contradictory verbal and nonverbal messages for a long period of time from someone you love can result in mental illness. For a person to believe that your expression of feelings is real and genuine, your verbal and nonverbal messages must be congruent.

EXERCISE 6.7
Expressing Your Feelings

Form a pair. Working with your partner, write down what the nonverbal cue would look like for each of the emotions named.

Nonverbal Cue	Love	Fear	Joy
Tone of voice	_____	_____	_____
Facial expression	_____	_____	_____
Posture	_____	_____	_____
Eye contact	_____	_____	_____
Gestures	_____	_____	_____
Spatial distance	_____	_____	_____
Touching	_____	_____	_____
Body movement	_____	_____	_____

EXERCISE 6.8
Can You Tell How I Feel?

The objective of this exercise is to demonstrate how the same verbal statement can change because of the nonverbal messages accompanying it. The procedure is as follows:

1. Form pairs. Flip a coin to decide who is person A and who is person B.

2. Each member of the pair will be given a statement to make to his or her partner.

3. Person A says to person B, "The rose is red" and then person B says to person A, "The rose is red." At this point try to be as neutral and nonexpressive as possible.

4. Person A says to person B, "1, 2, 3, 4, 5, 6, 7." and then person B says to person A, "1, 2, 3, 4, 5, 6, 7." At this point try to be as neutral and nonexpressive as possible.

5. Round 1: The statement is "The rose is red."
   a. Person A makes the statement while nonverbally communicating anger.
   b. Person B makes the statement while nonverbally communicating sadness.
   c. Person A makes the statement while nonverbally communicating happiness.
   d. Person B makes the statement while nonverbally communicating fear.
   e. Person A makes the statement while nonverbally communicating depression.
   f. Person B makes the statement while nonverbally communicating grief
   g. Person A makes the statement while nonverbally communicating hate.
   h. Person B makes the statement while nonverbally communicating love.

6. Round 2: The statement is "1, 2, 3, 4, 5 ,6, 7."
   a. Person A makes the statement while nonverbally communicating sadness.
   b. Person B makes the statement while nonverbally communicating happiness.
   c. Person A makes the statement while nonverbally communicating fear.
   d. Person B makes the statement while nonverbally communicating depression.
   e. Person A makes the statement while nonverbally communicating grief.
   f. Person B makes the statement while nonverbally communicating hate.
   g. Person A makes the statement while nonverbally communicating love.
   h. Person B makes the statement while nonverbally communicating anger.

Person	Round 1: "The Rose Is Red."	Round 2: "1, 2, 3, 4, 5, 6, 7."
A	Anger	Sadness
B	Sadness	Joy
A	Joy	Fear
B	Fear	Depression
A	Depression	Grief
B	Grief	Hate
A	Hate	Love
B	Love	Anger

7. Working as a pair, write down three conclusions about your experience.

8. Join with another pair and form a group of four. Share your conclusions. Listen to their conclusions. As a group of four, choose the three most meaningful conclusions.

EXERCISE 6.9
Off Balance

The purpose of this exercise is to experience mutual physical support with another person. The exercise is taken from the excellent book *Playfair,* written by Weinstein and Goodman (1980). The procedure is as follows:

1. Find a partner who was born in a different month from you. Make sure no walls, furniture, or objects are near you. This is an exercise that calls for starting slow, staying in complete control, and taking responsibility for your partner's well-being.

2. Stand facing your partner, firmly grasping each other's hands or wrists. The object of this exercise is for both of you to be off balance, yet totally supporting each other the whole time. Lean your weight backward so that if it were not for your partner supporting you, you would fall over. Be careful not to put too much strain on your partner. Work out an effective counterbalance between the two of you. Move around together, exploring different levels, different points of balance for your body. Use the support from your partner to do things you could not do by yourself.

3. Stand back-to-back with your partner, leaning into each other, so you are off balance and supporting each other's weight. Move around and explore this new position so that you are both continually off balance yet continually supporting each other.

4. Combine into a group of four with another pair. Repeat steps 2 and 3. Again, start out carefully. Make sure you do not have an unpleasant crash landing.

EXERCISE 6.10
Gaining Acceptance Nonverbally

Sometimes other people do not just give you acceptance; you have to earn it. You often spend a great deal of time and energy trying to gain the acceptance of individuals you like and admire. This exercise gives you an opportunity to experience gaining acceptance from the group nonverbally. Here is the procedure for the exercise:

1. One member volunteers to be an outsider. The other members of the group form a tight circle by locking arms and pressing close to each other's sides.

2. The outsider has to break into the group by forcing his or her way to the center of the circle. This is quite an active exercise. You should, therefore, be careful not to hurt anyone by becoming too rough. Anyone with a physical disability or injury should not take part in this exercise.

3. After everyone who wishes to has been an outsider, discuss the experience. The discussion may center on the following questions:
   a. How did you react to being an outsider? What did you learn about yourself from the experience?
   b. How did you react to trying to keep the outsider from gaining entry into the group? What did you learn about yourself from the experience?

EXERCISE 6.11

Expressing Acceptance Nonverbally

The purpose of this exercise is for you to have an opportunity to experience fully the acceptance felt toward you by others. At the same time, the members of the group are given an opportunity to express acceptance nonverbally. The procedure for the exercise is as follows:

1. One member volunteers to stand in the center of a circle made up of the other members of the group. She is to shut her eyes and be silent.

2. The other members of the group are all to approach her and express their positive feelings nonverbally in whatever way they wish. This may take the form of hugging, stroking, massaging, lifting, or whatever each person feels.

3. After everyone who wishes to has been the center of the circle, the group may wish to discuss the experience. The discussion may center on the following two areas:
   a. How did it feel to receive so much acceptance and affection? What were the reactions of each person in the center? Was it a tense situation for you or was it an enjoyable one? Why do you react as you do? What did you learn about yourself?
   b. How did it feel to give so much acceptance and affection to other members of the group? What are your reactions to such giving? Why do you react this way? What did you learn about yourself from this experience?

■ CHAPTER REVIEW

Test your understanding of the nonverbal expression of feelings by answering true or false to the following statements. The answers are at the end of the chapter.

True   False   1. It is possible to communicate verbally without giving nonverbal clues.

True   False   2. The verbal message is more believable than the nonverbal message.

True   False   3. In comparison with nonverbal actions, the verbal language is very limited.

True   False   4. Direct eye contact indicates dislike for the other person.

True   False   5. Feelings are misunderstood partly because the verbal and nonverbal messages are often incongruent.

True   False   6. Feelings are misunderstood partly because the nonverbal messages are often unclear.

True   False   7. Leaning away from another person is an expression of coldness.

True   False   8. Contradictions between verbal and nonverbal messages will tell the receiver that the sender is untrustworthy.

True   False   9. Contradictions between verbal and nonverbal messages will make the receiver suspicious.

True   False   10. Continued contradictory messages from a loved one can cause mental illness.

Self-Diagnosis

This chapter has focused on expressing feelings verbally. On a scale from 1 (poorly mastered) to 5 (highly mastered) rate the degree to which you have mastered each skill. Then choose two skills to improve on in the next week.

Rating	Skill
_____	Being aware of how I express my feelings nonverbally.
_____	Using nonverbal cues to express my feelings accurately.
_____	Being congruent in the way my verbal and nonverbal messages express feelings.
_____	Using nonverbal cues to express warmth.

Skills I Will Improve in the Next Week

1. _____

2. _____

Summary

In every relationship you decide which feelings you wish to communicate nonverbally to the other person and which you wish to keep private. We rarely communicate our feelings with words alone. Nonverbal messages are sent by our manner of dress, physique, posture, body tension, facial expression, degree of eye contact, hand and body movements, tone of voice, continuities in speech, spatial distance, and touch. Nonverbal messages are more powerful in communicating feelings than are verbal messages but are also more ambiguous and difficult to interpret accurately. It is important, therefore, to make your verbal and nonverbal messages congruent. Also, you should have developed skill in interpreting and expressing different feelings nonverbally. This skill will be helpful in the next chapter, which deals with how to listen and respond to others in a helpful way.

Answers

Exercise 6.6: Recognizing Cues for Affection or Hostility: 1. A; 2. H; 3. A; 4. H; 5. A; 6. A; 7. H; 8. A; 9. H; 10. A; 11. H; 12. A; 13. A; 14. H; 15. A; 16. H; 17. A; 18. H; 19. H; 20 H.

Chapter Review: 1. false; 2. false; 3. false; 4. false; 5. true; 6. true; 7. true; 8. true; 9. true; 10. true.

CHAPTER 7

Helpful Listening and Responding

Responding to Another Person's Problems

When someone is talking to you about something deeply distressing or of a real concern to her, how should you listen and respond in order to be helpful? How do you answer in ways that will both help the person solve her problem or clarify her feelings and at the same time help build a closer relationship between that person and yourself?

Perhaps the most important thing to remember is that you cannot solve other people's problems for them. No matter how sure you are of what the right thing to do is or how much insight you think you have into their problems, the other people must come to their own decisions about what they should do and achieve their own insights into the situation and themselves. So how do you listen and respond to ensure that other people will make their own decisions and gain their own insights?

Elements of Listening

Element	Explanation
Hearing	The physiological aspects of listening involve sound waves striking the ear at a certain frequency and volume.
Attending	Attention is focused on some messages and filters out others.
Understanding	The listener must interpret the messages similarly to the way the sender intended them.
Responding	The listener gives observable feedback to the sender.
Remembering	The listener is able to recall the content and meaning of the messages at a future time.

In listening and responding to other people's messages, there are two basic things that determine the effectiveness of your help:

1. Your intentions and attitudes as you listen and give your response.
2. The actual phrasing of your response.

The exercises that follow deal with both of these. Your intentions are the most important single factor in helping other people solve their problems. The appropriate phrasing of your response involves considerable skill, but skill alone is not enough. It is only when the skills in phrasing responses reflect your underlying attitudes of acceptance, respect, interest, liking, and desire to help that your response will be truly helpful. Your response is helpful when it helps the other person explore a problem, clarify feelings, gain insight into a distressing situation, or make a difficult decision. In order to examine the intentions or attitudes with which you can respond to someone asking for help with a problem or a concern, we will go through Exercise 7.1.

 EXERCISE 7.1
Listening and Response Alternatives

The objectives of this exercise are to (1) identify your response style, (2) understand the different types of responses you can use in a situation in which the sender has a problem he wants help with, and (3) determine when each type of response may be most effective in helping other people with their problems and in building a closer relationship between the other people and yourself. Each of the response alternatives used in this exercise communicates underlying intentions and attitudes. The procedure is as follows:

1. Using Answer Sheet A, and working by yourself, complete the Questionnaire on Listening and Response Alternatives. Specific instructions are on the answer sheet.

2. Using Answer Sheet B, and working by yourself, identify the underlying intent of each response given in the questionnaire. Specific instructions are on the answer sheet.

3. Using the Scoring Key in the Appendix, score Answer Sheet A. Write the number of times you used each type of response in the appropriate spaces on the answer sheet.

4. Read the next section, which is on intentions underlying the responses. Then divide into groups of three and score Answer Sheet B, discussing each response until everyone understands it.

5. Combine two triads into a group of six. On Table 7.1 (p. 228), mark the frequency with which each member of the group used each type of response.

6. Use the questions on page 228 to discuss with your group the results summarized in Table 7.1.

Answer Sheet A: Identifying Personal Responses

Read the twelve statements in the questionnaire and circle on this answer sheet the response that best represents what you would say to the speaker if you were trying to form a close relationship with him and to help him solve his problems.

1. a (b) c : d : e	7. a : b : c : d : e
2. a : b (c) d : e	8. a : b : c : d : e
3. a : b : c (d) e	9. a : b : c : d : e
4. a : b : c : d : e	10. a : b : c : d : e
5. a : b : c : d : e	11. a : b : c : d : e
6. a : b : c : d : e	12. a : b : c : d : e

Response	Frequency
E	_____
I	_____
S	_____
P	_____
U	_____

Answer Sheet B: Identifying the Intent of a Response

Study pages 222–228, on which the five basic intentions underlying the responses to the problems presented in the questionnaire are discussed. Then go back through the questionnaire and classify the responses to each problem according to the five categories. Read each of the twelve problem statements and identify the intent underlying each of the alternative responses by marking a *P* for probing, *I* for interpretative, *E* for evaluative, *S* for supportive, and *U* for understanding.

Item	a	b	c	d	e
1.					
2.					
3.					
4.					
5.					
6.					
7.					
8.					
9.					
10.					
11.					
12.					

Questionnaire on Listening and Response Alternatives

In this exercise, statements are made by several people about situations they face. Little or no information is presented about the nature of the person speaking. Following each statement is a series of five possible responses you might make in trying to help the person solve his or her problem. See Answer Sheet A for specific directions on how to complete this exercise.

1. **David.** "I'm determined to be a success, and I know I can do it if I just work hard enough. I may have to work 18 hours a day and stay chained to my computer, but if that's what it takes, I'll do it. My home life and my

family may suffer, but it will be worth it in the end. I will be a success, and that's all that matters."

   a. You seem to be a person who wants badly to succeed at your job. That is understandable, but it may stem from your insecurity about your own competence and ability.

   b. I guess we all, at some time or other, go through a period where we want to achieve success. Lots of people worry about whether their family will suffer while they work so hard. I'm sure everything will turn out all right for you and your family.

   c. I think you are right. Hard work always pays off. Keep at it!

   d. You see yourself as a very ambitious person. Yet you're unsure about whether you want your family to suffer because of the long hours you believe you will have to work in order to be successful.

   e. Can you tell me a little more about why success is important to you? What will you do when you've achieved this success? Will you be happy? Will it give you all that you want out of life?

2. **Roger.** "I never seem to have enough time to do the things I enjoy. Just as I'm ready to go enjoy a nice game of golf or tennis, my brother reminds me of some writing I need to do, or my wife saddles me with household chores. It's getting harder and harder to have the fun out of life that I expect to have. It's depressing!"

   a. Wanting to have fun is OK, but don't you think you should do some work too? I certainly wouldn't play golf if I thought that later I would regret not having worked. Life does have responsibilities.

   b. It's upsetting that your work and household responsibilities are increasing to the extent that you don't have time for the fun and recreation you want.

   c. Maybe your leisure activities are just a way of getting out of the unpleasant jobs you should do.

   d. I'm curious. How much time do you spend on your favorite sports?

   e. You're in a busy time of your life right now. I bet you will have more leisure time as you get older.

3. **Frank.** "I never have any luck with cars. Every car I've ever gotten has been a lemon. Not only have I paid a small fortune for the cars, but just when they are out of warranty, something goes wrong. The car I have now needs a new engine. What's wrong with me? Why should I have all the bad luck?"

   a. You're wondering if it is your fault somehow that every car you own breaks down and has to have costly repairs. All the money you have to pay for car repairs depresses and angers you.

   b. Your anger about the poor quality of the cars you have owned is being turned against yourself and experienced as depression. Aren't the companies that made the cars to blame?

   c. What kind of cars do you buy? How many cars have you owned?

d. Everyone has bad luck sometimes. I'm sure the next car you own will be more reliable. It's really not your fault the cars have turned out to be lemons. No one can tell how much repair a car will need when he first buys it.

e. You're always buying foreign cars. What you need is an American car that has a good warranty.

4. **Edythe.** "My older brothers pick on me constantly. They are always telling me what to do. I get pretty tired of their always harping at me to stand up straight or checking out my dates before I go out. What's worse, they tell things about me that are embarrassing. I've complained to my mother, and she tells them to stop, but they just keep on."

a. How often do you have serious talks with your brothers? Have you tried telling them how you feel?

b. You feel angry at your brothers because they pick on you, tell you what to do, are inconsiderate of your feelings, and want to pass judgment on your choice of dates, is that it? And you also feel helpless to change the situation, don't you?

c. I think you ought to be more understanding of your brothers. After all, they would not do it if they did not care about you.

d. Relax. Older brothers often act like that for a while. It's traditional. Once they see you have grown up, they will get off your back.

e. You resent being treated like a child. Part of establishing your independence as a person is feeling angry at people who don't treat you like an adult.

5. **Helen.** "When I was younger, I used to fight my parents because I wanted to get married. Now I'm married and I keep thinking of how good it was to be single and have no responsibilities to tie me down. I can't go anywhere without a bunch of kids clinging to me. It's rough, and there's nothing I can do about it."

a. I understand how you feel. I often feel that way too. But before long your children will grow up and then you will have all the freedom you want.

b. Let's explore how you arrange your time. How often do you wish to go somewhere without your children? How often do you hire babysitters?

c. You feel resentful and trapped because being married and having children don't allow you the freedom to go places and do things when you want to.

d. You say you fought your parents to get married. Now you feel resentful about the loss of freedom. Could it be that you are really angry at your parents for not stopping you from getting married in the first place?

e. Sounds to me as if you are stuck. You will just have to put up with the situation until your children are grown.

6. **Keith.** "I'm really depressed. I have a good job and I make an adequate salary, but I'm not happy. I guess working is not all it is cracked up to be. I have some money saved. I did not do too well in school before, but maybe I will quit work and go back to school. I don't know what I should do."

   a. How long have you felt this way? Have the feelings just started recently, or have you always felt depressed about what you were doing?

   b. In other words, you're depressed and puzzled because your job isn't fulfilling, but school wasn't either, and they are the only two alternatives you see yourself as having.

   c. Depression is often anger turned against oneself. Perhaps you're angry at yourself for not feeling fulfilled by what you are doing.

   d. If you didn't do so well in school before, you probably won't do any better now. You should be satisfied with having a good job; many people don't, you know.

   e. Lots of people have trouble making up their minds. There are a lot of people who don't like their jobs and who really don't want to go back to school. You don't need to feel depressed.

7. **Dale.** "I wish I could find a way to finish college without going to classes. I register each quarter, intending to go, but I get sidetracked and end up dropping out. I've been enrolled for 6 years. My parents would kill me if they knew how many credits I need to graduate!"

   a. It sounds as if you're just wasting time and money. You should probably just stop trying to go to school and get a good job instead.

   b. You feel guilty because you keep letting your parents think you are trying to finish college when in fact you are doing other things. It bothers you not to meet their expectations.

   c. Possibly if you tell me a little more about how you get sidetracked and what it is that you do while being sidetracked, we can get a clearer idea about what is involved.

   d. Many people have trouble finishing college. It's not unusual. Maybe you should quit. Your parents will understand if you explain things to them.

   e. Let's see if I understand you correctly. You're upset because you can't seem to finish college even though your parents really want you to, and you're worried about how they would react if you quit going to school. Right?

8. **David.** "All this work is driving me crazy! It seems as if I spend every waking moment working. I don't have any time to relax with my friends and family. No matter how hard I work I never seem to get caught up. I have so many responsibilities. I don't know how I'm going to get everything done."

   a. Don't feel so bad. I'm sure that if you just keep at it, you'll get things done and have the leisure you need.

b. You're obviously trying to do too much. What you need to do is cut down on your commitments so you'll have more free time.

c. You feel frustrated and angry that your work doesn't get finished and you can't enjoy your family and friends more; you work hard, but your responsibilities always seem to increase faster than your ability to meet them.

d. Can you tell me more about the specific nature of your responsibilities, the way you schedule your time, and how you acquire new responsibilities?

e. How you spend your time probably reflects your true values. Perhaps you prefer your work over your family and friends. Could it be that you consider your work more important than enjoying life?

9. **Roger.** "I never seem to get anywhere on time, I don't know why. People bug me about it, and sometimes they get pretty angry. I try to keep a schedule, but it never seems to work out. I have an important golf game coming up and I'm afraid I'm going to be late for it. I don't know what to do to change."

a. In other words, you feel frustrated with yourself because you always seem to be late and somewhat worried about the way other people react to your lateness.

b. I'm wondering if you have investigated ways of managing your schedule more effectively. How often are you late? Are there some things you are always late for and other things you are never late for?

c. You are obviously not very organized, and of course people will be angry when you treat them with such inconsiderateness. Perhaps you should ask someone more punctual to pick you up when you have an important engagement.

d. I really wouldn't worry. Being late is not so bad. I'm sure that no one is really angry about such a little thing as arriving late.

e. Being late is sometimes caused by passive-aggressiveness, where you want to punish other people but also are afraid to take responsibility for your actions.

10. **Frank.** "I just never seem to have any money. I have a good-paying job, but it seems as soon as I get my paycheck, it's gone. Then I have to scrimp and save the rest of the month. Now my car needs a new engine, and I don't know where I'm going to get the money to pay for it."

a. Tell me more about how you manage your money. Have you tried budgeting? What are your major expenses?

b. You're feeling depressed on account of your chronic lack of money and your uncertainty over how you are going to pay for your needed car repairs.

c. You may be wasting money on nonessentials. I think if you tried keeping a budget, you would be able to manage much better.

d. I'm sure the money for your new car engine will turn up. Don't worry. You have always managed in the past.

e. Depression such as you are experiencing often comes from a feeling of being helpless to solve your problems. Once you feel that you have some control over your financial problems, you'll feel better.

11. **Edythe.** "I just hate to bring my dates home to meet my family. I don't mind my boyfriends meeting my parents, but I wish there was some way to keep my older brothers out of the act. The way they give my dates the third degree scares them away. It's embarrassing."

a. Embarrassment is often caused by older siblings, especially when they view you as a little girl. We have to plan to get them to see you as an adult and start treating you as one.

b. It sounds as if they are pretty inconsiderate. Most people have siblings who embarrass them at some point, but your brothers sound as if they are really out of line.

c. Just wait. I bet that soon you will meet someone who won't be scared off by your brothers.

d. You feel angry about the way your brothers embarrass you by questioning your boyfriends, and you want to avoid such situations while at the same time allowing your parents to meet your dates.

e. Just what do your brothers do to your dates? What specific questions do they ask?

12. **Frances.** "I don't know about my children. David works too hard, Roger plays too much, Frank is always broke, Edythe married someone none of us have met, Helen got married too early, Keith quit school to work and now wants to quit work to go to school, and Dale isn't close to graduating after 6 years of college. You do your best and look how they turn out! It's enough to make a person give up."

a. You are worried about your children and yet feel helpless to change them. Each child seems to have some problem, and you are unsure how well their lives will turn out.

b. Can you explain further how you feel about your children?

c. Don't worry. I'm sure they will turn out all right. All parents must worry about their children some time or another.

d. Tell your children to straighten out. Either they listen to their mother, or else they aren't worth talking to.

e. You have certain expectations for each of your children, and they aren't living up to what you expect. These expectations are upsetting you.

Intentions Underlying the Responses

When other people want to discuss a problem or concern of theirs with you, there are at least five ways in which you can listen and respond:

1. Advising and evaluating
2. Analyzing and interpreting
3. Reassuring and supporting
4. Questioning and probing
5. Paraphrasing and understanding

Each of these alternative ways of responding communicates certain intentions. All of them, at one time or another, will be helpful. None of the responses can be labeled as good or bad, effective or ineffective. All have their place in helping other people solve their problems and gain insight into their difficulties. But some of the responses are more helpful than others in building friendships and helping people explore further their feelings and thoughts. In exploring the intentions underlying the responses in the preceding questionnaire, the person with the problem will be called the sender and the person giving the response will be the receiver.

Advising and Evaluating (E)

Giving advice and making a judgment as to the relative goodness, appropriateness, effectiveness, and rightness of what the sender is thinking and doing are among the most common responses we make when trying to help others. These responses communicate an evaluative, corrective, sug-

gestive, or moralizing attitude or intent. The receiver implies what the sender *ought* to do or *might* do to solve the problem. When advice is timely and relevant, it can be helpful to another person. Most often, however, when you give advice and evaluation you build barriers that keep you from being helpful and developing a deeper friendship.

For one thing, being evaluative and giving advice can be threatening to other people and make them defensive. When people become defensive they may closed-mindedly reject your advice, resist your influence, stop exploring the problem, and be indecisive. Why? Because giving advice and passing judgment often communicate that the receiver is assuming that her judgment is superior to that of the sender. When a person has a problem, she does not want to be made to feel inferior. For another thing, being evaluative often seems to be a way of avoiding involvement with another person's concerns and conflicts. While it is quick, fast, and easy, it also allows the receiver to generalize about the sender's problems, and this response communicates that the receiver does not care to take the time to understand the sender's problems fully. In addition, advice can encourage people not to take responsibility for their own problems. Even when praise is used to influence others, it can communicate that the sender must meet certain expectations before she is of value. Finally, advice and evaluation often tell more about the giver's values, needs, and perspectives than about the receiver's problems. Thus, if you wish to be helpful and further a relationship, you should usually avoid such phrases as "If I were you . . . ," "One good way is . . . ," "Why don't you . . . ?" "You should . . . ," "You ought to . . . ," "The thing to do is . . . ," and "Don't you think . . . ?"

It is important to avoid giving advice and evaluation in the early stages of helping other people understand and solve their problems and difficulties. There is a place for advising and evaluating, but there are other responses that are usually more helpful.

Analyzing and Interpreting (I)

When analyzing or interpreting the sender's problems and difficulties, the receiver's intentions are to teach, to tell the sender what his or her problem means, to inform the sender how the sender really feels about the situation, or to impart some psychological knowledge to the sender. In interpreting the sender's problems, the receiver implies what the sender might or ought to think. Analyzing or interpreting attempts to point out some deep hidden reason that makes the sender do the things he or she does. It attempts to give the person some additional insight through an explanation. Through such statements as, "Ah, ha! Now I know what your problem is," or, "The reason you are upset is . . . ," the receiver tries to teach the sender the meaning of the sender's behavior and feelings.

This suggestion will often make the sender defensive and will discourage him from revealing more thoughts and feelings for fear that these will also be interpreted or analyzed. Most of us react negatively when someone else implies that he knows more about us than we do. When the receiver tries to analyze or interpret the sender's behavior, thoughts, and feelings, the receiver may communicate "I know more about you than you know yourself." People will usually respond better when you help them think about themselves and their feelings than if you try to figure out what causes them to do the things they do. It also frees you from being an expert on human behavior.

Reassuring and Supporting (S)

Supportive and reassuring responses indicate that the receiver wants to reassure, be sympathetic, or reduce the intensity of the sender's feelings. When the receiver rushes in with support and reassurance, this response often denies the sender's feelings. Statements such as "It's always darkest just before the dawn," and "Things will be better tomorrow" frequently end up communicating a lack of interest or understanding. Supportive statements are, however, frequently used by people trying to help a friend, student, or child. It's distressing to see a friend depressed, so all too often a person will communicate, "Don't be depressed," rather than listening carefully and helping to clarify the causes and potential solutions for the depression. While there are times when other people need to be

reassured as to their value and worth or supported in their reactions and feelings, reassurance and support are often ways of saying, "You should not feel as you do."

Questioning and Probing (P)

Probing by asking questions indicates that the receiver wants to get further information, guide the discussion along certain lines, or bring the sender to a certain realization or conclusion the receiver has in mind. In asking a question, the receiver implies that the sender ought to or might profitably develop or discuss a point further. Questioning is, however, an important skill in being helpful to people who wish to discuss their problems and concerns with you. In using questions skillfully, it is necessary to understand the difference between an open and closed question and the pitfalls of the "why" question. An *open question* encourages other people to answer at greater length and in more detail. The *closed question* usually asks for only a simple yes or no answer. An example of an open question is "How do you feel about your job?" while an example of a

closed question is "Do you like your job?" Because open questions encourage other people to share more personal feelings and thoughts, they are usually more helpful.

When you intend to deepen a relationship or help other people understand and solve their problems, it is usually recommended that you avoid why questions. To encourage people to give a rational explanation for their behavior may not be productive because most people do not fully know the reasons they do the things they do. Being asked why can make people defensive and encourages them to justify rather than explore their actions. Why questions are also often used to indicate disapproval or to give advice. For example, the question, "Why did you yell at the teacher?" may imply the statement, "I don't think you should have yelled at the teacher." Because criticism and advice tend to be threatening, people may feel less free to examine the reasons that led them to a particular action or decision. Instead of asking people to explain or justify their actions through answering why, it may be more helpful to ask what, where, when, how, and who questions. These questions help other people to be more specific, precise, and revealing. For a more complete discussion of question asking, see Johnson (1979).

Asking questions skillfully is an essential part of giving help to other people who are discussing their problems and concerns with you. But questions, while they communicate that you are interested in helping, do not necessarily communicate that you understand. It may sometimes be more effective to change questions into reflective statements that encourage the person to keep talking. An example is changing a question, such as "Do you like swimming?" to a reflective statement, such as "You really like swimming." Reflective statements, which are discussed in the next subsection, focus on clarifying and summarizing without interrupting the flow of communication because they don't call for an answer.

Paraphrasing and Understanding (U)

An understanding and reflecting response indicates that your intent is to understand the sender's thoughts and feelings. In effect, this response asks the sender whether you, the receiver, have understood what the sender is saying and how she is feeling. This is the same as the paraphrasing response discussed in Chapter 4. There are three situations in which you will want to use the understanding response. The first is when you are not sure you have understood the sender's thoughts and feelings. Paraphrasing can begin a clarifying and summarizing process that increases the accuracy of understanding. The second is when you wish to ensure that the sender hears what he has just said. This reflection of thoughts and feelings often gives the sender a clearer understanding of himself and of the implications of his present feelings and thinking. Finally, paraphrasing reassures the sender that you are trying to understand his thoughts and feelings.

In order to be truly understanding, you may have to go beyond the words of the sender to the feelings and underlying meanings that accompany the words. It is the true meaning of the statement and the sender's feelings that you paraphrase.

After you have finished the procedure for scoring both answer sheets, record the frequency with which each member of the group used each type of response. This can be done by taking one member of the group, asking her how many times she used the evaluating response, placing a tally mark in the appropriate box, then asking the member how many times she used the interpreting response, and so forth. When the recording is completed, you will have a tally mark for each group member under each type of response. Then, as a group, discuss the results summarized in Table 7.1. The following questions may be helpful.

1. What are the most frequently used responses by the members of the group?
2. How frequently did each member use each of the responses?
3. How does a person trying to explain a problem to you react when you use each type of response?
4. When is each type of response most useful in helping other people with their problems and concerns and in building a relationship with them?
5. What responses tell the most about the receiver?

TABLE 7.1   *Frequency with Which the Group Members Used Each Type of Response*

Frequency	Evaluating	Interpreting	Supporting	Probing	Understanding	Total
0–2						
3–5						
6–8						
9–12						
Total	6	6	6	6	6	

EXERCISE 7.2

Practicing the Five Responses

This exercise provides you with a chance to practice each of the five types of responses. The exercise consists of two parts, one in which you are given a problem statement and you write down what you would say (assuming you wanted to respond with each of the five types of intentions), and one in which you and another person make statements and practice with each other giving the different types of responses.

Part 1

Read the following paragraphs and write a response for each category. Do this by yourself.

"Sometimes I get so depressed I can hardly stand it. Here I am, thirty-four years old and still not married. It's not as if I haven't had any chances, but I've never really wanted to marry any of the guys I've dated. All my friends are married; I can't understand why I'm not. Is there something wrong with me?"

>   Evaluative response
>   Interpretative response
>   Supportive response
>   Probing response
>   Understanding response

"I'm really concerned about a friend of mine named Jane. She never seems to take life seriously enough. She's dropped out of school, she gets a job, and then she quits after a week. She is using drugs, and I'm really worried that she's ruining her life. I don't know what I should do."

>   Evaluative response
>   Interpretative response
>   Supportive response
>   Probing response
>   Understanding response

"I need your advice about my relationship with June. She wants us to get very serious. But I don't even know if I like her. We spend a lot of time together, I have fun when I'm around her, but she's all the time pushing me not to date other women and to see her more often than I now do. I don't like to be pushed; but I don't want to hurt her by not dating her anymore. What would you do?"

> Evaluative response
> Interpretative response
> Supportive response
> Probing response
> Understanding response

Part 2

1. Divide into pairs. Discuss each other's answers, and make suggestions as to how they might be improved.

2. Think of a problem you now are having either at your job or in school. It may be a major problem, or it may be a minor one. Each person in the pair tells the other his problems. The receiver then gives an evaluative response, an interpretative response, a supportive response, a probing response, and then an understanding response.

3. Think of a problem you are having with your family. It may be either a minor or a major problem. Each person in the pair tells the other his problem. The receiver gives each of the five responses.

4. Think of a problem, either a major or a minor one, you are having with a friend. Each person in the pair tells the other his problem. The receiver gives each of the five responses.

5. In your pair, give each other the feedback concerning how well each of you can respond in the five ways discussed in this chapter. You may wish to continue practicing the different responses until you have mastered them to your satisfaction. This goal can be achieved by consciously applying them to your everyday conversations or by pairing up a member of your group and setting specific practice times for the two of you to increase your response skills.

■ COMPREHENSION TEST A

Test your understanding of responding to people's problems by answering true or false to the following statements. Answers are at the end of the chapter.

True False 1. If you try hard enough, you can solve other people's problems for them.

True False 2. The effectiveness of your help depends partly on your intentions and attitudes as you listen and give your response.

True   False   3. The phrasing of your response influences the effectiveness of your help.

True   False   4. Your intentions are of minor importance in helping people solve their problems.

True   False   5. A helpful response helps other people explore a problem, clarify feelings, gain insight, or make a difficult decision.

True   False   6. Giving advice is helpful to the sender's problems.

True   False   7. Telling the sender the underlying meaning of her feelings will bring a grateful response.

True   False   8. It's helpful to try and cheer up someone who's depressed.

True   False   9. Asking why questions will help the sender see the problem more clearly.

True   False   10. "You really hate your job" is a good example of a reflective statement.

Helping People Solve Their Problems

There are many times when a friend or acquaintance will wish to discuss a problem or concern with you. People do not often get very far in understanding their experiences and deciding how to solve their problems unless they talk things over with someone else. There is nothing more helpful than discussing a problem with a friend who is an effective listener. The first rule in helping other people solve their problems and understand distressing situations is to remember that all insights, understandings, decisions, and solutions occur within the other people, not within you. No matter how convinced you are that you know what the other people should do, your goal in helping must be to assist them in reaching their own decisions and forming their own insights.

The second rule in helping others solve their problems is to differentiate between an internal frame of reference (how the other person sees and feels about the situation) and an external frame of reference (how you see and feel about the other person's situation). You are able to give help to the extent that you understand and respond to the sender's frame of reference rather than imposing your frame of reference on the problem situation. It is not what makes you angry that is important, it is what makes the other person angry. It is not how you see things that matters, it is how the other person sees things. Your ability to be helpful to another person is related directly to your ability to view the situation from the other person's perspective.

Listening and responding in ways that help you understand the other person's perspective or frame of reference is always a tentative process. Many times the other person will not fully understand or be able to communicate effectively her perspective. While you are clarifying your own understanding of the other person's perspective, you will also be helping the other person understand herself better.

Listening and Responding Alternatives

The exercise on listening and responding alternatives is based on the work of Carl Rogers, a noted psychologist. He conducted a series of studies on how individuals communicate with each other in face-to-face situations (Rogers, 1965; Rogers & Roethlisberger, 1952). He found that the categories of evaluative, interpretative, supportive, probing, and understanding statements encompass 80 percent of all the messages sent between individuals. The other 20 percent of the statements are incidental and of no real importance. From his observations of individuals in all sorts of different settings—businesspeople, homemakers, people at parties and conventions, and so on—he found that the responses were used by individuals in the following frequency: (1) evaluative was most used, (2) interpretative was next, (3) supportive was the third most common response, (4) probing the fourth, and (5) understanding the least. Finally, he found that if a person uses one category of response as much as 40 percent of the time, then other people see him as *always* responding that way. This is a process of oversimplification similar to stereotyping.

The categories of response are in themselves neither good nor bad. It is the overuse or underuse of any of the categories that may not be functional or the failure to recognize when each type of response is appropriate that interferes with helping the sender and building a better friendship. If, in answering the response alternatives questionnaire, you use only one or two of the responses, it may be that you overuse some types of responses while you underuse others. You can easily remedy that imbalance by becoming more aware of your responses and working to become proficient in using all five types of responses when they seem appropriate.

When is each response appropriate? From your own experience and from listening to the discussion of your group, you may have some good ideas. In terms of what is appropriate in the early stage of forming a friendship, two of the possible responses to be most sensitive to are the understanding and the evaluative responses. Basically, the understanding response revolves around the notion that when an individual expresses a message, and that message is paraphrased in fresh words with no change of its essential meaning, the sender will expand upon or further explore the ideas, feelings, and attitudes contained in the message and achieve a recognition of previously denied meanings or feelings or move on to express a new message that is more meaningful to him. Even when the receiver has misunderstood and communicated a faulty understanding of the sender's ideas and feelings, the sender will respond in ways that will clarify the receiver's incorrect response, thus increasing the accuracy and clarity of communication between the two individuals.

It is the understanding response that is most likely to communicate to the sender that the listener is interested in the sender as a person and has an accurate understanding of the sender and of what she is saying, and it is this same response that most encourages the sender to go on and elaborate and further explore her problem. The understanding response may also be the most helpful for enabling the receiver to see the sender's problem from the sender's point of view. Many relationships or conversations are best begun by using the understanding response until a trust level is established; then the other categories of response can be more freely used. The procedures for engaging in the understanding response are rather simple (see Chapter 4), and anyone who takes the time and effort can become quite skillful in their use.

As has been discussed in Chapter 4, the major barrier to mutual understanding is the very natural tendency to judge, evaluate, approve, or disapprove of the messages of the sender. For this reason you should usually avoid giving evaluative responses in the early stages of a relationship or of a conversation about the sender's problems. The primary reaction to a value judgment is another value judgment (for example, "You say I'm wrong, but I think I'm right and you're wrong"), with each person looking at the issue only from his own point of view. This tendency to make evaluations is very much heightened in situations in which feelings and emotions are deeply involved, as when you are discussing a personal problem. Defensiveness and feelings of being threatened are avoided when the listener responds with understanding rather than with evaluative responses. Evaluative responses, however, may be helpful when you are specifically asked to make a value judgment or when you wish to disclose your own values and attitudes.

There will be times when another person tries to discuss an issue with you that you do not understand. *Probing responses* will help you get a clear definition of the problem before you respond. They may also be helpful if you do not think the sender is seeing the full implications of some of her statements. *Supportive responses* are useful when the person needs to feel accepted or when she needs enough support to try to engage in behavior aimed at solving her problem. Finally, *interpretative responses* are sometimes useful in confronting another person with the effect of her behavior on you; this situation will be further discussed in Chapter 8. Interpretation, if carried out with skill, integrity, and empathy, can be a powerful stimulus to growth. Interpretation leads to insight, and insight is a key to better psychological living. Interpretation is one form of confrontation.

■ COMPREHENSION TEST B

Test your understanding of effective listening and responding by answering true or false to the following statements. Answers are at the end of the chapter.

True   False   1. Give advice freely, remembering that the insights and under-standings happen within the receiver, not the sender.

True   False   2. There is a difference between how you see the situation and how the sender sees it.

True   False   3. Clarifying your understanding of the other person's perspec-tive will help the other person to understand herself better.

True   False   4. Ninety percent of all messages between two people are evalu-ative, interpretative, supportive, probing, and understanding.

True   False   5. The frequency of the responses from most-used to least-used is in this order: evaluative, interpretative, supportive, probing, and understanding.

True   False   6. If a person uses one category of response as much as 40 per-cent of the time, the person is seen as always responding that way.

True   False   7. Giving evaluative responses early is a barrier to mutual under-standing.

True   False   8. The understanding response best helps the receiver see the sender's point of view and encourages further communica-tion.

True   False   9. Probing responses help the receiver understand what the problem is.

True   False   10.. Interpretation is a form of confrontation.

Phrasing an Accurate Understanding Response

The second important aspect of listening with understanding is the phras-ing you use to paraphrase the message of the sender. The phrasing of the response may vary in the following ways:

1. **Content.** Content refers to the actual words used. Interestingly enough, responses that are essentially repetitions of the sender's statements do not communicate the receiver's understanding to the sender. It seems that repeating a person's words actually gets in the way of communicating an understanding of the essential meaning of the statement. It is more effective if the receiver para-phrases the sender's message in the receiver's own words and expressions.

2. **Depth.** Depth refers to the degree to which the receiver matches the depth of the sender's message in her response. You should not respond lightly to a serious statement, and correspondingly, you should not respond seriously to a shallow statement. In general, responses that match the sender's depth of feeling or that lead the sender on to a slightly greater depth of feeling are most effective.

3. **Meaning.** In the receiver's efforts to paraphrase the sender's statements, he may find himself either adding meaning or omitting meaning. Some of the obvious ways in which meaning can be added are (1) completing a sentence or thought for the sender, (2) responding to ideas the sender has used for illustrative purposes only, and (3) interpreting the significance of a message. Perhaps the most obvious way meaning can be omitted is by responding only to the last thing the sender said.

4. **Language.** The receiver should keep the language she uses in her response simple in order to ensure accurate communication.

EXERCISE 7.3

Phrasing an Accurate Understanding Response

This exercise provides you with an opportunity to classify responses according to their wording. The procedure for the exercise is as follows:

1. Each person should answer the questionnaire on the wording of an understanding response. The specific instructions are given on Answer Sheet A.

2. Study the categories of the understanding response given on page 239. Then categorize the responses for each item in the questionnaire as to the type of understanding response it represents. The specific instructions are given on Answer Sheet B.

3. Using the Scoring Key in the Appendix, score Answer Sheet B. Indicate in the appropriate space on the answer sheet the number of times you used each type of wording.

4. Form groups of three and score Answer Sheet B, discussing each type of wording until everyone in the triad understands it.

5. Combine two triads into a group of six. On Table 7.2 (p. 240), mark the frequency with which each member of the group used each type of wording.

6. Use the questions on page 240 to discuss the results summarized in Table 7.2.

Answer Sheet A: Identifying Personal Responses

Read the nine statements in the questionnaire and mark on this answer sheet the response that best represents what you would personally say to the speaker if you were trying to form a close personal relationship with him and help him solve his problems.

1. a : b : c : d
2. a : b : c : d
3. a : b : c : d
4. a : b : c : d
5. a : b : c : d

6. a : b : c : d
7. a : b : c : d
8. a : b : c : d
9. a : b : c : d

Response	Frequency
A	_____
S	_____
P	_____
I	_____

Answer Sheet B: Identifying the Phrasing of Understanding Responses

Study page 239 on which the four different phrasings of understanding responses are discussed. Then read each of the nine statements in the questionnaire and identify the category of each understanding response by: I = identical content, P = paraphrasing content, S = shallow or partial meaning, and A = additional meaning.

Item	a	b	c	d
1.				
2.				
3.				
4.				
5.				
6.				
7.				
8.				
9.				

Questionnaire on Accurate Understanding

In this exercise there are nine consecutive statements made by a young man who has sought help from a friend because of some things that have gone wrong in his life. Each statement is followed by four possible responses. In considering each alternative response, read it as a tentative, questioning statement that asks, "Do I understand you correctly; is this what you mean?" See Answer Sheets A and B for specific instructions on what to do with these statements.

1. "Boy, am I ever discouraged! Everything is going wrong in my life. It seems that everything I do is doomed to failure. I might as well not even try."
   a. You feel discouraged and ready to give up because of failure.
   b. Your whole life is a mess, and you feel suicidal.
   c. You are feeling discouraged because things aren't working out for you, is that right?
   d. You are feeling a little unhappy right now.

2. "For instance, yesterday at work I messed up my job, and the boss made me stay until I got it right. She was really mad at me. I felt awful."
   a. Your boss was in a bad mood.
   b. You messed up at work, and the boss made you stay late, and you felt awful.
   c. You were depressed because your boss was angry at you and saw you as not doing your job correctly.
   d. You're going to get fired because you can't do your job correctly.

3. "Because I had to stay late at work, I was late for my most important class. We had an exam, and I know I flunked it. I didn't even have time to finish the test. And I have to pass this class to graduate!"
   a. You are flunking out of school because you messed up at work.
   b. You think you did badly on a test.
   c. Staying late at work made you late for an important exam, which you didn't finish.
   d. You are worried about whether you will graduate after having done badly on an important exam in a required class.

4. "Then I went over to my girlfriend's house, and she was out on a date with someone else. That really tore me up! I started crying. I couldn't help it."
   a. You became even more depressed because when you needed someone to give you support and sympathy, your girlfriend was gone on a date with another man.
   b. You have really given up, haven't you?
   c. You are feeling discouraged.

   d. Your girlfriend was out on a date with someone else, and you cried about it.

5. "At this point I don't know whether to jump off a bridge or throw myself under a train. (Pause) What do you think?"
   a. You want me to tell you whether to jump off a bridge or get run over by a train, right?
   b. There doesn't seem to be any way out.
   c. You have decided to take revenge on the world by killing yourself, is that it?
   d. You want my advice.

6. "You know, I thought Carol really liked me. I can't believe she would be so dirty as to go out behind my back. Well, women are rotten, but I thought Carol was an exception."
   a. You don't have much confidence in women, but you thought Carol was different, and now you feel let down.
   b. You thought Carol was different from other women.
   c. Now you have proven that all women are rotten.
   d. You thought Carol really liked you until she went out behind your back.

7. "I really liked my job, too. The people are great to be around, and the boss is usually easygoing. (Pause) I guess I'm the rotten apple in the barrel. It can't be fun to work with someone as incompetent as I am. I guess if I don't quit, I will get fired."
   a. You don't think you will ever be able to do any job well.
   b. You feel discouraged because you don't think you are doing very well at your job, even though you like it. You are afraid your co-workers don't like you even though you like them.
   c. You like your job and the people you work with, but you feel you are incompetent and will get fired.
   d. You're going to quit your job.

8. "My parents are really going to be happy when they find out I flunked out of school. They always told me I was aiming too high and couldn't do it. They have never had any confidence in me. (Pause) I guess that is why I don't have much confidence in myself."
   a. Your parents' and your own expectations are going to be met by your doing badly in school.
   b. Your parents will be happy about your flunking out of school because they don't have any confidence in you, which is why you don't have confidence in yourself.
   c. You think you are going to flunk out of school.
   d. Your parents really hate you, don't they?

9. "If I could just get over this slump, maybe I could make it. Things have been bad for me before, and somehow I managed to muddle through. If I can just hang on, maybe things will turn out all right."
   a. You are going through a slump, and you have been through slumps before, and maybe things will turn out all right.
   b. You want to get out of this slump.
   c. You are confident about the future.
   d. You feel some hope that if you just stay with it, things will work out for you, as they have in the past.

Types of Phrasing of an Understanding Response

After you have completed Answer Sheet A, study and discuss the following categories of the understanding response. Do not proceed until you are sure you understand each of the categories.

In the beginning of this section we discussed four aspects of an understanding response: content, depth, meaning, and language. The questionnaire in Exercise 7.3 focuses on two of these dimensions—content (either identical or paraphrased) and meaning (either partial or additional). In this questionnaire, all of the alternatives following the statements are so phrased as to appear to be attempts to communicate an understanding intent. For each statement, however, the alternatives differ in the following ways:

Identical content (I): a response in which the attempt at understanding is implemented in large part by simply repeating the same words used by the sender

Paraphrasing content (P): a response in which the attempt at understanding is implemented by rephrasing in fresh words the gist of the sender's expression without changing either the meaning or the feeling tone

Shallow or partial meaning (S): a response in which the attempt at understanding is implemented in a limited way by bringing in only a part of what the sender expressed or by undercutting or watering down the feeling tone expressed

Additional meaning (A): a response in which the attempt at understanding actually goes beyond the meaning of the sender and adds meaning not expressed by the sender.

After you have finished the procedure for scoring both answer sheets, mark the frequency with which each member of the group used each type of phrasing. In the group, discuss the results summarized in Table 7.2 and

TABLE 7.2 *Frequency with Which the Group Members Used Each Type of Response*

Frequency of Response	Type of Responses			
	I	*P*	*S*	*A*
0–1	_____	_____	_____	_____
2–3	_____	_____	_____	_____
4–5	_____	_____	_____	_____
6–7	_____	_____	_____	_____
8–9	_____	_____	_____	_____

the consequences of using each type of phrasing. The following questions may be helpful:

1. What type of phrasing was most commonly used by the members of the group?
2. What would be my feelings if a person used each type of phrasing in discussing my problems and concerns?
3. How may I develop my skills in paraphrasing to ensure the most effective phrasing of my response?

 EXERCISE 7.4

Practicing the Phrasing of an Understanding Response

This exercise provides you with practice in the phrasing of an understanding response. The exercise has two parts: one in which you are given a problem statement and you write down what you would say, and one in which you and another person make statements and practice with each other giving an appropriately phrased understanding response.

1. Read the following paragraphs and write an understanding response for each one. Do this assignment by yourself. Be sure your response matches the paragraph in content, depth, language, and meaning.

a. "I'm really upset! That stupid professor gave me a C on my research paper! I worked on it for 6 weeks, and it was twice as long as the paper Joe turned in, yet he got an A. That paper represented a lot of learning on my part. And he had the nerve to give me a C! What does he want anyway? Or is it that I'm just dumb?"

b. "I need your help. There's a new woman who just moved in next door to you that I think I know. She may be a woman I dated several years ago; but I'm not sure, since I haven't been able to get a close look at her. If she is the same woman I want to meet her; if she isn't the same woman, I don't want to meet her. Can you find out her name, telephone number, and where she grew up?"

2. Divide into pairs. Discuss each other's responses and make suggestions as to how they might be improved.

3. Think of a problem you are having with a friend or a member of your family. It may be a major problem or a minor problem. Each person in the pair should share her problem; the receiver gives an understanding response that is appropriate in content, depth, language, and meaning.

4. In the pairs, give each other feedback concerning the appropriateness of the content, depth, language, and meaning of the understanding responses. You may wish to continue practicing the phrasing of the understanding response until you have mastered it to your satisfaction. This can be done by consciously applying it in your everyday conversations or by pairing up with a member of your group and setting specific practice times for the two of you to increase your skills.

 EXERCISE 7.5
Expressing Acceptance Verbally

The purpose of this exercise is to give you an opportunity to practice communicating acceptance to another person. The skills involved in expressing acceptance are listening with understanding and expressing warmth. In this exercise you will conduct a discussion in which you practice listening with understanding and the expression of warmth. The procedure is as follows:

1. Divide into trios. Two people will engage in a discussion; one person will observe. The role of the discussants is to express acceptance to each other. The role of the observer is to give the two discussants feedback concerning how successfully they communicated acceptance to each other. An Observation Sheet is provided for the observer's use.

2. The two discussants spend 10 minutes discussing how their current close friendships were initiated and developed. Or they may discuss any topic that is of real interest to the two of them; do not spend more than 1 minute, however, on the selection of a topic to discuss. During the discussion the two participants should be practicing both listening and understanding and expressing warmth. To listen with understanding is to paraphrase the other person's expressed feelings and ideas in your own words without any indication of approval or disapproval; this technique involves listening for meaning as well as listening to the other's words. To express warmth is to describe your feelings and to use the nonverbal cues of facial expression, tone of voice, posture, and so on in your discussion with your partner.

Observation Sheet: Expressing Acceptance

Listening with understanding	Person 1	Person 2
Paraphrased other's feelings and ideas in own words	_____	_____
Did not indicate approval or disapproval	_____	_____
Depth of response was appropriate	_____	_____
Did not add or subtract meaning	_____	_____
Did not change the feeling tone	_____	_____
Negotiated for meaning	_____	_____
Language was understandable and appropriate	_____	_____
Did a perception check for other's feelings	_____	_____

Expressing warmth	Person 1	Person 2
Direct description of own feelings	_____	_____
Tone of voice	_____	_____
Facial expression	_____	_____
Posture	_____	_____
Eye contact	_____	_____
Touching	_____	_____
Gestures	_____	_____
Spatial distance	_____	_____
Congruence between verbal and nonverbal expressions of feelings	_____	_____

3. At the end of the 10-minute discussion, the observer and the two discussants give the two discussants feedback about how well they expressed acceptance to each other. Be specific.

4. Next, the trio switches roles so that one of the former discussants is now the observer, and the other two members conduct a discussion. Follow the instructions given in step 2. This time discuss what your greatest fears and hopes are about initiating friendships.

5. Conduct a feedback session according to the instructions given in step 3.

6. Switch roles once more and conduct a discussion on why you need friends. Follow the instructions given in steps 2 and 3.

 EXERCISE 7.6
Level of Acceptance in Your Group

What is the level of acceptance in your group? You may wish to get everyone's opinion by completing the following questionnaire and summarizing the results. The purpose of this exercise is to provide a way in which the level of acceptance in your group may be assessed and discussed. Here is the procedure:

1. Each member of the group fills out the following questionnaire. Questionnaires should be unsigned so that no one's responses can be identified.

2. The results are tabulated in the Summary Table that follows the questionnaire.

3. Discuss the conclusions that can be drawn from the results.

4. What is contributing to the present high or low level of acceptance in the group?

5. How may the level of acceptance in the group be increased?

Questionnaire: Level of Acceptance

Think about the ways in which the members of your group normally behave toward you. Using the following scale, place the number corresponding to your perceptions of the group as a whole in the parentheses in front of the items.

5 = They *always* behave this way.
4 = They *typically* behave this way.
3 = They *usually* behave this way.
2 = They *seldom* behave this way.
1 = They *rarely* behave this way.
0 = They *never* behave this way.

My fellow group members

1. (_____) are completely honest with me.

2.   (_____) understand what I am trying to communicate.

3.*   (_____) interrupt and ignore my comments.

4.   (_____) accept me just the way I am.

5. (_____) tell me when I bother them.

6.*   (_____) don't understand things I say or do.

7.   (_____) are interested in me.

8.   (_____) make it easy for me to be myself.

9.*(_____) don't tell me things that would hurt my feelings.

10.   (_____) understand who I really am.

11.   (_____) include me in what they are doing.

12.*   (_____) evaluate whether I am acceptable or unacceptable.

13. (_____) are completely open with me.

14.   (_____) immediately know if something is bothering me.

15.   (_____) value me as a person, apart from my skills or status.

16.   (_____) accept my differences or peculiarities.

Totals:

(_____) Authenticity with me

(_____) Understanding of me

(_____) Valuing of me

(_____) Accepting of me

Add the total number of points in each column. Items with starred (*) numbers are reversed in the scoring—subtract from 5 the rating given to each before adding the totals for each column.

Summary: Level of Acceptance

Score	Authenticity	Understanding	Valuing	Accepting
0–4	_____	_____	_____	_____
5–8	_____	_____	_____	_____
9–12	_____	_____	_____	_____
13–16	_____	_____	_____	_____
17–20	_____	_____	_____	_____

■ CHAPTER REVIEW

Test your understanding of helpful listening and responding by answering true or false to the following statements. Answers are at the end of the chapter.

True   False   1. The aim of a receiver is to help the other person come to her own understanding and solution to her problem.

True   False   2. If your underlying attitude is not one of acceptance and liking, you won't be able to make a helpful response.

True   False   3. The most helpful response to help people explore their feelings and thoughts is the probing response.

True   False   4. "How do you feel about your job?" is an example of a closed question.

True   False   5. "Do you like your teacher?" should be changed to "You like your teacher" to become a reflective statement.

True   False   6. There is no difference between how you see and feel about a situation and how another person sees and feels about it.

True   False   7. Just repeating what the sender says is effective paraphrasing.

True   False   8. When you interpret the significance of a message, you are adding to the meaning of it.

True   False   9. You will communicate more accurately if you use simple language in your responses.

True   False   10. Responses that are slightly lighter in meaning than the sender's message are most effective.

True   False   11. If you paraphrase and express warmth and liking, you will be able to convince other people that you accept them.

True   False   12. If you are to accept another person, you must approve of the things he does.

Self-Diagnosis

This chapter has focused on listening in an appropriate way. On a scale from 1 (poorly mastered) to 5 (highly mastered) rate the degree to which you have mastered each skill. Then choose two skills to improve on in the next week.

Rating	Skill
_____	When appropriate, engage in the evaluative response.
_____	When appropriate, engage in the interpretative response.
_____	When appropriate, engage in the supportive response.
_____	When appropriate, engage in the probing response.
_____	When appropriate, engage in the understanding response.
_____	Match the message in paraphrasing content.
_____	Match the message in depth.
_____	Match the message in meaning.
_____	Match the message in language.
_____	Express acceptance verbally.

Skills I Will Improve in the Next Week

1. _____

2. _____

Summary

In every relationship you decide how to respond when the other person wishes to share a problem or a concern. When someone is talking to you about something deeply distressing or of a real concern to him or her, you need the skills to listen and respond in a helpful way. Your helpfulness depends on your attitude as you listen and the phrasing of your response. When other people are telling you about a problem, you can respond by (a) advising and evaluating, (b) analyzing and interpreting, (c) reassuring and supporting, (d) questioning and probing, and (e) paraphrasing and understanding. Each is appropriate under certain conditions. It is paraphrasing and understanding, however, that is most helpful in most circumstances. You should understand how to make reflective statements and ask open questions. You should also be able to match a message in content, depth, meaning, and language. The next chapter will expand on an important factor in being able to respond helpfully to others: the acceptance of others—and of yourself.

Answers

Comprehension Test A: 1. false; 2. true; 3. true; 4. false; 5. true; 6. false; 7. false; 8. false; 9. false; 10. true.

Comprehension Test B: 1. false; 2. true; 3. true; 4. false; 5. true; 6. true; 7. true; 8. true; 9. true; 10. true.

Chapter Review: 1. true; 2. true; 3. false; 4. false; 5. true; 6. false; 7. false; 8. true; 9. true; 10. false; 11. true; 12. false.

CHAPTER 8

Resolving Interpersonal Conflicts

You Must Negotiate

Not everything that is faced can be changed but nothing can be changed until it is faced.
—James Baldwin

Betsy is frustrated. She is a member of a learning group that includes Meredith, who is the bossiest student in the class. Whenever Betsy tries to contribute to the group's work, Meredith interrupts her and takes over. No one else gets to contribute his or her ideas and conclusions. Betsy wants to be an equal participant in the group but believes that Meredith will not let her. What is she to do?

Storms are a natural and unavoidable aspect of the earth's weather system, ranging in intensity from summer showers to hurricanes. Some are accompanied by gentle rain, others by thunder and lightning. Similarly, interpersonal storms are a natural and unavoidable aspect of life that vary in intensity from mild to severe, like that of Betsy in the example. Interpersonal storms have their origins in relationships among individuals. Especially when individuals work together to achieve shared goals, participate in a division of labor, have complementary roles such as student and teacher, and depend on each other's resources, storms will arise. Two people in a relationship are interdependent. What each does

249

influences what the other does. But at the same time, each person has different perspectives, goals, and needs. The combination of interdependence and differing perspectives makes it impossible for a relationship to be free from conflict.

To understand conflicts of interests, you must first understand what wants, needs, goals, and interests are (Johnson & Johnson, 1995a). There are many things each of us wants. A *want* is a desire for something. Each person basically has a unique set of wants. A *need* is a necessity for survival. Needs are more universal. Every person needs to survive and reproduce (water, food, shelter, sex), belong (loving, sharing, cooperating), have power, have freedom, and have fun (Glasser, 1984). On the basis of our wants and needs we set goals. A *goal* is an ideal state of affairs that we value and are working to achieve. Our goals are related through social interdependence. When we have mutual goals we are in a cooperative relationship; when our goals are opposed we are in a competitive relationship. Our **interests** are the potential benefits to be gained by achieving our goals.

Sometimes your interests and the interests of others are congruent and other times they are in conflict. A **conflict of interests** exists when the actions of one person attempting to reach his or her goals prevent, block, or interfere with the actions of another person attempting to reach his or her goals (Deutsch, 1973). See Table 8.1. Most conflicts of interests involve

1. Use of something (computer, book, clothes, car).
2. Obtaining something (money, clothes, computer games, power).
3. Agreeing on something (what movie to see, where to eat, what to do).

TABLE 8.1 *Understanding Conflicts of Interests*

Concept	Definition
Want	Desire for something
Need	Universal necessity for survival
Goal	Desired ideal state of future affairs
Interests	Potential benefits to be gained by achieving goals
Conflict of interests	The actions taken by person A to achieve goals prevent, block, or interfere with the actions taken by person B to achieve goals
Negotiation	A process by which persons who have shared and opposed interests and want to come to an agreement try to work out a settlement

In many classrooms teachers create a conflict of interests among students by having them compete for grades. Conflicts of interests are common both because they occur naturally and because they are deliberately created.

E X E R C I S E   8 . 1
My Past Conflict Behavior

Think back over the interpersonal conflicts you have been involved in during the past few years. These conflicts may be with friends, parents, brothers and sisters, girlfriends or boyfriends, husbands or wives, teachers or students, or your boss or subordinates. On a sheet of paper list the five major conflicts you can remember from your past and the strategies you used and the feelings you had in resolving them.

E X E R C I S E   8 . 2
Dividing Our Money

Some conflicts begin because there is only so much of something several people want, and no one can have as much as he or she would like. Salaries, promotions, office space, supplies, and even food are often the sources of such conflicts. When there is only so much money and several people have definite plans about how it should be used, not everyone has his or her plans adopted by the whole group. This exercise focuses on such a conflict. It requires three people to divide some money two ways.

1. Divide into groups of three. Each person contributes $1.00 to the group. The $3.00 is placed in the center of the group.

2. The triad decides how to divide the money between *two* members. One member must end up with no money. The majority rules. It is all right for one person to end up with all the money. A clear decision must be reached as to how the money is to be divided between not more than two people. The triad has 10 minutes to make this decision.
   a. No chance procedures are allowed. The group cannot draw straws or flip a coin to decide which two people get what amounts of money.
   b. No side agreements are allowed. The two who get the money cannot agree to buy lunch for the person left out.

3. The purpose of the exercise is to get as much money for yourself as you can. Try to convince the other two members of your triad to give you all the money. If the other two members agree to divide the money between themselves (leaving you out), offer one of them a better deal.

4. The majority rules. Whenever two members make a firm agreement to split the money a certain way, the decision is made. Be sure, however, to give the third person a chance to offer one of the two a better deal.

5. As soon as a decision is made, write your answers to these questions:
    a. What did I do to get the money? What strategies did I try?
    b. How did I feel during and after the negotiations?
    c. What strategies did the other two group members use?
    d. What did I learn about how I manage conflicts?

 EXERCISE 8.3
Nonverbal Conflict

Before you begin these exercises, please review the discussion of nonverbal exercises in Chapter 6. The following nonverbal exercises deal with various aspects of conflicts. They may be helpful in clarifying your feelings about conflict and your strategies of managing conflicts. Do not participate in the exercises if there is any physical reason why you should not (such as a recently broken arm and the like).

1. Pushing and shoving: Lock fingers with another person, with arms extended over your heads. Push against each other, trying to drive the other to the wall.

2. Thumb wrestling: Lock fingers with another person with your thumbs straight up. Tap your thumbs together three times and then try to pin the other's thumb so that the other cannot move it.

3. Slapping hands: A puts her hands out, palms down. B extends his hands, palms up, under A's hands. The object of the exercise is for B to try to slap the hands of A by quickly moving his hands from the bottom to the top. As soon as B makes a move, A tries to pull her hands out of the way before B can slap them.

4. Pushing down to the floor and helping up: In pairs, one person tries to push the other person down to the floor. No wrestling, but the person being pushed may resist if he or she wants to. After the person is pushed down to the floor, the pusher has to help the pushed person up. The person being helped up may still resist if he or she wants to. Reverse roles and repeat.

5. Unwrapping: Members choose partners. A makes him- or herself into a tight ball. B "unwraps" A, either partially or completely. A may struggle against being unwrapped, or may cooperate. Reverse roles and repeat.

EXERCISE 8.4
My Conflict Strategies

Different people learn different ways of managing conflicts. The strategies you use to manage conflicts may be quite different from those used by your friends and acquaintances. This exercise gives you an opportunity to increase your awareness of the conflict strategies you use and how they compare with the strategies used by other people.

1. For groups of six. Make sure you know the other members of your group. Do not join a group of strangers.

2. Working by yourself, complete the questionnaire "What Would I Do in a Conflict?"

3. Working by yourself, read the next section, "Conflict Strategies" (pp. 262–266).

4. Write the names of the other five members of your group on five slips of paper. On each slip of paper write one name and the conflict strategy that most fits the actions of the person named. After all group members are finished, pass out your slips of paper to the persons whose names are on them. Each member should end up with five slips of paper, each containing a description of your conflict strategy as seen by the other group members.

5. Score your questionnaire. Rank the five conflict strategies from the one you use most to the one you use least. This will give you an indication of how you see your own conflict strategy. The second most frequently used strategy represents your backup strategy to be used if your first strategy fails.

6. Each member describes the results of his or her questionnaire to the group. This is the person's view of his or her own conflict strategies. Then the person reads each of the five slips of paper on which are written the views of the group members about his or her conflict strategies. Then the person asks the group members to give specific examples of how they have seen him or her act in conflicts. The rules for constructive feedback should be used. Repeat this procedure for every member of the group.

7. Discuss the strengths and weaknesses of each of the conflict strategies.

What Would I Do in a Conflict?

For each conflict in the following list indicate which of the two alternatives you would most likely do. Circle the *a* or *b* of the statement that is most like what you would do. In some cases, you might not do either *a* or *b*, but please select the action that would be more likely to happen.

1. You and a classmate both want to use the computer at the same time.
   a. I would give up wanting it and give up on the classmate as a friend.
   b. I would try to force the classmate to let me use the computer first.

2. You and a classmate both want the same library book at the same time.
   a. I would give up on wanting it and give up on the classmate as a friend.
   b. I would listen carefully to why my classmate needed the book, and if his reasons were more important than mine, I would let him have it, because a good friend is important.

3. You and a classmate both want to sharpen your pencil at the same time.
   a. I would let the classmate go first and give up on her as a friend.
   b. I would ask for us to solve the problem by one person sharpening both pencils so both of us have to wait an equal amount of time.

4. You and a classmate both want to be first in the lunch line.
   a. I would let the classmate go first and give up on him as a friend.
   b. I would compromise by agreeing to alternate who goes first for an equal number of days.

5. You and a classmate both want the same chair at your favorite table in the library.
   a. I would try to force the classmate to let me have the chair, not caring if she was angry or upset with me.
   b. I would listen carefully to why my classmate wanted the chair, and if her reasons were more important than mine, I would let her have it, because a good friend is important.

6. You and a classmate are working on a group project. Both of you want to draw the illustrations, and neither wants to write the report.
   a. I would try to force the classmate to let me draw the illustrations, not caring if he was angry or upset with me.
   b. I would compromise by agreeing for each of us to draw half of the illustrations and write half of the report.

7. You and a classmate have been playing ball. Neither of you wants to put the equipment away.
   a. I would try to force the classmate to do it, not caring if she was angry or upset with me.
   b. I would ask for us to solve the problem by putting the equipment away together.

8. You and a classmate are making a video. Both of you want to run the camera, and neither wants to narrate.
   a. I would listen carefully to why my classmate wanted to do the filming, and if his reasons were more important than mine, I would let him do it, because a good friend is important.
   b. I would ask the classmate to compromise so that each of us filmed half of the time and each narrated half of the time.

9. You told a classmate a secret, and she told it to several other people.
   a. I would listen carefully to why my classmate told my secret, and if her reasons were more important than mine, I would forgive her, because a good friend is important.
   b. I would try to solve the problem by asking my classmate what happened and by working out an agreement about keeping secrets in the future.
10. You and a classmate both believe you did most of the work on a joint report.
   a. I would compromise by agreeing that we both did half.
   b. I would try to solve the problem by reviewing each aspect of the paper and decide who did how much on that aspect.

Scoring Procedure

Circle the letters below that you circled on each question. Then total the number of letters circled in each column.

Question	Withdrawing	Forcing	Smoothing	Compromising	Negotiating
1.	a	b			
2.	a		b		
3.	a			b	
4.	a				b
5.		a	b		
6.		a		b	
7.		a			b
8.			a	b	
9.			a		b
10.				a	b
Total	_____	_____	_____	_____	_____

EXERCISE 8.5
Confronting the Opposition

To resolve a conflict constructively, you and the other person have to discuss the conflict and negotiate a solution. For such a discussion to begin, one person must confront the other. Not all conflicts, however, can be successfully negotiated, and there may be times when it is advisable not to confront the opposition. The purpose of this exercise is to give you three specific examples of conflicts so that you can decide what you would do to make sure the conflicts are managed constructively. The procedure for the exercise is as follows:

1. Working by yourself, read the first example of a conflict. Then rank the five alternatives from the best (1) to the worst (5) way to resolve the conflict. In deciding what is the best strategy to use, take into account the following:
   a. What are the person's goals?
   b. How important are the goals to the person?
   c. How important is the relationship to the person?
   d. What is the best way to
      (1) improve the ability of the two people to relate to each other?
      (2) make their attitudes toward each other more positive?
      (3) reach an agreement that is satisfying to both people?
      (4) improve their ability to resolve future conflicts with each other?
   e. What is the most realistic thing to do?
2. Repeat this process for the second and third examples of conflicts.
3. Form a group of six members. In your group, rank the five alternative courses of action for the first example from the best (1) to the worst (5). Take into account the points listed in item 1.
4. Working as a group, list the interpersonal skills the person needs to discuss the conflict in a constructive way. You may wish to refer to the list of interpersonal skills summarized on pages 412–416.
5. Repeat this procedure for the second and third examples.
6. Be prepared to report to the other groups the following:
   a. In what order did the group rank the five alternatives for each conflict example?
   b. What reasons does your group have for your ranking?
   c. What interpersonal skills are needed for a constructive discussion of the conflict?

Mr. Smith

You are a salesperson for a tire company. You work under a highly emotional sales manager, with whom you have a formal relationship. He calls you by your first name, but you call him Mr. Smith. When he gets upset, he becomes angry and abusive. He browbeats you and your co-workers, and makes insulting remarks and judgments. These rages occur approximately once a week and last for about an hour. Most of the time, Mr. Smith is distant and inoffensive. He will tolerate no back talk at any time. So far, you and your co-workers have suffered in silence during his outbursts. Jobs are scarce, and you have a spouse and a seven-month-old son to support. But you feel like a doormat and really do not like what Mr. Smith says when he is angry. The situation is making you irritable. Your anger at Mr. Smith is causing you to lose your temper more and more with your co-workers and family. Today he starts in again, and you have had it!

Rank the following five courses of action from 1 to 5. Put a 1 by the course of action that seems most likely to lead to beneficial results, put a 2 by the next most constructive course of action, and so forth. Be realistic!

_____ I try to avoid Mr. Smith. I am silent whenever we are together. I show a lack of interest whenever we speak. I want nothing to do with him for the time being. I try to cool down while I stay away from him. I try never to mention anything that might get him angry.

_____ I lay it on the line. I tell Mr. Smith I am fed up with his abuse. I tell him he is vicious and unfair. I tell him he had better start controlling his feelings and statements because I'm not going to take being insulted by him any more! Whether he likes it or not he has to shape up. I'm going to make him stop or else I'll quit.

_____ I bite my tongue. I keep my feelings to myself. I hope that he will find out how his actions are hurting our department without my telling him. My anger toward him frightens me. So I force it out of my mind. I try to be friendly, and I try to do nice things for him so he won't treat me this way. If I tried to tell him how I feel, he would only be angry and abuse me more.

_____ I try to bargain with him. I tell him that if he stops abusing me I will increase my sales effort. I seek a compromise that will stop his actions. I try to think of what I can do for him that will be worth it to him to change his actions. I tell him that other people get upset with his actions. I try to persuade him to agree to stop abusing me in return for something I can do for him.

_____ I call attention to the conflict between us. I describe how I see his actions. I describe my angry and upset feelings. I try to begin a discussion in which we can look for a way to reduce (1) his rages and (2) my resentment. I try to see things from his viewpoint. I seek a solution that allows him to blow off steam without being abusive to me. I try to figure out what I'm telling myself about his actions that is causing me to feel angry and upset. I ask him how he feels about my giving him feedback.

Ralph Overtrain

You work as a technician repairing computers. You make service calls to the customers of your company. Ralph Overtrain is one of your closest co-workers. He does the same type of work that you do. The two of you are often assigned to work together on large repair projects. You are married and have two children. Ralph is single and often has trouble with his girlfriend. For the past several weeks, he has asked you to do part of his repair work because he feels too depressed and upset to concentrate on his work. You have agreed to such requests. Your wife is sick now, and you want to take some time off to visit her in the hospital. You ask Ralph if he would do part of your repair work so you can slip away and visit your wife. He refuses, saying that he is too busy and that it is your work, so you should do it. He says he sees no reason why he should do work you are getting paid for. You get more and more angry at Ralph. You see his actions as being completely selfish and ungrateful!

Rank the following five courses of action from 1 to 5. Put a 1 by the course of action that seems most likely to lead to beneficial results, put a 2 by the next most constructive course of action, and so forth. Be realistic!

_____ I try to avoid Ralph. I am silent whenever we are together. I show a lack of interest whenever we speak. I want nothing to do with him for the time being. I try to cool down while I stay away from him. I try never to mention anything that might make him angry or remind me of his un-gratefulness.

_____ I lay it on the line. I tell Ralph that I am fed up with his ungratefulness. I tell him he is selfish and a deadbeat. And I tell him he had better start paying back the favors I have done for him because I am not going to help him if he will not help me. Whether he likes it or not, he is going to do part of my work so I can visit my wife. I'm going to make him pay his debts to me.

_____ I bite my tongue. I keep my feelings to myself. I hope he will find out his behavior is wrong without my having to tell him. My anger toward him frightens me. So I force it out of my mind and try to be friendly. I try to do nice things for him so he will be willing to do a favor for me in the future when I need him to. If I tried to tell him how I feel, he would only be angry. Then he would be less likely to do me favors when I need him to in the future.

_____ I try to bargain with him. I tell him that if he does my work this time, I will do part of his work tomorrow. I seek a compromise that will allow me to visit my wife. I try to think of what I can do for him that will be worth it to him to take part of my work today. I tell him that other people don't see him as being reasonable and friendly. I try to per-suade him to agree to take part of my work today in return for some-thing I can do for him.

_____ I call attention to the conflict between us. I describe how I see his ac-tions. I describe my anger and upset feelings. I try to begin a discussion in which we can look for a way to be more cooperative regarding each other's needs and to reduce my anger. I try to see things from his view-point. I seek a solution that allows him to feel he is only doing his work while at the same time allowing me to visit my wife in the hospital. I try to figure out what I'm telling myself about his actions that is causing me to feel angry and upset. I ask him how he feels about my giving him feedback.

Donna Jones

In your upper-grade class this year, you have a student, Donna Jones, who seems to dislike you and everything about school. When you are interacting with her you can feel the resentment. She never seems to do anything overtly, but other students have reported incidences of Donna's making faces behind your back and making rude remarks about you and your assignments outside of class. On the morning of the math test, Donna has just dropped her papers on the floor for the third time and is disrupting the work of the other students. You have had enough, so you approach Donna and tell her to keep her papers on her desk, as she is interrupting the work of other students. As you turn to walk away, you notice grins on the faces of several students in front of you, and out of the corner of your eye you see Donna standing up and mimicking you behind your back.

Rank the five alternatives. Be realistic!

_____ I would ignore Donna and go back to my desk. I would arrange a way to seat her away from most of the other students and try to avoid any contact with her unless absolutely necessary. I would avoid any situation that could lead to conflict and hope that she changes as a result.

_____ I would turn around and "nail her" in the act. I'd tell her that I was fed up with her attitude and that it is time to shape up or ship out. If she's not able to work well in the classroom, she may find the principal's office more to her liking. Being firm and laying it on the line will change her behavior in a hurry.

_____ I would ignore Donna for the present, as I want to win her over to my side. Later I'd engage her in friendly conversation, find out what her hobbies are and about any pets she might have, establishing friendly feelings between us. She would then try harder on the tasks and not disrupt the class by ridiculing me anymore.

_____ I would take her up to my desk immediately and make a bargain with her that if she will stop disrupting the class and try to do the work, I'll let her be recess monitor for the week (something she has wanted to do for some time). I would continue to look for ways to trade off things she wanted to do for appropriate behavior in class.

_____ I would take her up to my desk and call attention to the conflict between us by describing how I saw her behavior and telling her that it makes me angry and upset. I'd explain what the problem is from my perspective and its effect on the other students and discuss possible solutions. I would ask for her perception of the conflict and what her feelings are, and I would keep discussing the situation until we had a solution that we both liked.

EXERCISE 8.6
Role-Playing the Conflicts

Now that you have discussed the three examples of conflicts, it may be helpful to role-play them. The purpose of this exercise is to role-play the entire negotiation of a solution of the conflict between the two people. Here is the procedure:

1. Form groups of six. Take the first conflict, between the salesperson and Mr. Smith. One member should volunteer to play the part of each character. There are three conflict episodes, so each group member will play one role during the three role-playing episodes.

2. Spend up to 10 minutes role-playing the conflict. Begin with the initiation of the strategy chosen by the group to be the most effective and continue through the entire negotiation of a solution to the conflict. The group members who are not playing a role observe in order to discuss the effectiveness of the person's actions in resolving the conflict.

3. In the group of six, discuss the role-playing episode:
   a. What were the strategies used to manage the conflict constructively?
   b. What interpersonal skills were used?
   c. What interpersonal skills were not used but might have been helpful?
   d. What changes in strategies would you make if you actually were in this situation?

4. Repeat this procedure for the second and third examples of conflicts.

5. What conclusions can your group make about managing conflicts on the basis of your role-playing? Be ready to share your conclusions with the other groups.

◼ COMPREHENSION TEST A

Seven words and seven definitions are listed. Your task is to match the correct definition with the correct word. You are to work cooperatively with other group members and come to a consensus about the correct definition for each word.

_____ 1. Conflict

_____ 2. Want

_____ 3. Need

_____ 4. Goal

_____ 5. Interests

_____ 6. Conflict of interests

_____ 7. Negotiation

a. A process by which persons who have shared and opposed interests and want to come to an agreement try to work out a settlement

b. Potential benefits to be gained by achieving goals

c. Incompatible activities—the actions taken by A obstruct the actions taken by B

d. Desire for something

e. When the actions of one person attempting to reach his or her goals prevent, block, or interfere with the actions of another person attempting to reach his or her goals

f. Universal necessity for survival

g. Desired ideal state of future affairs

What You Need to Know About Conflicts

To manage your interpersonal storms, you need to know several things about conflicts.

1. **You need to understand what is and is not a conflict.** Conflicts may involve struggles, disagreements, disputes, or quarrels. More precisely, conflicts occur as the actions of one person attempting to reach his or her goals prevent, block, or interfere with the actions of another person attempting to reach his or her goals (see Deutsch, 1973).

2. **You must accept conflicts as a natural part of life that must be faced and resolved in constructive ways.** You might as well try to stop the earth from turning on its axis as try to eliminate conflicts from your life. Conflicts arise no matter what you do. Conflicts are especially frequent whenever you have goals you care about and are involved in relationships you value.

3. **Whenever conflicts occur, destructive or constructive outcomes may result.** Obtaining constructive outcomes requires (a) a set of procedures for managing conflicts constructively, (b) the opportunity to practice, practice, practice the procedures until real skill and expertise in their use are attained, and (c) the support and encouragement to use the procedures by the norms and values of the school (and home).

4. **If conflicts are to be managed constructively, everyone needs to use the same procedures to resolve them and be skilled in their use.** All members of an organization (such as a school, business, or family) must use the same procedures.

5. **A constructive agreement must be reached.** This outcome is achieved when (a) the agreement maximizes joint benefits and everyone goes away satisfied and pleased, (b) disputants are better able to work together cooperatively and have more respect, trust, and liking for each other, and (c) disputants are better able to resolve future conflicts constructively.

6. **Because conflicts occur continually, and because so many people are so unskilled in managing conflicts, learning how to resolve conflicts constructively is one of the best investments you can make.** Once learned, conflict skills go with you to every situation and every relationship. Knowing how to resolve conflicts with skill and grace will increase your career success, quality of relationships with friends and colleagues, and happiness.

Conflict Strategies

When you become engaged in a conflict, two major concerns you have to take into account are

1. **Achieving your goals.** Each person has personal goals that he or she wishes to achieve. You are in conflict because your goals conflict with another person's goals. Your goal may be placed on a continuum from being of little importance to you to being highly important.

2. **Maintaining a good relationship with the other person(s).** Some relationships are temporary, and some are long-term. Some long-term relationships are vital and others are peripheral. Your relationship with the other person may be placed on a continuum from being of little importance to you to being highly important.

How important your personal goals are to you and how important the relationship is perceived to be determine how you act in a conflict. Given these two concerns within a relationship, there are five basic strategies that may be used to manage conflicts:

1. **The Turtle (Withdrawing).** If you act like a turtle, you give up both your goals and the relationship, and, therefore, you avoid the other person and the issue. Avoiding a hostile stranger may be the best thing to do. Or you may wish to withdraw from a conflict until you and the other person have calmed down and are in control of your feelings.

2. **The Shark (Forcing).** If you act like a shark, you try to achieve your goals at all costs, demanding that the other person let you have your way, no matter how much it hurts the relationship. When the goal is very important but the relationship is not, such as when you are buying a used car, you may want to act like a shark and use force. Never use force with someone you will have to relate to again soon.

3. **The Teddy Bear (Smoothing).** If you act like a teddy bear, you give up your goals in order to maintain the relationship at the highest level possible. When the goal is of no importance to you but the relationship is of high importance, you may want to act like a teddy bear and smooth. When a colleague feels strongly about something, and you couldn't care less, smoothing is a good idea. When you are smoothing, do so with good humor. Be pleasant about it. At times, to smooth you may need to apologize. Saying "I'm sorry" does not mean "I'm wrong." "I'm sorry" lets the other person know that you are sorry about the situation. When you think the other person's interests are much stronger or more important than yours, smooth and give the other person his or her way.

4. The Fox (Compromising). If you act like a fox, you give up part of your goals and sacrifice part of the relationship in order to reach an agreement. When both the goal and the relationship are moderately important to you and it appears that both you and the other person cannot get what you want, you may want to negotiate like a fox. When there is a limited amount of money, and both you and a fellow employee want a large raise, for example, negotiating a compromise may be the best way to resolve the conflict. You can meet in the middle, each taking half, or flip a coin and let chance decide who will get his or her way.

5. The Owl (Problem Solving/Negotiating). If you act like an owl, you initiate negotiations aimed at ensuring that you and the other person both fully meet your goals and maintain the relationship at the highest level possible. An agreement is sought that satisfies both you and the other person and resolves any tensions and negative feelings between the two of you. When both the goal and the relationship are highly important to you, you may want to act like an owl. Face the conflict. Negotiate to solve the problem. Think of solutions that will give both you and the other person what you want and will keep the relationship positive.

Each conflict strategy has its place. You need to be able to use any one of the five, depending on your goals and the relationship (see Figure 8.1). In deciding which of the five strategies to use within any one conflict, there are six rules to consider (Johnson & Johnson, 1995a, 1995b):

1. Do not withdraw from or ignore conflicts. When the goal is not important and you do not need to keep a relationship with the other person, withdrawing from the conflict may be appropriate. If the relationship is going to continue, however, ignoring a conflict keeps emotional energy tied up in resentment, hostility, or fear. In the long run, it is almost always easier to face a conflict in an ongoing relationship.

2. Do not engage in win-lose negotiations. When the goal is very important to you but the relationship is unimportant, forcing the other person to give in may be appropriate. In an ongoing relationship, however, you almost never go for the win because the loser may be resentful and want revenge. In the long run, it is almost always easier to ensure that the other person is satisfied and happy with the resolution of the conflict.

3. Assess for smoothing. When the goal is unimportant to you (or far more important to the other person than to you) and the relationship is very important, smoothing may be appropriate. Giving up your needs for the needs of another person only works in the long run if the other person reciprocates. It is a mistake, however, to smooth if in fact the goal is very important to you.

High Importance

FIGURE 8.1   *Conflict Strategies*

4. Compromise when time is short. When the goal and the relationship are of moderate importance to you, you may wish to compromise. Usually, compromising is used only when there is not enough time to solve the problem.

5. Initiate problem-solving negotiations. When both the goal and the relationship are important to you, you initiate negotiations to solve the problem. You ask the other person to join with you in problem-solving negotiations if he or she is rational and able to do so. The best time to problem solve is when the issue is small, concrete, and immediate. This way issues are dealt with when they are most easily resolved.

6. Use your sense of humor. Humor is very helpful in keeping conflicts constructive. Laughter usually does a great deal to resolve the tension in conflicts and helps disputants think more creatively about how to solve the problem.

In following those rules there are a number of guidelines to keep in mind. First, to be competent in managing conflicts, you must be able to engage competently in each of the five strategies. Each strategy is appropriate in certain circumstances, and you need to be good at all of them. Second, some of the strategies require the participation of the other disputant, and some may be enacted by yourself alone. You can withdraw or smooth alone, but you have to have the cooperation of the other person to force, compromise, or problem solve. Third, the strategies tend to be somewhat incompatible in the sense that choosing one of them makes choosing the others less likely. Forcing is not typically followed by smoothing. Fourth, certain strategies may deteriorate into other strategies. When you try to withdraw and the other person corners you, you are likely to respond with forcing. When you attempt to smooth, and the other person responds with forcing and anger, you may withdraw. Then you may force if the other person continues to be angry and competitive. Forcing creates counterforcing. Even negotiations may deteriorate into forcing when (a) the timing is wrong and the other person does not respond constructively or (b) the person negotiating lacks the skills necessary to keep the management of the conflict constructive. When time is short, negotiating sometimes deteriorates into compromise.

Fifth, in ranking the strategies from the one you use most frequently to the one you use least frequently, you need to be aware of your second as well as your first strategy. When you become very angry and upset, you will tend to regress to your backup strategy. You need to be sensitive to your backup strategy as well as your dominant one. Finally, the most competent business executives tend to be very relationship-oriented and primarily use smoothing and problem solving while the least competent business executives tend to be very goal-oriented and primarily use forcing and withdrawing. Competent people tend to be highly relationship-oriented, negotiating when the goals and needs involved in the conflict are important to them and smoothing when they are not. In ongoing relationships, even if you do not like the other person, it is usually a good idea to smooth or problem solve.

In some ways the five strategies present a simplified view of how most conflicts are managed. The complexities of the interaction between two individuals far exceed their initial approaches to the conflict. Conflicts can deteriorate. Within most conflicts there are initial strategies followed by backup strategies followed by other strategies that are based on what the other person is doing. You may wish to negotiate but when faced with a colleague who is forcing, you may force back.

One of the most difficult aspects of initiating problem-solving negotiations is managing emotions. Managing anger is especially problematic. If you try to hide it, very likely the problem will not be correctly identified and a wise agreement will not be reached. But if you express your anger destructively, the relationship may be severely damaged, if not ruined. Anger is the focus of the next chapter.

How Conflicts May Be Beneficial

The Chinese character for crisis represents a combination of the symbol for danger and the symbol for opportunity. Inherent in any conflict is the potential for destructive or constructive outcomes. On the *destructive* side, conflicts can create anger, hostility, pain, sadness, lasting animosity, and even violence. Conflicts can end in lawsuits, divorce, or war. Conflicts, however, carry the potential for many important positive outcomes.

Conflicts focus attention on problems that have to be solved. Conflicts energize and motivate us to solve our problems.

Conflicts clarify how you need to change. Patterns of behavior that are dysfunctional are highlighted and clarified by conflicts.

Conflicts clarify what you care about and are committed to. You only fight over wants and goals you value. And you fight much more frequently and intensely with people you value and care about. The more committed you are to your goals, and the more committed you are to the other person, the more frequent and intense the conflicts.

Conflicts clarify who you are and what your values are. It is through conflicts that your identity is developed.

Conflicts help you understand who the other person is and what his or her values are. It is through conflicts that the identity of your friends and acquaintances are clarified.

Conflicts (a) keep the relationship clear of irritations and resentments and (b) strengthen relationships by increasing your confidence that the two of you can resolve your disagreements. A good conflict may do a lot to resolve the small tensions of interacting with others and increase your confidence that the relationship can survive stress and adversity.

A conflict a day keeps depression away! Conflicts can release anger, anxiety, insecurity, and sadness that, if kept inside, makes us mentally sick.

Conflicts can be fun. Being in a conflict reduces boredom, gives you new goals, motivates you to take action, and stimulates interest. Life would be incredibly boring if there were no conflicts.

What determines whether a conflict is constructive or destructive are the procedures you use to manage your conflicts.

■ COMPREHENSION TEST B

Test your understanding of the conflict strategies by taking the following quiz. The answers are at the end of the chapter.

1. Match the conflict strategy with the situation in which it may be used appropriately.

    a. Withdraw   _____ Goal and relationship are both important.

    b. Force   _____ Goal and relationship are moderately important.

    c. Smooth   _____ Goal and relationship are both unimportant.

    d. Compromise   _____ Goal is important; relationship is not.

    e. Problem Solve _____ Goal is not important; relationship is important.

True   False   2. It is a good idea to act the same way in every conflict.

True   False   3. The conflict strategy you use depends on how important it is to maintain a good relationship and to achieve your goals.

True   False   4. The two most effective strategies are problem solving and compromising.

True   False   5. Appropriate humor helps you resolve conflicts constructively.

True   False   6. Your ability to come up with wise agreements depends on how well you understand the other person's goals, feelings, and interests.

True   False   7. The important thing about viewing the conflict from the other person's perspective is that it helps you persuade him or her to agree with you.

True   False   8. If you don't want to solve the problem, ignore the conflict.

True   False   9. If you get a chance to win, take it.

True   False   10. If time is short, smooth.

 EXERCISE 8.7
Which Strategy Would You Use?

Many people engage in conflicts without much conscious thought or planning. They just react when they should be thinking carefully about what is the most effective thing to do. When you find yourself in a conflict you have to choose a strategy that is appropriate and constructive. The following table indicates what to do, depending on how important the goal and the relationship are to you. Working with a partner, describe a conflict you are having with a schoolmate, friend, or family member. Then decide how important the goal is to you and how important the relationship is to you. Remember, any relationship is highly important that is ongoing (you will have to associate, interact, work, or live with the person throughout the foreseeable future).

Strategy-Choosing Table

Goal	+	Relationship	=	*Withdraw*
Goal	+	Relationship	=	*Force*
Goal	+	**Relationship**	=	*Smooth*
Goal	+	*Relationship*	=	*Compromise*
Goal	+	**Relationship**	=	*Problem Solve*

My Conflict Is _____

_____

Circle how important your goal is to you and how important the relationship is to you. Then look in the Strategy-Choosing Table and decide which strategy you should use.

Goal   Relationship

Goal   *Relationship*

Goal   **Relationship**

 EXERCISE 8.8
Using the Conflict Strategies

First, with a partner, write a story about two people who have a conflict. Second, write out five different endings for the story, one for each of the strategies. For each strategy, what would you do and what would you say?

	Actions and Behaviors	Phrases
Withdrawing		
Forcing		
Smoothing		
Compromising		
Problem Solving		

You need to be competent in using all five strategies. The most important, however, is problem solving. Working with a partner, write out what happens in each of the instances when two individuals use different strategies.

1. Problem solver against a withdrawer.
2. Smoother against a forcer.
3. Compromiser against a forcer.
4. Problem solver against a smoother.

Negotiating

Resolving a conflict of interests requires negotiation. **Negotiation** is a process by which persons who have shared and opposed interests, and want to come to an agreement, try to work out a settlement (Johnson & Johnson, 1995a). You spend a great deal of time negotiating, even when you do not think you are doing so. Negotiating occurs continually throughout your day, usually informally, without your full awareness that it is going on. There are two ways to negotiate: negotiating to win and negotiating to solve the problem.

Negotiating to Win (Forcing)

People . . . are trying to either shun conflict or crush it. Neither strategy is working. Avoidance and force only raise the level of conflict. . . . They have become parts of the problem rather than the solution.
    —DeCecco and Richards (1974)

There are times when you negotiate to win. Buying a used car is an example. In **win-lose negotiations** the goal is to make an agreement more favorable to you than to the other negotiator. You go for the win when your goals are important and when the relationship with the other person has no future. The ultimate goal of negotiating in such circumstances is to gain an advantage over the other person. You go for a win.

Helpful hints in going for the win are (a) make an extreme opening offer (if you are willing to pay $1,500, offer $500), (b) compromise slowly (try to get the other person to compromise first), (c) point out everything that is wrong and unreasonable about the other person's position, and (d) be ready to walk away with no agreement. You want to change the other's evaluation of how many concessions are required to reach an agreement through a combination of threats and promises. Tactics used to force the other to yield include making threats, imposing penalties that will be withdrawn if the other concedes, and taking preemptive actions designed to resolve the conflict without the other's consent (such as taking a book home

Important Points About Negotiations

1. **It takes two to negotiate.** You cannot negotiate without the consent and participation of the other disputant. There are two types of interdependence inherent in any negotiation. The first is *participation interdependence* (negotiations cannot take place without the cooperation of the other disputant), and the second is *outcome interdependence* (an agreement can only be achieved with the cooperation of the other disputant). No matter what happens disputants are dependent on each other to participate in the negotiating process and to reach an agreement.

2. **In any negotiations there are both cooperative and competitive elements.** The mixed-motive situation is created by the desire to reach an agreement and the desire to make that agreement as favorable to oneself as possible. Thus disputants face a *goal dilemma* between (a) maximizing their own outcomes and (b) reaching an agreement. The two goals can seriously interfere with each other.

3. **Both primary and secondary gains must be attended to in negotiations.** The *primary gain* is determined by the nature of the agreement. The *secondary gain* is determined by factors influencing the effectiveness of the working relationship between the two disputants and the impact of an angry and revengeful person on a disputant's quality of life.

4. **The disputants are dependent on each other for information about their wants, goals, and interests.** This information dependence creates two dilemmas. The first is a *dilemma of the trustworthiness* of the other disputant—will he or she tell the truth about his or her wants, goals, and interests? The second is the *dilemma of honesty and openness*—is the other truthfully revealing his or her own wants, goals, and interests?

5. **During negotiations contractual norms are developed that spell out the ground rules for conducting the negotiations and managing the difficulties involved in reaching an agreement.** Two common norms are the *norm of reciprocity* (a disputant should return the same benefit or harm given him or her by the other negotiators) and the *norm of equity* (the benefits received or the costs accrued by the disputants should be equal).

6. **Negotiations have important time dimensions.** There is a beginning, a middle, and an end. The strategies and tactics used to initiate negotiations, exchange proposals and information, and precipitate an agreement can be quite different and sometimes contradictory.

7. **Negotiations are an ever-present factor in human life.** Each person has to negotiate agreements every day. You cannot avoid negotiating.

8. **Negotiating is not easy to do well.** Using the procedures with skill, finesse, and grace takes years of practice and experience to achieve.

that the other insists is his). Tactics to persuade the other to yield include presenting persuasive arguments, imposing a deadline, committing oneself to an unalterable position, or making demands that far exceed what is actually acceptable.

It is often a mistake, however, to assume that you will *never* be interdependent with the other person again. It is also often a mistake to assume that the conflict cannot be redefined as a mutual problem to be solved. A famous example is the dispute between Israel and Egypt. When Egypt and Israel sat down to negotiate at Camp David in October 1978, it appeared that they had before them an intractable conflict. Egypt demanded the immediate return of the entire Sinai Peninsula; Israel, which had occupied the Sinai since the 1967 Middle East war, refused to return an inch of this land. Efforts to reach an agreement, including the proposal of a compromise in which each nation would retain half of the Sinai, proved completely unacceptable to both sides. As long as the dispute was defined in terms of what percentage of the land each side would control, no agreement could be reached. Once both realized that what Israel really cared about was the security that the land offered, while Egypt was primarily interested in sovereignty over it, the stalemate was broken. The two countries were then able to reach an integrative solution: Israel would return the Sinai to Egypt in exchange for assurances of a demilitarized zone and Israeli air bases in the Sinai.

There are very few times in your life when you negotiate with someone you will never interact with again. The majority of the time, therefore, you will want to engage in problem-solving negotiations.

Negotiating to Solve the Problem

Imagine that you and another person are rowing a boat across the ocean and you cannot row the boat by yourself. While the two of you may have conflicts about how to row, how much to row, what direction to row, and so forth, you seek food and water for the other person as well as for yourself. Otherwise, you may perish. Your conflicts become mutual problems that must be solved to both persons' satisfaction. You negotiate to solve the problem when (a) your goals are very important to you and (b) you have an ongoing cooperative relationship with the other person that must be maintained in good working order. In **problem-solving negotiations** the goal is to discover an agreement that will benefit everyone involved. Such agreements are called integrative solutions, which are advantageous because they:

1. **Maximize joint benefit.** Compromises, coin tosses, and other mechanical agreements are often unsatisfying to one or both parties and, therefore, create a situation in which the conflict is likely to appear again later.

2. **Strengthen the relationship between parties.** Strong relationships both help maintain agreements made and facilitate the development of integrative solutions in subsequent conflicts.

3. **Contribute to the welfare of the broader community** of which the two parties are members. For example, a college usually benefits as a whole when its students, faculty, and staff are able to reconcile their differences creatively.

You negotiate differently within ongoing relationships than you do with strangers or acquaintances. Within ongoing relationships you are expected to show considerable concern about the other person's interests. You are, after all, striving to achieve the same goals, and the productivity and quality of life for both of you are affected by how the conflict is managed. Helping the others achieve their goals is of some importance to you. How they can help you achieve your goals is of some importance to them.

Ongoing relationships are guided by a **norm of mutual responsiveness** (i.e., the rule that you should be committed to helping other people get what they want and fulfill their needs and they will do likewise). Within a work or personal relationship, there is an unspoken rule that each person is concerned about the other person's interests. A vigorous presentation of one's own interests, therefore, implies that these interests are genuinely important and the other person should agree if it is at all possible. **One-step negotiations** occur: Each person (a) assesses the strength of his or her interests, (b) assesses the strength of the other person's interests, and (c) agrees that whoever has the greatest need is given his or her way. If both people follow the norm of mutual responsiveness, each will decide that the other person's goals are more important than one's own goals about 50 percent of the time. If individuals are not equally responsive to each other's needs over time, the relationship breaks down.

 EXERCISE 8.9

Disagreeing—The Fallout Shelter

We often get into disagreements over what course of action to take in a situation. We then have to negotiate with others who represent different interests than we do. The purpose of this exercise is to increase your awareness of how you negotiate with others and increase your ability to give others feedback about their actions during negotiations.

1. Each person reads "The Fallout Shelter." Choose the two people you believe are most important to go into the fallout shelter and the two who are least important. Write down the reasons for your choices.

2. Form groups of four members. As a group, decide on the six people who are to go into the fallout shelter. You have 15 minutes to make the decision. During the discussion, try to negotiate your choices into the fallout shelter. The future of the human species may depend on your success in doing so.

3. As a group discuss what strategies each member used to negotiate their choices into the fallout shelter. Go around the group focusing on one member at a time (the focus person). Each member briefly describes how he or she perceived the focus person's actions during the group discussion. Use the rules for constructive feedback. Make sure everyone receives feedback.

The Fallout Shelter*

Your group is in charge of experimental stations in the far outposts of civilization. You work in an important government agency in Washington, D.C. Suddenly, World War III breaks out. Nuclear bombs begin dropping. Places all across the world are being destroyed. People are getting into the available fallout shelters. Your group receives a desperate call from one of your experimental stations. They ask for your help. There are ten people in this station. But their fallout shelter only holds six. They cannot decide which six people should enter the fallout shelter. They have agreed that they will obey your group's decision as to which six people will go into the fallout shelter. Your group has only superficial information about the ten people. Your group has 15 minutes to make the decision. Your group realizes that the six people chosen may be the only people left to start the human species over again. Your group's decision, therefore, is very important. If your group does not make the decision within the 15 minutes allowed, all ten people will die. Here is what you know about the ten people

Bookkeeper, male, thirty-one years old

His wife, six months pregnant

Second-year medical student, male, militant African American

Famous historian-author, male, forty-two years old

Hollywood actress who is a singer and dancer

Biochemist, female

Rabbi, fifty-four years old, male

Olympic athlete, all sports, male

College student, female

Policeman with gun (they cannot be separated)

*Source: D. W. Johnson & R. Johnson (1995c).

E X E R C I S E 8 . 1 0
Which Books Do We Take?

Scientists have suddenly discovered that a large comet is going to strike the earth. All life, if not the earth itself, will be destroyed. Your group (four members) has been picked to move from Earth to a new planet. The conditions on the new planet will be harsh and difficult. You will be starting life over, trying to develop a farming and technological society at the same time. Because of the limited room in the spaceship, you can only bring three books. "Think carefully," the captain says. "You will never return to Earth. You will never be able to get more books from Earth."

1. Work by yourself. First, decide which book you personally want to bring. Choose the book you think will be most (a) important to save and (b) helpful to starting a new civilization. Second, plan how to convince the other three members of your group that the book you have chosen should be chosen by the group.

2. Meet as a group. Only three books can go. You have to decide which three. You cannot take half of one and half of another. You cannot choose by chance (such as flipping a coin). Come to an agreement as to which three books your group will take and why. Each member should present the best case for the book he or she has chosen. The group must come to an agreement as to which three books they will take to the new planet. Each member must be able to explain the reasons why the three books were chosen.

3. As a group, first look up **conflicts of interests** and **negotiations** in this chapter. Explain how this situation is a conflict of interests that requires negotiation to be resolved. Second, decide on four pieces of advice for negotiating resolutions to conflicts of interests. Write them down. Each member of the group needs a copy.

4. Each member of the group pairs up with a member of another group. Pair members (a) present the four pieces of advice decided on by their groups, (b) listen carefully to each other's presentation, and (c) take the best ideas from both groups and decide on four pieces of advice for negotiating resolutions of conflicts. Both members need a copy.

5. Return to your group of four. Members share their new lists. As a group, make a new list of four pieces of advice for negotiating resolutions to conflicts of interests, taking the best ideas from all members.

Effective Problem-Solving Negotiating

A house divided against itself cannot stand.
—Mark 3:25

On the eve of the Revolutionary War, English political philosopher Edmund Burke eloquently asked members of the House of Commons to head off the coming conflict by negotiating with the colonials: "All government—indeed, every human benefit and enjoyment, every virtue, and every prudent act—is founded on compromise and barter." His observation is still accurate. Negotiation is woven into the daily fabric of our lives. On the interpersonal level, we buy and sell houses and cars, jointly decide where to eat dinner, bargain over salaries, and even decide where to eat lunch and what movie to see. On a larger scale, unions and management negotiate contracts, and nations arrange treaties and trade agreements. Failed negotiations may produce anything from minor inconveniences to a war.

Most people do not know how to negotiate effectively and, therefore, must be directly and purposefully taught how to do so. Not only do you need to know how to negotiate effectively to improve the quality of your immediate life, but you also need to know how to negotiate to be successful in your career. A recent survey conducted for Accountemps (a large accounting, bookkeeping, and data-processing temporary personnel service that is a division of Robert Half International, Inc.) of vice presidents and personnel directors of 100 of the nation's 1,000 largest corporations found that the people who manage America's leading corporations spend over four working weeks a year dealing with the problems caused by employees who cannot resolve their conflicts with each other. In answer to the question "What percent of management time is spent dealing with conflicts among employees," respondents revealed that executives spend an average of 9.2 percent of their time or, 4.6 weeks a year, attempting to deal with employee conflicts and the difficulties and disruptions they cause. In 1976, the American Management Association sponsored a survey on conflict management (Thomas & Schmidt, 1976). The respondents included 116 chief executive officers, 76 vice presidents, and 66 middle managers. They reported that about 24 percent of their time is spent dealing with conflict. The sources of conflicts they faced included misunderstandings, personality clashes, value and goal differences, substandard performance, disagreement over methods of work, lack of cooperation, competition, and noncompliance with rules and policies. School and hospital administrators, mayors, and city managers report that conflict resolution commands nearly 49 percent of their attention. In addition to taking up valuable management time, employee conflicts can seriously reduce any company's productivity and its ability to compete effectively in the marketplace. Knowing how to negotiate constructive resolutions to conflicts is an essential skill that will significantly enhance your career success.

That negotiating is not easy to do well even though it takes place frequently is a key to your success. *There are six basic steps in negotiating mutually beneficial agreements* (Johnson & Johnson, 1995a, 1995b):

1. Each person explains what he or she wants in a descriptive, nonevaluative way.
2. Each person explains how he or she feels in a descriptive, nonevaluative way.
3. Each person explains his or her reasons for wanting what he or she wants and feeling the way he or she does.
4. Each person reverses perspectives by summarizing what the other person wants and feels and the reasons underlying those wants and feelings.
5. The participants invent at least three good optional agreements that would maximize joint outcomes.
6. The participants choose the agreement that seems the wisest and agree to abide by its conditions.

Step One: Describing What You Want

If a man does not know to which port he is sailing, no wind is favorable.
—Seneca

Conflicts begin when two people want the same thing. When one person says, "I want the ice cream bar" and another person says, "I want the ice cream bar," a conflict exists. It is acceptable to want something. Every person has wants, needs, and goals. Every person every minute of the day wants something. To stand up for yourself, you have to let other people know what you want. Negotiating begins when you describe what you want. *Everyone has a perfect right to their wants, needs, and goals* (Alberti & Emmons, 1978). Two of the major mistakes in defining a conflict are to be **aggressive** by trying to hurt the other person or **nonassertive** by keeping your wants to yourself and saying nothing. You can **assert** your wants, needs, and goals directly to another person in an honest and appropriate way that respects both yourself and the other person. On the other hand, *everyone has a perfect right to refuse to meet your wants and needs or facilitate your goal accomplishment if they see it as destructive to their own interests to do so.* No one has to act against their best self-interests just to please someone else. Asserting your wants and goals does not include demanding that others act as you think they should. Providing others with information about your interests is different from trying to force others to act in the ways you wish them to. To clearly communicate your wants and goals to the other person,

1. Make personal statements that refer to *I, me, my,* or *mine.*

2. Be specific about your wants, needs, and goals, and establish their legitimacy.

3. Acknowledge the other person's goals as part of the problem. Describe how the other person's actions are blocking what you want. In doing so, separate the behavior from the person. More specifically, a **behavior description** includes
   a. A **personal statement** that refers to *I, me, my,* or *mine.*
   b. A **behavioral description** that includes the specific behaviors you have observed and does *not* include any judgment or evaluation or any inferences about the person's motives, personality, or attitudes.

4. Focus on the long-term cooperative relationship. During most conflicts of interest you will be discussing the current problems in your relationship. Negotiations within a long-term cooperative relationship include discussing how the relationship can be changed so the two of you can work together better. During such conversations, you will need to make relationship statements. A **relationship statement** describes some aspect of the way the two of you are interacting with each other. A good relationship statement indicates clear ownership (refers to *I, me, my,* or *mine*) and describes how you see the relationship. "I think we need to talk about our disagreement yesterday" is a good relationship statement (see Table 8.2).

TABLE 8.2 *Respect for Self and Others*

My Respect for Me	My Respect for You
I have a perfect right to:	You have a perfect right to:
My needs and wants	Your wants and needs
Tell you what I want	Tell me what you want
Tell you how I feel	Tell me how you feel
Refuse to give you what you want	Refuse to give me what I want

We Have a Perfect Right to Negotiate with Each Other

Besides communicating clearly and descriptively what you want, you must listen carefully to what the other person wants. There is no set of skills more important for negotiating than being a good listener. To listen to another person you must (a) face the person, (b) stay quiet (until your turn), (c) think about what the person is saying, and (d) show you understand. The keystone to good listening is paraphrasing. Often in a conflict it is helpful to follow the **paraphrasing rule:** Before you can reply to a statement, restate what the sender says, feels, and means correctly and to the sender's satisfaction. When you use paraphrasing, there is a rhythm to your statements. The rhythm is, "You said . . . ; I say. . . ." First you say what the sender said (You said). Then you reply (I say). Paraphrasing is often essential in defining a conflict so that a constructive resolution may be negotiated.

In communicating your wants and goals and carefully understanding what the other wants, you end up with a joint definition of the conflict (a) as a mutual problem and (b) in as small and specific a way as possible. Two drivers, coming from different directions, are roaring down a one-lane road. Soon they will crash head-on. If the two drivers define the situation as a competition to see who will chicken out, they tend to crash and both die. If the two drivers define the situation as a problem to be solved, they tend to see a solution in which they alternate giving each other the right-of-way. Even simple and small conflicts become major and difficult to resolve when they are defined in a competitive, win-lose way. Even major and difficult conflicts become resolvable when they are defined as problems to be solved. One of the most constructive things you can do in a conflict is to define the conflict as a mutual problem to be solved. Doing so will tend to increase communication, trust, liking for each other, and cooperation. No one tends to lose when you and the other person sit down to solve a mutual problem!

In defining a conflict, the smaller and more specific the definition, the easier it is to resolve. Think small. The more global, general, and vague the definition of the conflict, the harder the conflict is to resolve. Defining a conflict as, "She always lies," makes it more difficult to resolve than defining it as, "Her statement was not true." When it comes to resolving conflicts, small is easy, large is hard!

Joint Definition of a Conflict

I = Inform others of what you want and how you feel.

U = Understand the wants and feelings of the other person.

D = Define the conflict as a mutual problem.

Step Two: Describing Your Feelings

Many of us in business, especially if we are very sure of our ideas, have hot tempers. My father knew he had to keep the damage from his own temper to a minimum.
      —Thomas Watson, Jr.

It is not enough to say what you want in problem-solving negotiations. You also need to say how you feel. In conflicts everyone has feelings—you may feel angry, frustrated, or even afraid. Expressing and controlling your feelings is one of the most difficult aspects of resolving conflicts. It is also one of the most important. Both sides need to say how they feel. Both you and the other person have a perfect right to your feelings. The second step in problem-solving negotiations is to describe how you feel.

Within negotiations you must describe how you feel for at least two reasons. First, the only way other people can know how you are feeling and reacting is for you to tell them. Many people hide feelings and reactions in conflicts. You often do not want others to know how upset you really are. But if the conflict is to be resolved, you need to share your feelings and reactions. Such sharing helps other people understand how their actions are affecting you.

Second, unless feelings are openly recognized and expressed, the conflict will not be resolved. If individuals hide or suppress their anger, for example, they may make an agreement but keep their resentment and hostility toward the other person. Their ability to work effectively with the other person is damaged, as is their ability to resolve future conflicts constructively. And the conflict will tend to recur regardless of what the agreement is.

It is often difficult to express feelings, especially within conflict situations. Whenever there is a risk of being rejected or laughed at, expressing feelings becomes very difficult. The more personal the feelings, the greater the risk you may feel. It is also difficult to hide your feelings from other people. You may cry when you do not want to, get angry when it is best not to, or even laugh at a time that disturbs others. If you are angry and upset, typically the people you work with and the people around you will know. When you do not recognize, accept, and express your feelings, a number of difficulties may arise. Relationships may deteriorate, conflicts may fester, bias may creep into your judgments, and the insecurities of your colleagues may increase.

Besides communicating your interests and feelings clearly and descriptively, you must listen carefully to the other person's interests and feelings. To listen to another person you must (a) face the person, (b) stay quiet (until your turn), (c) think about what the person is saying, and (d) show you understand, probably through paraphrasing and perception-checking (see Chapter 3).

EXERCISE 8.11
Feelings in Conflicts

A basic aspect of any conflict is the feelings a person has while the conflict is taking place. Two common feelings are rejection and distrust. Many people are afraid of conflicts because they are afraid they will be rejected. And many people avoid conflicts because they do not trust the other person. The purposes of this exercise are to experience the feelings of rejection and distrust and to discuss how they influence your actions in conflicts. The procedure is as follows:

Part 1: Rejection

1. Form into groups of four.

2. Pass out the instructions (p. 281) to each member of your group. The group has 10 minutes to select one person to be rejected and excluded from the group.

3. Combine two groups of four into a group of eight. Discuss the following questions:
   a. Did you feel rejected by the other members of your group of four?
   b. What is it like to feel rejected? What other feelings result from being rejected?
   c. How do you act when someone is rejecting you?
   d. When you are in a conflict, how can you act to minimize feelings of rejection on both your part and the part of the other person?

Part 2: Distrust

1. Form pairs.

2. Give each member of the pair an instruction sheet (p. 281). Your pair has 5 minutes to interact after you have both read the instructions.

3. Combine three pairs into a group of six and discuss these questions:
   a. Did you feel distrusted by the other member of your pair?
   b. Did you distrust the other member of your pair?
   c. How do you act when someone distrusts you?
   d. What is it like to feel distrusted? What other feelings result from being distrusted?
   e. When you are in a conflict, how can you minimize the feelings of distrust on both your part and on the part of the other person?

4. Be prepared to share with other groups your conclusions about how to minimize rejection and distrust.

Part 1

You are to try to get the person sitting on your right rejected from the group. Use any reason you can think of—he misses too many meetings, she's the only one in the group wearing a sweater, she's the shortest person—anything you can think of. Stick to this, and try to convince the other group members that this is the person who should be rejected. You can listen to the arguments of other people in the group, but don't give in. Be sure you talk about the person and not about rules for rejecting.

Part 2

Instructions A

Do not share these instructions with the other person in your pair. Your task for the next five minutes is to talk as positively and warmly as you can to the other person. Say only positive and friendly things, showing especially that you want to cooperate and work effectively with him or her in the future. Your conversation is to concentrate on him or her about your impression of that person, and the need for cooperation between the two of you. Don't talk about yourself. No matter what happens, you say only positive things. Keep the conversation moving along quickly. You are to speak first.

Instructions B

Do not share these instructions with the other person in your pair. The other person will speak first. Your task for the next five minutes is to talk with the other person in a way that shows distrust of him or her. Whatever the other person says, say something in return that communicates suspicion, distrust, disinterest, defiance, disbelief, or contradiction. Talk only about the things the other person talks about, and avoid starting conversation or bringing up new topics. Try not to help the other person out in any way. As an example, should your partner comment, "Say, I like the shirt you're wearing," you might respond, "What do you say that for? It's ugly. I don't like it at all. What are you trying to accomplish by complimenting my shirt?"

Step Three: Exchanging Reasons for Positions

To be persuasive we must be believable; to be believable we must be credible; to be credible we must be truthful.
  —Edward R. Murrow

Once both you and the other person have expressed what you want and how you feel, have listened carefully to each other, and have jointly defined the conflict as a small and specific mutual problem, you must exchange the reasons for your positions. To do so, negotiators have to

1. **Express cooperative intentions and enlarge the shadow of the future.** One of the most constructive things you can do in resolving a conflict is to highlight the long-term cooperative relationship. The clear and unambiguous expression of cooperative intentions in negotiations results in higher quality agreements being reached in a shorter amount of time (i.e., better agreements faster). The other person becomes less defensive, more willing to change his or her position, less concerned about who is right and who is wrong, and more understanding of your views and ideas. The other person also tends to see you as an understanding and trustworthy person in whom he or she can confide.

Cooperative intentions may be communicated in three ways. The first is to stress your wish to deal with the conflict in a problem-solving way. Communicate that you and the other person will strive, side by side, to solve the problem rather than fight face-to-face to determine who wins. You want to say such things as, "This situation means that we will have to work together," "Let's cooperate in reaching an agreement," and "Let's try to reach an agreement that is good for both of us." The second is to stress your commitment to maximizing the joint outcome. Successful negotiation requires finding out what the other person really wants and needs and showing him or her a way to get it while you get what you want. The third is to enlarge the shadow of the future by stressing your commitment to the continuation and success of the cooperative efforts you and the other person are involved in. In doing so, you must wish to point out (a) your long-term mutual goals and (b) the ways the two of you are interdependent and how that interdependence will continue for the foreseeable future.

2. **Present your reasons; listen to the other person's reasons.** To say what you want and how you feel is not enough. You must also give your reasons for wanting what you want and feeling as you do. It is not enough to say, "I want to use the computer now and I'm angry at you for not letting me have it." You must also say, "I have an important homework assignment due today and this is my only chance to get it done." Your reasons are aimed at (a) informing the other person and (b) persuading him or her to agree with you. Once both of you have explained your reasons, either of you may agree or disagree to help the other person to reach his or her goals. The decision to help the other person reach his or her goals or keep negotiating is based on a comparison between (a) how important your goal is to you and (b) how important the other person's goal is to him or her (based on the reasons he or she presents). You must listen carefully to the reasons given and decide whether they are valid or not. If you decide that the other person's goals are far more im-

portant to him or her than yours are to you, then you may wish to switch from negotiating to smoothing. If neither you nor the other person is convinced to give up your own goals in order to fulfill the goals of the other person, then the two of you must reaffirm your cooperative relationship and explore each other's reasons at a deeper level.

3. Focus on wants and needs, not positions. The classic example of the need to separate interests from positions is that of a brother and sister, each of whom wanted the only orange available. The sister wanted the peel of the orange to make a cake; the brother wanted the inner part to make orange juice. Their positions ("I want the orange!") were opposed, but their interests were not. Often, when conflicting parties reveal their underlying interests, it is possible to find a solution that suits them both. The heart of negotiating is meeting the goals of the other person while ensuring your goals are being met. The success of negotiating depends on finding out what the other person really wants and showing him or her a way to get it while you get what you want. For a wise decision, therefore, reconcile wants, not positions. For every need or want, there usually exist several possible positions that could satisfy it. A common mistake is to assume that because the other person's position is opposed to yours, his or her goals must also be opposed. Behind opposed positions lie shared and compatible goals, as well as conflicting ones. To identify the other person's wants and needs ask, "Why?" and ask, "Why not?" and think about his or her choice, and realize that the other person has many different needs and wants.

4. Clarify the differences between your interests and the other person's interests before trying to integrate them into an agreement. Conflicts cannot be resolved unless you understand what you are disagreeing about. Only then will you be able to think of ways to satisfy both yourself and the other person so that the conflict can be resolved constructively. The more you differentiate between your interests and those of the other person, the better you will be able to integrate them into a mutually satisfying agreement. In discussing a conflict you try to find the answers to these questions: (a) What are the differences between my wants and goals and yours? (b) Where are our wants and goals the same? (c) What actions of the other person do I find unacceptable? (d) What actions of mine does the other person find unacceptable?

5. Empower the other person. Shared power and wise agreements go hand in hand. There are two ways to empower the other person. The first is by being open to negotiations and flexible about the option you like the best. If the other person can negotiate with you, then he or she has power and options. Willingness to negotiate is based on being open to the possibility that there may be a better option available than you now realize. Staying tentative and flexible means that you do not become overcommitted to any one position until an agreement is reached. Second, you empower through choice among options. Generate a variety of possible solutions before deciding what to do. If Susan says to Mr. Johnson, "You have to agree to let me not do my homework!" he will feel powerless. If Susan said, "Let's think of three possible agreements, and then choose the one that seems the best!" both she and Mr. Johnson feel powerful.

The psychological costs of being helpless to resolve grievances include frustration, anxiety, and friction. When a person is powerless, either he or she becomes hostile and tries to tear down the system or becomes apathetic and throws in the towel. You do not want the other person to do either one. We all need to believe that we have been granted a fair hearing and that we should have the power and the right to gain justice when we have been wronged. If it becomes evident that we cannot gain justice, then frustration, anger, depression, and anxiety may result.

 EXERCISE 8.12
Differentiating Between Positions and Interests

For each of the following situations identify and write out each person's position and interests that caused them to take that position. Then find a partner and come to agreement on the answers. One member will be chosen randomly to give the pair's answers.

1. Sue wants the orange so she can use the peel to make an orange cake. Jim wants the orange so he can use the inside to make orange juice.

	Sue	Jim
Position		
Interests		

2. Jeremy wants the book so he can read it. Andrew wants the book so he can sit on it and see better.

	Jeremy	Andrew
Position		
Interests		

3. Jennifer wants the computer so she can write her science report. Tyler wants the computer to practice keyboarding.

	Jennifer	Tyler
Position		
Interests		

4. Melissa wants the pencil so she can write with it. Sarah wants the pencil to erase mistakes.

	Melissa	Sarah
Position		
Interests		

5. Betsy wants the ball so she can practice catching it. Sam wants the ball so he can practice throwing it.

	Betsy	Sam
Position		
Interests		

Step Four: Understanding the Other's Perspective

The test of a first-rate intelligence is the ability to hold two opposed ideas in the mind at the same time, and still retain the ability to function.
—F. Scott Fitzgerald

In order to negotiate successfully with another person, you must be able to take the other person's perspective and understand how the conflict appears to the other person. **Social perspective-taking** is the ability to understand how a situation appears to another person and how that person is reacting cognitively and emotionally to the situation. The opposite of perspective-taking is **egocentrism** or being unaware that other perspectives exist, making one's own view of the conflict incomplete and limited.

Negotiation requires a realistic assessment of common and opposed interests. Often it requires the sacrifice of some of the opposed interests so that the common benefits, concerns, advantages, and needs may be built on. In order to be able to propose alternative agreements that will solve a problem, you must understand how the other person sees the problem and is thinking about it. In order to settle a conflict, it is necessary to have a clear understanding of all sides of the issue and an accurate assessment of their validity and relative merits. It is common to misunderstand the motivations behind the other person's actions. In order to understand the other person's actions and position, you will have to see the conflict from his or her perspective. To do so you must be sufficiently detached from your position that you can see the conflict from new perspectives. Understanding the other person's perspective, however, is not the same as agreeing with it.

To see the situation from the other's shoes, you need to understand several aspects of perspectives. *First, each person has a unique perspective (a way of viewing the world and his or her relation to it) that is different from the perspectives of others.* Your perspective results from the ways in which you respond to your experiences as an infant, child, youth, and adult. Other people have developed their perspectives based on their responses to their life experiences. This means that *different people have different perspectives.* No two people will see an issue in exactly the same way; each person will interpret identical events differently.

Second, a person's perspective selects and organizes what the person attends to and experiences. All experiences are interpreted and understood within the perspective in which they are viewed. People tend to see only what their perspective allows them to see. A rich person and a poor person may see a homeless person differently because they have two different perspectives. To make the situation worse, people tend to only see what they want to see. Out of a mass of detailed information, people tend to pick out and focus on those facts that confirm their prior perceptions and to disregard or misinterpret those that call their perceptions into question. Each side in a negotiation tends to see only the merits of its case, and only the faults of the other side. It is not enough to logically understand how the other person views the problem. *If you want to influence the other person, you also need to understand empathetically the power of his or her point of view and to feel the emotional force with which he or she believes in it.* You may see on the table a glass half full of water. The other person may see a dirty, half-empty glass about to cause a ring on the mahogany finish. Change a person's perspective and you change what the person attends to and the way the person interprets the events in his or her life. Understand the other's perspective, and you change your ability to find integrative solutions to the conflict.

Third, each person can have different perspectives at different times. If you have been lifting 5-gallon cans of paint and someone tosses you a 1-gallon can, it will seem very light. But if you have been lifting 1-quart cans, the 1-gallon can will seem very heavy. When you are hungry, you notice all the food in a room. When you are not hungry, the food does not attract your attention. As your job role, experiences, assumptions, physiological states, and values change, your perspective will change.

Fourth, the same message can mean two entirely different things from two different perspectives. If you provoke your co-worker, she may laugh. But if you provoke your boss, he may get angry and fire you! Different perspectives mean the message will be given different meanings. From one perspective, the same message may be interpreted as friendly teasing or as hostile insubordination. A person's perspective determines how a message will be interpreted.

Fifth, misunderstandings often occur because we assume that everyone sees things from the same perspective as we do. If we are interested in sports, we assume that everyone is interested in sports. If we get angry when someone laughs at our behavior, we assume that everyone will get angry when they are laughed at. If we think a teacher is stupid, we are surprised when a peer thinks the teacher is brilliant.

Failure to understand the other's perspective increases the likelihood of the conflict being managed destructively. It is important, therefore, to keep the other person's perspective in mind as well as your own when negotiating, for the following reasons (Johnson & Johnson, 1989). *First, perspective-taking improves communication and reduces misunderstandings and distortions by influencing how messages are phrased and received.* Negotiators often misunderstand and distort the positions of the others involved in the conflict due to poor communication. The better you understand the other person's perspective, the more able you are to phrase messages so the other person can easily understand them. If a person does not know what snow is, for example, you do not refer to "corn snow" or "fresh powder." In addition, understanding the other person's perspective helps you accurately understand the messages you are receiving from that person. For example, if the other person says, "That's just great!" the meaning reverses if you know the person is frustrated. You must be able to stand in the sender's shoes to understand accurately the meaning of the messages that person is sending you.

Second, perspective-taking is essential for a realistic assessment of common and opposed interests and an accurate assessment of their validity and relative merits. Often, reaching an agreement requires the sacrifice of some of the opposed interests so that the common benefits, concerns, advantages, and needs may be built on. To propose workable alternative agreements you must understand how the other person sees the problem.

Third, the more able you are to take the other person's perspective, the broader the picture you get of the issue.

Fourth, engaging in perspective taking tends to improve the relationship with the other person. You are liked and respected more when the other person realizes that you are seeing his or her perspective accurately and using it to create potential agreements that benefit both sides equally.

There is nothing more important to resolving conflicts constructively than understanding how the conflict appears from the other person's perspective. Overall (see Johnson & Johnson, 1989), perspective taking results in more information, both personal and impersonal, being disclosed; increases the capacity to phrase messages so that they are easily understood by the other; increases accurate comprehension of the other's messages; increases understanding and retention of the other's information and reasoning; facilitates the achievement of creative and high-quality problem solving; and promotes more positive perceptions of negotiations, the other person, and the joint cooperative efforts. Once you can view the conflict both from your own perspective and the other person's perspective, you can find mutually beneficial solutions. You can also communicate to the other person that you really understand his or her thoughts, feelings, and needs. It is usually easier to resolve a conflict when the other person feels understood. You ensure that you accurately see the situation from the other person's perspective by

1. Asking for clarification or correction to make sure your understanding is accurate. This is called **perception checking.**
2. Demonstrating your understanding of the other's wants and needs. This is often done by **paraphrasing.**
3. Presenting the other's position from his or her perspective.

The most effective way to gain insight into the other person's perspective is to present the other person's position and reasoning as if you were he or she. Then have the other person do the same. The more involved the two of you get in arguing for the other's position, the more you will understand how the conflict appears from the other person's viewpoint. Such role playing is invaluable in finding solutions that are mutually acceptable. A series of research studies on perspective reversal (Johnson, 1971) found that it increases cooperative behavior between negotiators, clarifies misunderstanding of the other's position, increases understanding of the other's position, aids one's ability to perceive the issue from the other's frame of reference, and helps achieve reevaluation of the issue and changes of attitude toward it. The studies also demonstrated that perspective reversal resulted in the role reverser being perceived as a person who tries to understand the other's position, as an understanding person in general who is willing to compromise, and as a cooperative and trustworthy person. Temporarily arguing your opponent's position does result in insight into your opponent's perspective and changes your attitudes about the issues being negotiated.

Once you can view the conflict both from your own perspective and the other person's perspective, you are in a position to find mutually beneficial agreements. You can also communicate to the other person that you really understand his or her thoughts, feelings, and needs. It is usually much easier to resolve a conflict when the other person feels understood. The more skilled you are in seeing things from other people's shoes, the more skilled you will be in resolving conflicts constructively.

EXERCISE 8.13

Old Lady/Young Girl

The objective of this exercise is to show how two people with different frames of reference can perceive the same event in two different ways.

1. Form groups of four. Divide each group into two pairs. Give each pair a picture (see Appendix, p. 419). One group receives Picture A and the other group receives Picture B.

2. Each pair writes out a description of the person in the picture, including such things as gender, clothing, hairstyle, and age. After they have finished their descriptions they hand back the copies of their pictures.

3. Each pair member meets with a member of the other pair. They have their descriptions, but no pictures. They are given a copy of Picture C. The two individuals are then asked to negotiate a common description of the person in the picture, including such things as gender, clothing, hairstyle, and age.

4. After an agreement is reached, the group of four discusses these questions:
   a. Did they see Picture C in the same way?
   b. Was it difficult to change their perceptions once they said it in one way?
   c. What impact do background, previous experience, expectations, and frame of reference have on how you see your own and the other's behavior in conflict situations?

EXERCISE 8.14

Your Point of View

Everyone has his or her own point of view. Some people like Chinese food. Some people do not. If you like Chinese food, you tend to assume that everyone does. If you like to be teased, you assume that everyone likes to be teased. In resolving conflicts it is important to understand the other person's point of view. An example of the need to understand others' points of view is given in the following paragraph. Read the story with your partner.

The Wise Men and the Buffalo

Once upon a time, four blind men who were considered to be very wise wanted to know what a buffalo looked like. When a buffalo was brought to their town, they all went to touch it. The first wise man grabbed hold of the buffalo's tail. "The buffalo is like a rope," he yelled. The second wise man rubbed his hands over the buffalo's side. "No, No! The buffalo is like a big furry rug," he cried. The third wise man grabbed hold of the buffalo's horn. "The buffalo is like a spear!" he shouted. "You are all wrong," the fourth man exclaimed. "The buffalo is like a table!" He was holding two of the buffalo's legs. "Rope!" "Rug!" "Spear!" "Table!" The blind men yelled at each other for the rest of the day. They never did agree on what a buffalo looked like.

Working in your pair, answer the following questions. Then join another pair and share your answers.

1. Which blind man was right? _____

2. What was their conflict based on? _____

3. Were they really wise? How do you tell if someone is wise? _____

   _____

4. How could the wise men have discovered what a buffalo really looks like? _____

   _____

5. What is the moral of the story? What does the story tell you about solving conflicts? _____

   _____

In your pair, rewrite the ending of the story to make it come out with a positive solution to the conflict. _____

_____

 EXERCISE 8.15
Perspective Reversal

Accurately understanding the conflict depends on gaining insight into the other person's perspective on the conflict. This may be done through **perspective reversal,** a procedure in which one or both disputants present the other's wants, feelings, and underlying interests. The specific actions involved in perspective reversal are (a) an understanding response while (b) expressing warmth. A variety of research studies have demonstrated that the use of perspective reversal can eliminate misunderstandings and reduce distortions of the other person's point of view (Johnson, 1971). The following procedure gives you an opportunity to practice perspective reversal:

1. Choose a current topic of interest on which there are differences of opinion in the class. Divide the class in groups of four. Divide each group of four into two pairs. Assign each pair one side of the issue.

2. The pairs meet separately for ten minutes to prepare a presentation of their side of the issue in negotiations with a member of the other pair.

3. Each pair member is assigned to a new pair with a person from the other pair.

4. In the negotiating pair, designate one member A and the other B. A presents her side of the issue for up to four minutes. B then presents his side of the issue for up to four minutes.

5. B then reverses his perspective and presents as complete and accurate a case for side A as possible. A then reverses perspectives and presents side B as completely and accurately as she can.

6. The pair is then given ten minutes to arrive at a negotiated settlement of the issue. During the ten minutes they must obey the paraphrasing rule: Before either can reply to a statement made by the other, he or she must accurately and warmly paraphrase the other's statement to the other's satisfaction.

7. Conduct a whole-class discussion on the impact of perspective reversal on your understanding and appreciation of the other side of the issue. Did perspective reversal help you reach an agreement? Did it affect how you felt about each other during the negotiations? Did you feel it contributed to reaching a mutually satisfying agreement?

Step Five: Inventing Options for Mutual Gain

One completely overcomes only what one assimilates.
   —André Gide

The fifth step of negotiating is to identify several possible agreements. One will rarely do. People have a tendency to agree to the first reasonable solution that is proposed. Doing so shuts off consideration of even more advantageous agreements. Thus, make sure you generate at least three good alternative agreements before deciding on which one to adopt. To invent a number of potential agreements, you must avoid a number of obstacles and you must think creatively.

The five major obstacles that inhibit the inventing of a number of options are (1) *judging prematurely* any new idea, (2) *searching for the single answer*—which leads to premature closure and fixation on the first proposal formulated as the single best answer, (3) *assuming a fixed pie* (the less for you, the more for me), (4) *shortsighted self-concern* with your own immediate needs and goals, and (5) *defensively sticking with the status quo* to avoid the fear of the unknown inherent in change.

To invent creative options, you need to invent first and judge later, gather as much information as possible about the problem, see the problem from different perspectives and reformulate it in a way that lets new orientations to a solution emerge, broaden the options on the table rather than look for a single answer, search for mutual gains, invent ways of making decisions easily, propose possible agreements, and test each proposed agreement against reality (What are its strengths and weaknesses? What does each person gain and lose? How does it maximize joint outcomes?)

Possible agreements include meeting in the middle; taking turns; sharing; letting the other person have it all; letting chance decide; package deals, in which several issues that are considered part of the agreement are settled; trade-offs, in which two different things of comparable value are exchanged; tie-ins, in which an issue considered extraneous by the other person is introduced and you offer to accept a certain settlement provided this extraneous issue will also be settled to your satisfaction; and carve-outs, in which a specific issue is taken out of a larger context, leaving the related issues unsettled. In inventing alternative agreements, it often helps to describe what you are doing and, neglecting to do that, create and continue the conflict. Knowing how your actions help create and continue the conflict is essential for planning how to resolve it. Neglecting to do something constructive helps create and continue the conflict just as much as doing something destructive. You may want the other person to change. But the easiest thing to change is your own actions. If you wish to resolve a conflict, you must begin with deciding how to change your actions. It would be nice if everyone else changed so you would never have to. But you do not have control over the actions of others. They do. What you do have is control over your own actions. You can change your actions much more easily than you can change the other person's actions!

Agreement Menu

1. Meeting in the middle.
2. Taking turns.
3. Sharing.
4. Letting the other person have it all.
5. Letting chance decide.
6. Package deal (several issues that are considered part of the agreement are settled).
7. Trade-off (two different things of comparable value are exchanged).
8. Tie-in (an issue considered extraneous by the other person is introduced and you offer to accept a certain settlement provided this extraneous issue will also be settled to your satisfaction).
9. Carve-out (a specific issue is taken out of a larger context, leaving the related issues unsettled).

Step Six: Reaching a Wise Agreement

I never let the sun set on a disagreement with anybody who means a lot to me.
—Thomas Watson, Sr.

Given that we are all separate individuals with our own unique wants and goals, whenever we interact with others we will have some interests that are congruent and other interests that are in conflict. It takes wisdom to manage the combination of shared and opposed interests and reach an agreement. **Wise agreements** are fair to all participants, are based on principles, strengthen participants' abilities to work together cooperatively, and improve participants' ability to resolve future conflicts constructively. Wise agreements are those that meet the following criteria:

1. **The agreement meets the legitimate needs of all participants and is viewed as fair by everyone involved.** The agreement should clearly specify the responsibilities and rights of everyone involved in implementing the agreement. These include:
   a. The ways each person will act differently in the future. These responsibilities should be stated in a way that is specific (tells who does what when, where, and how), realistic (each can do what he or she is agreeing to do), and shared (everyone agrees to do something different).
   b. How the agreement will be reviewed and renegotiated if it turns out to be unworkable. This includes (1) the ways in which cooperation will be restored if one person slips and acts inappropriately and (2) the times participants will meet to discuss whether the agreement is working and what further steps can be taken to improve cooperation with each other.

2. **The agreement is based on principles that can be justified on some objective criteria** (Fisher & Ury, 1981). The objective criteria may be that everyone has an equal chance of benefiting (such as flipping a coin, where one flips and the other chooses, or letting a third-party arbitrator decide), fairness (taking turns, sharing, equal use), scientific merit (based on theory, tested out, evidence indicates it will work), and community values.

3. **The agreement and the process of reaching the agreement strengthen participants' ability to work together cooperatively in the future.** The trust, respect, and liking among participants should be increased.

4. **The agreement and the process of reaching the agreement strengthen participants' ability to resolve future conflicts constructively.**

It is important that both you and the other person understand which actions trigger anger and resentment in the other. Criticism, put-downs, sarcasm, belittling, and other actions often trigger a conflict. If the two of you understand what not to do as well as what to do, the conflict will be resolved much more easily. Sometimes people find out later that they have made a bad agreement. You may have agreed to something you should not have, or you may have changed your mind, or you may have found out you cannot keep your side of the bargain. At that point, you re-open negotiations and try to find a workable resolution to the conflict.

Try, Try Again

Difference of opinion leads to inquiry, and inquiry to truth.
—Thomas Jefferson

When you fail at negotiating an integrative agreement that is wise, the next step is to start over. To be successful at negotiating in a problem-solving way, you must remember to try, try again. No matter how far apart the two sides seem, no matter how opposed your interests seem to be, keep talking. With persistent discussion a viable and wise decision will eventually become clear.

 EXERCISE 8.16
Problem-Solving Negotiations

Conflicts end when a wise agreement is reached that is fair to everyone involved. To reach an agreement, you and the other person must negotiate. The more skillful you are in using the problem-solving negotiation procedure, the easier it will be to reach a wise agreement. The purpose of the following role playing is to provide you with practice situations in which you may use the six-step problem-solving negotiation procedure.

Person One	*Person Two*
I want	I want
I feel	I feel
My reasons are	My reasons are
My understanding of your wants, feelings, and reasons is	My understanding of your wants, feelings, and reasons is
Three plans to solve the problem are	Three plans to solve the problem are
We choose a plan and agree	We choose a plan and agree

Role Plays

1. You have enrolled in a large lecture class. You arrive for class a little early and take an aisle chair. Before the class begins you place your books on your chair and leave to get a drink of water. When you get back, you find your books sitting in the aisle and another student in your chair. What do you do? Role-play the exchange using the six steps of problem-solving negotiations.

2. You are standing in the hallway when another student runs into you. You are thrown against the wall and drop your books. The other student laughs. What do you do? Role-play the exchange using the six steps of problem-solving negotiations.

3. You tell a friend in confidence about someone you would like to go out with. The next day several people comment on it. You get your friend alone to talk about it. What do you do? Role-play the exchange using the six steps of problem-solving negotiations.

4. Chris borrows your history book. The next day, when Chris returns your book, it is muddy and the cover is torn. You believe that when you borrow something, you are responsible for taking care of it. You have to spend 20 minutes cleaning the book and taping the cover back together. Chris laughs and calls you a neatness freak. What do you do? Role-play the exchange using the six steps of problem-solving negotiations.

Role-Playing Procedure

1. Form groups of four. Divide each group into two pairs. One pair is assigned the role of the complainant and the other pair is assigned the role of the perpetrator.

2. The pair prepares to role-play the assigned character by reading the description of the situation and writing out the answers to the following questions:
   a. What do you want?
   b. How do you feel?
   c. What are your reasons for wanting what you want and feeling like you do?

3. One member of each pair meets with a member of the other pair and engages in the role play while using the six-step problem-solving negotiation procedure.

4. The group of four discusses how effectively the problem-solving negotiation procedure was used.

EXERCISE 8.17

Hamlet and His Father's Ghost

1. Form groups of four. Divide each group into two pairs. One pair is as-signed the role of Hamlet, and the other pair is assigned the role of the ghost.

2. The pair prepares to role-play the assigned character by reading the de-scription of the situation and writing out the answers to the following questions:
   a. What do you want?
   b. How do you feel?
   c. What are your reasons for wanting what you want and feeling like you do?

3. One member of the Hamlet pair meets with a member of the Ghost pair. They role-play a negotiation between Hamlet and his father's ghost, using the six-step problem-solving negotiation procedure.

4. The group of four discusses how effectively the problem-solving negotia-tion procedure was used.

Role-Playing Situation

The scene is the battlements of the castle of the king of Denmark. It is mid-night, the witching hour. The ghost of Hamlet's father appears and beckons Hamlet to follow the ghost for a private talk. They have a conflict that must be resolved. Decide which pair will play Hamlet and which will play his father. Then resolve the conflict using the problem-solving negotiation procedure.

Ghost

I am your father's spirit. Listen to me. If you ever loved me you must avenge my foul, strange, and most unnatural murder. I was not bitten by a poisonous snake. The serpent that bit me now wears my crown. He is an incestuous beast. He seduced your mother, a seemingly virtuous queen. Then, when I was asleep in the garden, he poured poison into my ear. My own brother, your uncle, killed me to gain both my crown and my wife. This is horrible! Hor-rible! You must kill him! You are my son and it is your duty to avenge my death. I cannot rest in my grave until my murder is avenged. You must fulfill your obligation and put me to rest. Denmark will not prosper with such a man on the throne. The king must be committed to the welfare of Denmark, not himself. And besides, if he has a son you will lose your birthright.

Hamlet

I did not know you were murdered. I thought you died of a snakebite. This is a complete surprise to me. The fact that my uncle murdered you is even more a surprise. I have a relationship with this man. I certainly want justice, but let's not be hasty. Asking me to kill him is a serious request. First, I may be too young and inexperienced to do it right. You would do better to ask one of your generals to do it. Second, killing my uncle could seriously damage my future career options and quality of life. Don't be so bloodthirsty. Think of my future! Third, this is not the time for me to kill someone. I am a carefree youth! I am in love. I'm still in school. I have years of learning and maturing left before I will be ready to kill someone. Fourth, I would never rest in my grave, and I might even go to hell, if I killed my uncle. Finally, killing my uncle is a complex task. I have to catch him alone doing something wicked so his soul will go to hell. What use is it if I kill him when he is doing something virtuous and he goes to heaven? This is not one of the usual "walk into the room and stab him" killings. This one is very complex and difficult. I'm not sure I want to do that much work!

Refusal Skills: This Issue Is Nonnegotiable

Not every issue is negotiable. You need to know when an issue is and is not negotiable and to be able to say no. *Negotiable issues* include conflicts over (a) the use of something (computer, book, car, clothes), (b) agreeing on something (what to do, what to have for dinner, what movie to see), and (c) obtaining something (money, power, fame, clothes, friends). On most issues you benefit from negotiating and reaching an agreement.

There are times, however, when you will not want to negotiate. You may feel this way because you do not like the other person, you see the issue as being nonnegotiable, you are uncomfortable with the issue, or you cannot do what the other person wants. You always have the option of saying no in negotiations. And you do not always need a clear reason. When you think someone is trying to manipulate you instead of solving a real problem, do not negotiate and do not make an agreement (see Table 8.3).

TABLE 8.3 *Reasons for Saying No*

Clear	Unclear
Illegal	My intuition tells me "no"
Inappropriate	I am not sure
It will hurt other people	The right option is not there
I will not be able to keep my word	I have changed my mind

EXERCISE 8.18
Negotiable Versus Nonnegotiable Issues

1. Form pairs. Draw two columns on a sheet of paper. Label the first column *Negotiable* and the second column *Nonnegotiable*. In the first column write "Eat a salad for lunch." In the second column write "Shoplift." What you eat for lunch is negotiable. Breaking the law is not negotiable. Each pair lists five issues that are negotiable and five issues that are not negotiable. Both members need a copy.

2. Find a new partner. *Share* your list of negotiable and nonnegotiable issues. *Listen* to his or her list. *Create* a new list from the best ideas of both of you.

3. Role-play a situation in which someone is trying to get you to do something you do not want to do. Pick one of the nonnegotiable issues. Try to negotiate it with your partner. Your partner should say, to your every attempt, "No, I won't do it. That issue is nonnegotiable." Then reverse roles. Your partner tries to negotiate one of the nonnegotiable issues with you. You reply to his or her every attempt, "No, I won't do it. That issue is nonnegotiable."

Meredith	*Margaret*
Help me cheat on this test.	No, I won't. That issue is nonnegotiable.
It's only one test. No one will ever know.	No, I won't. That issue is nonnegotiable.
If you're my friend, you'll help me cheat.	No, I won't. Cheating is nonnegotiable.

EXERCISE 8.19
What Are the Rules?

In previous times there were rules for engaging in conflicts. In the Middle Ages, for example, individuals who were involved in a conflict could fight a duel. A duel is a prearranged combat with deadly weapons (usually swords or pistols) between two persons. It took place under formal arrangements and in the presence of witnesses for each side, called seconds. Whoever won was considered to win the argument or dispute as well as the duel. There were strict rules as to how the duel was arranged, how it began and ended, and how duelists were allowed to behave during the duel. Failure to follow the rules would result in losing the duel. These rules were shared, so that all duelists followed them.

Boxing is an athletic contest between two persons, each of whom uses fists to try to knock the other unconscious or to inflict enough punishment to cause the opponent either to quit or to be judged beaten. A boxing match is conducted under established rules and procedures and has a referee, judges, and a timekeeper. If one boxer is knocked down and cannot rise in ten seconds, then he has lost. Hitting is only allowed above the belt. Hitting begins and ends in three-minute intervals called rounds. If a boxer breaks the rules he is declared the loser. The most famous set of rules was established by the Eighth Marquis of Queensberry. Boxers had to wear gloves. They could not wrestle, gouge with their thumbs, hug to squeeze the breath out of their opponents, hit below the belt, or hit while opponents were helpless or after the round ended. These rules were shared, so that all boxers followed them.

Although dueling had clear rules, and boxing has clear rules, many children are not taught the rules for engaging in conflicts. In classrooms and schools, there tend to be no shared rules and procedures that are followed by all students and faculty.

What Conflict Rules Do You Follow?	What Rules Do Your Peers Follow?

Negotiation: A Review of the Rules

You negotiate to resolve conflicts of interests. *Conflicts of interests* exist when your actions interfere with or block another person from achieving his or her goal. In a conflict of interests there are two concerns—achieving your goals and maintaining an effective working relationship with the other person. These two concerns result in five possible strategies: forcing, withdrawal, smoothing, compromise, and problem solving. The most important and most difficult strategies involve negotiation. *Negotiation* is a process by which persons who have shared and opposed interests, and want to come to an agreement, try to work out a settlement. Negotiations are inevitable. You negotiate every day, and sooner or later you negotiate with everyone in your life. There are two types of negotiations. *Win-lose negotiations* occur when participants want to make an agreement more favorable to themselves than to the other persons. It is appropriate primarily when you will never have to work with the other person in the future, such as when buying a used car. The majority of the time, however, you negotiate within an ongoing relationship. That requires *problem-solving negotiations,* where the goal is to reach an agreement that benefits everyone involved. Within ongoing relationships individuals are committed to the well-being of the other person as well as to their own well-being. In order to negotiate mutually beneficial agreements participants must state what they want and how they feel, state the reasons why they want what they do, reverse perspectives and summarize the other's position and interests, invent a series of possible agreements, and finally reach a wise decision. In order to negotiate mutually beneficial agreements participants must

1. State what they want and listen carefully to what the other person wants. Participants agree on a definition of the conflict that specifies it as a small and specific mutual problem to be solved. You inform, understand, and define (IUD).

2. State how they feel and listen carefully to how the other person is feeling.

3. State the reasons why they want what they do and feel how they do. Participants exchange reasons for their positions by expressing cooperative intentions, focusing on interests, not positions, exploring how their interests are incompatible and compatible, and empowering each other by giving choices.

4. Present the opposing perspective as completely and accurately as they can, summarizing the other's position and interests. Participants gain an understanding of the other person's perspective by paraphrasing and checking their perceptions of the other person's interests and reasons.

5. Invent creative options for mutual gain by avoiding the obstacles to creative problem solving.

6. Reach a wise agreement that meets the legitimate needs of all participants, is based on principles that can be justified on some objective criteria, enhances their ability to work together cooperatively, and strengthens their ability to resolve future conflicts constructively.

7. Try, try again until a wise agreement is reached.

To negotiate in good faith you need to build a reputation of someone who is honest, truthful, and trustworthy. Not all issues, however, are negotiable. You must know the difference between a negotiable and a nonnegotiable issue. And you must be able to say, "No, I will not negotiate on this issue," when it is appropriate to do so. One of the most problematic aspects of negotiating is to ensure that both people want to negotiate at the same time. Motivation to negotiate often must be coordinated.

Managing emotions, especially anger, is one of the most difficult aspects of negotiating. Managing your own anger and your responses to the anger of other individuals is covered in the next chapter.

■ CHAPTER REVIEW

Test your understanding of resolving interpersonal conflicts by taking the following quiz. Answers are at the end of the chapter.

True   False   1. If the relationship is really good, you will never have conflicts.

True   False   2. Conflicts can help you understand yourself and deepen a relationship.

True   False   3. It's a sign of weakness to explain the reasons for your wants.

True   False   4. You should avoid conflicts whenever possible.

True   False   5. Problem solving begins with honestly describing what you want.

True   False   6. A wise agreement is fair to everyone and strengthens the relationship.

True   False   7. The first agreement suggested is usually the best.

True   False   8. It's easier to resolve conflicts constructively if you hide your feelings.

True   False   9. Conflicts give you energy and make your life more interesting.

True   False   10. Trying to understand the other's perspective creates confusion.

True   False   11. Everything is negotiable.

True   False   12. If you hide your anger, resolving the conflict is difficult.

True   False   13. You need to think of several possible agreements to find a wise one.

True   False   14. Intuitively you will know what the agreement should be.

True   False   15. First you inform, then you understand, and then you define.

True   False   16. Larger problems are surprisingly easier to resolve than smaller ones.

True   False   17. You should focus on positions, not wants and goals.

True   False   18. People have to empower themselves; you can't do it for them.

Self-Diagnosis

In this chapter you have studied the two concerns inherent in conflicts, the five strategies for managing conflicts, the two types of negotiating, and the six-step problem-solving negotiation procedure. What have you mastered, and what do you need more work on? On a scale from 1 (poorly mastered) to 5 (highly mastered) rate the degree to which you have mastered each skill. Then choose two skills to improve on in the next week.

Rating	Skill
_____	Understanding there are two concerns in conflicts—goals and relationships.
_____	Withdrawing when both the goal and the relationship are of low importance.
_____	Forcing when the goal is important but the relationship is not.
_____	Smoothing when the goal is unimportant and the relationship is very important.
_____	Engaging in problem-solving negotiations when both the goal and the relationship are important.
_____	Compromising when both the goal and relationship are important but time is short.
_____	Understanding the difference between "win-lose" and "problem-solving" negotiations.
_____	Describing what I want.
_____	Describing how I feel.
_____	Explaining my reasons for wanting and feeling as I do.
_____	Taking the perspective of the other party.
_____	Developing several optional agreements that maximize joint gain.
_____	Determining which alternative agreement is most wise and agreeing to adopt it.
_____	Saying no when the issue is nonnegotiable.

Skills I Will Improve in the Next Week

1. _____

2. _____

Summary

In every relationship you decide how to manage the conflicts that arise. Perhaps the most difficult interpersonal skills to master are those involved in resolving conflicts constructively. When faced with a conflict, you have two concerns: achieve your goals and maintain the relationship. These two concerns identify five strategies for resolving conflicts: you can withdraw, try to force the other person to do what you want, do anything to maintain the relationship, compromise, or negotiate. The most important and most difficult strategy is negotiation. **Negotiation** is a process by which persons who have shared and opposed interests and want to come to an agreement try to work out a settlement. There are two types of negotiations. **Win-lose negotiations** occur when participants want to make an agreement more favorable to themselves than to the other persons. **Problem-solving negotiations** occur when participants want to make an agreement beneficial to everyone involved. Within ongoing relationships, conflicts should be resolved through problem-solving negotiations. In order to negotiate mutually beneficial agreements, participants must state what they want and how they feel, state the reasons why they want what they do, reverse perspectives and summarize the other's position and interests, invent a series of possible agreements, and finally reach a wise decision. In the next chapter you will study how to manage your anger in constructive ways.

Answers

Comprehension Test A: 1. c; 2. d; 3. f; 4. g; 5. b; 6. e; 7. a.

Comprehension Test B: 1. e, d, a, b, c; 2. false; 3. true; 4. false; 5. true; 6. true; 7. false; 8. false; 9. false; 10. false.

Chapter Review: 1. false; 2. true; 3. false; 4. false; 5. true; 6. true; 7. false; 8. false; 9. true; 10. false; 11. false; 12; true; 13. true; 14. false; 15. true; 16. false; 17. false; 18. false.

CHAPTER 9

Anger, Stress, and Managing Feelings

If you are patient in one moment of anger, you will escape a hundred days of sorrow.
   —Chinese proverb

The Nature of Stress

We are always under some stress, as long as we are alive. Sometimes the stress is low—when we are asleep, for instance; and sometimes the stress is high—for instance, when we are being attacked by muggers. But as long as we are alive, we are experiencing stress. Stress cannot be avoided, and our stress level is never at zero.

Besides the fact that stress is unavoidable, there are several aspects of stress that you should understand. One is that both too high and too low a stress level is damaging. If we experience too high a stress level for too long, physiological problems such as headaches, ulcers, and muscle pains can develop. But boredom can make us just as sick as high distress. A certain amount of stress is necessary for meeting the challenges of our lives and for providing the energy required to maintain life, resist aggression, and adapt to constantly changing external influences.

Humans, as a species, are stress-seeking. We seem to long for new experiences and new challenges. Traveling to the North Pole, climbing mountains, living in deserts, and exploring the bottom of the oceans are all activities for which we are biologically and socially ill-adapted, but we do them anyway. Humans seek out certain types of stress and enjoy them.

Another important aspect of stress is that the human body reacts to stress in a stereotyped, physiological way. Stress results in an emergency discharge of adrenaline and corresponding changes in the hypothalamus, pituitary, and thymus glands. Briefly, the autonomic nervous system and the endocrine system combine to speed up cardiovascular functions and slow down gastrointestinal functions. This response equips us to take physical action to restore the situation and our internal physiological state to normal. It really does not matter whether we are reacting with great joy or great fear; our physiological response is the same. To understand stress fully, homeostasis must first be understood. Homeostasis is the ability to stay the same. The internal environment of our bodies (our temperature, pulse rate, blood pressure, and so forth) must stay fairly constant, despite changes in the external environment, or else we will become sick and may even die. Stress alerts our bodies that action is needed to adapt to the external environment by changing our internal environment. The body then strives to restore homeostasis. Stress, therefore, can be defined as a nonspecific, general response of the body, signaling a need to perform adaptive functions so homeostasis can be restored.

There are many stressful events in our lives, from the death of a loved one to getting a speeding ticket. Stress affects both sexes and all ages. People in late adolescence or their twenties may be accumulating the effects of stress, effects that may not be apparent until their forties or fifties. Stress disorders are based on the slow developmental accumulation of psychological and physical stress responses throughout an individual's life. On the one hand, how you manage stress has great influence on your ability to reach out to other people, build a relationship, and maintain it over a long period of time. On the other hand, the quality of your relationships determines how much stress you experience.

Managing Stress and Anger

The Nature and Value of Stress

The Nature and Value of Anger

Managing Anger Constructively

Recognize and acknowledge your anger.

Decide whether to express your anger.

Express anger directly when possible.

Express anger indirectly when needed.

Stay focused on the task.

Analyze and understand your anger.

Congratulate yourself.

Express other emotions.

Expressing Anger Constructively

Clarify other's intent.

Describe other's behavior.

Describe your feelings of anger.

Make verbal and nonverbal messages congruent.

Be assertive, not aggressive.

Assess impact of your anger on other person.

Eliminate Unwanted Feelings Such As Anger in One's Life

Irrational beliefs underlie anger and blaming.

Dispose of feelings.

Deal with Another Person's Anger

Don't return anger or aggression.

Giving the other the "right" to feel angry.

See other's anger as feeling helpless.

Separate other's anger from aggression.

Focus other's attention on task.

Express respect or affection for other.

Explain the situation in a rational way.

Seek help in managing other.

Anger and Negotiations

EXERCISE 9.1

Can Friends Help You Stay Well?*

What is the level of stress and support in your life? You may wish to get an idea by completing the following questionnaires (California Department of Mental Health, 1981). The procedure is to complete stress-level and support-network-strength questionnaires, score them, and plot the results on the chart.

Stress Level

Circle each stress event that you have experienced within the last 12 months. Then add the scores for each item you circled.

Personal

(6)   Serious injury or illness

(6)   Alcohol, drug, or emotional problem

(4)   Marriage

(4)   Death of close friend

(2)   Trouble with friends or neighbors

(2)   Begin or end school or training program

Work and Finances

(6)   Lost job, retired

(4)   Sold or bought home

(2)   Changed jobs, promotion

(2)   Trouble with boss

Family

(10) Death of spouse or immediate family member

(8)   Divorce

(6)   Reconciliation or separation

(4)   Serious illness or injury of family member

(4)   Pregnancy or birth

(4)   Family arguments or trouble with in-laws

(4)   Child enters or leaves home

(2)   Relative moves into household

(2)   Moved to new residence

Stress Total:

Support Network Strength

Circle *one* response for *each* item. Then add the scores next to each item you circled.

1. At work, how many persons do you talk to about a job hassle?

    none (or not employed) (0)   one or two (3)   two or three (4)

    four or more (5)

---

*Exercise 9.1 was reprinted with permission of the California Department of Mental Health from *Friends can be good medicine*. Sacramento: State of California, Technical Report, 1981.

2. How many neighbors do you trade favors with (loan tools or household items, share rides, babysitting, etc.)?

   none (0)   one (1)   two or three (2)   four or more (3)

3. Do you have a spouse or partner?

   no (0)   several different partners (2)   one steady partner (6) married or living with someone (10)

4. How often do friends and close family members visit you at home?

   rarely (0)   about once a month (1)   several times a month (4) once a week or more (8)

5. How many friends or family members do you talk to about personal matters?

   none (0)   one or two (6)   three to five (8)   six or more (10)

6. How often do you participate in a social, community, or sports group?

   rarely (0)   about once a month (1)   several times a month (2) once a week or more (4)

Support Total:

Draw a line across each barometer where your scores for stress level and network strength fall.

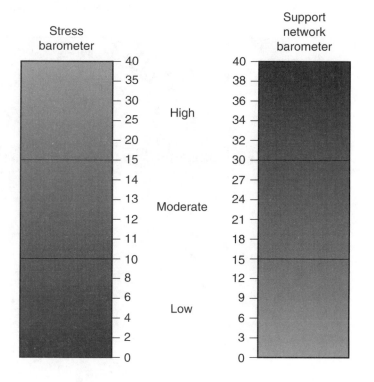

If your STRESS LEVEL score is

Less than 10:
You have a *low stress level* and your life has been stable in most areas.

10–15:
You have a *moderate stress level* and there has been a lot of change in your life.

16 or more:
You have a *high stress level* and there have been major adjustments in your life.

If your SUPPORT NETWORK score is

Less than 15:
Your support network has *low strength* and probably does not provide much support. You need to consider making more social contacts

15–29:
Your support network has *moderate strength* and likely provides enough support except during periods of high stress.

30 or more:
Your support network has *high strength* and it will likely maintain your well-being even during periods of high stress.

The chart on this page illustrates the relationship between stress and the support we get from others. Using your ranking *(high, moderate, low)* from the previous exercise, put an *x* where your stress level and support network

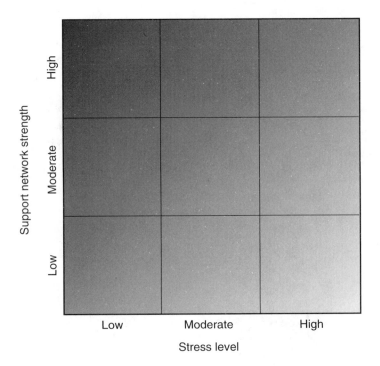

strength scores intersect. When your stress level is *lower* than your network strength, your score will be in the darker area of the chart. When your stress level is *higher* than your support strength, your score will fall in the lighter area. Darker colors indicate a greater likelihood of remaining well. Lighter colors indicate a higher risk of becoming ill.

Managing Stress Through Social Support Systems

One of the most effective ways to manage stress is to utilize social support systems involving other people who care about you or are sympathetic to your plight. Discussing stressful situations with friends and clarifying one's feelings through describing them to a sympathetic person are some of the most helpful strategies for managing stress. One of the first actions you should take when you find yourself experiencing stress, therefore, is to seek out friends and sympathetic acquaintances with whom to discuss the situation and your feelings.

There is a biological precedent for such a procedure. In the course of evolution, colonies of individual cells combined to form a single cooperative community in which competition was amply overcompensated by mutual assistance (because each member of the group could depend on the others for help). Different cells specialized, each undertaking different functions, some to look after food intake and digestion, others to provide the means for respiration, locomotion, and defense, still others to coordinate the activities of the entire colony. The evolution of diverse species was largely dependent on the development of processes that permitted many cells to live in harmony, with a minimum of stress between them, serving their own best interests by ensuring the survival of the entire complex structure. Stress within the body is managed through this complex division of labor in which different specialized cells work collaboratively to deal with threats to the productiveness of the entire colony. The indispensability of disciplined, orderly, mutually cooperative support is illustrated by its opposite—the development of cancer, whose most characteristic feature is that it cares only for itself. Cancer feeds on the other parts of the biological system to which it belongs until it kills the entire system, thus committing biological suicide, since a cancer cell cannot live except within the body in which it started its egocentric development.

Loneliness, isolation, and lack of social support during periods of stress create physiological damage and aggravate the effects of stress. Isolating ourselves during stressful times is the equivalent of committing social suicide, since destroying or failing to maintain our relationships when we need them the most is self-destructive. When we are experiencing stress, we need other people to turn to for support. Yet many people have too few relationships they can count on as sources of support. In our complex, technological, bureaucratic world, a broad base of interpersonal support is important. In addition to whatever family we may have, we need friends and acquaintances who respect us, challenge us, provide resources for us, and will be our mentors, evaluators, experts, and energizers. When we are experiencing stress, it is important to feel that we are not alone and to realize that by discussing situations with other people we can alleviate stress and provide ourselves with relief from pain.

The Nature and Value of Anger

Jim and Sam have been in the same classes for two years. Repeatedly Sam pushes Jim, teases him, takes his pencils, and generally bothers him. Today Jim has had enough. When Sam grabs his pencil, Jim loses his temper, jumps up, and tries to grab his pencil back. The teacher quickly intercedes, but Jim keeps yelling at Sam to leave him alone.

Emotions are always involved in conflicts, and one of the most common is anger. **Anger** is a defensive, emotional reaction that occurs when we are frustrated, thwarted, or attacked. You get angry when other people obstruct your goal accomplishment, frustrate your attempts to accomplish something, interfere with your plans, make you feel belittled and rejected, or indicate that you have no value or importance. When you get angry at other people the results can be either destructive or constructive. Anger tends to be *destructive* when (a) you express anger in a way that creates dislike, hatred, frustration, and a desire for revenge on the part of the other person or (b) it is repressed and held inside (a habit that tends to create irritability, depression, insomnia, and physiological problems such as headaches and ulcers). Anger tends to be *constructive* when you feel more energy, motivation, challenge, and excitement, and the other person feels friendship, gratitude, goodwill, and concern. In this chapter we shall examine the nature of anger and how it can be managed in constructive rather than destructive ways.

Anger both causes and accompanies distress. Anger can result in tight muscles, teeth grinding, piercing stares, headaches, heart attacks, loud voices, projectiles, and other forms of violence. When we are angry our "blood boils," we are "fit to be tied," we have "reached the end of our rope," and what happened is "the last straw." Anger is an emotion that occurs regularly in the life of every person, more often and with greater intensity at some times than at others. Failure to manage anger constructively can lead to alienation of loved ones, disrupted work performance, and even cardiovascular disorder. Proper recognition, understanding, acceptance, and channeling of anger can make life more comfortable, productive, and exciting.

In order for anger to be managed constructively, its components must be identified, and its major functions must be understood. The useful and constructive aspects of anger must be promoted while the destructive and useless aspects of anger are quelled. Rules for constructive anger management must be followed.

The main components involved in most human anger are as follows:

1. Anger is usually a defense against something.

2. Anger occurs when we are not getting something we want or would like. We get angry when we are frustrated, thwarted, or attacked.

3. Anger contains a sense of righteousness and a belief that one's personal rights have been violated. When we are angry, we usually believe that we are rightfully angry because the other person has acted unjustly or irrationally.

4. There is a narrowing of perceptual focus and priorities when we are angry. All our attention is focused on the person and behavior we are angry with.

5. There is a demanding aspect to anger. It makes us insist that we get our way.

6. There is considerable physiological arousal that demands expression in physical action. We are not only ready to fight or flee, but there is a demand that we actually do so.

When we plan how to manage our anger constructively, we need to keep in mind that anger is a righteous but defensive reaction to frustration and aggression based on a unidimensional perceptual focus, a physical demand to take action, and a belief that we must have our way.

There are at least eight major functions of anger. A brief description of each follows.

1. Anger gives us energy and increases the strength with which we act. Anger mobilizes us for action and thereby provides considerable physical energy to apply toward achieving our goals.

2. Anger disrupts ongoing behavior by making us agitated and impulsive as well as interfering with our ability to process information and attend to what is taking place. Anger disrupts behavior. It causes people to focus continually on the injustice that has been done to them or on the attack they are defending against. Someone who is angry has trouble attending to the tasks at hand and has difficulty comprehending new information. Anger often results in impulsive actions aimed at correcting the situation.

3. Anger makes it easier to express negative feelings and give negative feedback that might not be expressed if we were not angry. Expressing negative feelings often provides information needed to define problems accurately. Anger is a sign that something is going on that needs to be changed. Expressing anger constructively can increase trust by showing that the relationship is strong enough to handle strains. Healthy relationships depend on the ability of both partners to give accurate but negative feedback to each other, and anger helps them to do so. But the potential negative aspect of such forthrightness is that the strength of the negative feelings or feedback may be inappropriate to the provocation, may be overstated, or may be stated in such an offensive and threatening way that the conflict is escalated and the other person becomes fearful and angry.

4. Anger is defense against being vulnerable. Anger changes internal anxiety to external conflict. Anger can overcome anxiety and fear and encourage us to take actions we would never take otherwise. A small child may strike out in anger against a much bigger peer. A subordinate may confront a boss she is afraid of. A very shy person, when angry, may introduce himself to strangers.

5. Anger makes us more aggressive and antagonistic. Feeling angry can be a signal that aggressive actions are called for. Many times we become aggressive through habit when faced with a provocation and strike out verbally or physically at the other people in the situation.

6. Anger can be a signal that an event is a provocation or that something frustrating or unpleasant is taking place. Discovering that we are angry can help clarify what is taking place within a situation.

7. Anger helps us maintain a sense of virtue and righteousness in the face of opposition. Anger helps us maintain a belief that we are right, justified, and superior.

8. Anger can intimidate other people and is therefore a source of interpersonal power and influence. When we want to overpower another person, get our way, or dominate a situation, being angry can often help us to do so.

Being angry at another person can be an unpleasant experience. We can make the other person resentful and hostile when we express anger. We can become anxious after we have expressed anger as we anticipate rejection, counter-anger, and escalation of the conflict. Yet anger can have many positive effects on our problem solving if we learn to manage it constructively.

■ COMPREHENSION TEST

Test your understanding of stress and anger by answering true or false to the following statements.

True   False   1. We are under stress only when we are angry.

True   False   2. Very high stress is damaging, but very low stress is beneficial.

True   False   3. The body reacts to stress by slowing down the heart and speeding up the digestion.

True   False   4. Most of our stress originates from interaction with other people.

True   False   5. Repressing anger can cause insomnia, headaches, and ulcers.

True   False   6. Although anger gives us energy, it disrupts our ongoing behavior.

True   False   7. Anger changes our internal anxiety into external conflict.

True   False   8. Feelings of anger are a signal that something frustrating or unpleasant is taking place that you need to be aware of.

True   False   9. If you avoid discussing an issue, it will appear later in a different form.

True   False   10. "You are two hours late for our date, and I'm feeling angry" is a more constructive expression of anger than "I'm going to stomp on you for being late."

Rules for Managing Anger Constructively

Aesop tells of a bear roaming through the woods in search of berries who happened on a fallen tree in which a swarm of bees had stored their honey. The bear began to nose around the log very carefully to find out if the bees were at home. Just then one of the swarm came home from the clover field with a load of pollen. Guessing what the bear was after, the bee flew at him, stung him sharply, and then disappeared into the hollow log. The bear immediately lost his temper and sprang on the log tooth and claw to destroy the nest. But this action only brought out the whole swarm. The poor bear had to take to his heels, and he was able to save himself only by diving into a pool of water. Sometimes it is wiser to bear a single hurt in silence than to provoke a thousand injuries by flying into a rage. In managing your anger constructively, there is a set of rules to follow.

Rule One: Recognize and Acknowledge That You Are Angry

The first rule in managing anger is to recognize and acknowledge the fact that you are angry. Anger is a natural, healthy, normal human feeling. Everyone feels it. You need not fear or reject your anger. For one thing, repressed, denied anger does not vanish but often erupts suddenly in verbal and physical assaults on people and property as well as overreactions to minor provocations. In addition, repression and denial of your anger can create headaches, ulcers, muscle pains, and other physiological ailments. Remember that anger and aggression are not the same thing. You can express anger without being aggressive.

Rule Two: Clarify the Other's Intent

Do not jump to conclusions. Clarify the other person's intent and make sure the provocation is deliberate. Make sure you get all the facts before you react. Do not assume that aggression was intended without checking it out. It may be a misunderstanding. Use perception checks to make sure that you are not making false assumptions about the other person's feelings and intentions ("My impression is that you are not interested in trying to understand my ideas. Am I wrong?" "Did my last statement bother you?"). When negotiating the meaning of the other person's actions and when clarifying both your feelings and the feelings of the other person, use paraphrasing to make sure you accurately understand the other person and that the other person feels understood and listened to. If it was not a misunderstanding, you decide whether to express your anger directly or indirectly.

Rule Three: Decide What to Do with Your Anger

> *I was angry with my friend:*
> *I told my wrath, my wrath did end.*
> *I was angry with my foe:*
> *I told it not, my wrath did grow.*
> —William Blake

Expressing anger constructively can be one of the most difficult aspects of resolving conflicts because of the risks inherent in expressing your anger, the risks inherent in not expressing your anger, and the advantages of directly expressing your anger in a constructive way.

There are risks in directly expressing your anger. When you express anger, you have to worry about alienating the other person or making the person angry at you. Expressing anger could lead to losing the relationship or even losing your job. To express anger constructively you must first be aware that you are angry, accept anger as natural and normal, and decide to express it. Because of the risks, you usually pause before expressing anger because anger makes you impulsive (impulsive, antagonistic acts can escalate conflict and get you into trouble), decreases your information-processing capacity (making your decision about how to respond somewhat suspect), and creates a sense of righteousness (making you believe the other person deserves to be punished), all of which can influence you to express your anger at times when it would be better to calm down before dealing with the issue.

There are also risks in not expressing your anger. Keeping anger buried is usually harmful, causing a number of problems. First, hidden anger does not solve the problem and tends to add to your discomfort. This approach is not sensible. Second, anger distracts you from planning a constructive course of action. Being angry fills your thoughts with ways of getting even, not with how to get others to behave differently towards you. The net result is that things get worse and worse as you become angrier and angrier. Third, concealed anger is often displaced onto other persons. Not expressing anger at a friend or acquaintance can lead to displacing anger on your friends, family, or some stranger. Hidden anger does not vanish, but often suddenly erupts. Fourth, anger can make you physically sick. Headaches, high blood pressure, and physical pains often result. Fifth, repeated failure to express anger in words sometimes gives the impression that you don't care. In the long run, keeping anger to yourself will only hurt you and your relationships.

There are advantages to expressing anger directly. Anger conveys to other people what your commitments are. Expressing anger can clear the air so that positive feelings can once again be felt and expressed. Problems that are being ignored are brought to the surface and highlighted through the expression of anger. Expressing your anger while the provocation is small prevents anger from building up and becoming a problem in and of itself. Anger can override fear and feelings of vulnerability and lead you to act more competently in troublesome situations. Directly expressing your anger, however, takes skill.

Rule Four: Express Your Anger Directly When It Is Appropriate

The fourth rule is to express your anger directly and descriptively when it is appropriate to do so. To express your anger constructively, you describe the other person's behavior, you describe your feelings, and you make your nonverbal messages congruent with your words. You focus on the problem (not the person), assert your anger without being aggressive, assess the impact of your anger on the other person, and let your anger go (so you are free from negative emotions).

Describing the Other Person's Behavior

Express your anger to the appropriate person. Do not generalize. Be specific about the provocation and make your description of the other person's actions accurate and to the point. A **behavioral description** is a combination of describing the other person's actions and a personal statement to take ownership of your observations. In describing the other person's provocative actions, you observe what actually occurred and describe it clearly and specifically. You must describe visible evidence (the actions of the other person), behavior that is open to anyone's observation. Using personal statements is also a good idea so that it is clear that you are taking ownership of your observations. An example of a good behavior description is "Jim, by my count, you have just interrupted me for the third time." (Not, "Jim, you are really being rude," which is negative labeling or, "Jim, you always want to be the center of attention," which imputes an unworthy motive.) In describing another person's behavior, you (a) take responsibility for your anger (the other person did not make you become angry, your anger resulted from your interpretation of the causes of the other person's behavior) and (b) make your anger part of initiating problem-solving negotiations. Unless you are willing to become more involved with the other person and the situation, you should not express your anger.

Describing Your Feelings of Anger

You describe your feelings by using personal statements (referring to *I, me,* or *my*) and specifying the feeling by name or by action-urge, simile, or some other figure of speech. Your description will be more helpful and effective if it is specific rather than general ("You bumped my arm" rather than "You never watch where you are going"), tentative rather than absolute ("You seem unconcerned about completing our project" rather than "You don't care about the project, and you never will"), and informing rather than demanding ("I haven't finished yet" rather than "Stop interrupting me"). This latter point needs reemphasizing because of its importance; the description of your anger should be noncoercive and should not be a demand that the other person change. Avoid judgments of the other person ("You are egocentric"), name-calling, or trait-labeling ("You're a phony"), accusations and imputing undesirable motives to the other person ("You always have to be the center of attention"), commands, demands, and orders ("Stop talking and listen!"), and sarcasm ("You're really considerate, aren't you?" when the opposite is meant). By describing your feelings about the other person's actions, your feelings are seen as temporary and capable of change rather than as permanent. It is better to say, "At this point, I am very annoyed with you" than "I dislike you, and I always will."

Taking clear ownership of your feelings avoids a common trap in expressing anger. When anger is accusatory and "you" messages are used, the conflict tends to escalate and the person is likely to respond with counter-anger (Kubany et al., 1992). Avoid saying, "You're frustrating me," or, "You're making me mad." "You" statements tend to evoke anger, antagonism, defiance, and alienation in the other person, and fuel your own anger and instigate aggressive acts that may haunt you later.

Making Your Verbal and Nonverbal Messages Congruent

When directly expressing your anger, use both verbal and nonverbal messages skillfully. Nonverbal messages are more powerful than words in expressing feelings, but they are also more difficult to understand. You need to be able to make your words and nonverbal messages congruent. In describing your feelings you need to make your nonverbal messages similar to your verbal ones. When you express anger verbally, your facial expression should be serious, your tone of voice neutral to cold, your eye contact direct, and your posture rather stiff. Contradictory verbal and nonverbal messages may indicate to the other person that you are untrustworthy, and you may often make the other person anxious.

Focusing on the Task

You can usually be far more effective in expressing your anger when you stay focused on the goal to be achieved. The more focused you are on the task and issue, the less angry you will be. Do not let yourself get sidetracked or baited into a quarrel. There is evidence that anger directed toward a person will be far more destructive than anger directed toward an issue. Viewing an incident as a personal affront is likely to result in disruptive and defensive anger, while viewing an incident as a problem to be solved is likely to result in discriminative, expressive, and energizing anger.

Assertiveness Versus Aggressiveness

All people have a perfect right to express their thoughts, feelings, opinions, and preferences and to expect that other people will treat them with respect and dignity. In interpersonal situations involving stress and anger, you may behave nonassertively, aggressively, or assertively. In general, it is a good idea to raise your restraints and inhibitions against aggressive and nonassertive behavior and to lower any inhibitions, restraints, or anxieties you have about being assertive. When you behave **nonassertively,** you say nothing in response to a provocation, keeping your feelings to yourself, hiding feelings from others, and perhaps even hiding your feelings from yourself. Nonassertive behavior is often dishonest and involves letting other people violate your personal right to be treated with respect and dignity.

Aggressive behavior is an attempt to hurt someone or destroy something. It infringes on the rights of others and involves expressing your feelings indirectly through insults, sarcasm, labels, put-downs, and hostile statements and actions. Aggressive behavior involves expressing thoughts, feelings, and opinions in a way that violates others' rights to be treated with respect and dignity.

Assertive behavior involves describing your feelings, thoughts, opinions, and preferences directly to another person in an honest and appropriate way that respects both yourself and the other person. It enables you to act in your own best interests, to stand up for yourself without undue anxiety, to express honest feelings comfortably, and to exercise personal rights without denying the rights of others. Assertive behavior is direct, honest, self-enhancing self-expression that is not hurtful to others and is appropriate for the receiver and the situation.

When you are angry at another person's actions, it is important that you are assertive, but not aggressive.

Assessing the Impact of Your Anger on Another Person

Take into account the impact your anger will have on the other person. While you will usually feel better after expressing anger constructively and directly to another person, the other person may feel alienated and resentful. After expressing anger directly, it is important to make sure that the other person has a chance to respond and clarify his or her feelings before the interaction is ended. Give the other person a chance to explain. Show that you are interested in what he or she has to say by listening attentively, without showing signs of impatience, boredom, or hostility.

The purpose of asserting your anger is to create a shared understanding of the relationship so it may be improved or so you may be more effective in achieving your goals. You want the other person to know how you perceive and feel about his or her actions, and you wish to end up knowing how the other person perceives and feels about your actions. You want to discuss the situation until you and the other person have a common perspective or frame of reference in viewing the relationship and your interactions with each other. You assess the impact of your anger on the other person to ensure that it promotes problem solving, not defensive withdrawal or counter-anger.

Letting Go of the Anger

Make the expression of anger cathartic. **Catharsis** is the release of pent-up emotion either by talking about feelings or engaging in active emotional release by crying, laughing, or shouting. Anger needs to be expressed in a way that terminates it. Anger is not a feeling to hold on to. Once you have expressed your anger constructively, let it go.

Expressing other emotions in addition to anger helps you let your anger go. Besides expressing negative feelings, it is important to express positive feelings while discussing a conflict. There are positive feelings, such as liking, appreciation, and respect that strengthen your relationship with the other person. The more you focus on your positive feelings for the other person, the less angry both of you will be.

Direct-Expression-of-Anger Summary

To express anger constructively, first describe the other person's provocative behavior and then describe your anger verbally while making your nonverbal messages congruent with your words. An example would be, "Jim, by my count you have just interrupted me for the third time in the past half hour, and I am both frustrated and angry as a result" (while maintaining a serious facial expression, a neutral to cold tone of voice, direct eye contact, and a rather stiff posture). You should then be ready to negotiate on the meaning of Jim's actions and on whether or not anger is the appropriate feeling to have.

In expressing anger your attitude should not be "Who's right and who's wrong?" but rather "What can each of us learn from this discussion that will make our relationship more productive and satisfying?" You stay focused on the task to be completed, not on the other person's provocations. As a result of the discussion, each of you will act with fuller awareness of the effect of your actions on the other person as well as with more understanding of the other person's intentions.

Finally, make sure the timing of the expression of your anger is appropriate. Generally, express your anger when there is time enough to discuss the situation and the provocation. The closer in time your reaction

Expressing Anger Constructively

Clarify the Other Person's Intent

Describe the Other Person's Behavior

Describe Your Feelings of Anger

Make Your Verbal and Nonverbal Messages Congruent

Focus on the Problem, Not the Person

Be Assertive, Not Aggressive

Assess the Impact of Your Anger on the Other Person

Let Go of the Anger

is expressed to the provocation, the more constructive the discussion will tend to be. If you express your anger appropriately, you should be able to let it go and free yourself from its effects.

Rule Five: Express Your Anger Indirectly When Direct Expression Is Inappropriate

The fifth rule of managing your anger constructively is to express it indirectly or to react in an alternative way when direct expression is inappropriate. There are times when you cannot express your anger directly to the people provoking you. You still need to free yourself from the anger before discussing the conflict with the appropriate people. Feelings do need to be expressed. The stronger the feeling, the stronger the need for expression. However, the expression can be indirect. You do not want to stay angry forever. The sooner you get rid of the feelings, the happier your life will be. Expressing and terminating anger indirectly usually involves the following:

1. **Physical exercise.** There is a general maxim that when one is angry and wants to feel better tomorrow, then one should exercise today. Vigorous exercise like jogging, swimming, tennis, or volleyball provides physical release of energy that is important in releasing anger.

2. **Private physical expression.** Strongly express the feeling in private by shouting, swearing, crying, moaning, throwing pottery, pillow fights, and even hitting a pillow against a wall while yelling. Such actions will provide a physical release of energy and anger.

3. **Psychological detachment.** You can detach by
   a. Resolving the situation in your mind or resigning yourself to it. Hanging on to the negative feelings only makes your life unpleasant. Give up thoughts of revenge and getting back at other people; you want to resolve the problem. Remember, you gain power and influence when you keep calm and refuse to get angry.
   b. Telling yourself things that help you let the negative feelings go. You can put up with an unfair instructor; an obnoxious peer is not really that bad. Since anger is sometimes due to doubting yourself or letting yourself feel threatened by someone else, it is important to remember that you are a worthwhile person and that you have many strengths and competencies. Doing so can keep you from feeling angry.
   c. Changing the way you view the provocation, thereby changing your feelings of anger. Through modifying your interpretations of what the other person's behavior means, you can control your feelings, responding with amusement or indifference rather than with anger.

4. **Relaxation.** Learn to relax when you wish. You cannot be relaxed and angry at the same time. When your anger is triggered,
relax. As you learn to relax more easily, your ability to regulate
your anger will improve.

By learning alternative ways of reacting to provocations and indirect ways
of expressing anger, you will be able to choose the most effective response.
Such freedom gives you an advantage in situations in which other people
are trying to provoke you. The best way to take charge of such a situation
is not to get angry when most people would expect or even want you to
do so.

Rule Six: Analyze and Reflect on Your Management of Anger

The sixth rule is to analyze, understand, and reflect upon your anger. Get to know
yourself so that you recognize (a) the events and behaviors that trigger
your anger and (b) the internal signs of arousal that signal you are becoming angry. It is important for you to understand the regularities of your
anger patterns—when, in what circumstances, and with whom you become angry. You can then plan how to avoid frustrating, anger-provoking
situations. The more sharply tuned you are to the signs of internal arousal,
the greater your ability to stop your anger before it develops.

*Finally, congratulate yourself when you have succeeded in managing your
anger constructively.* Feel good about your success. Don't focus on your mistakes and failings or on the nastiness of other people. Focus on your ability to manage your anger constructively.

 EXERCISE 9.2
Understanding My Anger

Being aware of our feelings is an important and somewhat difficult task. Many
of us were taught to hide our feelings. We learned to pretend we did not have
them. This is especially true of feelings we consider negative, such as anger.
We often keep our anger inside and act as if it were not there. We deny to
ourselves that we are angry. In order to be aware of our anger and express it
appropriately, we must understand what makes us angry. The purpose of this
exercise is to increase your awareness of what makes you angry. The procedure is as follows:

1. Working by yourself, complete the statements listed under "My Anger"
   on a separate sheet of paper. Be sure to write out your answers fully.

2. Form groups of four. Take the first statement and discuss the answers of
   each member. Then go on to the second statement.

3. After you have finished discussing all 16 statements, write down
   a. Five major things that make your group members angry.
   b. Five major ways in which your group members express their anger.
   c. Five major conclusions your group has come to about what happens when anger is expressed.

4. Share your conclusions with the other groups, while they share their conclusions with you.

5. In your group of four, discuss how your group's conclusions compared with the conclusions of the other groups.
   a. Do you all feel anger for the same reasons?
   b. Do you all express your anger in the same way?
   c. Do you all feel the same way when someone is angry at you?
   d. Do you all agree on what consequences will result from expressing anger?

My Anger

Complete the following statements. Be specific. Try to think of times when you were angry or someone was angry at you. You may wish to substitute "co-workers," "students," or "colleagues" for "friends" and "boss" or "parent" for "teacher."

1. I feel angry when my friends . . .

2. When I'm angry at my friends, I usually . . .

3. After expressing my anger, I feel . . .

4. The way I express anger usually makes my friends . . .

5. When my friends express anger toward me, I feel . . .

6. When I feel that way, I usually . . .

7. After reacting to my friends' anger, I feel . . .

8. My reactions to my friends' anger usually results in . . .

9. I feel angry when my teacher . . .

10. When I'm angry at my teacher, I usually . . .

11. The way I act when I'm angry at my teacher makes me feel . . .

12. The way I act when I'm angry at my teacher usually results in my teacher . . .

13. When my teacher expresses anger at me, I feel . . .

14. When I feel that way I usually . . .

15. After reacting to my teacher's anger, I feel . . .

16. My reactions to my teacher's anger usually result in my teacher . . .

EXERCISE 9.3

Defusing the Bomb

The purpose of this exercise is to discuss how you manage provocations. Here is the procedure for the exercise:

1. Divide into groups of three.

2. Read the following incident and as a group answer these questions:
   a. How would you feel?
   b. What would you do?
   c. How would you maximize positive outcomes and minimize negative outcomes?
   d. What would you say to yourself to manage your feelings constructively?

Incident

You are a teacher at a suburban junior high school. You are sitting in your office when a parent, Ms. Jones, walks in without an appointment. Ms. Jones, in a very loud and angry voice, begins to demand that you reprimand one of your students, stating that the student is vicious and picks on Ms. Jones's son (who is a student in your class). Ms. Jones refuses to listen to your explanations, criticizes your ideas, and even brags about how well she understands teaching and child development. For the most part, she is uninterested in anything you have to say. Finally, as you present your view once again, Ms. Jones calls you a "stupid jerk."

 EXERCISE 9.4

Talking to Yourself to Manage Provocations

Any meeting to discuss a conflict can be divided into four states:

1. Preparing emotionally for the meeting.

2. Listening to the other person's angry statements.

3. Coping with the arousal and agitation resulting.

4. Congratulating yourself for coping successfully.

For each stage, there are a number of statements you should make to yourself to help you manage the provocation successfully. The assumption is that through controlling what you say to yourself before, during, and following a provocation, you can change your conflict behavior and instruct yourself in more constructive behavioral patterns. The purpose of this exercise is to give you some practice in differentiating among the self-statements for each stage and applying them to a conflict situation you have recently been involved in. The procedure is as follows:

1. Form groups of three. Working as a group, classify the self-statements according to the four stages of managing a provocation constructively. Place a 1 for statements that you would say to yourself to prepare emotionally for the meeting, a 2 for statements that you would say to yourself while listening to the other person express his or her anger toward you, and so forth.

2. Read the two case studies that follow the list of self-statements, and for each plan what your group would say to yourselves to manage the provocation. All members of the group need to agree on what you would say.

3. Have each member of the triad identify a conflict situation that usually creates anger and distress in him or her.

4. Working as a triad, take each conflict situation and work out a series of self-statements that can be used during each stage of managing the provocation constructively. Each member of the triad should develop a set of self-statements that will help him or her manage the conflict situation more constructively next time it appears.

Managing Provocations by Talking to Yourself

The following list contains statements you could say to yourself to help yourself manage a conflict situation constructively. Working as a triad, classify each statement as belonging in one of the four stages of managing a provocation constructively. Check your group's answers against the key provided on p. 420 of the Appendix.

Stage	What I Say to Myself
1. _____	Dealing with her anger is only a minor annoyance.
2. _____	Listen carefully for the issue, not the feelings.
3. _____	Getting upset will not work. Stay relaxed.
4. _____	I did that well!
5. _____	I got through that without getting angry. Way to go!
6. _____	What does she want?
7. _____	It is not worth getting upset over.
8. _____	Listening to her anger will be easy.
9. _____	I will be able to manage the situation.
10. _____	He is trying to get me angry. I am not going to.
11. _____	I did not take anything personally. Good job!

Stage   *What I Say to Myself*

12. _____ What is the issue? Do not get distracted into a quarrel.

13. _____ I am excellent at managing provocations.

14. _____ So he is insulting me. So what? The issue is more important.

15. _____ Calm down. I can't expect people to act the way I want them to.

16. _____ Take a few deep breaths and relax before we start.

17. _____ Good for me!

18. _____ It will be easy.

19. _____ What does she want?

20. _____ Relax.

Were You Talking About Me?

One of your friends, John, has asked to meet with you. He has heard that you have been spreading negative rumors about him. He is very hurt, angry, and upset. In talking with another friend, you did mention several good points and a couple of inadequacies about John in a general discussion, but John has heard only that you were criticizing him behind his back. In preparing for the meeting, what are statements you can make to yourself to

1. Prepare emotionally for the meeting?
2. Prepare to listen to John's angry statements?
3. Cope with your arousal and agitation during the meeting?
4. Congratulate yourself for coping successfully with his anger?

I Didn't Do It!

Sally is an acquaintance who continually bothers other people. She pushes, nudges, pokes, and trips her classmates regularly. A good friend, Jane, came to you crying with a cut lip and a bruised knee, complaining that Sally tripped her. You sit down with Sally to have a talk with her about her behavior. Sally is extremely angry, saying that she did not touch Jane and Jane is lying. Sally sees you as being completely out of line in wanting to meet with her. You know that once you start to talk to her, she will start yelling and calling you names. In preparing for the meeting, what are statements you can make to yourself to

1. Prepare emotionally for the meeting?
2. Prepare to listen to Sally's angry statements?
3. Cope with your arousal and agitation during the meeting?
4. Congratulate yourself for coping successfully with her anger?

EXERCISE 9.5

Anger Arousers

In discussing conflicts there are certain actions that can make other people angry. Given below is a list of statements. Each represents one type of anger arouser. Working with a partner, match the statement with the type of anger arouser it represents.

Statement

Juan: "Don't worry, I'll pay you back!"
Pam: "You never, ever pay back money you owe someone!"

Nancy: "Sorry your jacket got dirty."
Megan: "You are such a jerk!"

Bill: "I think . . . "
Sam: "What you think doesn't matter, it's what you did that counts."

Jane: "This would be fair."
Jan: "Oh yes, that's fair all right. That's really fair! The whole world will stand up and shout 'That's fair!' "

Jeff: "I'm sorry."
Julie: "I know you, and you are a liar."

Chris: "You should apologize to me!"
Jean: "You are so wrong, so very, very wrong!"

Miguel: "I'm really worried I hurt Karl's feelings."
Judy: "So what? Can you loan me $5.00?"

Gene: "I don't know what you're talking about!"
Raymond: "It's all your fault and you should be penalized!"

Anger Arouser

Sarcasm is a harsh form of put-down or ridicule. In a conflict, sarcasm almost always makes the other person angry.

Negative Judgment is stating that the other person is wrong or bad.

Interrupting is cutting the other person off before he or she has finished speaking.

Ignoring is doing something else while someone is talking to you or brushing off what another person is saying as unimportant.

Globalizing is attaching a negative label to a person by saying, "You always do this" or "You never do that."

Blaming/Accusing is stating the problem is someone's fault and that person needs to be punished.

Insulting/Name-Calling is attaching a negative label to the person as part of a personal attack.

Stating Opinion as Fact is stating your opinion as if it were the absolute truth, leaving no room for discussion.

Eliminating Unwanted Feelings from Your Life

I have known a great many troubles, but most of them never happened.
—Mark Twain

When it is not wise to express anger directly, you need to be able to eliminate unwanted anger from your life. You do so by (a) recognizing that you can change yourself more easily than you can change the world,

Tips on Survival

Want to live a long time? Research studies on survival in concentration camps, in prisoner-of-war camps, on cancer and heart-disease victims, and on old age indicate there are five factors that are important to survive and live a long life.

1. **Have deeply held goals and commitments.** These goals and commitments need to involve relationships with other people. People who lived the longest in concentration and prisoner-of-war camps, for example, were people who turned their concern outward and worked to help other people survive.

2. **Share your distress with other people.** Quiet, polite, passive, accepting, and well-behaved persons die. A person who openly shares his or her suffering with other people and is aggressive in getting his or her needs met will tend to live longer.

3. **Maintain high morale.** Depression kills. In concentration camps, in POW camps, and among cancer patients, people who become depressed die.

4. **Engage in physical activity.** Keeping yourself physically active helps you survive.

5. **Maintain friendships and love relationships.** Lonely people die. Isolated people die. People with good friends and loving relationships survive. Many psychologists believe that loneliness is the biggest personal adjustment problem in the United States.

Want to live a long and happy life? Then build goals and commitments that are important to you and that involve other people's welfare. Share your moments of distress and discomfort with other people. Learn how to talk with other people about how you feel. Avoid depression and keep your morale high. Keep physically active. Constantly build and renew friendships and love relationships. We will all die someday. Let us hope that we do not die from lack of commitments, passivity, depression, inactivity, or loneliness.

(b) avoiding irrational beliefs that create and intensify unwanted anger, and (c) disposing of unwanted feelings such as anger.

You have some choice as to how long you stay angry. If you deal with your feelings constructively, they will not last long. Depending on how you manage your feelings, you can be angry or depressed all the time by turning small events into tragedies, or you can quickly eliminate unwanted feelings from your life and feel good most of the time.

To change negative or destructive feelings, you have two choices. You can choose to try to change things outside of yourself: You can change jobs, friends, location, and careers. Or you could choose to change things within yourself: You can change your interpretations of what is happening in your life. Changing your interpretations will change your feelings. In choosing whether to try to change something outside of yourself or inside yourself, it is important to remember: *The easiest thing to change in your life is yourself.*

Let's take an example. Sam believes his boss is always picking on him. He thinks that his boss gives him the dirtiest jobs to do. Sam thinks that his colleagues are not made to work as hard as he is. The boss always seems to be criticizing Sam but not his colleagues. All this makes Sam angry, depressed, worried, and frustrated. Sam also feels that the situation is hopeless. "What can I do?" asks Sam. "My boss has all the power. He can fire me, but I can't do anything to him." Sam has two choices. He can try to change his boss, or he can try to change his feelings. Psychologists would tell Sam it is easier to change his feelings than to change his boss. What do you think?

Irrational Beliefs Underlying Anger and Blaming

Long-term anger is based on two irrational beliefs. The first is that you must have your way and that it is awful not to get everything you want. This is known as **catastrophizing.** The second is that people are bad and should be severely dealt with if they have behaved wrongly. If you see the cause of your frustration as being wicked people who deserve to be punished for their evil acts, you are stuck in a blame orientation. A blame orientation distracts you from finding a solution to your frustration.

A blame orientation is especially destructive when it is applied to yourself. **Self-blame** exists when you say "bad me" to yourself or when you judge your basic self-worth on the basis of your inadequate or rotten behavior. Self-blame is in effect being angry at yourself. Self-blame involves a double attack: one against your actions and the other against yourself as a person. If you spill coffee on your desk, you can see your behavior as being uncoordinated, or you can see your behavior as clumsy and yourself as rotten and no good. Self-blame is similar to giving yourself a grade on the basis of a behavior you do not like. When you blame yourself, you believe it is catastrophic that you are not getting what you want, that it is your fault, and therefore you are a bad person who should be severely punished. When you blame yourself (or others), you have to carry the anger around inside you, subjecting yourself to a great deal of stress and even making yourself sick. Perhaps most important, blaming yourself distracts you from finding a solution to your problems. All the punishment in the world does not promote creative insight into how a situation may be more constructively managed.

You should never blame yourself (or others) for

1. **Not having the intelligence to do as well as you would like.** If the intellectual ability is not there, you cannot blame yourself. Either it is in your genes, or it is not.

2. **Being ignorant.** Ignorance means that you have not yet learned a skill. You cannot blame yourself if you did not know better.

3. **Having behaved badly.** You should separate your behavior and your self-worth. You are not your actions. Engaging in a bad behavior does not make you a bad person.

4. **Not being perfect.** In perfectionism, you attempt to be all things rather than who you are. A perfectionist never has developed an internal sense of how much is good enough. Only when you can stop trying to be perfect do you ever become free to be who you are.

5. **Being psychologically disturbed at the time.** Everyone at times enters psychological states such as anger, depression, grief, fear, and even extreme tiredness that result in behaving in ways destructive to the best interests of ourselves or others. Psychological problems do not result from being possessed by demons. Being psychologically disturbed does not make you an evil person.

To combat a blame orientation you must first change your basic assumptions that (a) it is a catastrophe when you do not get what you want and (b) whoever is to blame must be severely punished. Second, you must engage in an internal debate to replace your old assumptions with the new, more constructive ones. Never blame anyone (including yourself). Always separate the person from the actions. Third, you must forgive yourself (and others) for everything. The sooner you forgive yourself the better. Sooner or later you forgive yourself and those you disagree with. Since you will eventually forgive, the sooner you do so the better for you. Finally, you must be problem oriented. Focus on the problem to be solved, not on the failure of you or others to live up to your expectations. Remember that when you blame others they become much more hostile and angry with you, escalating the conflict into destructive directions.

Disposing of Feelings: Like It or Dump It

Habits can not be thrown out the upstairs window. They have to be coaxed down the stairs one step at a time.
—Mark Twain

The five aspects of expressing feelings discussed are these:

1. Gather information through your five senses (sight, hearing, smell, touch, taste). For example, you see and hear someone yelling at you while feeling the person grabbing your arm.

2. Interpret the meaning of the information gathered. Then you decide the person is angry and is trying to obstruct your progress.

3. Experience the feelings appropriate to your interpretations. You may, for instance, feel threatened and angry.

4. Decide how you intend to express your feelings. You may decide to pull your arm free and ask the person to explain.

5. Express your feelings. Then you could step back and sharply pull your arm (freeing it) and ask, "What is wrong?"

Feelings are not caused by events and people around you; they are caused by the ways in which you interpret your experiences. Your friends and acquaintances cannot upset you; only the interpretations you make about their behavior can upset you. Therefore, you can control your feelings. You can decide which feelings you would like to keep and expand. You can decide which feelings you would like to get rid of. Your feelings are disposable!

Through your senses you strive for accurate and complete information about the situation. Through your interpretations, you can either feel challenge or enjoyment, or you can feel angry, depressed, anxious, or helpless. When your interpretations result in feelings that contribute to a painful and troubled life, you are managing your feelings destructively. The assumptions you make about what is good or bad, what you do or do not need, and what causes what in the world tend to control your interpretations. Your assumptions can be irrational or rational. An **irrational assumption** is a belief (accepted without proof) that makes you depressed, anxious, or upset most of the time. If you believe that you have to be perfect or else you are absolutely worthless, you have an irrational assumption. If you believe that everyone in the world has to think you are absolutely marvelous or else you will be miserable, you have an irrational assumption. Irrational assumptions can only make you feel miserable because they lead to depressing interpretations. *All you have to do to ruin your life is to make a few irrational assumptions and refuse to change them no matter how much pain they cause!*

A **rational assumption** is a belief that makes you feel satisfied, content, happy, and proud most of the time. A rational assumption is that it would be nice if everyone liked you, but you can live a perfectly happy and wonderful life whether they do or not. Adopting rational assumptions also provides you with more energy to live a happy life. It takes energy to have destructive feelings. It takes energy to hold onto irrational assumptions. It takes energy to make interpretations that lead to miserable feelings. It takes energy to try to ignore, deny, and hide these miserable feelings. The fewer irrational assumptions you have, the more energy you will have for enjoying yourself and your relationships! The more quickly you get rid of your irrational assumptions and the destructive feelings they cause, the more energy you have for enjoying yourself and your relationships! To eliminate unwanted feelings from your life you need to

1. Be aware of your assumptions.
2. Understand how your assumptions determine your interpretation of the information gathered by your senses.
3. Be able to tell how rational or irrational your assumptions are. You become highly aware of when you are making an irrational assumption and think of a rational assumption that is much more constructive.
4. Dump your irrational assumptions for rational ones through a process of arguing with yourself (against the irrational assumption and for the rational one).

Irrational assumptions are learned. Usually they are learned in early childhood. They were taught to you by people in your past. Irrational assumptions are bad habits. What was learned as a child can be unlearned as an adult. If you keep arguing against your irrational assumptions, you will soon develop rational ones! Do not let yourself feel bad just because you have developed bad thinking habits in the past!

 EXERCISE 9.6

Assumptions, Assumptions, What Are My Assumptions?

What are common irrational assumptions? How do you know if your assumptions are rational or irrational? One way is to compare them with the following list of rational and irrational assumptions taken from the writings of Albert Ellis (1962). Do you make any of these assumptions? Do you have any of the irrational assumptions that are listed? Do you make any of the rational assumptions in the list? Can you tell the difference between the rational and the irrational ones?

Read each of the listed statements. Write *yes* for any assumption that describes how you think. Write *no* for any assumption that does not describe how you think. Then reread each statement. Write *R* for the rational assumptions. Write *I* for the irrational assumptions. Keep your answers. You will use them in a later lesson.

Common Assumptions

_____ 1. I must be loved, liked, and approved of by everyone all the time or I will be absolutely miserable and will feel totally worthless.

_____ 2. It would be nice if I were liked by everyone, but I can survive very well without the approval of most people. It is only the liking and approval of close friends and people with actual power over me (such as my boss) that I have to be concerned with.

_____ 3. I have to be absolutely 100 percent perfect and competent in all respects if I am to consider myself worthwhile.

_____ 4. My personal value does not rest on how perfect or competent I am. Although I'm trying to be as competent as I can, I am a valuable person regardless of how well I do things.

_____ 5. People who are bad, including myself, must be blamed and punished to prevent them from being wicked in the future.

_____ 6. What is important is not making the same mistakes in the future. I do not have to blame and punish myself or other people for what has happened in the past.

_____ 7. It is a total catastrophe and so terrible that I can't stand it if things are not the way I would like them to be.

_____ 8. There is no reason the world should be the way I want it to be. What is important is dealing with what is. I do not have to bemoan the fact that things are not fair or just the way I think they should be.

_____ 9. If something terrible could happen, I will keep thinking about it as if it is actually going to take place.

_____ 10. I will try my best to avoid future unpleasantness. Then I will not worry about it. I refuse to go around keeping myself afraid by saying, "What if this happened?" "What if that happened?"

_____ 11. It is easier to avoid difficulties and responsibilities than to face them.

_____ 12. Facing difficulties and meeting responsibilities are easier in the long run than avoiding them.

_____ 13. I need someone stronger than myself to rely on.

_____ 14. I am strong enough to rely on myself.

_____ 15. Since I was this way when I was a child, I will be this way all my life.

_____ 16. I can change myself at any time in my life, whenever I decide it is helpful for me to do so.

_____ 17. I must become upset and depressed about other people's problems.

_____ 18. Having empathy with other people's problems and trying to help them does not mean getting upset and depressed about their problems. Overconcern does not lead to problem solving. How can I be of help if I am as depressed as others are?

_____ 19. It is terrible and unbearable to have to do things I don't want and don't like to do.

_____ 20. What I can't change I won't let upset me.

 EXERCISE 9.7

Interpretations

The assumptions we make greatly influence our interpretations of the meaning of events in our lives. These interpretations determine our feelings. The same event can be depressing or amusing, depending on the assumptions and interpretations we make. The purpose of this exercise is to focus a group discussion on the ways in which assumptions affect our interpretations and how we feel.

1. Form groups of four. Take the ten episodes that follow and discuss the following questions:
   a. What irrational assumptions is the person making?
   b. How do these assumptions cause the person to feel the way he or she does?
   c. What rational assumptions does the person need in order to change his or her feelings into more positive feelings?

2. In your group, discuss assumptions each of you have that influence your feelings of depression, anger, frustration, distress, and worry. When you are experiencing each of these feelings, what assumptions are causing you to feel that way? How can you change these assumptions to make your life happier?

Episodes

1. Sally likes to have her co-workers place their work neatly in a pile on her desk so that she can add her work to the pile, staple it all together, and give it to their supervisor. Her co-workers, however, throw their work into the supervisor's basket in a very disorderly and messy fashion. Sally then becomes very worried and upset. "I can't stand it," Sally says to herself. "It's terrible what they are doing. And it isn't fair to me or our supervisor!"

2. Jill has been given responsibility for planning next year's budget for her department. This amount of responsibility scares her. For several weeks she has done nothing on the budget. "I'll do it next week," she keeps thinking.

3. John went to the office one morning and passed a person he had never met in the hallway. He said, "Hello," and the person just looked at him and then walked on without saying a word. John became depressed. "I'm really not a very attractive person," he thought to himself. "No one seems to like me."

4. Dan is an intensive-care paramedic technician and is constantly depressed and worried about whether he can do his job competently. For every decision that has to be made, he asks his supervisor what he should do. One day he came into work and found that his supervisor had quit. "What will I do now?" he thought. "I can't handle this job without her."

5. Jane went to her desk and found a note from her supervisor that she had made an error in the report she worked on the day before. The note told her to correct the error and continue working on the report. Jane became depressed. "Why am I so dumb and stupid?" she thought to herself. "I can't seem to do anything right. That supervisor must think I'm terrible at my job."

6. Heidi has a knack for insulting people. She insults her co-workers, her boss, customers, and even passersby who ask for directions. Her boss has repeatedly told Heidi that if she doesn't change she will be fired. This depresses Heidi and makes her very angry at her boss. "How can I change?" Heidi says. "I've been this way ever since I could talk. It's too late for me to change now."

7. Tim was checking the repairs another technician had made on a television set. He found a mistake and became very angry. "I have to punish him," he thought. "He made a mistake and he has to suffer the consequences for it."

8. Bonnie doesn't like to fill out forms. She gets furious every day because her job as legal secretary requires her to fill out form after form after form. "Every time I see a form my stomach ties itself into knots," she says. "I hate forms! I know they have to be done in order for the work to be filed with the courts, but I still hate them!"

9. Bob is very anxious about keeping his job. "What if the company goes out of business?" he thinks. "What if my boss gets angry at me?" "What if the secretary I yelled at is the boss's daughter?" All day he worries about whether he will have a job tomorrow.

10. Jack is a very friendly person who listens quite well. All of his co-workers tell their problems to Jack. He listens sympathetically. Then he goes home deeply depressed. "Life is so terrible for the people I work with," he thinks. "They have such severe problems and such sad lives."

EXERCISE 9.8
Changing Your Feelings

Now that you have discussed how people can make their assumptions more constructive, you may want to apply your own advice to yourself. The purpose of this exercise is to give you a chance to discuss your own negative feelings and see what assumptions are causing them. Here is the procedure:

1. Form groups of four. Draw straws to see who goes first in your group. Then go around the group in a clockwise direction. Each member completes the following statements:
   a. What depresses me about school or work is . . .
   b. When I get depressed about school or work I . . .
   c. The assumptions I am making that cause me to be depressed are . . .
   d. Constructive assumptions I can adopt to change my depression to more positive feelings are . . .
   Listen carefully to what each group member says. If he is not sure of his assumptions, help him clarify them. Give support for making his assumptions more constructive.

2. Now go around the group again and discuss how each member completes these statements:
   a. The things I worry about are . . .
   b. What I do when I get worried is . . .
   c. The assumptions I am making that cause me to be worried are . . .
   d. Constructive assumptions I can adopt to change my worry to more positive feelings are . . .

3. Now try anger.
   a. The things I get angry about are . . .
   b. What I do when I get angry is . . .
   c. The assumptions I am making that cause me to be angry are . . .
   d. Constructive assumptions I can adopt to change my anger to more positive feelings are . . .

4. Let's see how you feel about your career!
   a. The negative feelings I have when I think about my career are . . .
   b. The things I do when I have those feelings are . . .
   c. The assumptions I am making that cause the feelings are . . .
   d. Constructive attitudes I can adopt to change these feelings to more positive ones are . . .

5. Discuss in your group what the members learned about themselves and the ways in which they manage their feelings.

EXERCISE 9.9

How Do I Manage My Feelings?

There are five questions in this exercise. Each question has two parts. Check *a* if your way of managing feelings is best described by the *a* part of the question. Check *b* if your way of managing feelings is best described by the *b* part of the question. Think about each question carefully. Be honest. No one will see your answers. The results are simply for your own self-awareness.

1. _____ a. I am fully aware of what I am sensing in a given situation.

   _____ b. I ignore what I am sensing by thinking about the past or the future.

2. _____ a. I understand the interpretations I usually make about other people's actions. I investigate my feeling by asking what interpretation is causing it. I work to be aware of interpretations I am making.

   _____ b. I deny that I make any interpretations about what I sense. I ignore my interpretations. I insist that I do not interpret someone's behavior as being mean. The person *is* mean.

3. _____ a. I accept my feeling as being part of me. I turn my full awareness on it. I try to feel it fully. I take a good look at it so I can identify it and tell how strong it is. I keep asking myself, "What am I feeling now?"

   _____ b. I reject my feeling. I ignore it by telling myself I'm not angry, upset, sad, or even happy. I deny my feeling by telling myself and others, "But I'm not feeling anything at all." I avoid people and situations that might make me more aware of my feelings. I pretend I'm not really feeling the way I am.

4. _____ a. I decide how I want to express my feeling. I think of what I want to result from the expression of my feeling. I think of what is an appropriate way to express the feeling in the current situation. In my mind, I review the sending skills.

   _____ b. Since I've never admitted to having a feeling, I don't need to decide how to express it! I don't think through what might happen after I express my feelings. I never think about what is appropriate in a situation. When my feelings burst I am too emotional to remember good sending skills.

5. _____ a. I express my feelings appropriately and clearly. Usually, this means describing my feeling directly. It also means using nonverbal messages to back up my words. My words and my nonverbal messages communicate the same feeling.

_____ b. I express my feelings inappropriately and in confusing ways. Usually, this means I express them indirectly through commands, accusations, put-downs, and evaluations. I may express feelings physically in destructive ways. My nonverbal messages express my feelings. I shout at people, push or hit them, avoid people, refuse to look at them, or don't speak to them. I may hug them, put my arm around them, give them gifts, or try to do favors for them. My words and my nonverbal messages often contradict each other. I sometimes smile and act friendly toward people I'm angry at. Or I may avoid people I care a great deal for.

How to Deal with an Angry Person

Everybody gets angry. You do, and so do other people. Figuring out what to do when someone is expressing anger to you is tough. What do you do? Letting your anger or the other person's anger get out of hand is disastrous. But so is hiding it. Hidden anger only smolders until it explodes later *"for no good reason."*

Here are some suggestions for dealing with an angry person. Some of them are designed to help the other person avoid unnecessarily frustrating situations. Some are on-the-spot actions you can take when you see the other person is having a problem.

1. **Do not get angry or aggressive back.** When the other person gets angry at you, the first step is for you to control your own feelings. Breathe deeply and slowly. Imagine an invisible wall between yourself and the other person's anger. View the other person from an objective perspective. Be cool. Being hurtful toward the other person can damage his or her dignity, self-respect, confidence, courage, and peer standing. Often it will escalate the situation and influence the person to be even more destructive in his or her behavior.

2. **Give the other person the right to feel angry.** Remember that anger is a natural human feeling. The other person has a *right* to feel and express anger as well as happiness, joy, sadness, grief, and pain. So do you.

3. **Recognize the other's anger is a sign of feeling weak and helpless.** Anger is a strong defensive emotion that signals the person feels frustrated, thwarted, or attacked. It may be unpleasant to listen to, but it does not infringe on the rights of others when it is communicated appropriately. Identify the source of the frustration or attack.

4. **Separate the other's anger from aggression.** Remember that anger is different from aggression. **Aggression** is an attempt to hurt someone or destroy something. It infringes on the rights of others. This distinction may help you to react appropriately to the many kinds of upsetting things an angry person may say and do.

5. **Keep focusing your own and the other person's attention on the task or problem.** Do not get distracted by the other person's anger. Stay focused on what must be done to complete the task or solve the problem. Taking insults personally distracts you from your goals and involves you in unnecessary conflict. Recognize what the other person is doing, but do not be provoked by it. Keep bringing his or her attention back to the decision to be made or action to be taken to solve the problem.

6. **Use other emotions such as respect or affection to help the angry person regain control.** Sometimes a sudden show of respect or affection will change the other person's mood.

7. **Present a rational explanation of the situation.** Understanding the situation can help the other person understand the cause of his or her anger and begin to calm down. Your explanation can include telling the person how you feel and asking for consideration. An example is "Yelling usually does not bother me, but today I have a headache; could you please keep your voice volume down?"

8. **Model expressing anger constructively.** Perhaps the other person will calm down and follow your example.

9. **Talk to yourself.** Prepare yourself for the experience by saying such things to yourself as "I'm good at managing others' anger"; ignore the anger by saying such things to yourself as "His anger is a minor annoyance, not a major catastrophe"; cope with your arousal and agitation by saying such things to yourself as "Breath deep, relax, slow your pulse down"; and reward yourself for coping successfully by saying such things to yourself as "You were terrific; you were calm during the whole conversation!"

10. **When you cannot handle a situation, seek help.** Do not hesitate to seek help when you need to. Call the instructor, administrator, boss, or colleagues to help deal with the angry person. In extreme cases, when a person is about to become violent, call the police to physically restrain the person. In preparing to meet with the angry person find a friend or adviser to talk through the situation in order to think more creatively about how to handle the emotionally unstable person.

EXERCISE 9.10
Handling Put-Downs

Everyone gets put down. Often put-downs are presented as humor and sometimes they are funny. Other times they just hurt. We all need to learn how to manage put-downs so that our self-esteem is not damaged and the attacker is not encouraged to do it again. First, we determine whether the put-down is a valid or invalid accusation. If it is invalid, then it is the other person's mistake. If the put-down is valid, then there is no reason to feel hurt because valid feedback helps (not hurts) us. Besides, no one is perfect. Second, to discourage the attacker from putting us down in the future, we should do the following:

1. *The very best thing to do when you are put down is to ignore it and the person doing it.* Most times people make put-downs to get attention. Being ignored is the thing that attackers dislike most.

2. *But, if you must say something to the person who put you down, do not respond with a put-down.* Insulting back only escalates the situation and results in more put-downs.

3. *It is better to cut the person off by giving a quick comeback that is not nasty and shows that you are unaffected by the put-down.* "I don't agree." "Really? I didn't know that." "Big deal." "So what?" "Who cares?"

4. *You could also agree with the person.* "How did you know?" "You know, you're right." "Who told you?" "I never noticed that before."

5. *Finally, you could make a joke of it.* "Would you put that in writing?" "That was supposed to be a secret." "Watch it or I'll call my lawyer." "Are you talking to the right person?"

EXERCISE 9.11
Protecting Yourself from Put-Downs

When you are put down you can (a) feel hurt, rejected, and ashamed, (b) become angry at the other person, or (c) avoid both through the images you think of and the things you say to yourself. Practice the following:

1. Imagine yourself protected from put-downs by
   a. A suit of armor.
   b. An invisible cape.
   c. A bulletproof vest.

2. Imagine the put-down is something you can sidestep:
   a. A breeze that sails by without touching you.
   b. An arrow or bullet that speeds by and misses you.

3. Ignore what the other person says and say things to yourself that are true:
   a. About the other person:
      (1) "Something must be bugging him (her)."
      (2) "Someone who puts others down usually feels bad about himself (herself)."
      (3) "Poor person. He (she) must not like himself (herself)."
      (4) "He (she) is trying to impress others. He (she) must need friends."
   b. About yourself:
      (1) "No matter what they say, I'm still an OK person."
      (2) "I know it isn't true."
      (3) "I won't let this bother me. I know I'm a good person."
      (4) "Sticks and stones will break my bones, but words will never hurt me."
      (5) "If they really knew me, they wouldn't say that."

Anger and Negotiations

Managing your anger and responding to the anger of others are two of the most difficult aspects of resolving conflicts. In win-lose negotiations anger is used strategically to force the other person to give up. In problem-solving negotiations anger is described and presented as part of the problem to be resolved. Negotiations do not end until anger and any other negative feelings are resolved and the relationship is as good as or better than ever. In both types of negotiations, however, anger is potentially problematic. Loss of control in win-lose negotiations can result in self-defeating actions. Hiding anger in problem-solving negotiations can result in a failure to resolve the conflict. If you perfect your skills in managing your anger and in responding to the anger of others constructively, you will tend to be a highly competent negotiator even under the most difficult conditions.

Managing Anger Constructively: A Checklist

1. Anger occurs when we are not getting something we want or would like (when we feel frustrated, thwarted, attacked, belittled, devalued).
2. Anger can
   a. Add to your frustrations. This response is not sensible. Getting angry over a frustration does not usually remove the frustration and always adds to your discomfort.
   b. Prevent you from solving problems. Being angry often fills your thoughts with ways of getting even with others, not with how to get others to behave differently toward you. The net result is that things get worse and worse as you become angrier and angrier.
   c. Make you physically sick.

3. Beware of its
   a. Narrowing of perceptual focus and priorities.
   b. Righteousness, blame orientation, and desire to punish.
   c. Demand that you get your way.
   d. Physiological arousal.
4. Rules for managing your anger constructively:
   a. Recognize and acknowledge your anger.
   b. Decide whether you wish to express it. Know how to detach and let it go if you decide not to.
   c. When it is appropriate to do so, express anger directly and descriptively. Once you have expressed your anger constructively, let it go.
   d. Express it indirectly, or react in an alternative way when direct expression is not appropriate.
      (1) Physical exercise.
      (2) Private physical expression.
      (3) Psychological detachment.
      (4) Relaxation.
   e. When the other person is angry, stay focused on the task or issue. Do not get distracted into his or her anger.
   f. Analyze, understand, and reflect upon your anger.
5. Anger is based on two irrational beliefs:
   a. You must have your way. It is awful not to get everything you want.
   b. People are bad and should be severely dealt with if they have behaved wrongly. They are wicked for frustrating you and deserve to be punished.
6. Express your anger constructively by
   a. Describing the other person's behavior.
   b. Describing your anger.
   c. Making your verbal and nonverbal messages congruent.
   d. Checking your perceptions of the other person's behavior and the assumptions you are making about the meaning of the behavior.
   e. Paraphrasing the other person's replies.
7. Manage the anger of others by
   a. Not getting angry or aggressive back.
   b. Giving the other person the right to feel angry.
   c. Recognizing that the other's anger is a sign of his or her feeling weak and helpless.
   d. Separating the other's anger from aggression.
   e. Focusing your own and the other person's attention on the task or problem.
   f. Expressing emotions such as respect or affection to help the other regain control.
   h. Explaining the situation in a rational way.
   i. Modeling how to express anger constructively.
   j. Seeking help.

■ CHAPTER REVIEW

Test your understanding of anger, stress, and managing your feelings by answering true or false to the following statements. Answers are at the end of the chapter.

True   False   1. A certain amount of stress is beneficial.

True   False   2. Only crazy people talk to themselves.

True   False   3. When you cannot express anger directly, hard exercise is a good idea.

True   False   4. Long-term anger tends to be rational.

True   False   5. If someone gets angry at you, get angry back.

True   False   6. To have feelings, you first gather information through your senses.

True   False   7. All anger is aggressive.

True   False   8. You describe the other person's behavior in expressing your anger.

True   False   9. When you or someone else makes a mistake, blaming is OK.

True   False   10. Anger is usually a defense against something.

Self-Diagnosis

This chapter has focused on anger. On a scale from 1 (poorly mastered) to 5 (highly mastered) rate the degree to which you have mastered each skill. Then choose two skills to improve on in the next week.

Rating	Skill
_____	An understanding of stress and how to deal with it.
_____	An understanding of the nature of anger.
_____	An understanding of the rules for expressing anger constructively.
_____	The ability to express anger constructively. I can describe the other person's behavior, describe my anger, and make my verbal and nonverbal messages congruent.
_____	The ability to identify irrational beliefs and change to rational ones.
_____	The ability to dispose of unwanted feelings.
_____	The ability to deal with another person's anger directed at me.
_____	The ability to express anger appropriately in negotiations.

Skills I Will Improve in the Next Week

1. _____

2. _____

Summary

In every relationship you decide how to manage the stress and anger that arise. Stress is unavoidable. You are always under some stress. Social support is key to managing stress. Conflict is a source of stress, and anger is a typical response. **Anger** is a defensive, emotional reaction that occurs when we are frustrated, thwarted, or attacked. When you get angry with other people, the results can be either destructive or constructive. To manage anger constructively you recognize and acknowledge that you are angry. Then decide whether or not you wish to express your anger. You express it indirectly or react in an alternative way when direct expression of anger is not appropriate. To express anger constructively you describe the other's actions and you describe your angry feelings verbally while making your nonverbal messages congruent with your words. Long-term anger is based on two irrational beliefs—that you must get your way and that the other person must be punished. To ensure that you do not keep anger long-term, you decide to change yourself (rather than the other person), control how you interpret the information you receive through your senses, change your assumptions, and thereby free yourself from your anger. Finally, in a conflict you must control your reactions to other people's anger toward you as well as your anger toward them. You give them the "right" to feel angry, you try not to get angry back, and you focus your attention on the task. You describe the situation and talk to yourself to keep yourself calm. As you practice the suggestions in this chapter, you will find that you have more constructive control over your anger and relationships. In the next chapter you will learn how to interact effectively with diverse peers.

Answers

Comprehension Test A: 1. false; 2. true; 3. false; 4. true; 5. true; 6. true; 7. false; 8. true; 9. false; 10. true.

Chapter Review: 1. true; 2. false; 3. true; 4. false; 5. false; 6. true; 7. false; 8. true; 9. false; 10. true.

CHAPTER 10

Building Relationships with Diverse Individuals

Introduction

We live in one world. The problems that face each person, community, and country cannot be solved without global cooperation and joint action. Economically, for example, the globalization of business is reflected in the increase in multinational companies, coproduction agreements, and offshore operations. As globalization becomes the norm, more and more companies must translate their local and national perspectives into a world view. Companies that are staffed by individuals skilled in building relationships with diverse peers will have an advantage in the global market.

Interacting effectively with peers from different cultures, ethnic groups, social classes, and historical backgrounds does not come naturally. For 200,000 years humans lived in small hunting and gathering groups, interacting only infrequently with other nearby small groups. Today we are required to communicate effectively with people across those subtle but pervasive barriers of culture, religion, generations, ethnicity, gender, handicapping conditions, and social class. No wonder this requirement feels uncomfortable—we have never had to deal with such heterogeneity before!

Diversity among your acquaintances, classmates, co-workers, neighbors, and friends is increasingly inevitable. North America, Europe, and many other parts of the world are becoming more and more diverse in terms of culture, ethnicity, religion, age, physical qualities, gender, and so forth. In order to build relationships and interact effectively with diverse individuals you must

1. Recognize that diversity exists and is a valuable resource.
2. Seek out relationships with different individuals within a cooperative context (not a competitive or individualistic one).
3. Include in your identity your historical and cultural heritage.
4. Respect and appreciate the historical and cultural heritage of others.
5. Establish superordinate identity that unites all relevant groups.
6. Reduce the internal cognitive barriers to building positive relationships with diverse individuals (such as stereotyping and prejudice).
7. Understand how to resolve conflicts constructively and skillfully use the procedures for doing so.
8. Learn and internalize pluralistic, democratic values including the commitment to the equal worth of all persons and each individual's inalienable right to life, liberty, and the pursuit of happiness.

EXERCISE 10.1
Relating to Diverse Individuals

How skillful in relating to diverse individuals are you? The following steps are a framework for understanding how to interact effectively with diverse individuals. Rate yourself on a scale from 1 (low skills) to 5 (high skills). The higher your score, the more you see yourself as having the skills to interact effectively with diverse individuals. After you have answered the questions and determined your score, find a partner and (a) explain why you answered each question the way you did and (b) listen to his or her explanations.

_____ 1. I recognize that diversity exists, and I value it as an important resource.

_____ 2. I can create a cooperative context in which I work with diverse individuals to achieve mutual goals.

_____ 3. An important part of my identity is my historical and cultural heritage.

_____ 4. I recognize, respect, and value the historical and cultural heritage of others.

_____ 5. I highlight the superordinate identity that unites us all into one society.

_____ 6. I work constantly to reduce my internal barriers (such as stereotyping and prejudice) to interacting effectively with diverse individuals.

_____ 7. I know the procedures for resolving conflicts constructively, and I am skillful in using them.

_____ 8. I am committed to the pluralistic values that recognize the equal worth of all persons and each individual's inalienable right to life, liberty, and the pursuit of happiness.

_____ **Total**

Step One: Recognize and Value Diversity

The first step in managing diversity well is to recognize that diversity exists and to value and respect fundamental differences among people. Diversity is a necessary requirement for living a productive, effective, successful, and fulfilling life. Walter Lippmann once said, "Where all think alike, no one thinks very much." Diversity contributes to achievement and productivity, creative problem solving, growth in cognitive and moral reasoning, perspective-taking ability, and general sophistication in interacting and working with peers from a variety of cultural and ethnic backgrounds (Johnson & Johnson, 1999). Within a relationship, a community, an organization, a society, or a world, the goal is not to make everyone alike. The goal is to work together to achieve mutual goals while recognizing cultural diversity and learning to value and respect fundamental differences.

EXERCISE 10.2
My Attitudes Toward Diversity

On the lines that follow, list several things you like about having diverse friends and several things you dislike about having diverse friends.

Benefits of Diverse Friends   *Detriments of Diverse Friends*

_____   _____

_____   _____

_____   _____

_____   _____

_____   _____

Step Two: Interact with Diverse Individuals in a Cooperative Context

We are going to have to find ways of organizing ourselves cooperatively, sanely, scientifically, harmoniously, and in regenerative spontaneity with the rest of humanity around earth. . . . We are not going to be able to operate our spaceship earth successfully nor for much longer unless we see it as a whole spaceship and our fate as common. It has to be everybody or nobody.
—R. Buckminster Fuller

Your second step in building effective relationships with diverse individuals is to ensure your interaction takes place within a cooperative context. The discords of diversity are not automatically transformed into a symphony when people are brought face-to-face. Prejudice, stereotyping, and discrimination often increase with proximity. What largely determines whether interaction results in positive or negative relationships is the context within which the interaction takes place. Basically, the context can be cooperative, competitive, or individualistic. In a **cooperative** context individuals work together to achieve mutual goals. In a **competitive** context individuals strive to outperform each other. In an **individualistic** context individuals seek their own benefit independently of what others are doing. You create a cooperative context by identifying and highlighting

1. Important goals that everyone wants to achieve.
2. A set of common procedures and norms that help coordinate efforts to achieve the goals.

Cooperative interaction has very powerful and positive effects on relationships. Friendships are based largely on the ability of two people to define mutual goals (even if the goal is to fall in love) and then to cooperate in obtaining them. When people cooperate, they tend to like each other more, trust each other more, be more candid with each other, and be more willing to listen to and be influenced by each other. When people compete or work individualistically, then liking, trust, influence, and candor tend to decrease. There is considerable evidence that cooperative experiences, compared with competitive and individualistic ones, promote more positive, committed, and caring relationships regardless of differences in culture, language, religion, ethnicity, social class, gender, ability, or other areas (Johnson & Johnson, 1989). In addition, joint efforts to achieve mutual goals (that is, cooperation) increase individuals' self-esteem and psychological health, ability to act independently and be autonomous, and appropriately use interpersonal and small-group skills.

Casey Stengel, one of the most successful baseball managers in history, once said, "It's easy to get the players. Getting them to play together, that's the hard part." It is not difficult to get diverse individuals in the same city, neighborhood, company, or school. Getting them to work together in effective and constructive ways, that is the hard part. In a competitive or individualistic context, diversity easily becomes a problem. In a cooperative context, diversity is a vital resource that benefits all. Establishing the cooperative context is a necessary condition for ensuring that diversity enriches rather than divides.

Step Three: Build Pride in Your Historical and Cultural Identity

What lies behind us and
What lies before us are
Small matters compared
To what lies within us.

 —Ralph Waldo Emerson

The third step is to develop an awareness and appreciation of your own historical, cultural, ethnic, and religious background. To appreciate the heritage of others and build collaborative relationships with them, you must appreciate your own heritage and be confident that diverse others will also. Your historical and cultural heritage is part of your identity. Your **identity** is a consistent set of attitudes that defines "who you are." It is a type of cognitive structure called a **self-schema** (a generalization about the self, derived from past experience, that organizes and guides your understanding of the information you learn about yourself from interacting with others).

There are several points to understand about your identity. First, your identity consists of various aspects of your current self and the potential selves you would like to be or that you imagine you might be. These potential selves include ideals that you would like to attain and standards that you feel you should meet. Second, the aspects of your identity are arranged in a hierarchy. The more important an aspect of your identity is, or the higher it stands in the hierarchy, the more likely it is to influence your choices and your behavior.

Third, your identity consists of multiple subidentities or self-schemas that are organized into a coherent, stable, and integrated whole. Your subidentities include your view of your *physical characteristics* (height, weight, sex, hair and eye color, and general appearance), your *social roles*

(student or teacher, child or parent, employee or employer, and so forth), *the activities you engage in* (playing the piano, dancing, reading and so forth), your *abilities* (skills, achievements), your *attitudes and interests* (liking rock and roll, favoring equal rights for females), and your *general personality traits* (extrovert or introvert, impulsive or reflective, sensible or scatterbrained).

Your subidentities also include your **gender identity** (fundamental sense of maleness or femaleness), **cultural identity** (sense of origins and membership in a culture), **ethnic identity** (sense of belonging to one particular ethnic group), **religious identity** (sense of belonging to one particular religious group), **social class identity** (sense of belonging to one particular social class), and so forth. Each of these subidentities should be recognized and valued, and they need to be organized and integrated into a coherent and stable sense of self.

Fourth, your identity defines your membership in certain groups and places you in relationship to other groups. Eric Erikson (1950), for example, stated that a person's identity has to be grounded in a cultural identity if it is to facilitate psychological health. He believed that identity is located in the core of communal culture and that as a member of a community, an important part of identity was exemplifying the moral code of the community, which he referred to as "character."

Fifth, each aspect of your identity helps you understand who you are in relation to your relationships with other people. Some of these relationships are positive and some are negative. You define yourself through your family, friends, and people who like you, but you also define yourself through your enemies and the people who dislike you.

Finally, each aspect of your identity has positive or negative connotations. You generally look at yourself in an evaluative way, approving or disapproving of your behavior and characteristics. This process is referred to as *self-esteem*. The word *esteem* comes from the Latin *aestimare*, which means "to estimate or appraise." Self-esteem thus means to appraise the worth of your behavior and characteristics.

Historically, identity has existed only as being a member of communities and groups. On the basis of these memberships, everyone knew exactly who he or she was. In the Middle Ages, for example, self-definition was based on ten sources:

1. The geographical location of your community. ("I am a citizen of this city, region, country.")

2. The family you are part of. ("I am someone's son or daughter, someone else's cousin or uncle.")

3. Who you are married to. ("I am this person's husband/wife.")

4. Your occupation. ("I am a member of this or that guild, profession, organization.")

5. Your social rank. ("I am a nobleman/serf.")

6. Your gender. ("I am a man/woman.")

7. Your age. ("I am young/old.")

8. Your bodily characteristics. ("I am tall and strong.")

9. Your moral goodness. ("I am an honest, decent person.")

10. Your religion. ("I am Catholic.")

There are a number of reasons why having a clear identity is important. *First, your identity provides consistency to your self-view.* Generally, you work to minimize any contradictions in your view of yourself by organizing and revising incoming information to make it consistent with your view of yourself. You do so by adding relevant information or by altering inconsistent information. People tend to twist what they perceive so that it fits into their existing schemas.

Second, your identity provides stability to your life. The world can change, other people can change, your career and family life can change, but there is something about yourself that remains the same. Even though

Culture and Communication

Not all cultures communicate in the same way. Anglo-American culture, for example, values assertiveness, encourages the direct expression of feelings, sees time as a scarce commodity not to be wasted, and emphasizes learning how to express oneself verbally clearly and completely. Zuni-American culture, in contrast, values reticence (which is respect for privacy), encourages keeping feelings private (expressing feelings publicly is similar to undressing in front of other people), sees time as unlimited, and emphasizes listening carefully and speaking infrequently.

your identity expands during infancy, childhood, adolescence, and early adulthood (due to physical growth, more complex relationships, new responsibilities, and cognitive and social development), your personal identity remains coherent and unified.

Third, your identity directs your attention toward certain information out of all the information available. Information congruent with your self-view is processed easily, while information that contradicts your view of yourself is resisted and may be screened out entirely. If you see yourself as intelligent, for example, and you receive two A's and two C's, you tend to focus on the A's and ignore the C's.

Fourth, your identity facilitates the retention of information relevant to your view of yourself. You remember what is consistent with your identity and forget what is not. You may remember your successes, for example, and forget your failures. Your memories may even be reconstructed so the events you remember fit your view of yourself.

Fifth, you seek out information and experiences that will validate your identity. When you see yourself as intelligent, you seek out evidence "proving" that you are an intellectually superior person.

Finally, your identity provides the means for dealing with stressful events. The more complex your identity, the greater the buffer against stress and adversity. The complexity of your identity reduces the stress you experience and helps you cope with existing stress. People with more complex identities are less prone to depression and illness; they also experience less severe mood swings following success or failure in one particular area of performance.

Building pride in your historical and cultural identity is an important step in enriching your life with diverse friends and increasing your competence in interacting with diverse individuals. How you define your historical identity, however, has implications for the way you view other cultural groups.

EXERCISE 10.3
Who Am I?

	Personal Characteristics	Demographic Characteristics	Abilities, Competencies
1.	_____	_____	_____
2.	_____	_____	_____
3.	_____	_____	_____
4.	_____	_____	_____
5.	_____	_____	_____
6.	_____	_____	_____
7.	_____	_____	_____
8.	_____	_____	_____
9.	_____	_____	_____
10.	_____	_____	_____

EXERCISE 10.4
My Identity

The following list presents ten methods of self-definition during the Middle Ages. Define yourself according to each category. Then rank order the ten characteristics from 1 (most important) to 10 (least important) to your identity.

Who Am I	My Answers	Rank
Geography	_____	____
Family	_____	____
Marriage	_____	____
Occupation	_____	____
Social rank	_____	____
Gender	_____	____
Age	_____	____
Bodily characteristics	_____	____
Moral goodness	_____	____
Religion	_____	____

EXERCISE 10.5
Aspects of Self

Rank the following benefits of yourself from most important to you (1) to least important to you (11).

_____ Physical characteristics (height, weight, sex, hair and eye color, and general appearance)

_____ Social roles (student or teacher, child or parent, employee or employer, and so forth)

_____ Activities you engage in (playing the piano, dancing, reading, and so forth)

_____ Abilities (skills, achievements)

_____ Attitudes and interests (liking rock and roll, favoring equal rights for females)

_____ Personality traits (extrovert or introvert, impulsive or reflective, sensible or scatterbrained)

_____ Gender identity (fundamental sense of maleness or femaleness)

_____ Cultural identity (sense of origins and membership in a culture)

_____ Ethnic identity (sense of belonging to one particular ethnic group)

_____ Religious identity (sense of belonging to one particular religious group)

_____ Social class identity (sense of belonging to one particular social class)

Step Four: Appreciate Others' Historical and Cultural Backgrounds

Between people, as among nations, respect for each other's rights ensures peace.
—Benito Juarez

The fourth step is to develop an appreciation for the historic, cultural, ethnic, and religious backgrounds (and other important personal characteristics) of others. Other heritages may be seen positively or negatively, and members of different heritage groups may be seen as collaborators or as competitors. A critical aspect of developing a historical, cultural, and ethnic identity is whether ethnocentricity is inherent in your definition of yourself. An in-group identity must be developed in a way that does not lead to rejection of out-groups. There are many examples where being a member of one group requires the rejection of other groups. There are also many examples where being a member of one group requires valuing and respecting other groups. Out-groups need to be seen as collaborators and resources rather than competitors and threats. You should see yourself as a person who respects diverse backgrounds and values them as resources that increase the quality of your life and the viability of society.

EXERCISE 10.6
Cultural, Historical, and Ethnic Heritage Assignment

1. My cultural, historical, ethnic heritage is _____

   _____

2. Find the other members of this class who share your cultural heritage.

3. Plan a 15- to 20-minute class presentation on your cultural heritage that includes the following:
   a. Definition of cultural identity. (Who are we?)
   b. History of culture. (What is our history?)
   c. Traditions of culture. (What are our traditions?)
   d. Aspects of culture (food, songs, art). (Examples of our culture are . . . !)
   e. Personal experiences as member of the culture. (My personal experiences as a member of this culture are . . . !)
   f. Continuing traditions you are following.

EXERICSE 10.7
Comparing Cultural Identities

What do we have in common? How are we different? Shown here are two overlapping circles. Such a figure is known as a Venn diagram.

1. In the first circle write down the aspects of your cultural, historical, and ethnic identity that are unique and different from that of the other person.

2. In the second circle write down the aspects of the other person's cultural, historical, and ethnic identity that are unique and different from yours.

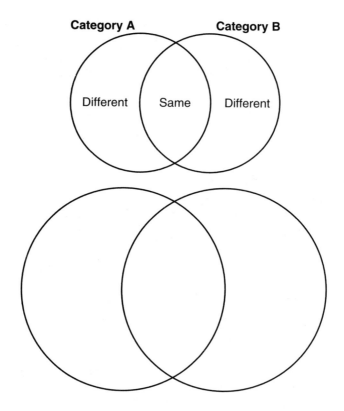

3. In the overlapping part of the circles, write down the aspects of both your cultural, historical, and ethnic identities that are similar.

4. Discuss how you are different and what you have in common.

5. Find a new partner and repeat the procedure.

Step Five: Establish a Superordinate Identity

Your fifth step in building effective relationships with diverse individuals is to unite your own historical identity and the historical identities of others under a strong superordinate identity. Your own historical identity and the historical identities of others need to be subparts of a larger identity as, for example, "Americans." America is a nation of Norwegian-Americans, Italian-Americans, Chinese-Americans, Black Americans, and so forth. This diversity illustrates that being an American is creedal rather than racial or ancestral. The superordinate identity of "American" comes from believing that *all humans are created equal and endowed by their creator with certain inalienable rights* (i.e., our commitment to the Constitution, Bill of Rights, and Declaration of Independence of the United States). Each cultural group is part of the whole. The common commitment to "equality, justice, and liberty for all" unites Americans as one people, even though they are the descendants of many cultures, races, religions, and ethnic groups. The superordinate identity unites all citizens in a shared community where each individual recognizes that he or she is part of a broader community that all wish to preserve. Each individual recognizes that members of the broader community share key values and norms despite important differences in other areas.

To become an American, individuals immigrate to the United States and adopt the values underlying its democratic system. Members of each new immigrant group, while modifying and enriching the United States, learn they are first and foremost Americans. America is one of the few successful examples of a pluralistic society where different groups clashed but ultimately learned to live together through achieving a sense of common beliefs and nationhood. In American diversity, there has always been a broad recognition that Americans are one people. Whatever their origins, all citizens are Americans.

 EXERCISE 10.8

Was de Tocqueville Right or Wrong?

Without common belief . . . there still may be men, but there is no social body. In order for society to exist . . . and prosper . . . it is necessary that the minds of all men should be held together by certain predominant ideas.
—de Tocqueville

_____ Agree   _____ Disagree

De Tocqueville believed that a common set of values and ideals held American society together. Do you agree or disagree? Write down your reasoning for your answer. Find a partner, share your opinion and reasoning, listen carefully to his or her opinion and reasoning, and come to agreement as to what is necessary for our society to exist and prosper.

What Would You Add and Why?

Alexis de Tocqueville called civic values "the habits of the heart." Consider carefully his recommendations. Add five other "habits of the heart" that you think all American children and adolescents should learn in school, and write down the reasons why. Find a partner. Share your five additions and reasons. Listen carefully to his or her five additions and reasons. Create a list of five additional habits of the heart that both can agree on.

Alexis de Tocqueville	*My Additions*
1. Taking responsibility for the common good.	_____
2. Trusting others to take responsibility for common good.	_____
3. Being honest.	_____
4. Having self-discipline.	_____
5. Reciprocating good deeds.	_____

EXERCISE 10.9
American Values

The preambles from the Declaration of Independence and the Constitution of the United States are shown.

1. List the values contained in these statements. Find a partner. Explain your list. Listen to his or her list. Come up with a combined list that is as accurate as possible.

2. Working as a pair, list the ways that schools can teach these values to every child and adolescent in the United States.

Declaration of Independence

When in the Course of human events, it becomes necessary for one people to dissolve the political bands which have connected them with another, and to assume among the Powers of the earth, the separate and equal station to which the Laws of Nature and of Nature's God entitle them, a decent respect to the opinions of mankind requires that they should declare the causes which impel them to the separation.

We hold these truths to be self-evident, that all men are created equal, that they are endowed by their Creator with certain unalienable Rights, that among these are Life, Liberty, and the pursuit of Happiness. That to secure these rights, Governments are instituted among Men, deriving their just powers from the consent of the governed, that whenever any Form of Government becomes destructive of these ends, it is the Right of the People to alter or to abolish it, and to institute new Government, laying its foundation on such principles and organizing its powers in such form, as to them shall seem most likely to effect their Safety and Happiness.

Constitution of the United States

We the People of the United States, in Order to form a more perfect Union, establish Justice, insure domestic Tranquility, provide for the common defense, promote the general Welfare, and secure the Blessings of Liberty to ourselves and our Posterity, do ordain and establish this Constitution for the United States of America.

Values	*Ways to Teach Them*
_____	_____
_____	_____
_____	_____
_____	_____
_____	_____
_____	_____

Step Six: Reduce Internal Barriers to Constructive Interaction

Your sixth step is to reduce your internal barriers to valuing diversity, such as stereotyping, prejudice, and blaming the victim. Your internal barriers begin with categorization. In order to understand other people and yourself, categories must be used. **Categorizing** is the cognitive process of conceptualizing objects and people as members of groups. People are categorized on the basis of *inherited traits* (culture, sex, ethnic membership, physical features) or *acquired traits* (education, occupation, lifestyle, customs). Categorization and generalizing are natural processes that cannot be avoided and are often helpful in processing information and making decisions. At times, however, they malfunction and result in such cognitive barriers as stereotyping, prejudice, and blaming the victim. Unless you are aware of the dynamics of such cognitive barriers, you may be unable to interact effectively with diverse peers.

Stereotyping

Stereotypes are everywhere, and everyone has them. Stereotypes are a product of the way the mind stores, organizes, and recalls information, and, therefore, the use of stereotypes cannot be avoided. Stereotypes are used to describe differences among groups and to predict how others will behave. Stereotypes reduce complexity, help us make quick decisions, fill in the gaps in what is known, help us make sense of who we are and what is happening, and help create and recognize the patterns needed to draw conclusions. Unfortunately, stereotypes can also support unfairness and injustice.

The world is simply too complicated to attend to every detail, and, therefore, the perceiver relies on stereotypes to simplify social perception. A **stereotype** is a belief that associates a whole group of people with certain traits. Stereotypes reduce the complexity of the social environment and make it more manageable. Women have been stereotyped as being more emotional than men. Men have been stereotyped as being more competitive than women. Tall, dark, and handsome men have been stereotyped as being mysterious.

You form stereotypes by (a) categorizing (you sort single objects into groups rather than thinking of each as unique) and (b) differentiating between the in-group (the group with which you identify) and out-groups. You commonly assume that the members of out-groups are quite similar while realizing that the members of the in-group are quite diverse (*out-group homogeneity effect*). The failure to notice differences among out-group members may result from lack of personal contact with a representative sample of the out-group. A white person, for example, may see all Hispanics as being alike, but someone with a wide variety of Hispanic friends may see little similarity among Puerto Ricans, Cubans, Mexicans, and Argentineans.

An efficient cognitive system does more than simply make things easy for people at all costs. Rather, it distributes limited resources in ways that maximize the informational value gained for the effort expended. There are several reasons why stereotyping is efficient. First, the social categorization that precedes stereotyping reduces the amount of information that must be attended to. When you group social stimuli together and treat them as functionally equivalent, you reduce the need to form individualized impressions of each category member. Second, stereotypes expand your base of knowledge by allowing you to infer a person's attributes without having to attend carefully to the person's behavior. Through the relatively simple act of social categorization, stereotypes allow you to gain a large amount of "functionally accurate" information, thus resulting in a beneficial ratio of information gained to effort expended. Stereotypes are particularly useful when processing capacity is constrained, processing resources are scarce, and accurate social perception is difficult to achieve. Stereotypes facilitate the encoding of both stereotype-consistent and stereotype-inconsistent information when processing capacity is low. The energy saved by encoding stereotype-consistent information is then used to understand stereotype-inconsistent information. Stereotypes may be automatically activated when people experience a threat to their self-image.

People who hold strong stereotypes are prone to the **fundamental attribution error**. They attribute negative behavior on the part of a minority group member to dispositional characteristics and positive behavior by a minority group member to situational factors, while one's own negative behavior is attributed to situational causes and one's own positive behavior is viewed as dispositional. When a minority group member acts in an undesirable way, the attribution is "that's the way those people are" or "those people are born like that." If the minority group member is seen engaging in desirable behavior, the person holding the stereotype can view the minority person as an exception to the rule or view the minority person's behavior as due to luck, the situational context, or extraordinary motivation and effort.

Stereotypes not only affect the ones who hold them; stereotypes also affect the ones targeted. When a widely known negative stereotype (e.g., poor intellectual ability) exists about a group, it creates for its members a burden of suspicion that acts as a threat (*stereotype threat*). This threat arises whenever individuals' behavior could be interpreted in terms of a stereotype, that is, whenever group members run the risk of confirming the stereotype. If a group is stereotyped as having low intellectual ability, for example, when members are taking academic tests, there may be a "situational pressure" to disconfirm the stereotype that distracts them and depresses their academic performance. The possibility of being judged by a stereotype can cause so much anxiety that intellectual performance is disrupted.

To change your stereotypes, and to minimize your stereotypes, you

1. Interact on a personal as well as a professional level. The more personal information you have about someone, the less you stereotype.

2. Commit considerable time and energy to the relationship. The more time and energy you apply to considering a person's characteristics and behavior, the less you stereotype.

3. Consciously work to form an accurate impression of the other person. The more motivated you are to form an accurate impression of someone, the less you stereotype.

4. View the other person as a typical member of the other group. The more you perceive the person to be typical of the stereotyped group, the more your interaction will change your stereotypes.

For your stereotypes to change, you need to interact with members of different groups for prolonged periods of time under conditions where you get to know each other personally and see each other as being typical members of your groups.

EXERCISE 10.10
Why Do Stereotypes Endure?

Several reasons why stereotypes persist are listed. Rank them from most important (1) to least important (7). Write down your rationale for your ranking. Find a partner and share your ranking and rationale, listen to his or her ranking and rationale, and cooperatively create a new, improved ranking and rationale. Then find another pair and repeat the procedure in a group of four.

_____ The tendency for people to overestimate the association between variables that are only slightly correlated or not correlated at all is known as **illusionary correlation**. Many people, for example, perceive that being poor and being lazy are associated. Any poor person who is not hard at work the moment you notice him or her may be perceived to be lazy. Low-power groups can acquire negative traits easily, and once acquired, the stereotype is hard to lose.

_____ Your prejudice makes you notice the negative traits you ascribe to the groups you are prejudiced against, and you believe information that confirms your stereotypes more readily than evidence that challenges them. People tend to process information in ways that verify existing beliefs. This tendency is known as the *confirmation bias* (the tendency to seek, interpret, and create information that verifies existing beliefs).

_____ You have a **false consensus bias** when you believe that most other people share your stereotypes (see poor people as being lazy). You tend to see your own behavior and judgments as quite common and appropriate, and to view alternative responses as uncommon and often inappropriate.

_____ Your stereotypes tend to be **self-fulfilling**. Stereotypes can subtly influence intergroup interactions in such a way that the stereotype is behaviorally confirmed. You can behave in ways that elicit the actions you expect from out-group members, thus confirming your stereotype.

_____ You dismiss individuals who do not match your stereotype as exceptions to the rule or representatives of a subcategory.

_____ Your stereotypes often operate at an implicit level without your conscious awareness.

_____ You often develop a rationale and explanation to justify your stereotypes and prejudices.

EXERCISE 10.11

Stereotyping

Once you realize that everyone is socialized to be prejudiced and to stereotype others, you need to clarify just what stereotypes you now hold. This exercise is aimed at clarifying (a) what stereotypes you have been taught about other groups, (b) what stereotypes they have been taught about you, and (c) how the process of stereotyping works.

1. Post the following list of words on sheets of paper around the room:

Male	Female
Teenager	Over age 70
Asian American	African American
Native American	Hispanic American
Blind	Deaf
Lower income	Middle income
Roman Catholic	Protestant
Southern	Midwestern

2. Each participant is to circulate around the room, read the various categories, and write one stereotype he or she has heard under each heading. Participants are told not to repeat anything that is already written down. They are not to make anything up. They are to write down *all* the stereotypes they have heard about each of the groups listed.

3. After everyone is done writing, participants are to read all the stereotypes under each category.

4. Participants discuss
   a. Their personal reactions.
   b. How accurate the stereotypes of their identities are.
   c. What they have learned about stereotyping others.

EXERCISE 10.12

Interacting on the Basis of Stereotypes

Stereotypes are rigid judgments made about other groups that ignore individual differences. The purpose of this exercise is to demonstrate how stereotypes are associated with primary and secondary dimensions of diversity.

1. Divide participants into groups of five. The group is to role-play a discussion among employees of a large corporation of the ways in which the percentage of people of color and women in higher level executive positions may be increased from 10 percent to 50 percent.

2. Give each member of the group a headband to wear with a particular identity written on it for other group members to see. *Group members are not to look at their own headbands.* The five identities are

   Single mother of two young children, unemployed
   Physically disabled employee
   Woman, age 72
   White male, company president
   Black female, union official

3. Stop the discussion after 10 minutes or so. Then have the groups
   a. Guess what the label on their headband was.
   b. Discuss their personal reactions.
   c. Discuss the participation pattern of each member—who dominated, who withdrew, who was interrupted, who was influential.
   d. Discuss what they have learned about stereotyping others.

Prejudice

To know one's self is wisdom, but to know one's neighbor is genius.
—Minna Antrim

Stereotyping can result in prejudice. To be prejudiced means to prejudge. **Prejudice** can be defined as an unjustified negative attitude toward a person based solely on that individual's membership in a group other than one's own. Prejudices are judgments made about others that establish a superiority/inferiority belief system. If one person dislikes another simply because that other person is a member of a different ethnic group, sex, or religion, we are dealing with prejudice.

One common form of prejudice is ethnocentrism. **Ethnocentrism** is the tendency to regard your own ethnic group, culture, or nation as better or more "correct" than others. The word is derived from **ethnic**, meaning a group united by similar customs, characteristics, race, or other common factors, and **center**. When ethnocentrism is present, the standards and values of our culture are used as a yardstick to measure the worth of other ethnic groups. Ethnocentrism is often perpetuated by **cultural conditioning**. Children are raised to fit into a particular culture and are conditioned to respond to various situations similarly to the way others in the culture react. In addition to ethnocentrism, there are many other types of "isms." **Sexism** is prejudice directed at a person because of his or her gender. **Ageism** is prejudice against the elderly. **Racism** is prejudice directed at people because of their ethnic membership.

Of all the isms, racism may have received the most attention. Racism deals with the forming of unfounded or inaccurate opinions about a group, leading to biased behavior against members of that group. Racism gives permission to individuals to treat "racial groups" differently because it mistakenly assumes that (a) humans may be divided into clearly defined racial groups and (b) these groups vary in capabilities and aptitudes. Traditional racism directly and explicitly contains negative evaluations of minorities and uses the "natural world order" as a justification ("Nature intended it to be this way"). The same is true for traditional sexism. Modern racism camouflages prejudices within more sophisticated principles of meritocracy and justice. *Modern racism* posits that if you scratch the apparently nonracist surface of many people, you will find bigotry lurking beneath. Modern racism arises because people can see themselves as being fair, humanitarian, and egalitarian while at the same time holding a somewhat negative view of members of groups other than their own. Having prejudiced thoughts, however, does not necessarily make you a racist. Even people who completely reject prejudice may sometimes experience unintentional prejudiced thoughts and feelings due to prior learning. In this case, racism is like a lingering bad habit that surfaces despite people's best efforts to avoid it. As with all bad habits, with enough commitment and support, racism can be eliminated and the errors listed in Table 10.1 can be avoided.

When prejudice is put into action, it is discrimination. **Discrimination** is an action taken to harm a group or any of its members. It is a negative, often aggressive action aimed at the target of prejudice. Discrimination is aimed at denying members of the targeted groups treatment and opportunities equal to those afforded to the dominant group.

Blaming the Victim

It is commonly believed that the world is a just place where people generally get what they deserve. If you win the lottery, it must be because you are a nice person who deserves some good luck. If you are robbed, it must be because you were careless and wanted to be punished for past misdeeds. Any person who is mugged in a dark alley while carrying a great deal of cash may be seen as "asking to be robbed." Most people tend to believe that they deserve what happens to them. Most people also believe that others also get what they deserve in the world. It is all too easy to forget that victims do not have the benefit of hindsight to guide their actions.

But what happens when situations appear to be unjust? One method is to blame the victim by convincing ourselves that no injustice has occurred. When someone is a victim of prejudice, stereotyping, and discrimination, all too often they are seen as "doing *something* wrong." **Blaming the victim** occurs when we attribute the cause of discrimination or mis-

TABLE 10.1   *Errors in Making Decisions About Diverse Others*

Building an impression of another person requires collecting information from your perceptions and making conclusions about what it means. In doing so there are numerous ways errors can occur.

Errors in Making Inferences

Relying on small samples	Small samples are highly unreliable.
Relying on biased samples	People often ignore clear information about how typical and representative a sample is.
Underutilization of base-rate information	People tend to pay more attention to a single concrete instance than to valid base-rate information, perhaps because the single concrete instance is vivid and salient and thus more compelling.

Errors from Cognitive Heuristics

Availability heuristic	Estimating the frequency of some event by the ease with which you can bring instances to mind; people tend to overestimate the frequency of events that are easy to remember.
Representativeness heuristic	Seeing how well the information matches some imagined average or typical person in the category; the closer the person is to the prototype, the more likely we are to judge the person to be in the category.

Weighing Information

Positive frame	People avoid risks and opt for a "sure thing."
Negative frame	People take risks to avoid "costs."
Post-decision rationalization	Alternative chosen becomes more attractive, and alternatives not chosen become less desirable.

fortune to the personal characteristics and actions of the victim. The situation is examined for potential causes that will enable us to maintain our belief in a just world. If the victim can be blamed for causing the discrimination, then we can believe that the future is predictable and controllable because we will get what we deserve.

Attributing Causes

Blaming the victim occurs when we attempt to attribute a cause to events (see Tables 10.2 and 10.3). We constantly interpret the meaning of our behavior and of events that occur in our lives. Many times we want to figure out *why* we acted in a particular way or *why* a certain outcome occurred. If we get angry when someone implies that we are stupid, but we couldn't care less when someone calls us clumsy, we want to know why we are so sensitive about our intelligence. When we are standing on a street corner after a rainstorm and a car splashes us with water, we want to know whether it was caused by our carelessness, the driver's meanness, or just bad luck. This process of explaining or inferring the causes of events has been termed **causal attribution**. An **attribution** is an inference drawn about the causes of a behavior or event. Any behavior or event can have a variety of possible causes. We observe the behavior or event and then infer the cause. When a person trips and falls, for example, we can attribute his or her behavior to a preoccupied mood, being in too much of a hurry, clumsiness, or someone tripping him. Early in childhood we begin observing our own behavior and drawing conclusions about ourselves. We seem to have a fundamental need to understand both our own behavior and the behavior of others. In trying to understand why a behavior or event occurred, we generally choose to attribute causes either to

1. Internal, personal factors (such as effort and ability) or
2. External, situational factors (such as luck, task difficulty, or the behavior or personality of other people).

TABLE 10.2 *Dimensions of Attributions*

	Stable	Unstable
Internal	Ability	Effort
External	Task difficulty	Luck

TABLE 10.3 *Success Orientation*

	Stable	Unstable
Success	Ability	Effort
Failure	Task difficulty	Luck

For example, if you do well on a test, you can attribute your success to hard work and great intelligence (an internal attribution) or to the fact that the test was incredibly easy (an external attribution). When a person drops out of school, you can attribute the departure to a lack of motivation (an internal attribution) or lack of money (an external attribution).

People make causal attributions to explain their successes and failures. Frequently such attributions are **self-serving**, designed to permit us to take credit for positive outcomes and to avoid blame for negative ones. We have a systematic tendency to claim that our successes are due to our ability and efforts while our failures are due to bad luck, obstructive people, or task difficulty. We also have a systematic tendency to claim responsibility for the success of group efforts ("It was all my idea in the first place, and I did most of the work") and avoid responsibility for group failures ("If the other members had tried harder, this would not have happened").

Attribution theorists assume that how people explain their successes and failures determines how hard they work on subsequent tasks. If minority students, for example, attribute academic failure to lack of ability, it can eventually lead to *learned helplessness* (the feeling that no amount of effort can lead to success). If minority students think through why they succeeded or failed, however, and conclude that their failure is caused by either (a) a lack of effort or (b) using the wrong strategy, they will be empowered to succeed in the future.

We can attribute a person's poverty to laziness, or a person's involvement in an accident to carelessness, or a person's cancer to his or her being angry and mean. Doing so maintains a belief in justice and fairness. Not everyone, however, gets what he or she deserves. Attributing the causes of others' failure and misfortune to their actions rather than to prejudice and discrimination can be a barrier to building constructive relationships with diverse peers. Bad things do happen to good people. Racism does exist. Innocent bystanders do get shot.

Step Seven: Resolve Conflicts Constructively

In the first century of the common era, a skeptic approached the great rabbi Hillel and asked Hillel to teach him the full meaning of the Torah in a single proposition. Hillel responded, "Do not do unto your fellow man what you would not have him do unto you. This is the essence; the rest is commentary." No advice could be better for resolving conflicts constructively.

Your seventh step in building effective relationships with diverse individuals is to resolve conflicts constructively. This is the focus of Chapter 8. In conflicts you must work to achieve your goals and maintain effective relationships with the other person. You do so by mastering five strategies (forcing, withdrawing, smoothing, compromising, and negotiating). Negotiating is a process by which persons who have shared and opposed interests and want to come to an agreement, try to work out a settlement. You may negotiate to win (forcing) or to solve the problem. In problem-solving negotiations agreements are sought that maximize joint benefit, strengthen relationships, and contribute to the welfare of the broader community. To negotiate to solve the problem you describe what you want, describe how you feel, explain your reasons for wanting what you do and feeling as you do, reverse perspectives, invent at least three good optional agreements, and choose the agreement that seems the wisest. In interacting with diverse individuals conflicts are sure to arise. They must be managed with skill to ensure that constructive outcomes result.

Step Eight: Internalize Pluralistic Values

Your eighth step in building effective relationships with diverse individuals is to adopt a set of pluralistic values. The previous seven steps are implicitly based on values that must be adopted and internalized. The values necessary for building and maintaining positive relationships, especially among diverse individuals, are part of the superordinate identity, cooperative efforts, and constructive conflict resolution that unite diverse individuals (Johnson & Johnson, 1999).

In the United States, the superordinate identity of "American" is based on a set of common, pluralistic values specified in the Constitution, Bill of Rights, and Declaration of Independence. To interact effectively with diverse individuals, you must value democracy, freedom, liberty, equality, justice, the rights of individuals, and the responsibilities of citizenship. It is these values that form the American creed. All individuals are free to speak their minds and give their opinions. All individuals are considered to be of equal value. Every member has the right and responsibility to contribute his or her resources and efforts to achieving the group's goals and to take responsibility for the common good. Each member has a right to expect other individuals to be considerate of his or her needs and wants. All individuals are expected to reciprocate good deeds. All individuals must at times put the good of the group above their own needs and desires. All individuals have the right to participate in civic activities, including voting in elections. As Americans, we respect basic human rights, listen to dissenters instead of jailing them, and have a mul-

Aristotle's Golden Mean

Almost two and a half millennia ago, Aristotle wrote his *Nicomachean Ethics* in which he explores the question of "moral virtue" ("What constitutes good behavior? What ways of acting enable us to function effectively in the world?") He states that an important dimension of virtuous behavior is moderation ("an intermediate between excess and deficit, equidistant from the extremes, neither too much nor too little"). Each person must determine his or her own extremes and act in a relatively moderate way. Thus a person who easily loses his or her temper must strive to be more calm, while a person who rarely expresses feelings ought to become more expressive. Each must seek his or her own golden mean.

tiparty political system, a free press, freedom of speech, freedom of religion, and freedom of assembly. These values were shaped by millions of people from many different backgrounds. Americans are a multicultural people knitted together by a common set of political and moral values.

Relationships among diverse individuals exist within a community. For a community to exist and sustain itself, members must share common goals and shared values aimed at increasing the quality of life and defining appropriate behavior. A community cannot exist if it is dominated by (a) competition where individuals are taught to value striving for their personal success at the expense of others or (b) individualistic efforts where individuals value only their own self-interests. Rather, diverse individuals are bound together by the values underlying cooperation and problem-solving negotiations, such as commitment to the common good and the well-being of other community members, a sense of responsibility to contribute one's fair share of the work, respect for the efforts of others and for them as people, behaving with integrity, caring for other members, compassion when other members are in need, and appreciation of diversity. Such civic values both underlie and are promoted by cooperation and constructive conflict resolution.

The value systems underlying constructive conflict resolution promote the values of subjecting one's conclusions to challenge, viewing issues from all perspectives, reaching agreements that are satisfying to and beneficial for all disputants, and maintaining effective and caring long-term relationships (see Table 10.4). In other words, constructive conflict resolution inherently teaches a set of civic values aimed at ensuring the fruitful continuation of the community.

TABLE 10.4 *Key Values*

Source	Key Value
Superordinate identity	**Human equality:** American citizens are equally entitled to just treatment, respect, consideration for their needs, and freedom of conscience, thought, and expression. They are also entitled to be free of coercion. No matter how different individuals' historic and cultural background, they are all equal as Americans. This shared community exists despite differences of culture, ethnicity, language, ancestry, religion, gender, handicapping conditions, and so forth.
Cooperative community	**Reciprocity of good deeds:** If other citizens promote your success and well-being, it is expected that you will also promote their success and well-being. It is reciprocity that underlies the golden rule ("Do unto others what you would have others do unto you"). It requires that each citizen treat others with the fairness he or she would expect from them.
Problem-solving negotiations	**Wise agreements:** Conflicts should be resolved by agreements that maximize joint outcomes and benefit everyone concerned, improve the relationship among the individuals involved, and improve participants' ability to resolve conflicts constructively in the future.

Other Aspects of Diversity

In addition to the eight steps, there are three aspects of diversity that need to be noted. Within relationships among diverse individuals, there are frequent culture clashes and misunderstandings. It is through relationships with diverse individuals, however, that sophistication is increased.

Culture Clash

Another aspect of building relationships with diverse peers is cultural clashes. **Culture clash** is conflict over basic values that occurs among individuals from different cultures. The most common form occurs when members of minority groups question the values of the majority. Common reactions by majority group members when their values are being questioned are feeling

1. **Threatened:** Their responses include avoidance, denial, and defensiveness.

2. **Confused:** Their responses include seeking more information in an attempt to redefine the problem.

3. **Enhanced:** Their responses include heightened anticipation, awareness, and positive actions that lead to solving the problem.

Many cultural clashes develop from threatening, to confusing, to enhancing. Once they are enhancing, they are no longer a barrier.

As prejudice, stereotyping, and discrimination are reduced, as the tendency to blame the victim is avoided, and as cultural clashes become enhancing, the stage is set for recognizing and valuing diversity.

Clarifying Miscommunications

Imagine that you and several friends went to hear a speaker. Although the content was good, and the delivery entertaining, two of your friends walked out in protest. When you asked them why, they called your attention to the facts that the speaker continually used "you guys" even though half the audience were women, used only sports and military examples, quoted only males, and joked about senility and old age. Your friends were insulted.

Communication is actually one of the most complex aspects of managing relationships with diverse peers. To communicate effectively with people from a different cultural, ethnic, social-class, and historical background you must increase your

1. **Language sensitivity:** knowledge of words and expressions that are appropriate and inappropriate in communicating with diverse groups. The use of language can play a powerful role in reinforcing stereotypes and garbling communication. To avoid this problem, individuals need to heighten their sensitivity and avoid using terms and expressions that ignore or devalue others.

2. **Awareness of stylistic elements of communication:** knowledge of the key elements of communication style and how diverse cultures use these elements to communicate. Without awareness of nuances in language and differences in style, the potential for garbled communication is enormous when interacting with diverse peers.

Your ability to communicate with credibility to diverse peers is closely linked to your use of language. You must be sophisticated enough

to anticipate how your messages will be interpreted by the listener. If you are unaware of nuances and innuendoes contained in your message, then you will be more likely to miscommunicate. The words you choose often tell other people more about your values, attitudes, and socialization than you intend to reveal. Receivers will react to the subtleties conveyed and interpret the implied messages behind your words. The first step in establishing relationships with diverse peers, therefore, is to understand how language reinforces stereotypes and to adjust your usage accordingly.

You can never predict with certainty how every person will react to what you say. You can, however, minimize the possibility of miscommunicating by following some basic guidelines:

1. Use all the communication skills discussed in this book.

2. Negotiate for meaning whenever you think the other persons you are talking with have misinterpreted what you said.

3. Use words that are inclusive rather than exclusive such as *women, men, participants*.

4. Avoid adjectives that spotlight specific groups and imply the individual is an exception, such as *black doctor, woman pilot, older teacher, blind lawyer*.

5. Use quotes, references, metaphors, and analogies that reflect diversity and are from diverse sources—for example, from Asian and African sources as well as from European and American.

6. Avoid terms that define, demean, or devalue others, such as *cripple, girl, boy, agitator*.

7. Be aware of the genealogy of words viewed as inappropriate by others. It is the connotation the receiver places on the words that is important, not your connotation. These connotations change over time, so continual clarification is needed. There are "loaded" words that seem neutral to you but highly judgmental to people of diverse backgrounds. The word *lady*, for example, was a compliment even a few years ago, but today it fails to take into account women's independence and equal status in society and, therefore, is offensive to many women. Words such as *girls* or *gals* are just as offensive.

Gaining Sophistication Through Relationships

Some people are **sophisticated** about how to act appropriately within many different cultures and perspectives. They are courteous, well-mannered, and refined within many different settings and cultures. Other people are quite **provincial**, knowing only how to act appropriately within their narrow perspective. To become sophisticated a person must be able to see the situation from the cultural perspective of the other people involved. Much of the information about different cultural and ethnic heritages and perspectives cannot be attained through reading books and listening to lectures. Only through knowing, working with, and personally interacting with members of diverse groups can individuals really learn to value diversity, utilize diversity for creative problem solving, and work effectively with diverse peers. While information alone helps, it is only through direct and personal interaction among diverse individuals and developing personal as well as professional relationships with them that such outcomes are realized. Understanding the perspective of others from different ethnic and cultural backgrounds requires more than information. It requires the personal sharing of viewpoints and mutual discussion of situations.

To gain the sophistication and skills required to build relationships with diverse peers, you need to develop friends from a wide variety of cultural, ethnic, social-class, and historical backgrounds. Many aspects of relating to individuals different from you are learned only when a friend is candid about misunderstandings you are inadvertently creating. To gain the sophistication and skills you need to relate to diverse peers, work with them, and become friends with them, you need

1. **Actual interaction:** Seek opportunities to interact with a wide variety of peers. You do so because you value diversity, recognize the importance of relating effectively to diverse peers, and recognize the importance of increasing your knowledge of multicultural issues.

2. **Trust:** Build trust by being open about yourself and your commitment to cross-cultural relationships and being trustworthy when others share their opinions and reactions with you. Being trustworthy includes expressing respect for diverse backgrounds and valuing them as a resource that increases the quality of your life and adds to the viability of your society.

3. **Candor:** Persuade your peers to be candid by openly discussing their personal opinions, feelings, and reactions with you. There are many events that seem neutral to you that are offensive and hurtful to individuals from backgrounds different from yours. To understand what is and is not disrespectful and hurtful, your peers must be candid about their reactions and explain them to you.

If you are not sophisticated and skilled in building relationships with diverse peers, you are in danger of unconsciously colluding with current patterns of discrimination. **Collusion** is conscious and unconscious reinforcement of stereotypic attitudes, behaviors, and prevailing norms. People collude with discriminatory practices and prejudiced actions through ignorance, silence, denial, and active support. Perhaps the only way not to collude with existing discriminatory practices is to build the friendships with diverse peers that allow you to understand when discrimination and prejudice occur.

Friendships

All human beings have an innate need for friendships. Friendships, however, are not easy. They are not easy to initiate, build, or maintain. Real friendships mean hard work. They are even harder work when the friendship is between individuals from different heritages. Friendship means participating in intimate conversations in which both hopes and fears are shared, being honest and trustworthy, committing to the other person and the relationship, really listening to each other, working together to achieve shared goals, and negotiating and problem solving when you do not agree. Friendships take more effort than being in physical proximity to another person, talking with them, or sharing a meal. All friendships share several fundamental characteristics.

Friendship Pattern	Explanation
Enduring friendships	Many people sustain friendships longer than might be predicted by conventional wisdom and theory.
Rotating friendships (moving from friend to friend)	Blend of positive and negative behaviors, including some that attract friends (such as playful teasing and knowing interesting gossip) and others that destabilize relationships (such as bossiness, aggression, and untrustworthiness shown by sharing secrets).
Chronically friendless individuals	Behave in ways that discourage interaction and subvert relationships, such as being socially inhibited and disengaged (e.g., shy, timid), emotionally uncontrolled (easily angered), or self-centered (less caring, less honest).

 ## Characteristics of Friendships

Rank the following characteristics of friendships from most important to you (1) to least important to you (5).

_____ Commitment (intentionally give time and energy to relationship and work to increase trust and caring)

_____ Honesty (disclosure of who you are)

_____ Equality (everyone has the same value, not necessarily the same interests, and each is given equal consideration)

_____ Autonomy (friends revel in their differences; they allow each other to be separate and distinct individuals)

_____ Resolving conflicts (listen carefully to each other, become informed about each other's needs, resolve conflicts through problem-solving negotiations to find solutions that maximize joint gain and benefit everyone)

■ CHAPTER REVIEW

Demonstrate your understanding of the following concepts by matching the definitions with the appropriate concept. Find a partner. Compare answers.

Concept	Definition
_____ 1. Prejudice	a. Belief that associates a whole group of people with certain traits.
_____ 2. Ethnocentrism	
_____ 3. Stereotype	b. An action taken to harm a group or any of its members.
_____ 4. Illusionary correlation	c. Unjustified negative attitude toward a person based solely on that individual's membership in a group other than one's own.
_____ 5. Discrimination	
_____ 6. Blaming the victim	d. Attributing the cause of discrimination or misfortune to the personal characteristics and actions of the victim.
_____ 7. Collusion	
_____ 8. Scapegoat	e. Conflict over basic values that occurs among individuals from different cultures.
_____ 9. Racism	
_____ 10. Cooperation	f. Conscious or unconscious reinforcement of stereotypic attitudes, behaviors, and prevailing norms.
_____ 11. False consensus bias	
_____ 12. Stereotype threat	g. Tendency for people to overestimate the association between variables that are only slightly correlated or not correlated at all.
_____ 13. Culture clash	
	h. Prejudice directed at people because of their ethnic membership.
	i. Believing that most other people share one's own stereotypes.
	j. Guiltless but defenseless group that is attacked to provide an outlet for pent-up anger and frustration caused by another group.
	k. Working together to achieve mutual goals.
	l. Tendency to regard ones's own ethnic group, nation, religion, culture, or gender as being more correct than others.
	m. Whenever group members run the risk of confirming the stereotype.

Self-Diagnosis

This chapter has focused on interacting with diverse individuals. On a scale from 1 (poorly mastered) to 5 (highly mastered) rate the degree to which you have mastered each of the steps presented. Then choose two skills to improve on in the next week.

Rating	Skill
_____	I recognize that diversity exists and value it as a vital resource.
_____	I establish a cooperative context for my interactions with individuals from diverse backgrounds.
_____	I understand my historical and cultural heritage and view it as a central aspect of my identity.
_____	I respect and appreciate the historical and cultural heritages of others.
_____	I highlight and treasure the superordinate identity that unites us all into one society, one country, and one world.
_____	I am cognizant of my stereotypes and prejudices, and I consciously work to reduce them.
_____	I understand the procedures for resolving conflicts constructively and practice them frequently enough to become quite skillful in their use.
_____	I believe in and am committed to the pluralistic values that underlie the previous seven steps.

Skills I Will Improve in the Next Week

1. _____

2. _____

Summary

In a global village highly diverse individuals interact daily, study and work together, and live in the same community. Diversity among your acquaintances, classmates, co-workers, neighbors, and friends is increasingly inevitable. You are expected to interact effectively with people from a wide variety of backgrounds and characteristics. In order to gain the sophistication and skills needed to do so, you must take eight steps. You must appreciate the benefits from interacting with diverse individuals. You must ensure that the context for your interaction with diverse individuals is cooperative, not competitive or individualistic. You must include your historical and cultural heritage as a central aspect of your identity. You must respect and appreciate the historical and cultural heritages of other people. You must understand and accept the superordinate identity that unites all citizens despite their differences. You must constantly work to reduce your stereotypes and prejudices that interfere with your interacting effectively with diverse individuals. You must understand the procedures for resolving conflicts constructively and very skillfully use them when conflicts with diverse individuals arise. Finally, you must commit yourself to and internalize the pluralistic values that underlie the previous seven steps. Despite the cultural clashes and misunderstandings that inevitably occur when individuals with diverse heritages interact, positive relationships are quite possible and very sophisticating.

Answers

Chapter Review: 1. c; 2. l; 3. a; 4. g; 5. b; 6. d; 7. f; 8. j; 9. h; 10. k; 11. i; 12. m; 13. e.

CHAPTER 11

Barriers to Interpersonal Effectiveness

We pay a heavy price for our fear of failure. It is a powerful obstacle to growth. It assures the progressive narrowing of the personality and prevents exploration and experimentation. There is no learning without some difficulty and fumbling. If you want to keep on learning, you must keep on risking failure—all your life. It's as simple as that.
—John Gardner

Introduction

There are a number of barriers to engaging in effective interpersonal interaction that have their origins in interpersonal relationships. When you are troubled by these barriers, your interpersonal effectiveness is seriously impaired. The barriers are

1. Fear and anxiety.
2. Shyness.
3. Self-blame.

Fear and anxiety, more than any other emotions, incapacitate interpersonal interaction. They cause avoidance of the anxiety-provoking situation and an immobilization of interpersonal interaction within the situation. Fears can persist year after year, chronically interfering with constructive relationships and effective interaction. Learning to overcome fear and anxiety is an essential ingredient of being effective interpersonally. One specific type of problem arising from fear and anxiety is shyness. The excessive caution and undue self-consciousness in interpersonal relationships produced by shyness can stand as a major barrier to developing and maintaining friendships and effective working relationships. When interpersonal interaction is inhibited, interpersonal skills either never appear or are underutilized. Finally, self-blame, the directing of anger toward yourself for not living up to your expectations and hopes, results in depression that interferes with effectively relating to other people. This chapter focuses on overcoming the inhibition and avoidance created by these three barriers.

Managing Anxiety and Fear

Of all the emotions humans experience, fear is perhaps the most chronic and troublesome. All of us, many times during our lives, are afflicted with fear, anxiety, nervousness, phobia, or worry. Anger can quickly flare up and quickly die down. Depression may hang on, but sooner or later it will be replaced with a neutral feeling or even a positive one. A fear of failure, however, can influence practically everything you do every day of your life. It may not hurt as much as depression, or flare up like anger, but it will be there all the time, ready to disturb, year in and year out. It is fear that has the unique power of preventing you from fulfilling your potential. It is fear that can suppress talents and prevent genius from being actualized. Stage fright can prevent a great singer from being recognized; fear of failure can prevent an Einstein from entering a doctoral program or beginning a research project; fear of humiliation can prevent a young inventor from submitting his or her ideas to a potential manufacturer. Fear can be devastating in a special way that anger and depression cannot.

Fear exists when a person is afraid and knows what he or she is afraid of. **Anxiety** exists when a person is afraid but does not know what he or she is afraid of. The fears and anxieties that rule our lives the most are not spectacular ones. Most of us do not chronically fear having to fight a great white shark with a letter opener. What we do fear is being rejected and failing. We all experience anxiety at times—a troubled uneasiness of mind mixed with uncertainty and doubt. But when the feeling is persistent, with an intensity out of proportion to the object or situation that caused it, the anxiety is called a **phobia.** Phobias can develop in at least three ways. They can result from anxiety attacks, because people associate their feelings of panic with the places and situations in which they occur. A panic attack that occurs while you are driving your car, for example, may result in a phobia about driving. Phobias can also grow out of specific experiences. If you were bitten by a dog when you were a young child, for example, you may develop a phobia about dogs. Finally, phobias can be learned from others, such as by observing parents who fear lightning or bugs. In some cases the fear involved in a phobia is projected from its original source to a different place or situation. A fear of falling in social status, for example, may be repressed and projected into a fear of falling in an elevator.

Fear and anxiety usually involve two kinds of pain. One type of pain comes from doing what you are afraid of. The other type of pain comes from avoiding what you are afraid of. Either way you experience pain. The pain connected with doing an activity is generally less in the long run than the pain connected with avoiding an activity. Replacing the unpleasantness of rejection with the pain of loneliness usually is not a good bargain. Simply avoiding anxiety-provoking situations does not remove discomfort. There is discomfort in combatting the fear and there is discomfort in giving in to the fear. The discomfort connected with overcoming your fears has an ending, whereas the annoyance connected with not changing your fears can persist for as long as you live.

The procedures for managing and overcoming your fears and anxieties include the following:

1. Do not fear anxiety. Once you become afraid that your anxiety may come back, it will. Fearing that you may become anxious creates anxiety. The more you worry about the possibility of experiencing an anxiety attack, the more likely it is that you will have one. Generally, the more you worry about something, the worse it gets.

2. Accept your fear and anxiety as natural feelings that are to be experienced but not fought or resisted. The key to managing fear and anxiety is simply to accept them. The harder you fight them the worse they become. The more you try to fight to get rid of your fears, the more unacceptable and shameful you see them to be, the worse they will become. The more you ignore them, pay no attention to them, and accept them for what they are, the less hold they will have over you.

3. Own your fear and anxiety. Accept them as your feelings. Do not view anxiety as "it," something separate and apart from you that descends on you and takes control, but rather as one of your feelings that you sometimes experience and is within you and, therefore, subject to your control.

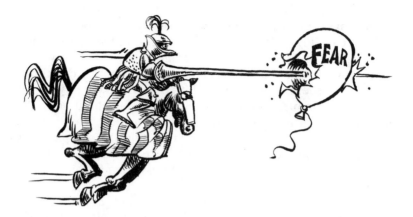

4. Accept yourself as you are. Rejection from others cannot hurt unless you reject yourself as a result. Failing cannot hurt unless you reject yourself for it. Being an anxious person or a person who has anxiety attacks does not make you a horrible outcast. You do not have to be loved and accepted by others to like yourself, you do not have to be perfect in order to respect yourself, and you do not have to be in perfect control of your feelings in order to feel worthwhile.

5. Recognize that fear is learned and, therefore, it may be unlearned.

6. Challenge the idea that you must worry over something unpleasant just because it *might* happen to you. Do not engage in "What if . . . ?" Avoid the neurotic idea that it is important to think about a possible danger. Fight the idea that you should constantly think of, dwell upon, and worry over a frightening situation. Do not fix upon a grain of truth and magnify it out of proportion. Vigorously attack the mental nonsense (neurotic misconceptions) that
   a. You ought to be terribly upset about something.
   b. Worrying helps.
   c. The more you focus on the dreaded event, the better it is; that is, it is important to think about potential danger just because it *might* happen.
   d. Outside events can upset you. Remember that it is your thinking about things that disturbs you, not the things themselves.

7. Avoid catastrophizing. The moment you tell yourself that something is awful or terrible, or that you are facing a catastrophe, you are going to become disturbed. The two things you can do are
   a. Convince yourself that the situation is not a catastrophe after all. Accept your fear as being a minor, not a major, inconvenience.

b. Convince yourself that even if the situation is a catastrophe there is really no need to become terribly upset over it because being upset only makes your situation worse.

8. Remember that being afraid does not mean that you are crazy. Many people fear that experiencing an anxiety attack will drive them crazy. They are afraid that experiencing anxiety means that they are losing their minds. They see themselves as going out of control and running berserk down the street. Being afraid and being psychotic are two separate things entirely. An anxiety attack may feel strange and puzzling, but it does not mean you are going crazy.

9. View the fear and anxiety as a problem to be managed and solved, not as a catastrophe to hide from. When you overreact and become overconcerned, the anxiety takes control. When you are working on solving a problem, you are merely concerned.

10. Systematically desensitize yourself to the fearful situation by doing the following:
    a. Learn how to relax systematically. A relaxed person cannot be an anxious person.
    b. After you are relaxed, imagine yourself overcoming your fears by engaging in the behavior you are afraid of.

11. Flood yourself with actual experiences of doing what you are most afraid of. Such flooding involves at least three elements:
    a. Taking risks by repeatedly exposing yourself to the very thing you are most afraid of. You overcome your fear when you do the thing you are afraid to do and are willing to face the dangers involved. People who do not take risks in facing their fears live in a constant state of anxiety and apprehension. If you are afraid of riding an elevator, you must do so anyway. People who have ridden in elevators thousands of times do not have the same nervousness as a person who rarely takes an elevator.
    b. Not blaming yourself if you perform less than perfectly in the situation. Separate your actions and performance from yourself.
    c. Practicing facing the fearful situation and then practicing some more. Practice makes you the master. If you have not mastered the situation you are afraid of, you have not practiced it enough. To master an activity you have to
       (1) Practice it.
       (2) Examine the performance to find out where you can improve.
       (3) Change.
       (4) Practice it again.

In other words, stick your neck out and do the thing you are afraid of. Then, after you have done less than perfectly, sit back objectively and look over your mistakes so that you can improve next time. Progress is built on mistakes. The person who does not make mistakes does not learn.

12. Distract yourself when the anxiety becomes too high. It is impossible to be upset about something unless you are thinking about it. Anything that diverts you from your troubles will give you relief.

13. Work on developing a broad view of life and a wide variety of experiences. The more you know about the world, and the more you have experienced, the more comfortable you tend to be in any situation. The person with the most experiences is the person who can compare the next experience to those that he or she has already had.

14. Do not be afraid of being independent. Do not ask for sympathy from other people. There is a tendency to use one's fear and anxiety to control others by expecting them to feel sorry for you or to make excuses and exceptions for you, because you are terrified. People who are afraid and who lean upon others to help them with their fears are not always quick to give them up, because to do so means they have become independent, which they are sometimes reluctant to do.

15. Accept reality. Life is full of danger, heartache, and injustice. Every living creature has to go through some suffering, and you are no different. If you are not facing some suffering today, you will be tomorrow. There is no need to be terrified or nervous or worried about these possibilities. Remind yourself that
    a. Most frustrations are really not as bad as you think they are.
    b. Even if some are that bad, you do not have to lose your mind over them and thus make matters worse. If you focus on danger, heartache, and injustice unduly, you will create unnecessary additional suffering for yourself and for the people around you.

16. Do not expect great improvement. Measure your improvement in terms of
    a. Duration of anxiety.
    b. Intensity of anxiety.
    c. Frequency of anxiety.

17. Others will be too busy to pay much attention to how you are doing on your self-improvement program. Reward yourself for your progress.

18. As you confront your fears, they will get worse for a while. Learning usually takes place in an erratic way, and you will never know from one time to the next just how you are going to do.

19. Watch out for spontaneous recovery. There is a strong tendency for neurotic symptoms to return after you think you have gotten rid of them. Such backsliding usually means you have gotten careless about fighting your fear.

Breathing

Breathing is essential to life. Proper breathing is an antidote to stress. It is through proper breathing that your blood is purified of waste products, infused with oxygen, and purged of carbon dioxide. Poorly oxygenated blood contributes to anxiety states, depression, and fatigue, making it many times more difficult to cope with stressful situations. Proper breathing habits not only are essential for good mental and physical health but also are a key to relaxing effectively. When you are faced with an anxiety-provoking situation, deep and proper breathing is one of your first lines of defense. Breathing exercises have been found to be effective in reducing anxiety, depression, irritability, muscular tension, and fatigue.

 EXERCISE 11.1
Learning How to Breathe Deeply

The objective of this exercise is to help you relax systematically when you are anxious by controlling your breathing. You may wish to complete this exercise with a partner. Take turns reading the exercise while the other does it. The procedure for the exercise is as follows:

1. Sit up straight with good posture in a hard-backed chair.

2. Slowly breathe inward through your nose, counting from one to four as you do so.
   a. First, fill the lower section of your lungs. Your diaphragm will push your abdomen outward to make room for the air.
   b. Second, fill the middle part of your lungs. As you do so you will feel your lower ribs and chest move slightly forward to accommodate the air.
   c. Third, fill the upper part of your lungs. Raise your shoulders and collarbone slightly so that the very tops of your lungs are replenished with fresh air.

   Practice until these three steps are performed in one smooth, continuous inhalation.

3. Hold your breath for 4 seconds.

4. Exhale slowly, counting to eight while you do so. Pull in your abdomen slightly and lift it slowly as the lungs empty. When you have completely exhaled, relax your abdomen and chest.

5. Continue deep breathing for about 5 to 10 minutes at a time.

6. Scan your body for tension. Compare the tension you feel at this time with the tension you felt at the beginning.

7. Use this deep-breathing procedure whenever you feel yourself getting tense.

Progressive Muscle Relaxation

You cannot have a warm feeling of well-being and relaxation in your body and at the same time experience anxiety and psychological stress. As your muscles relax, your pulse rate becomes slower, your blood pressure drops, and you breathe deeper and slower. When it is successfully learned, deep-muscle relaxation is an excellent antidote to anxiety and fear.

There are two steps in using deep-muscle relaxation:

1. Learning to distinguish between sensations of tension and deep relaxation.

2. Learning to relax any major muscle group on demand, even within highly anxiety-provoking situations.

 EXERCISE 11.2

Systematic Muscle Relaxation

The objective of this exercise is to train you in a procedure for systematic muscle relaxation. You may wish to complete this exercise with a partner. Take turns reading the exercise while the other does it. Go through the following procedure daily until you have it memorized and are able to relax any set of muscles at will. Then use it whenever you are in an anxiety-provoking situation. Here is the procedure:

1. Lie down on a blanket or rug or sit in a comfortable chair with a back high enough to support your head. When you tense a muscle group, do so enough to clearly feel the tension, but do not strain any muscles.

2. Tense your hands, forearms, and biceps by clenching both fists and curling both arms as if you were in a body builder's pose. Hold for 5 to 7 seconds. Concentrate on how the tension feels. Notice each detail of the tension in your hands, forearms, and biceps. Feel the tension.

3. Relax your hands and arms, letting them rest on the floor or on the arms of the chair. Concentrate on relaxing your hands, forearms, and biceps as much as possible. Continue the relaxation for 20 to 30 seconds. Notice the difference between the tension and relaxation. Enjoy the pleasant and soothing feeling of relaxation.

4. Repeat this procedure.

5. Tense all your facial, neck, throat, and shoulder muscles by wrinkling up your forehead and, at the same time, press your head as far back as possible, rotate it clockwise in a complete circle, and then rotate it counterclockwise in a complete circle. Now wrinkle up the muscles of your face by frowning, squinting your eyes, pursing your lips, pressing your tongue on the roof of the mouth, and trying to touch your ears with your shoulders. Hold for 5 to 7 seconds. Notice the tension. Study how it feels. Enjoy it.

6. Relax all the muscles in your face, neck, throat, and shoulders. Concentrate on how the relaxation feels. Continue the relaxation for 20 to 30 seconds. Enjoy the relaxation and study each detail of how each relaxed muscle feels.

7. Repeat the procedure.

8. Tense your chest, stomach, and lower back muscles by arching back as you take a deep breath into your chest. Hold your breath for 5 to 7 seconds. Study how the tense muscles feel. Then relax for 20 to 30 seconds. Notice the difference between the tension and the relaxation. Take a deep breath, pressing out your stomach, and tensing your muscles. Hold your breath and the tension for 5 to 7 seconds. Then relax for 20 to 30 seconds. Notice the difference between the tension and the relaxation. Study the difference. Enjoy the soothing and enjoyable feeling of relaxation.

9. Repeat this procedure.

10. Tense your thighs, buttocks, calves, and feet by pointing your feet and toes back toward your face and tightening your shins. Hold for 5 to 7 seconds. Study the tension. Then relax the muscles. Let them go completely relaxed. Notice the difference between the tension and relaxation. Enjoy the warm and soothing feeling of relaxation. Now curl your toes downward while at the same time tightening your calves, thighs, and buttocks. Hold for 5 to 7 seconds. Study the details of how each tensed muscle feels. Then relax. Let the muscles go completely relaxed. Notice and enjoy the difference between the tension and relaxation.

11. Repeat this procedure.

12. Let your whole body go completely relaxed. Feel the relaxation in your hands and arms, your face and neck, your chest and stomach, and your legs and feet. Notice how comfortable and enjoyable it feels.

Shyness

Every person, experiencing as he does his own solitariness and aloneness, longs for union with another.
—Rollo May

There is no joy except in human relationships.
—Antoine de Saint Exupéry

Answer the following questions yes or no:

_____ 1. I often become anxious when I am the center of attention.

_____ 2. I am often concerned about being rejected by others.

_____ 3. I tend to be very self-conscious in interacting with other people.

_____ 4. When I am with people I do not know, I hesitate before expressing my thoughts and feelings.

_____ 5. I am very conscious of whether people like me or not.

_____ 6. I need to be more aggressive in forming relationships with other people.

If you answered yes to several of these questions, you may be suffering from a very common problem—shyness. **Shyness** is an excessive caution in interpersonal relations. Specifically, shy people tend to (1) be timid about expressing themselves, (2) be overly self-conscious about how others are reacting to them, (3) embarrass easily, and (4) experience physiological symptoms of their anxiety, such as a racing pulse, blushing, or an upset stomach (Zimbardo, 1977). Shyness involves excessive caution in social interaction and may include timidity, self-consciousness, anxiety, and sensitivity to embarrassment.

If you are shy, you are not alone. Most people have been shy during some stage of their lives, and up to 40 percent of Americans report being currently troubled by shyness. Most people, furthermore, experience shyness only in certain situations, such as when asking someone for help, when interacting with a member of the opposite sex, or when attending large parties. Shyness has a number of undesirable consequences, such as contributing to difficulty in making friends, being lonely and depressed, and being sexually inhibited. It is no surprise, therefore, that the vast majority of shy people do not like being shy.

Shyness can be successfully overcome. Although shyness tends to be a deeply entrenched part of an individual's personality and it takes a great deal of hard work to overcome, most shy people believe that they have succeeded in conquering their shyness. The two steps in doing so are (1) understanding your shyness and (2) building your self-esteem.

Understanding Your Shyness

To understand why you are shy, you should analyze your shyness. Try to pinpoint exactly what kinds of people tend to elicit your shy behavior. In his study on shyness, Zimbardo (1977) found the people who generated shyness (in order of decreasing importance) were

1. Strangers.
2. Members of the opposite sex.
3. Authorities by virtue of their knowledge.
4. Authorities by virtue of their role.
5. Relatives.
6. Elderly people.
7. Friends.
8. Children.
9. Parents.

Next, try to ascertain what situations tend to elicit your shyness. Situations in which people tended to feel shy (in order of decreasing importance) were when they were

1. The focus of attention of a large group (such as when giving a speech).
2. A member of a large group.
3. Of lower status than the other people present.
4. In social situations in general.
5. In new situations in general.
6. In situations requiring assertiveness.
7. In situations in which one was being evaluated.
8. The focus of attention of a small group.
9. In small social groups.
10. In one-to-one interactions with a member of the opposite sex.
11. Vulnerable (needing help).
12. In small task-oriented groups.
13. In one-to-one interactions with a member of the same sex.

Once you understand which people and situations cause your shyness, you are ready to work on overcoming it.

Building Your Self-Esteem

Your shyness lies primarily within your evaluation of your self-worth. Increased self-confidence is an important aspect of combating shyness. Some of the guidelines for building higher self-esteem are as follows:

1. **Control your self-esteem through how you see yourself.** Changing the way in which you think about yourself will change your self-esteem.

2. **Set your own standards for evaluating yourself.** Do not fall into the common trap of letting others set the standards by which you evaluate yourself. People with low self-esteem tend to be particularly susceptible to persuasion and too readily accept others' standards for their own.

3. **Set realistic goals.** Do not demand too much of yourself. Do not expect yourself to perform always at your best. Compare your performance against that of average individuals, not superstars.

4. **Modify negative self-talk and attributions.** Individuals with low self-esteem tend to think in counterproductive ways and make negative statements to themselves. When they succeed at something, for example, they may attribute it to good luck rather than to their ability and effort. Make sure you take credit for your successes and consider seriously the possibility that failures may not be your fault. Make self-enhancing conclusions about the way in which you applied your abilities and effort and tell yourself what a competent and good person you are.

5. **Emphasize your strengths.** People with low self-esteem often derive little satisfaction from their accomplishments and virtues. They pay little heed to their good qualities while emphasizing their defeats and faults. Accept your personal shortcomings that you are powerless to change and work to change those that are changeable. At the same time, you should increase your awareness of your strengths and learn to appreciate them.

6. **Work to improve yourself.** Efforts at self-improvement can be used to boost your self-esteem. Many personal shortcomings can be conquered. Although it is important to reassess your goals and discard those that are unrealistic or are imposed by others, this book is an example of how you can improve your interpersonal skills and your confidence in relating to others.

7. **Approach others with a positive outlook.** Negativism toward yourself can result in negativism toward others. Faultfinding and criticism destroy relationships with others. They lead to tension, bitter exchanges,

and rejection, which, in turn, lower your self-esteem. When you approach people with a positive, supportive outlook, you will promote rewarding interactions and gain acceptance. There is nothing that enhances self-esteem more than acceptance and genuine affection from others.

 EXERCISE 11.3
Understanding Your Shyness

The objective of this exercise is to help you analyze not only the social situations in which you feel shy but also the causes of your shyness. Without understanding your shyness you cannot build an effective strategy to overcome it. The procedure for the exercise follows:

1. Divide into pairs. Complete the following steps for both of you.

2. *Specify your target behaviors.*
   a. Examine the list of Zimbardo's findings on which people and situations tend to generate reticence in others (see p. 393). List the ones that seem most characteristic of you. Add any others that apply to you.
   b. Decide which of the following may be reasons for your shyness:
      Concern about negative evaluation
      Fear of rejection
      Lack of self-confidence
      Lack of specific interpersonal skills
      Fear of intimacy
      Preference for being alone
      Emphasis on and enjoyment of nonsocial activities
      Personal inadequacy or disability
      Other _____
   c. Which of the following negative thoughts are typical of you and help prevent you from pursuing relationships in an active and positive way? Each of these thoughts undermines or precludes productive interpersonal behavior.
      I am undesirable.
      I am dull and boring.
      If I ever admitted this thought to anyone, that person would reject or ridicule me.
      Other people are not interested in my thoughts and feelings.
      I cannot relax, be spontaneous, and enjoy myself.
      I cannot seem to get what I want from this relationship.

> If I said how I feel, that person might leave me and I would be all alone.
> I will not risk being hurt again.
> There must be something wrong with me if he/she left me.
> I do not know how to act around other people.
> I will make a fool of myself.
> Other _____

d. Generate a number of specific behaviors you wish to increase in frequency within the problem situations and with the problem people. Initiating a conversation, asking someone to dance, and paraphrasing a person's remarks are examples.

3. *Gather baseline data.* The **baseline period** is a span of time, before the actual beginning of your efforts to change, during which you systematically observe your target behaviors. Gathering baseline data includes (1) measuring the specific frequency of the behaviors targeted to be increased, (2) noting the situations or events that happen before the targeted behavior, and (3) noting the typical consequences of the targeted behavior.

   a. Place yourself in the situation in which you feel shy. Count how often you engage in the behavior targeted to be increased (such as initiating a conversation). You need to know the initial frequency of the target behavior in order to evaluate later how effectively you are increasing it. Because it is crucial that you have accurate data about the initial frequency of your behavior, it is important that you be honest with yourself and count all instances of the targeted behavior. It may be necessary to carry a portable device for recording your behavior, which may be simply an index card. The information should then be transferred to a permanent written record sheet or a graph. Carry out this procedure for a week or for a minimum of five times.

   b. For each instance of the targeted behavior, note the situations, events, feelings, or thoughts that precede the occurrence of your targeted behavior. These questions may help:
      > What did I think or say to myself?
      > What behavior of other people occurred?
      > What were the physical circumstances of the past few minutes?

4. Based on your tentative conclusion as to the causes of your shyness and the data you have gathered about the frequency with which you naturally initiate and build a relationship, design a plan to increase the frequency of your targeted behavior. The plan should include

   a. How you will reinforce or reward yourself for engaging in the desired behavior.

   b. The conditions you have to meet in order to earn the reward. Set a behavioral target and frequency that are both challenging and realistic.

5. Complete a contract for each member of the pair.

Self-Change Contract

I, _____, do hereby agree to initiate my action plan as of (date) _____ and to continue it for a minimum period of (weeks) _____ or until (date) _____.

My specific action plan is to _____

_____ .

I will do my best to complete this action plan to my utmost ability and to evaluate its effectiveness only after it has been honestly tried for the specified period of time.

For every _____ times I successfully comply with my action plan, I will reward myself with _____ .

I hereby request that the witness who has signed below support me in my action plan and encourage me to comply with the specifics of the contract.

Signed _____

Witness _____

Avoiding Self-Blame

A major threat to self-acceptance and good interpersonal relationships is a blame orientation. **Self-blame** exists when you say "bad me" to yourself or when you judge your basic self-worth on the basis of your inadequate or rotten behavior. Self-blame is, in effect, being angry at yourself. Blame involves a double attack: one against your actions and the other against yourself as a person. As discussed in the chapter on anger (Chapter 9), you should never blame yourself (or others) for: (1) not having the intelligence to do as well as you would like; (2) being ignorant; (3) having behaved badly; (4) not being perfect; and (5) being psychologically disturbed at the time.

Again, to combat self-blame, first, do not assume that it is a catastrophe when you do not get what you want and that whoever is to blame must be severely chastised. Instead, engage in replacing your old assumptions with new, more constructive assumptions (the specific procedures for doing so are covered in Chapter 9). Second, forgive yourself (and others) for everything. The sooner you do this the better for all concerned. And finally, be problem-oriented, not blame-oriented or fault-oriented. As much as possible, separate the person from their actions. This will help you focus on the problem to be solved. Do not focus on your own or others failure to live up to your expectations. And remember that when you blame others, you risk their becoming hostile and angry with you and escalating the conflict into a destructive direction.

Mistakes and Self-Talk

Many people, when they make a mistake, make discouraging, critical, and blaming statements to themselves almost automatically. You may be one of them. In many cases it is difficult for you to identify your negative self-talk. But in order to feel better, it is important to train yourself to engage in positive self-talk after making mistakes. This behavior change can be initiated by

1. Looking at negative self-talk in general.
2. Identifying as best you can your negative self-talk.
3. Formulating productive self-talk.
4. Practicing it until it becomes automatic.

The purpose of these four steps is to develop an ongoing, energetic, encouraging inner speech.

There are times when many people are really hard on themselves when they make a mistake. They forget that while it feels good to succeed, it is not awful to make a mistake. Mistakes tell them that certain things may need to be done in a different way or with more time and concentration. Mistakes are the means for learning to do things better. Mistakes are an important part of long-term success, especially when people challenge themselves to accomplish something difficult.

You have a choice. You may see mistakes as negative (something awful that proves you are stupid, a loser, or a failure) or as positive (a source of information about how to modify current behavior to be more effective in the future). What choice you make determines how you react to your mistakes. Genuine happiness is only possible to the degree that you feel good about yourself despite your mistakes and failures. The sooner you realize that failure is not bad in itself but is rather a natural part of achieving and living, the better able you will be to challenge yourself, grow, develop, and achieve.

Critical Thoughts	Encouraging Thoughts
(Circle the self put-down that you might use when you make a mistake.)	(Circle the comments you like best for handling a mistake.)
You stupid idiot. Why can't you do something right!	That didn't work. What shall I try next?
I'll never get it.	Everyone makes mistakes. Just try it again.
I really blew it this time.	I'll see if I can do better next time.
I hate myself.	I only did one thing poorly. Look at everything I did right!
Why am I such a loser?	I'm learning from my mistakes and that makes me a winner!

EXERCISE 11.4

Being Positive About Yourself While Trying Again

1. Form a group of three.

2. Ask members to identify a failure or two they have experienced recently. These failures need to be written out on a slip of paper. Place all the failures in a hat.

3. Each member draws a failure out of the hat. The member then
   a. Makes a series of negative self-statements about the failure.
   b. Makes a series of positive self-statements about the failure.

4. This procedure is repeated until every member has gone through the sequence at least twice.

5. Discuss how hard or easy it is to change negative self-statements to positive ones and how important it is to learn to do so.

■ CHAPTER REVIEW

Demonstrate your understanding of barriers to interpersonal effectiveness by matching each definition with the appropriate characteristic. Check your answers with a partner, and explain the reasoning for your answers. The answers are at the end of the chapter.

Concept	Definition
_____ 1. Fear	a. When you say "bad me" to yourself or when you judge your basic self-worth on the basis of your inadequate or rotten behavior.
_____ 2. Anxiety	
_____ 3. Phobia	
_____ 4. Catastrophizing	b. Telling yourself that what you are facing is so awful and terrible that you cannot bear it
_____ 5. Shyness	c. Excessive caution in interpersonal relations.
_____ 6. Self-blame	d. When a person is afraid but does not know what he or she is afraid of
	e. Anxiety with an intensity out of proportion to the object or situation that caused it.
	f. When a person is afraid and knows what he or she is afraid of.

Self-Diagnosis

This chapter has focused on overcoming the barriers to interpersonal effectiveness. On a scale from 1 (poorly mastered) to 5 (highly mastered) rate the degree to which you have mastered each skill. Then choose two skills to improve on in the next week.

Rating	Skill
_____	Reducing fear and anxiety through deep breathing and progressive muscle relaxation.
_____	Reducing shyness by building your self-esteem.
_____	Avoiding self-blame by avoiding catastrophizing, through self-forgiveness, and by increasing encouraging thoughts.

Skills I Will Improve in the Next Week

1. _____

2. _____

Summary

In every relationship you decide how to manage the internal barriers to relating effectively to the other person. Barriers to interpersonal effectiveness include (a) fear and anxiety, (b) shyness, and (c) self-blame. **Fear** exists when a person is afraid and knows what he or she is afraid of. **Anxiety** exists when a person is afraid but does not know what he or she is afraid of. Managing fear and anxiety includes accepting them as natural feelings and viewing them as problems to be solved, not as catastrophes to hide from. Learning how to engage in deep breathing, progressive relaxation, and visualizing yourself overcoming your fears are also helpful. **Shyness** is an excessive caution in interpersonal relations. To overcome your shyness, you determine which people and situations cause it, you build your self-esteem, and you improve your interpersonal skills. Helping others learn interpersonal skills involves specifying the target behavior, gathering baseline data, designing your program, executing and evaluating your program, and terminating the training. **Self-blame** exists when you say "bad me" to yourself or when you judge your basic self-worth on the basis of your inadequate and rotten behavior. You reduce self-blame by changing your assumptions and forgiving yourself. Finally, people successful in gaining a high level of interpersonal skills are willing to take risks, tolerate failure, persist, and celebrate success.

Answers

Chapter Review: 1. f; 2. d; 3. e; 4. b; 5. c; 6. a.

CHAPTER 12

Epilogue

Importance of Interpersonal Skills

In 1955, Edward Banfield lived for nine months in a small town in southern Italy that he called "Montegrano." What Banfield noticed most was the town's alienated citizenry, grinding poverty, and pervasive corruption. He concluded that the primary source of Montegrano's plight was the distrust, envy, and suspicion that characterized its inhabitants' relations with each other. They viewed communal life as little more than a battleground. Town members consistently refused to help one another unless it would result in material gain. Many actually tried to prevent their neighbors from succeeding, believing that others' good fortune would inevitably undercut their own. Consequently, they remained socially isolated and impoverished, unable to cooperate to solve common problems or pool their resources and talents to build viable economic enterprises.

Montegrano's citizens were not inherently more selfish or foolish than people elsewhere. But for a number of complex historical and cultural reasons, they lacked the norms, habits, attitudes, and networks that encourage people to work together for the common good. They lacked what Alexis de Tocqueville called "the habits of the heart." Habits of the heart include taking responsibility for the common good, trusting others to do the same, being honest, having self-discipline, reciprocating good deeds, and perfecting the interpersonal skills necessary for interpersonal effectiveness and self-actualization.

There is no way to overemphasize the importance of interpersonal skills and their use to build constructive and effective relationships. **Interpersonal skills** are the sum total of your ability to interact effectively with other people. Your interpersonal skills allow you to take appropriate social initiatives, understand people's reactions to them, and respond accordingly. To live is to reach out to others. We all need other people. Striving to maximize the quality of our life requires that we also strive to maximize the quality of the lives of our neighbors, colleagues, friends, and loved ones. We engage in relationships because we have goals we wish to pursue that require the participation of other people as well as ourselves. Building and maintaining effective and fulfilling relationships requires that you

1. Disclose yourself to others to let them recognize you as a distinct and unique individual.
2. Build trust between yourself and others.
3. Communicate your ideas and thoughts effectively.
4. Communicate your feelings verbally.
5. Communicate your feelings nonverbally.
6. Listen to others' problems constructively and respond in helpful ways.
7. Face conflicts with the other person and resolve them constructively.
8. Manage anger and stress in constructive ways.
9. Value diversity and build relationships with individuals who are different from you.
10. Overcome the internal barriers to relating effectively with others.

No matter whether we are interacting with many people or just one, whether the situation is formal or informal, or whether the relationship is personal or impersonal, you need your interpersonal skills.

 EXERCISE 12.1

Planning for Improvement

The following section is a summary of the major interpersonal skills you need to interact effectively with other people, build friendships, and actualize your potential. Write an essay describing your strengths and weaknesses for each of the ten sets of skills. Then write out a plan for improving each of the ten sets of interpersonal skills over the next three months or so.

Interpersonal Effectiveness, Self-Actualization, and Interpersonal Skills

Your interpersonal skills are a necessary requirement for creating the relationships within which you increase your interpersonal effectiveness and actualize your potential to the fullest. It is through your relationships that you become more effective interpersonally. **Interpersonal effectiveness** is the degree to which the consequences of your behavior match your intentions. You take action in interacting with another person, assess the consequences of your behavior and obtain feedback from others, reflect and decide whether those consequences match your intentions, and then engage in a modified action in the relationship, and repeat the process. It is through your interpersonal skills that you build the relationships within which you can increase your interpersonal effectiveness.

It is through your relationships that you actualize your potential. **Self-actualization** is the drive to actualize your potential to the fullest extent and take joy and a sense of fulfillment from being all that you can be. It rests upon your ability to build good relationships, live fully in the present (as opposed to the past or future), and be autonomous by applying your values and principles flexibly in order to act in ways that are appropriate to the current situation (as opposed to being inner-directed or outer-directed). It is through your interpersonal skills that you build the relationships that promote your self-actualization.

There are at least ten sets of interpersonal skills that you must master to become more interpersonally effective and actualize your potential to its fullest extent.

Self-Disclosure

In every relationship you decide how well you wish the other person to know you and build an appropriate level of openness. To be open with another person you must (a) be aware of who you are, (b) accept yourself, and (c) take the risk of trusting the other person to be accepting of you (O = S A T). There are two sides of openness: How open you are with other persons (disclosing yourself to them) and how open you are to others (listening to their disclosures in an accepting way). **Self-disclosure** is revealing to another person how you perceive and are reacting to the present situation and giving any information about yourself and your past that is relevant to an understanding of your perceptions and reactions to the present. Self-disclosure focuses on the present, includes feelings as well as facts, has both breadth and depth, and should be reciprocal in the early stages of a relationship. Healthy relationships are built on self-disclosure.

You cannot disclose unless you are self-aware. Self-awareness leads to self-knowledge and self-understanding. **Self-awareness** comes from focusing your attention on yourself and receiving feedback on how others perceive you. **Feedback** is information that allows you to compare your actual performance with standards of performance. There are rules for both giving and receiving feedback, such as focusing on behavior, not personality and being descriptive, not judgmental.

You only disclose what you accept. **Self-acceptance** is viewing yourself and your actions with approval or satisfaction, or having a high regard for yourself. There is a reciprocal relationship among self-disclosure, self-awareness, and feedback. The more self-aware and self-accepting you are, the more you can let others know about you, the better the feedback you can receive, which increases your self-awareness.

Self-disclosure can be selective so that you present a certain impression to other people. **Self-presentation** is the process by which you try to shape what others think of you and what you think of yourself. Finally, self-disclosure is a risk. Taking the risks involved in disclosing yourself requires trust.

Trust

In every relationship you decide what level of trust you will build and maintain. Friendships and other effective relationships require a high level of trust. When you **trust** another person you perceive that (a) the choice can lead to gains or losses, (b) whether you will gain or lose depends upon the behavior of the other person, (c) the loss will be greater than the gain, and (d) the other person will probably behave in such a way that you will gain rather than lose. There are two parts to trust: Being trusting and being trustworthy. Trust is increased when a person takes a risk and acts in a trusting way and the other person responds supportively in a trustworthy way. The key to trust is being trustworthy. Trust is dynamic; it is never set but changes constantly as individuals interact. While difficult to build, trust is easy to destroy. Trust has to be appropriate.

Communication

In every relationship you decide what you wish to communicate to the other person. **Interpersonal communication** is the sending of a message to a receiver with the conscious intent of affecting the receiver's behavior. Communication contains seven basic elements (sender's intentions, sender's encoding of message, sending the message, channel through which message is sent, the receiver's decoding of the message, the receiver's internal response, and the amount of noise in the process). Communication is effective when the receiver interprets the sender's message the way the sender intended it. Communication is not a step-by-step linear process. Everything takes place simultaneously. Effective communication requires both sending and receiving skills. Sending messages effectively requires taking clear ownership of your message and describing (not judging) the other person's behavior. Statements about the relationship are important for improving the quality of interaction. Two-way communication tends to take more time but is far more effective than one-way communication. Communication is enhanced when you make the message appropriate to the receiver's frame of reference. Other sending skills include describing your feelings and making your verbal and nonverbal messages congruent with each other. The more credible you are, the more effective your communication tends to be. Receiving messages effectively requires paraphrasing and negotiating for meaning. These skills take continual practice to perfect.

Expressing Feelings Verbally

In every relationship you decide which feelings you wish to communicate verbally to the other person and which you wish to keep private. **Feelings** are internal physiological reactions to your experiences. Having feelings is a natural and joyful part of being alive. You cannot enjoy or consciously communicate your feelings, however, if you are not aware of them. There are five aspects to being aware of your feelings: gathering information through your senses, deciding what the information means, experiencing the appropriate feeling, deciding how to express your feeling, and expressing it. Feelings may be expressed verbally and nonverbally. Expressing feelings verbally must include (a) a personal statement and (b) a description of the feeling. Four ways to describe a feeling include identifying or naming it, using sensory descriptions, describing an action urge, or using a figure of speech. Indirect expression of feelings creates ambiguity and misunderstandings. When clarifying other people's feelings, you may use a **perception check**, which has three parts (describing your perception of the other's feelings, asking whether your perception is correct, and refraining from expressing approval or disapproval).

Expressing Feelings Nonverbally

In every relationship you decide which feelings you wish to communicate nonverbally to the other person and which you wish to keep private. We rarely communicate our feelings with words alone. Nonverbal messages are sent by our manner of dress, physique, posture, body tension, facial expression, degree of eye contact, hand and body movements, tone of voice, continuities in speech, spatial distance, and touch. Nonverbal messages are more powerful in communicating feelings than are verbal messages but are also more ambiguous and difficult to interpret accurately. It is important, therefore, to make your verbal and nonverbal messages congruent.

Helpful Listening and Responding

In every relationship you decide how to respond when the other person wishes to share a problem or a concern. When someone is talking to you about something deeply distressing or of a real concern to him or her, you need the skills to listen and respond in a helpful way. Your helpfulness depends on your attitude as you listen and the phrasing of your response. When other people are telling you about a problem, you can respond by (a) advising and evaluating, (b) analyzing and interpreting, (c) reassuring and supporting, (d) questioning and probing, and (e) paraphrasing and understanding. Each is appropriate under certain conditions. It is paraphrasing and understanding, however, that are most helpful in most circumstances. You should understand how to make reflective statements and ask open questions. You should also be able to match a message in content, depth, meaning, and language.

Resolving Interpersonal Conflicts

In every relationship you decide how to manage the conflicts that arise. Perhaps the most difficult interpersonal skills to master are those involved in resolving conflicts constructively. When faced with a conflict, you have two concerns: achieve your goals and maintain the relationship. These two concerns identify five strategies for resolving conflicts: you can withdraw, try to force the other person to do what you want, do anything to maintain the relationship, compromise, or negotiate. The most important and most difficult strategy is negotiation. **Negotiation** is a process by which persons who have shared and opposed interests and want to come to an agreement try to work out a settlement. There are two types of negotiations. **Win-lose negotiations** occur when participants want to make an agreement more favorable to themselves than to the other persons. **Problem-solving negotiations** occur when participants want to make an agreement beneficial to everyone involved. Within ongoing relationships, conflicts should be resolved through problem-solving negotiations. In order to negotiate mutually beneficial agreements, participants must state what they want and how they feel, state the reasons why they want what they do, reverse perspectives and summarize the other's position and interests, invent a series of possible agreements, and finally reach a wise decision.

Managing Your Anger, Stress, and Feelings

In every relationship you decide how to manage the stress and anger that arise. Stress is unavoidable. You are always under some stress. Social support is key to managing stress. Conflict is a source of stress, and anger is a typical response. **Anger** is a defensive, emotional reaction that occurs when we are frustrated, thwarted, or attacked. When you get angry with other people the results can be either destructive or constructive. To manage anger constructively you recognize and acknowledge that you are angry. Then decide whether or not you wish to express your anger. You express it indirectly or react in an alternative way when direct expression of anger is not appropriate. To express anger constructively, you describe the other's actions, and you describe your angry feelings verbally while making your nonverbal messages congruent with your words. Long-term anger is based on two irrational beliefs—that you must get your way and the other person must be punished. To ensure that you do not keep anger long-term, you decide to change yourself (rather than the other person), control how you interpret the information you receive through your senses, change your assumptions, and thereby free yourself from your anger. Finally, in a conflict you must control your reactions to other people's anger toward you as well as your anger toward them. You give them the "right" to feel angry, you try not to get angry back, you focus your attention on the task. You describe the situation, and talk to yourself to keep yourself calm.

Building Relationships with Diverse Others

In every relationship you decide how to manage the differences between the two of you. Diversity among your acquaintances, classmates, co-workers, neighbors, and friends is increasingly inevitable. Such diversity is an opportunity that can have positive or negative consequences, depending on your engaging in an eight-step program. The first step is to recognize that diversity exists and is a valuable resource. The second step is to build cooperative relationships with diverse individuals. Cooperation promotes a process of acceptance while competitive and individualistic efforts tend to promote a process of rejection. The third step is to include your historical and cultural heritage in your identity. The fourth step is to respect and appreciate the historical and cultural heritage of others. The fifth step is to establish a superordinate identity that unites all relevant groups into one. In the United States, the superordinate identity as an American binds all citizens together. The sixth step is to reduce the internal cognitive barriers to building positive relationships with diverse individuals. The barriers include stereotyping, prejudice, and blaming the victim. The seventh step is resolving all conflicts that arise from cultural clashes and other aspects of diversity in constructive ways. Finally, you must learn and internalize a set of pluralistic values including the commitment to the equal worth of all persons and each individual's inalienable right to life, liberty, and the pursuit of happiness. These are some of the values inherent in the Declaration of Independence and the Constitution of the United States.

Barriers to Interpersonal Effectiveness

In every relationship you decide how to manage the internal barriers to relating effectively to the other person. Barriers to interpersonal effectiveness include (a) fear and anxiety, (b) shyness, and (c) self-blame. **Fear** exists when a person is afraid and knows what he or she is afraid of. **Anxiety** exists when a person is afraid but does not know what he or she is afraid of. Managing fear and anxiety includes accepting them as natural feelings and viewing them as problems to be solved, not as a catastrophe to hide from. Learning how to engage in deep breathing, progressively relaxation, and visualizing yourself overcoming your fears are also helpful. **Shyness** is an excessive caution in interpersonal relations. To overcome your shyness you determine which people and situations cause it, you build your self-esteem, and you improve your interpersonal skills. Helping others learn interpersonal skills involves specifying the target behavior, gathering baseline data, designing your program, executing and evaluating your program, and terminating the training. **Self-blame** exists when you say "bad me" to yourself or when you judge your basic self-worth on the basis of your inadequate and rotten behavior. You reduce self-blame by changing your assumptions and forgiving yourself. Finally, people successful in gaining a high level of interpersonal skills are willing to take risks, tolerate failure, persist, and celebrate success.

Looking Forward

These ten sets of interpersonal skills are the heart of initiating, building, and maintaining effective, caring, and committed relationships. Mastery of these skills does not take place in a few hours, days, weeks, or even years. It takes at least one lifetime. Every day, in every interaction, in every relationship you could be, should be, working to improve your interpersonal skills. *At the end of this book you are at a new beginning.* Becoming more and more skillful and sophisticated in using interpersonal skills is the key to the quality of your life and the lives of the people with whom you interact.

EXERCISE 12.2
Your Relationships and Your Skills

1. Choose three relationships you are currently involved in. One should be a close, personal friendship, the second should be a good relationship but not a friendship, and the third should be a relationship that is currently not going very well.

2. Consider how each of the skills is being used in each relationship.

3. Formulate at least three goals for using the skills appropriately to improve the quality or effectiveness of each relationship.

EXERCISE 12.3
Relationship Survey

The objectives of this exercise are to help you become more aware of the qualities of the relationships in your life and to commit you to applying the skills and insights you have gained from this book to increase the richness of your relationships. You will need a large sheet of paper and a felt-tipped pen for the exercise. The procedure is as follows:

1. Form a group of four.

2. Write your name at the top of the paper and divide it into two columns. On one side list four of your relationships that you value highly, and on the other side write what it is that you value about the relationship. These could be relationships you are currently involved in or ones you have had in the past.

3. Share this information with the group. This gives each member an opportunity to practice self-disclosure and listening skills. After each member has shared his or her information, the other group members should suggest what they perceive as the essential qualities of a good relationship for that person. The person should then write down the group mates' suggestions in the appropriate column on the sheet of paper.

EXERCISE 12.4
Self-Contract

Write a description of yourself as a person skillful in interacting with other people. Mention all the strengths and skills you can think of, and mention the areas in which you need to increase your skills. Then make a contract with yourself to make some changes in your life; the contract can involve starting something new, stopping something old, or changing some present aspect of your life. It should involve applying your interpersonal skills to actual situations you are now facing, or working to develop certain skills further. It may involve initiating new relationships or terminating old relationships. In making the contract, pick several relationships you now have and set a series of goals concerning how you will behave to increase your effectiveness and satisfaction in these relationships. Write the contract down, place it in an envelope, address the envelope to yourself, and open it three months later.

Summary of Interpersonal Skills

This book has focused on the interpersonal skills you need for interpersonal effectiveness and self-actualization. On a scale from 1 (poorly mastered) to 5 (highly mastered) rate the degree to which you have mastered each skill. Then create a plan to improve your interpersonal skills continuously.

1. Self-Disclosure

_____ a. Be aware of your thoughts, feelings, needs, and actions.

_____ b. Accept your thoughts, feelings, needs, and actions.

_____ c. Express your thoughts, feelings, reactions, and needs to other people when it is appropriate; let other people know you as you really are.

_____ d. Seek out feedback from other people.

_____ e. Give feedback to other people when they request it.

2. Trust

_____ a. Take risks in self-disclosure when it is appropriate.

_____ b. Respond with acceptance and support to other people's self-disclosure.

_____ c. Reciprocate other people's self-disclosures.

3. Communication

_____ a. Speak for yourself by using personal pronouns when expressing thoughts, ideas, reactions, and feelings.

_____ b. Describe other people's actions without making value judgments.

_____ c. Use relationship statements when they are appropriate.

_____ d. Take the receiver's perspective into account when sending your messages.

_____ e. Ask for feedback about the receiver's understanding of your message.

_____ f. Paraphrase accurately without making value judgments about the sender's thoughts, reactions, perceptions, needs, and feelings.

_____ g. Negotiate the meaning of the sender's messages.

_____ h. Understand what the message means from the sender's perspective.

4. Expressing Feelings Verbally

_____ a. Understand the process of having and expressing feelings (sensing, interpreting, feeling, intending, expressing).

_____ b. Describe your feelings (making a personal statement and describing a feeling by name, simile, action urge, figure of speech).

_____ c. Use perception checks (describe your perception of other's feelings, ask whether perception is correct, without indicating approval or disapproval).

_____ d. Avoid the indirect expression of feelings through commands, questions, accusations, and so on.

5. Expressing Feelings Nonverbally

_____ a. Be aware of how you express feelings nonverbally.

_____ b. Use nonverbal messages to communicate your feelings clearly.

_____ c. Use nonverbal cues to express warmth.

_____ d. Make your nonverbal and verbal messages congruent.

6. Listening and Responding

_____ a. When appropriate, engage in an evaluative response.

_____ b. When appropriate, engage in an interpretative response.

_____ c. When appropriate, engage in a supportive response.

_____ d. When appropriate, engage in a probing response.

_____ e. When appropriate, engage in an understanding response.

_____ f. Match the message in paraphrasing content.

_____ g. Match the message in depth.

_____ h. Match the message in meaning.

_____ i. Match the message in language.

_____ j. Express acceptance verbally.

7. Acceptance and Support

_____ a. Describe other people's strengths when it is appropriate to do so.

_____ b. Appropriately express acceptance of other people.

_____ c. Describe your strengths when it is appropriate to do so.

8. Influence

_____ a. Reinforce others' actions in order to increase, decrease, or maintain the frequency of their behavior, depending on what is in their best interests.

_____ b. Arrange for your behavior to be reinforced in order to increase, decrease, or maintain the frequency of desired behavior.

_____ c. Model interpersonal skills for others who wish to acquire them.

9. Conflicts

_____ a. Be aware of your two concerns in a conflict (achieving your goals and maintaining the relationship in good working order) and choose one of five strategies accordingly (withdrawal, forcing, smoothing, negotiating, compromising).

      _____ (1) Understand that there are two concerns in conflicts—goals and relationships.

      _____ (2) Withdraw when both the goal and the relationship are of low importance.

      _____ (3) Force when the goal is important but the relationship is not.

      _____ (4) Smooth when the goal is unimportant and the relationship is very important.

      _____ (5) Engage in problem-solving negotiations when both the goal and the relationship are important.

      _____ (6) Compromise when both the goal and relationship are important but time is short.

_____ b. Understand the difference between "win-lose" and "problem-solving" negotiations.

_____ c. When negotiating with a person you have an ongoing relationship with, negotiate to solve the problem (do not negotiate to win). Seek a solution that achieves both your own goals and the goals of the other person. Try to improve your relationship with the other person while resolving the conflict. You engage in problem-solving negotiations by

      _____ (1) Describing what you want.

      _____ (2) Describing how you feel.

_____ (3) Explaining my reasons for wanting and feeling as you do.

_____ (4) Taking the perspective of the other party.

_____ (5) Developing several optional agreements that maximize joint gain.

_____ (6) Determining which alternative agreement is most wise and agreeing to adopt it.

_____ d. Say "no" when the issue is nonnegotiable.

10. Stress and Anger

_____ a. Follow the rules for the constructive management of anger.

_____ (1) Recognize and acknowledge that you are angry.

_____ (2) Decide whether or not you wish to express your anger.

_____ (3) Have ways of responding to provocations other than anger and depression.

_____ (4) Express your anger directly and effectively when it is appropriate to do so.

_____ (a) Make the expression cathartic.

_____ (b) Ask for clarification before responding to a provocation.

_____ (c) Make it to the point and express it to the appropriate person.

_____ (d) Take responsibility for the anger, owning it as yours and becoming more involved with the other person in expressing it.

_____ (e) Remember that heightened anger makes you agitated and impulsive.

_____ (f) Beware of the righteousness of your anger.

_____ (g) Stay task oriented rather than letting yourself get sidetracked by taking others' actions personally.

_____ (h) Take into account the impact your anger will have on the other person.

_____ (i) Use the skills of accurate communication and constructive feedback.

_____ (j) Express positive feelings as well as your anger while discussing the situation.

_____ (5) Express your anger indirectly when direct expression is not appropriate.

_____ (6) Analyze, understand, and reflect on your anger.

_____ (7) Congratulate yourself when you have succeeded in managing your anger constructively.

_____ b. Assert your anger through behavior descriptions, descriptions of your own feelings, congruent nonverbal messages, and good listening skills.

_____ c. Manage your feelings constructively.

_____ (1) Recognize your irrational assumptions that lead to negative feelings.

_____ (2) Build more rational assumptions.

_____ (3) Argue with yourself, replacing your irrational assumptions with rational ones.

11. Interacting with Diverse Individuals

_____ a. Recognize that diversity exists and value it as an important resource.

_____ b. Create a cooperative context in which you work with diverse individuals to achieve mutual goals.

_____ c. Include your historical and cultural heritage as an important part of your identity.

_____ d. Recognize, respect, and value the historical and cultural heritage of others.

_____ e. Highlight the superordinate identity that unites us all into one society.

_____ f. Work constantly to reduce your internal barriers to interacting effectively with diverse individuals (such as stereotyping and prejudice).

_____ g. Know the procedures for resolving conflicts constructively, and use them skillfully.

_____ h. Be committed to the pluralistic values that recognize the equal worth of all persons and each individual's inalienable right to life, liberty, and the pursuit of happiness.

12. Reducing Barriers to Effective Interaction

_____ a. Reduce fear and anxiety through deep breathing and progressive muscle relaxation.

_____ b. Reduce shyness by building your self-esteem.

_____ c. Avoid self-blame by avoiding catastrophizing, through self-forgiveness, and by increasing encouraging thoughts.

Appendix

Instructions: The sender is to study the figure on the left. With his back to the group, he is to instruct the members of the group on how to draw it. He should begin with the top square and describe each in succession, taking particular note of the placement relationship of each to the preceding one. No questions are allowed.

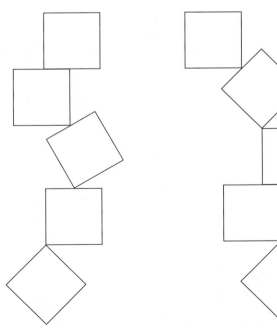

Square Arrangement I:
One-Way Communication

Square Arrangement II:
Two-Way Communication

SCORING KEY
Identifying the Intent of a Response

After you have completed Answer Sheet 7.1B, use this scoring key to score the types of responses you gave for each item on Answer Sheet A. Then divide into groups of three and score the accuracy with which you identified the different responses for each item on Answer Sheet B. In groups of three, discuss each answer until everyone understands it.

Item	a	b	c	d	e
1.	I	S	E	U	P
2.	E	U	I	P	S
3.	U	I	P	S	E
4.	P	U	E	S	I
5.	S	P	U	I	E
6.	P	U	I	E	S
7.	E	I	P	S	U
8.	S	E	U	P	I
9.	U	P	E	S	I
10.	P	U	E	S	I
11.	I	E	S	U	P
12.	U	P	S	E	I

Instructions: The sender is to study the figure to the right on page 417. Facing the group, she is to instruct the members on how to draw it. She should begin with the top square and describe each in succession, taking particular note of the placement relationship of each to the preceding one. She should answer all questions from participants and repeat her descriptions if necessary.

SCORING KEY

Phrasing an Accurate Understanding Response

After you have completed Answer Sheet 7.3B, use this scoring key to score the type of phrasing you personally gave for each item on Answer Sheet A. Then divide into groups of three, score the accuracy with which you identified the different types of phrasing for each item on Answer Sheet B, and discuss each answer in your group until everyone understands it.

Item	a	b	c	d
1.	I	A	P	S
2.	S	I	P	A
3.	A	S	I	P
4.	P	A	S	I
5.	I	P	A	S
6.	P	S	A	I
7.	A	P	I	S
8.	P	I	S	A
9.	I	S	A	P

PICTURE A

PICTURE B

PICTURE C

Managing Provocations by Talking to Yourself

Stage   *What I Say to Myself*

1.   1   Dealing with her anger is only a minor annoyance.
2.   2   Listen carefully for the issue, not the feelings.
3.   3   Getting upset will not work. Stay relaxed.
4.   4   I did that well!
5.   4   I got through that without getting angry. Way to go!
6.   1   What does she want?
7.   3   It is not worth getting upset over.
8.   2   Listening to her anger will be easy.
9.   1   I will be able to manage the situation.
10.   3   He is trying to get me angry. I am not going to.
11.   4   I did not take anything personally. Good job!
12.   2   What is the issue? Do not get distracted into a quarrel.
13.   4   I am excellent at managing provocations.
14.   3   So he is insulting me. So what? The issue is more important.
15.   3   Calm down. I can't expect people to act the way I want them to.
16.   2   Take a few deep breaths and relax before we start.
17.   4   Good for me!
18.   1   It will be easy.
19.   1   What does she want?
20.   2   Relax.

Glossary

Above average effect bias   The vast majority of people consider themselves as being above average in any socially desirable category or trait.

Acceptance   The communication of high regard for another person and his or her statements.

Action theory   A theory as to what actions are needed to achieve a desired consequence in a given situation.

Ageism   Prejudice directed against the elderly.

Aggressive behavior   To attempt to hurt someone or destroy something.

Anger   A defensive emotional reaction that occurs when we are frustrated, thwarted, or attacked. Anger is a righteous but defensive reaction to frustration and aggression based on a unidimensional perceptual focus, a physical demand to take action, and a belief that we must get our way.

Antecedents   Situations or events that typically come before the target behavior.

Anxiety   A feeling that exists when you are afraid but you do not know what you are afraid of.

Arbitration   The submission of a dispute to a disinterested third party who makes a final and binding judgment as to how the conflict will be resolved.

Assertive behavior   Describing your feelings, thoughts, opinions, and preferences directly to another person in an honest and appropriate way that respects both yourself and the other person.

Asyndetic response   Acknowledging another's statement but using it only as a polite way of introducing your own ideas into the conversation.

Attribution   An inference about the cause of a person's action.

Attribution theory   A social psychological explanation of how individuals make inferences about the causes of behaviors and events.

Autonomy   Ability to decide how to apply personal values and principles flexibly in order to act appropriately in the current situation.

Baseline period   A span of time before the actual start of an intervention program during which the target behavior is systematically observed.

Basic self-acceptance   A belief that you are intrinsically and unconditionally acceptable.

Behavior description   A statement that includes a personal statement (referring to *I, me,* or *my*) and a description of the specific behaviors you have observed.

Behavioral deficit   A response that is a problem because it does not occur often enough.

Behavioral excess   A response that is a problem because it occurs too often.

Belief in a just world   A belief that there is an appropriate fit between what people do and what happens to them.

Beneffectance   The tendency to take credit for success and deny responsibility for failure; from *beneficent* plus *effectance.*

Blame   Believing that the cause of your frustration is wicked people (including yourself) who deserve to be punished for their evil acts.

Blaming the victim   Attributing the cause of discrimination or misfortune to the personal characteristics and actions of the victim.

Catastrophizing   Believing that you must have your way and that it is awful not to get everything you want.

Categorizing   A basic human cognitive process of conceptualizing objects and people as members of groups.

Catharsis   The release of pent-up emotion either by talking about feelings or engaging in active emotional release by crying, laughing, or shouting.

Causal attribution   The process of explaining or inferring the causes of events.

Channel   A means of conveying the message to the receiver; the sound waves of the voice or the light waves of seeing words on a printed page are examples of channels.

Cognitive conservatism   Effect where, once your view of yourself has developed, there is a conservative tendency to maintain and reinforce it and to resist changing it.

Collusion   Conscious and unconscious support of prejudice, stereotypes, and discrimination, and prevailing norms. People collude with discriminatory practices and prejudiced actions through ignorance, silence, denial, and active support.

Communication   A message sent by a person to a receiver(s) with the conscious intent of affecting the receiver's behavior.

Communication networks   Representations of the acceptable paths of communication between persons in a group or organization.

Competitive goal structure   A negative correlation among group members' goal attainments; when group members perceive that they can obtain their goals if and only if the other members with whom they are competitively linked fail to obtain their goal.

Compliance   Behavior in accordance with a direct request. Behavioral change without internal acceptance.

Compromising   Giving up part of your goal while the other person does the same in order to reach an agreement. You seek a solution in which both sides gain something and settle on an agreement that is the middle ground between your two opening positions.

Conditional self-acceptance   Making conclusions about yourself on the basis of how well you meet external standards and expectations.

Confirmation   A response from other people indicating that we are normal, healthy, and worthwhile.

Conflict of interests   When the actions of one person attempting to maximize his or her needs and benefits prevent, block, interfere with, injure, or in some way make less effective the actions of another person attempting to maximize his or her needs and benefits.

Conformity   Changes in behavior that result from group influences. Yielding to group pressures when no direct request to comply is made.

Confrontation   The direct expression of one's view of the conflict and one's feelings about it and at the same time an invitation to the opposition to do the same.

Consensual validation   Comparing our perceptions and reactions with those of others.

Consensus A collective opinion arrived at by a group of individuals working together under conditions that permit communications to be sufficiently open and the group climate to be sufficiently supportive for everyone in the group to feel that he or she has had a fair chance to influence the decision.

Cooperation The means by which you and other people engage in joint action to accomplish a goal you all want.

Cooperative goal structure A positive correlation among group members' goal attainments; when group members perceive that they can achieve their goal if and only if the other members with whom they are cooperatively linked obtain their goal.

Cooperative intention The expression that you want to work together to achieve a mutual goal.

Coorientation Operating under the same norms and adhering to the same procedures.

Cultural conditioning The way in which we, as children, are taught to respond to a given situation as we see others in our culture react so that we may fit into a particular culture.

Cultural identity Your sense of origins and membership in a culture.

Culture clash Conflict over basic values that occurs among individuals from different cultures. The most common form occurs when members of minority groups question the values of the majority.

Cycle of social interaction Perceiving the other person's actions, deciding how to respond, taking action, and perceiving the other person's response.

Discrimination An action taken to harm a group or any of its members.

Double standard Believing what you do is legitimate while identical actions by the opponent in a conflict are illegitimate.

Effective communication When the receiver interprets the sender's message in the same way the sender intended it.

Egocentrism Embeddedness in one's own viewpoint to the extent that one is unaware of other points of view and of the limitations of one's perspectives.

Emotional isolation Not having deep relationships.

Ethnic identity Your sense of belonging to one particular ethnic group.

Ethnocentrism The tendency to regard our own ethnic group, culture, or nation as better or more correct than others.

Experiential learning Generating an action theory from your own experiences and then continually modifying it to improve your effectiveness.

False consensus bias A belief (often false) that most other people think and feel very much as we do, such as sharing our stereotypes (such as believing that poor people are lazy).

Fear A feeling that exists when you are afraid and you know what you are afraid of.

Feedback Disclosing how you are perceiving and reacting to another person's behavior to provide him or her with constructive information to help the person become aware of the effectiveness of his or her actions.

Feelings Internal physiological reactions to your experiences.

Forcing Overpowering opponents by requiring them to accept your solution to the conflict. You seek to achieve your goals at all costs and without concern for the needs of others.

Fundamental attribution error   The attribution of the causes of other's behaviors to personal (disposition) factors and the causes of one's own behavior to situational (environmental) factors. In explaining the causes of the other's behavior the attributer overestimates the causal importance of personality, beliefs, attitudes, and values, and underestimates the causal importance of situational pressures. The opposite is done in explaining the causes of one's own behavior.

Gender identity   Your fundamental sense of your maleness or femaleness.

Goal   The end toward which your effort is directed, based on your needs, interests, personality, and relevant roles.

Hit-and-run   Starting a conversation about the conflict, giving your definition and feelings, and then disappearing before the other person has a chance to respond.

Identity   A consistent set of attitudes that defines who you are.

Illusion of control   When you ascribe rational reasons to events occurring purely by chance.

Illusory correlation   An overestimation of the strength of a relationship between two variables. Variables may not be related at all, or the relationship may be much weaker than believed.

Impression management   The process by which you behave in particular ways to create a desired social image.

Individualistic goal structure   No correlation exists among group members' goal attainments; group members perceive that obtaining their goal is unrelated to the goal achievement of other members.

Ingratiation   Acts that are motivated by the desire to get along and be liked.

Inner-directed   Controlled by a small number of values and principles set early in life that are rigidly adhered to, no matter what the situation.

Integration   Combining several positions into one new, creative position.

Intentions   Guides to action, immediate goals as to what you want to have happen.

Interdependence   Sharing mutual goals and needing to coordinate actions to achieve a goal.

Interest   Need, goal, benefit, profit, advantage, concern, right, or claim.

Interpersonal communication   A message sent by a person to a receiver with a conscious intent to affect the receiver's behavior.

Interpersonal effectiveness   The degree to which the consequences of your behavior match your intentions.

Interpersonal skills   The sum total of your ability to interact effectively with other people.

Interpersonal Trust Scale   Developed by Rotter to distinguish between people who have a tendency to trust and those who tend to distrust.

Interpretation   Deciding what the information gathered by your senses means.

Irrational assumption   A belief that makes you depressed, anxious, or upset most of the time.

Looking-glass self   The self that is created by adopting, over time, other's views of you.

Message Any verbal or nonverbal symbol that one person transmits to another.

Mirror image Both parties in a conflict believing they are an innocent victim who represents truth and justice and who is being attacked maliciously by an evil enemy.

Mood A conscious state of mind based on personality, past events, another's behavior, physical setting, and the significance of the interaction.

Mote-beam mechanism Each person in a conflict seeing all the vicious acts of the opponent while being blind to identical actions he or she is taking.

Negative judgment Stating that the other person is wrong or bad.

Negative reinforcement Withdrawing or removing an object or event that, by its removal, encourages or strengthens a response.

Negotiation A process by which persons who have shared and opposed interests and want to come to an agreement try to work out a settlement.

Noise Any element that interferes with the communication process.

Nonnegotiable norms Norms individuals are expected to follow without exception, such as those outlawing physical violence against oneself or another person, public humiliation and shaming, and lying and deceit.

Nonassertiveness Saying nothing in response to a provocation, keeping your feelings to yourself, hiding feelings from others, and perhaps even hiding your feelings from yourself.

Norm of mutual responsiveness Rule that you should be committed to fulfilling each other's goals and concerned about each other's interests.

Norm of reciprocity A norm that a negotiator should return the same benefit or harm given him or her by the other negotiator; "an eye for an eye and a kiss for a kiss" is an example of a norm of reciprocity.

Norms Shared expectations about the behavior that is appropriate within the situation.

Objective self-awareness Becoming aware of some aspect of yourself and evaluating it by considering how it measures up to some internal rule or standard.

One-step negotiations Each person (a) assesses the strength of his or her interests, (b) assesses the strength of the other person's interests, and (c) agrees that whoever has the greatest need is given his or her way.

Open self-presentation Letting others see us as we believe ourselves to be.

Openness The sharing of information, ideas, thoughts, feelings, and reactions to the issue being discussed.

Outer-directed Controlled by other's expectations and pressure to conform.

Overjustification effect Effect that occurs when external influences on a given behavior are so conspicuous that their influence on the behavior is underestimated.

Paraphrasing Restating, in your own words, what the person says, feels, and means.

Paraphrasing rule Before replying to a statement, restate what the sender says, feels, and means correctly and to the sender's satisfaction.

Perceiving/perception The process of gathering sensory information and assigning meaning to it.

Perception check   To ask for clarification or correction to make sure your understanding is accurate. It involves describing what you think the other person's feelings are, asking whether or not your perception is accurate, and refraining from expressing approval or disapproval of the feelings.

Personal statements   Statements that refer to *I, me, my,* or *mine.*

Perspective   A person's way of viewing the world and his or her relation to it.

Perspective reversal   Presenting the perspective and position of another person as if it were yours.

Phobia   Persistent anxiety with an intensity out of proportion to the object or situation that caused it.

Polarized thinking   An oversimplified view of a conflict in which everything you do is good and everything the other person does is bad.

Positive reinforcement   Presenting an object or event that increases, strengthens, or maintains a response.

Prejudice   An unjustified negative attitude toward a person based solely on that individual's membership in a group.

Problem-solving negotiations   When each negotiator has as his or her goal the reaching of an agreement that benefits everyone involved. You negotiate to solve the problem when you have an ongoing cooperative relationship with the other person, must negotiate an agreement to resolve the current conflict, and then will continue the cooperative efforts and the relationship.

Provincial   Knowing how to act appropriately only with one's own narrow perspective and culture.

Psychological health   The ability to build and maintain cooperative, interdependent relationships with other people.

Racism   Any attitude, action, or institutional structure that subordinates a person because of his or her ethnic membership.

Rational assumption   A belief that makes you feel satisfied, content, happy, and proud most of the time.

Real-ideal comparison   A judgment about how your real self compares with your ideal self.

Reflected self-acceptance   Making conclusions about yourself on the basis of how you think other people see you.

Reinforcement   Rewards given for approved behavior that tend to increase the likelihood that the behavior will be repeated.

Reinforcement contingencies   The conditions that have to be met in order for the person to earn the rewards.

Relationship statements   Personal statements that describe some aspect of the way the two of you are interacting with each other.

Religious identity   Your sense of belonging to one particular religious group.

Role   A set of expectations defining appropriate behaviors associated with a position within a group. The *part* played by a member of a group. Rules or understandings about the tasks persons occupying certain positions within a group are expected to perform.

Role reversal   Having two participants in a conflict reverse roles and play each other during a role play.

Sarcasm   A harsh form of put-down or ridicule that, in conflict, almost always makes the other person angry.

Self-acceptance   A high regard for yourself or, conversely, a lack of cynicism about yourself.

Self-actualization   The drive to develop our potential to its fullest extent to find joy and a sense of fulfillment.

Self-awareness   The paying attention to and being aware of oneself. Focused self-attention.

Self-blame   Judging your basic self-worth on the basis of your inadequate or rotten behavior.

Self-disclosure   Revealing how you are reacting to the present situation and giving any information about the present that is relevant to an understanding of your reactions to the present.

Self-evaluation   Your estimate of how positively your attributes compare with those of your peers.

Self-fulfilling prophecy   A set of actions that provokes the other into engaging in behavior that confirms one's original assumptions. An example is assuming that the other is belligerent and then proceeding to engage in hostile behavior, thereby provoking the other into belligerent actions that confirm the original assumption.

Self-monitoring   The tendency to regulate your behavior to meet the demands of social situations.

Self-perception theory   Observing yourself in order to understand how you are feeling and reacting and what is causing these feelings and reactions.

Self-presentation   The process by which we try to shape what others think of us, and even what we think of ourselves.

Self-promotion   Acts that are motivated by a desire to get ahead and be respected for one's competence.

Self-schema   A set of cognitive generalizations about the self, derived from past experience, that organizes and guides the processing of self-related information.

Self-serving attribution bias   The tendency to accept greater personal responsibility for positive outcomes than for negative outcomes.

Self-verification   Presenting yourself to others as you believe yourself to be.

Sender credibility   The attitude that the receiver has toward the sender's trustworthiness.

Sensing   Gathering information through your five senses—seeing, hearing, touching, tasting, and smelling.

Sexism   Any attitude, action, or institutional structure that subordinates a person because of his or her gender.

Sharing   The offering of your resources to other people in order to help them achieve their goals.

Shyness   Excessive caution in interpersonal relations.

Smoothing   Giving up your goals and letting the other person have his or her way in order to maintain the relationship at the highest level possible. When the goal is of no importance to you but the relationship is of high importance, you smooth.

Social comparison   Using another person for comparison so that one can evaluate one's own attitudes and abilities.

Social identity   Your sense of belonging to one particular social class.

Social interaction   Patterns of mutual influence linking two or more persons.

Social isolation   Not having a network of friends who share your interests and concerns and help provide a sense of community.

Social loafing   A reduction of individual effort when working with others on an additive group task.

Social perspective-taking   The ability to understand how a situation appears to another person and how that person is reacting cognitively and emotionally to the situation.

Social sensitivity   The ability to perceive and respond to the needs, emotions, and preferences of others.

Social skills training   A structured intervention designed to help participants to improve their interpersonal skills. It is generally conducted in group settings.

Sophistication   Knowing how to act appropriately (in courteous, well-mannered, refined ways) within many different cultures, perspectives, and settings.

Stereotype   A set of beliefs about the characteristics of the people in a group that is applied to almost all members of that group.

Strategic self-presentation   When we attempt to shape others' impressions of us in specific ways in order to gain influence, power, sympathy, or approval.

Superordinate goals   Cooperative goals that neither person can accomplish alone, but that are so compelling each person will join in to achieve them.

Support   The communication to another person that you recognize he or she has the capability and strength to manage a given situation productively.

Time-competent   Able to tie the past and the future to living fully in the present.

Triggering event   An event (such as two group members being in competition or the expression of criticism on a sensitive point) that triggers the occurrence of a conflict.

Trust   Perception that a choice can lead to gains or losses, that whether you will gain or lose depends on the behavior of the other person, that the loss will be greater than the gain, and that the person will likely behave so that you will gain rather than lose.

Trusting behavior   Openness and sharing.

Trustworthy   Expressing acceptance, support, and cooperative intentions.

Two-factor theory of emotion   You first experience physiological arousal and then seek an appropriate label for the feeling. The label you apply to the feeling may not be accurate.

Win–lose dynamic   Seeing every action of the other as a move to dominate.

Win–lose negotiations   When the goal of the negotiation is to make an agreement more favorable to you than to the other person.

Wise agreements   Those that are fair to all participants, are based on principles, strengthen participants' abilities to work together cooperatively, and improve participants' ability to resolve future conflicts constructively.

References

Alberti, R., & Emmons, M. (1978). *Your perfect right.* San Luis Obispo, CA: Impact.

Ambady, N., & Rosenthal, R. (1992). The slices of expressive behavior as predictors of interpersonal consequences: A meta-analysis. *Psychological Bulletin, 111,* 256–274.

Baron, R., Kerr, N., & Miller, N. (1992). *Group process, group decision, group action.* Pacific Grove, CA: Brooks/Cole.

California Department of Mental Health. (1981). *Friends can be good medicine.* Sacramento: State of California, Technical Report.

Center for Public Resources. (1982). *Basic skills in the U.S. workforce.* Washington, DC.

DeCecco, J., & Richards, A. (1974). *Growing pains: Uses of school conflict.* New York: Aberdeen Press.

Deutsch, M. (1962). Cooperation and trust: Some theoretical notes. In M. R. Jones (Ed.), *Nebraska Symposium on Motivation,* pp. 275–320. Lincoln: University of Nebraska Press.

Deutsch, M. (1973). *The resolution of conflict.* New Haven, CT: Yale University Press.

Ellis, A. (1962). *Reason and emotion in psychotherapy.* Secaucus, NJ: Lyle Stuart.

Erikson, E. (1950). *Childhood and society.* New York: W. W. Norton.

Fenigstein, A., Scheier, M., & Buss, A. (1975). Public and private self-consciousness: Assessment and theory. *Journal of Consulting and Clinical Psychology, 43,* 522–527.

Fisher, R., & Ury, W. (1981). *Getting to yes.* Boston: Houghton Mifflin.

Gergen, K. (1991). *The saturated self: Dilemmas of identity in contemporary life.* New York: Basic Books.

Glasser, W. (1984). *Control theory.* New York: Harper & Row.

Goffman, E. (1959). *The presentation of self in everyday life.* Garden City, NY: Doubleday.

Hamachek, D. (1971). *Encounters with the self.* New York: Holt, Rinehart, & Winston.

Jackson, D. (1959). Family interaction, family homeostasis, and some implications for conjoint family therapy. In J. Masserman (Ed.), *Individual and familial dynamics,* pp. 112–141. New York: Grune & Stratton.

Johnson, D. W. (1971). Role reversal: A summary and review of the research. *International Journal of Group Tensions, 1,* 318–334.

Johnson, D. W. (1974). Communication and the inducement of cooperative behavior in conflicts. *Speech Monographs, 41,* 64–78.

Johnson, D. W. (1991). *Human relations and your career* (3rd ed.). Englewood Cliffs, NJ: Prentice Hall.

Johnson, D. W. (1979). *Educational psychology.* Englewood Cliffs, NJ: Prentice Hall.

Johnson, D. W., & Johnson, F. (2000). *Joining together: Group theory and research* (6th ed.). Boston: Allyn & Bacon.

Johnson, D. W., & Johnson, R. (1989). *Cooperation and competition: Theory and research.* Edina, MN: Interaction Book Company.

Johnson, D. W., & Johnson, R. (1992). *Positive interdependence: The heart of cooperative learning.* Edina, MN: Interaction Book Company.

Johnson, D. W., & Johnson, R. (1994). *Joining together: Group therapy and research* (5th ed.). Boston: Allyn & Bacon.

Johnson, D. W., & Johnson, R. (1995a). *Teaching students to be peacemakers* (3rd ed.). Edina, MN: Interaction Book Company.

Johnson, D. W., & Johnson, R. (1995b). *My mediation notebook* (3rd ed.). Edina, MN: Interaction Book Company.

Johnson, D. W., & Johnson, R. (1995c). *Creative controversy: Intellectual challenge in the classroom* (3rd ed.). Edina, MN: Interaction Book Company.

Johnson, D. W., & Johnson, R. (1997). *Nuts and bolts of cooperative learning.* Edina, MN: Interaction Book Company.

Johnson, D. W., & Johnson, R. (1999). *Human relations: Valuing diversity.* Edina, MN: Interaction Book Company.

Johnson, D. W., & Matross, R. (1977). The interpersonal influence of the psychotherapist. In A. Gurman and A. Razin (Eds.), *Effective psychotherapy: A handbook of research* (pp. 395–432). Elmsford, NY: Pergamon Press.

Johnson, D. W., & Noonan, P. (1972). Effects of acceptance and reciprocation of self-disclosures on the development of trust. *Journal of Counseling Psychology, 19,* 411–416.

Knapp, M., & Vangelisti, A. (1995). *Interpersonal communication and human relationships.* Boston: Allyn & Bacon.

Kramer, R. (1999). Trust and distrust in organizations: Emerging perspectives, enduring questions. In J. Spence, J. Darley, & D. Foss (Eds.), *Annual review of psychology,* vol. 50, pp. 569–598. Palo Alto, CA: Annual Reviews.

Kubany, E., et al. (1992, Fall). Verbalized anger and accusatory "you" messages as cues for anger and antagonism among adolescents. *Adolescence, 505.*

Ladd, G. (1999). Peer relationships and social competence during early and middle childhood. In J. Spence, J. Darley, & D. Foss (Eds.), *Annual review of psychology,* vol. 50, pp. 333–359. Palo Alto, CA: Annual Reviews.

Leavitt, H. (1958). *Managerial psychology.* Chicago: University of Chicago Press.

Luce, R., & Raiffa, H. (1957). *Games and decisions.* New York: Wiley.

Luft, J. (1969). *Of human interaction.* Palo Alto, CA: National Press.

Martin, R., & Poland, E. (1980). *Learning to change.* New York: McGraw-Hill.

Miller, S., Nunnally, E., & Wachman, D. (1975). *Alive and aware: Improving communication in relationships.* Minneapolis: Interpersonal Communication Programs.

Novaco, R. (1975). *Anger control.* Lexington, MA: D. C. Heath.

Parker, J., & Seal, J. (1996). Forming, losing, renewing, and replacing friendships: Applying temporal parameters to the assessment of children's friendship experiences. *Child Development, 67,* 2248–2268.

Powell, J. (1969). *Why am I afraid to tell you who I am?* Niles, IL: Argus.

Rogers, C. (1965). Dealing with psychological tensions. *Journal of Applied Behavioral Science, 1,* 6–25.

Rogers, C., & Roethlisberger, F. (1952). Barriers and gateways to communication. *Harvard Business Review,* July-August: 28–35.

Rotter, J. (1971). Generalized expectancies for interpersonal trust. *American Psychologist, 26,* 443–452.

Thomas, K., & Schmidt, W. (1976). A survey of managerial interests with respect to conflict. *Academy of Management Journal, 19,* 315–318.

Tjosvold, D. (1991). *Team organization.* New York: Wiley.

Weinstein, M., & Goodman, J. (1980). *Playfair.* San Luis Obispo, CA: Impact.

Zimbardo, P. (1977). *Shyness.* Reading, MA: Addison-Wesley.

Index

Abilities, 352
Acceptance, 81, 96, 97, 414
  gaining through self-disclosure, 50
  group level of, 243–245
  nonverbal acquisition of, 208–209
  nonverbal expression of, 209
  supportive responses for, 233
  verbal expression of, 241–243
Accusations, 328
  communicating feelings with, 178
Acquired traits, 361
Action
  anger as motivation for, 313
  feedback on, 60
  feelings promoting, 173
  overt, 187
Action theories, 25
Adversity management. *See also* Conflict resolution
  with self-disclosure, 49
Advice, 60
Advising and evaluating responses (E), 222–223
Affection, nonverbal cues of, 204–205
Aggression, 276
  versus assertiveness, 319–320
  resulting from anger, 314
Agreement, 261
  invention of, 291–292
  wise, 293–295, 373
Alcohol, reducing self-awareness with, 54
Analyzing and interpreting responses (I), 223–224
Anger, 415–416
  acknowledging, 316
  constructive management of, 315–327
  constructive versus destructive, 312
  dealing with angry persons, 339–342
  describing, 318–319
  direct expression of, 317–322
  eliminating, 329–330
  functions of, 313–315
  impact of, 320
  indirect expression of, 322–323
  irrational beliefs underlying, 330–331
  long-term, 409
  management of, 265, 307, 409
  nature of, 312–315
  and negotiations, 342
  repression of, 317
  triggers of, 294, 328
  understanding patterns of, 323–325
Antagonism, resulting from anger, 314
Antisocial behavior, from psychological problems, 14
Anxiety, 284, 384, 410
  breathing exercises for, 389–390
  management of, 384–389
  muscle relaxation for, 390–391
Approval, communicating feelings with, 178
Aristotle, 372
Assertiveness, 276
  versus aggressiveness, 319–320
Assumptions, 172
  effect on interpretations, 335–336
  rational verus irrational, 332–335
Attending, 154–155, 214
Attitudes, 352
  message perception, influence on, 156
  underlying responses, 214–221
Attributions, 369–370
  about self, 394

Autonomy, 5–6
Availability heuristic, 368

Banfield, Edward, 403
Baseline period, 396
Basic self-acceptance, 63
Behavior
  anger as disrupter of, 313
  bad, 331, 398
  controlling, 52–53
  describing versus judging, 133, 137
  focusing feedback on, 59
  nonverbal, 197
Behavior descriptions, 277
  for anger management, 318
Being, versus feeling, 184–185
Beliefs, influence on message perception, 156
Blame orientation, 328, 330–331
  irrational beliefs underlying, 330–331
  self-blame, 397–398
Blaming the victim, 367–370
Body language, 194–195
Body orientation, 197
Boredom, 306
Breathing, 389–390
Buber, Martin, 10
Burke, Edmund, 275

Cancer-prone persons, emotional characteristics
  of, 19
Candor, 377
Career, negotiation skills for, 275–276
Carve-outs, 292
Catastrophizing, 330, 386–387
Categorization, 361
  social, 362
Catharsis, 320
Causal attribution, 369–370
Cells, cooperation of, 311
Character, 352
Clarification, 153
Closed questions, 225
Clothing
  as a communication tool, 197
  perceptions of, 64–65
Cognitive development, and relationships, 14
Cognitive heuristics, errors in, 368
Coldness, nonverbal expression of, 201–202
Collusion, 377
Commands, communicating feelings with, 178
Commitment to relationship, 21
  and feedback, 60
Communication, 124–128, 406–407, 412–413
  channels of, 126
  excessive, 130
  mistakes in, 151–152
  versus misunderstandings, 128–130
  one-way, 144–147
  principles of, 128
  sending messages effectively, 132–148, 407
  stylistic elements of, 374–376
  two-way, 133, 144–147
Communication behavior, observing, 158–160
Communication skills, 132
  improving, 161
  receiving, 148–151, 408
  and self-awareness, 53
  sending, 132–148, 407

Communities, 372
    cooperation in, 373
Competition, 250
    from distrust, 103
    responding to, 100
    and trust, 95
Competitive context, 350
Compromise, 263, 264
Conditional self-acceptance, 63
Confirmation bias, 364
Conflict resolution, 249–302, 408
    constructive, 370–371
    role playing, 260
    strategies for, 253–255, 262–266, 267–269
Conflicts of interest, 250, 278, 414–415
    benefits of, 266
    characteristics of, 261
    confronting, 263
    from distrust, 102
    nonverbal, 252
    over money, 251–252
    past strategies for handling, 251
    rules of, 298–299
    from suppression of feelings, 176
Confrontation, 255–259
    interpretation as, 233
Consensual validation, 49
Content, 234
    identical, 239
    paraphrasing, 239
Contexts, 350
Cooperation, 13, 250
    in communities, 373
    with diverse individuals, 350–351
    and perspective reversal, 288
    for stress management, 311
    and trust, 95
Cooperative intentions, 96, 282
Credibility, reestablishing, 100
Critical thoughts, 399
Criticism, 394–395
Crude law of relationships, 20
Cultural conditioning, 366
Cultural identity, 352
    comparing, 357–358
Culture. *See also* Diversity
    and differences in emotional expression, 195
    and nonverbal communication, 197
    pride in, 351–356
Culture clashes, 373–374

de Tocqueville, Alexis, 359, 403
Deep breathing, 389–390
Defensiveness, from evaluative responses, 223
Deindividuation, 55
Demands, implying, 177
Depression, from high self-awareness, 54
Depth of response, 235
Desensitization, 387
Detachment, psychological, 322
Dilemmas, in negotiation, 270
Disagreements, 272–273
Disapproval, communicating feelings with, 178
Discrimination, 367
Display rules, of emotional expression, 195
Disrespect, 99
Distance, interpersonal, 195, 197
Distinctiveness, of personal versus impersonal
    relationships, 11
Distrust, 97, 102. *See also* Trust
    during conflicts, 280
Diverse individuals
    appreciation of, 356–358
    blaming, 367–370
    clarifying miscommunications with, 374–376
    constructive conflict resolution with, 370–371
    cooperative interaction, barriers to, 361–370
    cooperative interaction with, 350–351
    evaluating relations with, 348–349

    friendships among, 377–378
    pluralistic values for relating to, 371–373
    prejudice against, 366–367
    relating to, 348–349, 409–410, 416
    stereotyping, 361–366
    superordinate identities, uniting, 358–361
Diversity, 348, 409
    and culture clashes, 373–374
    and pride in identity, 351–356
    recognizing and valuing, 349
    and sophistication, 376–377
    and stereotypes, 365–366. *See also* Stereotypes
    valuing, barriers to, 361–370
Divorced persons, health risks of, 17–18
Dominance, 83
Double binds, 196
Dyadic interaction, 10

Effective communication, 129–130
Egocentrism, 285
Elaboration, 153
Ellis, Albert, 333
Emotional expression. *See also* Feelings, nonverbal
    expression of; Feelings, verbal expression of
    self-awareness of, 199–201
Emotional isolation, 21
Emotional maturity, 185
Emotional trust, 102–103
Emotions. *See also* Feelings
    expressing, 49
Employability, and interpersonal skills, 16
Employees, conflicts among, 275
Empowerment, in negotiation, 283–284
Encouraging thoughts, 399
Equity, norm of, 270
Erikson, Eric, 352
Ethnic identity, 352
Ethnocentrism, 356–357, 366
Evaluative responses, 222–223, 232–233
Expectations, influence on message perception,
    156
Experiential learning, 24–26
Expression of feelings. *See* Feelings, nonverbal
    expression of; Feelings, verbal expression of
External frame of reference, 231
External influences, 55–56
Eye contact, 195–197

Facial expressions, 195, 197
False consensus bias, 364
Family history, sharing, 68–70
Fantasy situations, for increasing self-awareness,
    76–77
Fear, 97, 384, 410
    management of, 384–389
    muscle relaxation for, 390–391
Feedback, 27, 79, 406
    in communication process, 147
    gaining self-awareness through, 57–61
    giving, 59–60
    on messages, 133
    negative, 314
    receptivity to, 40–45
    requesting, 57, 61
    and self-disclosure, 57–58, 74
Feeling, 173
    versus being, 184–185
Feelings, 169
    ambiguity in expression of, 186–187
    awareness of, 170–175
    changing, 173, 330, 337
    communicating, 133
    controlling, 174
    describing, 179–185, 279–281
    disposing, 332–333
    explaining to others, 56
    expressing, 167–175, 168–169, 206
    indirect expression of, 178
    managing, 338–339

negative, 180
negative, expression of, 314
nonverbal expression of, 193–197, 407–408, 413
power of, 167–168
repression of, 173–174, 176–177
sharing, 47, 60
verbal expression of, 178–180, 407, 413
Firestone, Harvey S., 28
First impressions, 65
Forcing, 262, 265, 269, 271
Forgiveness, 331
Formality, 10
Fox (compromising) strategy, 263
Frames of reference, internal versus external, 231
Friction, 284
Friendship Relations survey, 41–45
Friendships
characteristics of, 378
creating, 7
with diverse individuals, 377–378
ingredients of, 18
shared activities of, 18
trust in, 102–103
Frustration, 284
Fundamental attribution error, 363

Gains, primary and secondary, 270
Gender identity, 352
Generalization, 361
Genetic traits task, 109–110
Gestures, 197
Globalizing, 328
Goal dilemma, 270
Goals, 250, 329
common, 48
communicating, 277
conflicting, 262
rights to, 276
Goffman, Erving, 63–64
Golden mean, 372
Good deeds, reciprocity of, 373
Groups, trust in, 103
Guided practice, 27

Habits of the heart, 359–360, 403
Health. See Physical health; Psychological health
Hearing, 214
Heart-disease-prone persons, emotional characteristics of, 19
Heritage
appreciating others', 356–358
pride in, 351–356
Hillel, 370
Historical identity, uniting with others', 358–361
Homeostasis, 306
Honesty, dilemma of, 270
Hostility, nonverbal cues for, 204–205
Humanness, and relationships, 13
Humor, in conflict resolution, 264

Identity, 351–353, 354, 355
development of, 15
in-group, 356–357
superordinate, 358–361
Ignorance, 331, 398
Ignoring, 328
Illusionary correlation, 364
Impersonality of life, 21–22
Impression management, 64
Impressions, clarifying, 79
Impulsiveness, 55
resulting from anger, 313, 317
In-group identity, 356–357
Independence, 388
Individualistic context, 350
Inferences, errors in, 368
Influence, 414
Information, weighing, 368
Ingham, Harry, 57

Ingratiation, 65
Inherited traits, 361
Initial interactions, 47
Inner-directed people, 6
Insults, 328
Integration, in personal versus impersonal relationships, 11
Integrative solutions, 271–272
understanding perspective for, 286
Intentions, 174–175
clarifying, 316
for helping others, 214
inferences drawn from, 129
underlying responses, 222–231
Interaction, 9–10
gaining self-awareness from, 56
Interests, 250, 352
clarifying, 283
conflicts of, 250
versus positions, 283–285
Internal frame of reference, 231
Interpersonal communication, 124–125, 127. See also Communication
Interpersonal distance, 195
Interpersonal effectiveness, 405
barriers to, 383–401, 410, 416
improving, 5
self-diagnosis of, 4
Interpersonal relations, patterns in, 82–83
Interpersonal skills, 7, 412–416
dynamic nature of, 6
importance of, 12, 403–404
power of, 1–2
steps to learning, 26–29
Interpersonal Trust Scale, 102
Interpretations, 171–173, 233, 332
assumptions, influence of, 335–336
changing, 330
Interpretive responses, 223–224, 233
Interruptions, 328
Intimacy, seeking and avoiding, 48
Introspection, 55
Irrational assumptions, 332–335
Isolation, stress resulting from, 311

Johari Window, 40, 57–58
Johnson Trust Diagram, 106
Joint action, 48
Journals, 32
Judgments. See also Stereotypes
avoiding, 133, 137, 152
biased, 176
versus descriptions, 59
negative, 328
prejudice in, 366–367
responding with, 222–223

Labels, 72
communicating feelings with, 178
Language, of responses, 235
Language sensitivity, 374–376
Large-group interaction, 10
Laughter, and conflicts, 264
Learned helplessness, 370
Lippmann, Walter, 349
Listening, 151–155, 213–214, 279, 408, 413
alternatives for, 222–231
elements of, 214
for meaning, 154–155
for negotiation, 278
partial, 154
for problem solving, 232–233
selective perception, 155–156
with understanding, 241–242
Loneliness, 21
causes of, 22, 23
physical effects of, 17
potential for, 20
stress from, 311

Looking-glass self, 57
Luft, Joe, 57

Manchester, William, 194
Meaning
    additional, 239
    listening for, 154–155
    perspective-based nature of, 141
    of responses, 235
    shallow or partial, 239
Meaning response, negotiating for, 154–155, 156
Messages, 126
    appropriateness of, 133
    clarifying and elaborating on, 153
    contradictory verbal and nonverbal cues, 178,
        195–196, 205–206, 319
    encoding, 126
    feedback on, 133
    nonverbal, 133
    ownership of, 132–133, 135–136
    phrasing of, 141
    repeating, 134
    sending, 132–148
Miscommunications, clarifying, 374–376
Mistakes, and self-talk, 398–400
Misunderstandings
    versus communication, 128–130
    and perspective, 140, 287
Moderation, 372
Modern racism, 367
Moral development, and relationships, 14
Moral virtue, 372
Morale, maintaining, 329
Motivation to continue, in personal versus
        impersonal relationships, 11
Muscle relaxation, 390–391

Name calling, 178, 328
Needs, 250
    right to, 276
Negotiable issues, 297–298
Negotiation, 154–155, 250, 263, 269–272, 408.
        See also Conflict resolution
    and anger, 342
    with diverse individuals, 371
    feedback on, 272–273
    forcing, 269, 271
    interdependence of, 270
    norms in, 272
    one-step, 272
    for problem solving, 271–288
    refusals, 297–299
    review of, 299–301
    starting over, 294
    steps to, 276–294
    win-lose, 263, 269, 300, 408
Noise, 126, 129
Nomadic life style, 21
Nonassertiveness, 276, 319–320
Nonverbal communication, 193–197
    ambiguity of, 195–196, 198
    congruence with verbal messages, 205–206,
        319
    contradictory to verbal messages, 178, 195–196
    practice exercise for, 202–204
Nonverbal cues
    for affection versus hostility, 204–205
    interpretation of, 199
    for warmth versus coldness, 201–202
Nonverbal messages, 133
    and verbal messages, congruence of, 178,
        195–196, 205–206, 319
Norm of mutual responsiveness, 272
Norms, 64
    in negotiation, 270

One-step negotiations, 272
One-way communication, 144–147
Open questions, 225

Openness, 45–51, 405–406
    dilemma of, 270
    nonreciprocation of, 99
    in personal versus impersonal relation-
        ships, 11
    and trust, 96
Opposition, confronting, 255–259
Options, in negotiation, 291–292
Oral explanations, 56
Out-group homogeneity effect, 362
Out-groups, 357
Outcome interdependence, 270
Outer-directed people, 6
Overt actions, 187
Owl (problem solving/negotiating) strategy, 263

Pain, from fear and anxiety, 385
Paraphrasing, 152–153, 227, 234, 278, 288
Paraphrasing and understanding responses (U),
        227–228
Parents, feedback from, 59
Participation interdependence, 270
Peers, feedback from, 59
Perception checks, 187–188, 288, 407
    for anger management, 316
Perceptions
    of others' feelings, 187–188
    sharing, 60
    validating through self-disclosure, 49
Perfectionism, 331, 398
Personal development, and relationships, 14–15
Personal identity, and relationships, 15
Personal responses. See also Responses
    identifying, 236
Personal statements, 135–136
    in behavior descriptions, 277
Personality traits, 352
Perspective reversal, 288, 290–291
Perspective taking, 140, 141, 285
Perspectives, 286–287
    assumptions and, 172
    interpretations and, 172
    understanding others', 140–144, 285–291
    uniqueness of, 286
Phobias, 384–385
Physical characteristics, 351
Physical exercise, 329
    for releasing anger, 322
Physical expression, private, 322
Physical health
    anger, effects of, 312
    and breathing, 389
    and expression of feelings, 168, 173
    and relationships, 17–19
    stress-related problems, 306
Physical support, mutual, 208
Physiological systems
    feelings, effect on, 173
    stress, reaction to, 306
Pluralistic values, 371–373
Points of view, 289–290
Positions, in negotiations
    describing reasons for, 281–285
    versus interests, 283–285
Positive outlook, 394–395
Posture, 197
Power, from anger, 314
Power struggles, 177
Prejudice, 366–367
Primary gains, in negotiation, 270
Prisoner's dilemma game, 110–114
Probing responses, 225–227, 233
Problem orientation, 398
Problem solving, 231–232, 263
    listening and responding in, 213–221, 232–233
Problem-solving negotiation, 264, 265, 271–288, 300,
        373, 408
Productivity, and relationships, 16
Professional relationships, openness of, 45

Provocation
  management of, 325–327
  self-talk for, 420
Psychological detachment, from anger, 322
Psychological health
  and conflict, 266
  and congruence of nonverbal and verbal messages,
    206
  and cultural identity, 352
  and expression of feelings, 168, 173
  and relationships, 13–14
  and self-acceptance level, 63
Psychological problems, 331, 398
Put-downs, handling, 341–342

Quality of life, and relationships, 16–17
Quality of relationships, 10
  and self-disclosure, 49
Questioning and probing responses (P), 225–227
Questions, 225–227
  communicating feelings with, 178

Racism, 366–367
Rational assumptions, 333–335
Rationalization, post-decision, 368
Reactions
  explaining to others, 56
  to feelings, 170–175
  to nonverbal cues, 199
  sharing, 46–47
Real-ideal comparison, 63
Reality, shared perceptions of, 14
Reasons, in negotiations, 282–283
Reassuring and supporting responses (S), 224–225
Receiver, 126
  perspective of, 141
Receiving skills, 148–151, 407
Reciprocity
  norm of, 270
  of self-disclosure, 47
Recognition, 81
Reflected self-acceptance, 62
Reflective statements, 226–227
Refusal skills, 297–299
Rejection, 99
  during conflicts, 280
Relationship problems, barriers to constructive
  solutions, 176
Relationship statements, 137–139, 407
  for negotiations, 277
Relationships
  benefits of, 13–19
  difficulty in forming, 19–23
  humanizing elements of, 13
  importance of, 2–3
  initiating, 66–67
  interpersonal skills for, 3
  open versus closed, 83–85
  perception of importance, 262
  personal versus impersonal, 10, 11
  quality of, 5, 10, 411
  trust in, 95
Relationships diagram, 33
Relaxation, for releasing anger, 323
Reliability, 102–103
Religious identity, 352
Remembering, 214
Replaceability, of personal versus impersonal
  relationships, 11
Representativeness heuristic, 368
Resentment, triggers of, 294
Resource interdependence, 100
Respect, for self and others, 277
Response style, identifying, 214–221
Responses, 151–155, 213–214, 235, 408, 413
  alternatives for, 222–231
  asyndetic, 154
  content of, 234
  depth of, 235

intent of, 216, 418
irrelevant versus relevant, 149–151
language used in, 235
over- or underuse of, 232
phrasing, 419
practicing, 229–230
for problem-solving situations, 232–233
selective perception in, 155–156
Ridicule, 99
Righteousness, 313
Risk taking, response to, 115
Risks
  of expressing anger, 316–317
  of expressing feelings, 169
Rogers, Carl, 232
Role playing, for conflict resolution, 260

Samples, unreliable, 368
Sarcasm, 328
  communicating feelings with, 178
Scaffolding, 27
Secondary gains, in negotiation, 270
Selective perception, 155–156
  from denial of feelings, 176
Self
  actual versus ideal, 54
  aspects of, 64, 356
  enduring nature of, 65
  labeling, 185
  looking-glass, 57
  potential, 351
  respect for, 277
  stability of, 353–354
  trust, proclivity to, 102
Self-absorption, 54
Self-acceptance, 386, 406
  increasing, 79
  measuring, 81–82
  and self-disclosure, 39, 62–63
Self-actualization, 5–6, 53, 405
Self-alienation, 173
Self-awareness, 406
  of anger, 323–325
  benefits of, 52–53
  dangers of, 54
  of emotional expression, 199–201
  from feedback, 57–61
  increasing level of, 55–57
  increasing with self-disclosure, 49
  lack of, 55
  and self-disclosure, 39, 51–57, 70–71
  of unknown areas, 71–72
Self-awareness theory, 54
Self-blame, 330–331, 410
  avoiding, 397–398
Self-contract, 411–412
Self-description, 85, 86
Self-diagnosis, 4
Self-disclosure, 39, 45–66, 405–406, 412
  adjective checklist for, 74–75
  appropriateness of, 50–51
  benefits of, 48–50
  and feedback, 57–58
  impact of, 47–48
  lack of, 48
  reciprocating, 97
  responding to, 46
  risks of, 45–46, 115
  and self-acceptance, 62–63
  and self-awareness, 51–57, 70–71
  and self-presentation, 63–66
  and trust, 96, 115–116
Self-discrepancy, from self-awareness, 54
Self-esteem, 353
  building, 394–395
Self-evaluation, 63
Self-fulfilling prophecies
  stereotypes as, 364
  of trust, 101–102

Self-identity, 353–356
Self-improvement, 394
Self-monitoring, 53
Self-perception theory, 55–56
Self-presentation, 406
    open, 65
    and self-disclosure, 63–66
    strategic, 64
Self-promotion, 65
Self-schema, 351
Self-serving attributions, 370
Self-talk, 420
    with mistakes, 398–400
    negative, 394
Self-understanding, 53
Self-verification, 65
Self-view, 353
Sender, 126
    dynamism of, 134
    frame of reference of, 231
    perspective of, 141
Sender credibility, 134
Sending skills, 132–148, 407
Sensing, 171
Sexism, 366
Shakespeare, William, 63
Shared perceptions, 14
Sharing, 96
Shark (forcing) strategy, 262
Shyness, 384, 392, 410
    self-esteem, building, 394–395
    understanding, 393, 395–397
Skill development process, 26–28
Small-group interaction, 10
Smoothing, 262, 263, 265, 283
Sociability, 83
Social class identity, 352
Social comparison, 56
Social control, and self-disclosure, 49
Social development, and relationships, 14
Social isolation, 21
Social perspective-taking, 285
Social roles, 351–352
Social science research, application to interpersonal
    skills, 23–24
Social sensitivity, 53
Social suicide, 311–312
Social support, 15–16. See also Support networks
Space, during communication, 195, 197
Stengel, Casey, 351
Stereotypes, 361–366
    clarifying, 365
    colluding with, 377
    interactions based on, 365–366
    minimizing, 363
    persistence of, 364
Strengths, 79
    clarifying, 157
    emphasizing, 394
Stress, 305–311, 415–416
    anger resulting from, 312–315
    determining level of, 308–311
    and self-identity, 354
    sharing, 329
    support networks for, 311–312
Stress disorders, 306
Stress management, 307, 409
    and relationships, 15–16
    and self-awareness, 53
    with self-disclosure, 49
Success orientation, 369
Superordinate goals, 100
Superordinate identity, 358–361
    human equality, 373
Support, 96
Support networks, 409
    strength of, 308–311
    for stress management, 311–312

Supportive responses, 224–225, 233
Survival, tips on, 329

Teddy Bear (smoothing) strategy, 262
Tie-ins, 292
Time-competence, 5
Time dimensions, of negotiations, 270
Torah, 370
Touch, 197
Trade-offs, 292
Trust, 94, 406, 412
    appropriateness of, 100–103, 112
    and communication process, 129
    destroying, 99
    developing, 94–95, 119
    emotional trust, 102–103
    in friendships, 102–103
    gaining sophistication with, 377
    in groups, 103
    increasing, 114
    maintaining, 94–95
    mutual, 112
    nonverbal, 116–119
    openly discussing, 114–116
    reestablishing, 100
    reliability, 102–103
    and self-disclosure, 39
    as self-fulfilling prophecy, 101–102
Trust actions, 106–108
Trust behaviors, 108
Trust building, 97–99, 108–110
Trust circle, 117
Trust cradle, 118
Trust fall, 118–119
Trust passing, 119
Trust walk, 117–118
Trustworthiness, 95, 96–97, 406
    and congruence of nonverbal and verbal
        messages, 206
    dilemma of, 270
    evaluating, 105–108
Turtle (withdrawing) strategy, 262
Two-factor theory of emotion, 56
Two-way communication, 133, 144–147

Understanding, 214
Understanding responses, 227–228, 232–233
    phrasing of, 234–244

Value judgments, 184. See also Judgments
    reactions to, 233
Values, 373
    clarifying, with conflicts, 266
    pluralistic, 360–361, 371–373
Venn diagram, 357–358
Verbal messages, congruence with nonverbal
        messages, 178, 195–196, 205–207, 319
Voice, 197
    tone of, 195
Vulnerability, anger as defense against, 314

Wants, 250
    communicating, 277
    message perception, influence on, 156
    right to, 276
Warmth
    expression of, 241–243
    nonverbal expression of, 201–202
Why questions, 226
Win-lose negotiations, 263, 269, 300, 408
Withdrawal, 262
Workplace, conflicts in, 275–276
Worry, 386

You statements, 319